Hellenic Studies 64

BETWEEN THUCYDIDES AND POLYBIUS

Recent Titles in the Hellenic Studies Series

http://chs.harvard.edu/chs/publications

BETWEEN THUCYDIDES AND POLYBIUS

THE GOLDEN AGE OF GREEK HISTORIOGRAPHY

EDITED BY
GIOVANNI PARMEGGIANI

CENTER FOR HELLENIC STUDIES
Trustees for Harvard University
Washington, D.C.
Distributed by Harvard University Press
Cambridge, Massachusetts, and London, England
2014

Between Thucydides and Polybius
  Edited by Giovanni Parmeggiani
Copyright © 2014 Center for Hellenic Studies, Trustees for Harvard University
All Rights Reserved.
Published by Center for Hellenic Studies, Trustees for Harvard University,
  Washington, D.C.
Distributed by Harvard University Press, Cambridge, Massachusetts, and London,
  England
Production: Nancy Wolfe Kotary
Cover design: Joni Godlove
Printed by Edwards Brothers Malloy, Ann Arbor, MI

LIBRARY OF CONGRESS CATALOGING-IN-PUBLICATION DATA

Between Thucydides and Polybius : the golden age of Greek historiography / edited by
  Giovanni Parmeggiani.
    pages cm -- (Hellenic studies ; 64)
  ISBN 978-0-674-42834-8 (alk. paper)
  1. Greece--Historiography. I. Parmeggiani, Giovanni. II. Series: Hellenic studies ; 64.

DF211.B48 2014
938.007--dc23

2014013063

Contents

Contents

Acknowledgments

The papers collected in this volume originate from two conferences held at Harvard University and at the University of Bologna in 2007 and organized by Nino Luraghi and Riccardo Vattuone. Support for the events and for a particularly long editorial process has been provided by the Loeb Fund of the Department of the Classics, Harvard University, the Magie Fund of the Department of Classics, Princeton University, the University of Bologna, and the Banca Popolare dell'Emilia Romagna, and is here gratefully acknowledged. For complex editorial work, thanks are due to Daniel Tober and Jessica Wright (both Princeton) and Pietro Liuzzo (Bologna). Jill Curry Robbins of CHS has provided help, guidance, and editorial and more generally moral support well beyond any reasonable definition of the call of duty. The contributors to this enterprise have showed matchless patience. It is the editor's hope that they will consider their forebearance rewarded at least in part by the present volume.

Giovanni Parmeggiani
Università di Ferrara

1

Introduction

Giovanni Parmeggiani

IN THE MODERN reception of ancient Greek history, the fourth century BCE has always been seen as a period of transition from the golden Classical age of the fifth century to the Hellenistic period: an appendix to the former, a prologue to the latter. Given this peculiar and unfavourable intermediary position, the fourth century has often been seen in a negative light, and has never really gained the status of an age with a proper, legitimate identity.

It is a widespread opinion that, as often happens with periods of transition, the fourth century was, above all, a time of decadence (decadence of the Greek *polis*, and of Greek historiography). Considering that many political and cultural changes did take place in the period 404–323 BCE, however, the concept of decadence is hardly helpful. On the contrary, since it has been brought into play in order to explain the transition from the greatness of the Classical to the Hellenistic age, it appears to reflect the prejudice that the fifth century was the pinnacle of the Greek cultural experience as a whole. It goes without saying that such a perspective is affected by a classicist bias and is, in every respect, questionable. The idea that the time when founders of Western thought such as Plato and Aristotle lived, and also the literature they shared, was decadent does not seem particularly convincing.

The fourth century has always suffered from comparison with the fifth. This is an initial difficulty that every modern scholar has to deal with when studying fourth-century historiography and, more generally, the way that fourth-century literature dealt with the past. Indeed, one could speak of the shadow that the fifth century casts on the fourth. Just as Photius the Patriarch was puzzled by Theopompus of Chios' self-praise, observing that the superiority Theopompus claimed for himself over fifth-century predecessors was inconceivable because of the undisputed greatness of Herodotus and Thucydides,[1]

---

[1] Photius *Bibliotheca* 176.121a (Theopompus FGH 115 F 25).

similarly Felix Jacoby stated in 1926 that Greek historiography reached its perfection with Thucydides, thus implying that historians of the fourth century could not match the greatness of their predecessor.[2] "Abstieg nach Thukydides," *dixit* Jacoby, and once again the concept of decadence creeps in, as a consequence of the preconceived superiority of the fifth century. Things do not appear to have changed much since the time of Photius (ninth century CE).

Classicist prejudices are prevalent even today. But a closer examination of Theopompus' own words as they have been transmitted to us by Photius would suffice to make clear that Theopompus was not simply praising himself, but also the literature of his time, seemingly regardless of genre boundaries. If we cannot agree *a priori* with Theopompus (for in so doing we would simply reverse the classicist bias), we should meditate on this statement and take it as a starting point for a careful reexamination of fourth-century culture.

A survey of the *Trümmerfeld* ("field of ruins") of ancient Greek historiography—as Hermann Strasburger memorably called it[3]—and of fourth-century historiography in particular, gives discouraging results. The most important works of that time, admired by the ancients for centuries, survive only in scanty fragments, mostly citations by later authors. This obviously complicates interpretation, since the manner of citation is diverse and often driven by agendas and interests that have nothing to do with those of the original author. Recent studies, for example, have shown how the various biases of Polybius, Athenaeus, and Diodorus distort our image of the lost historical works that they made use of and quoted.[4] The shadow projected by the citing author over the author cited presents a second difficulty in dealing with the fourth century: the 'cover text', as Guido Schepens taught us some time ago,[5] and as is illustrated in various papers collected in the present volume, always requires a careful approach and in-depth study.

On top of this, there is a third difficulty we need to consider: the tendency of modern critics to use inadequate concepts for defining and understanding fourth-century literature. This approach has obviously led to serious misunderstandings, as in the case of Isocrates (Marincola, this volume) and Xenophon (Nicolai, this volume). The concept of 'rhetorical historiography' is a major case in point. It rests on the false premises that Isocrates, as the teacher of Ephorus and Theopompus, was the proponent of an historiographical program and that devoting attention to style and using historical *exempla* are practices

---

[2] See Jacoby 1909 and 1926.
[3] Strasburger 1977.
[4] On Polybius, see Schepens and Bollansée 2005. On Athenaeus, see Lenfant 2007. On Diodorus, specifically in relation to Ephorus, see now Parmeggiani 2011.
[5] See Schepens 1997:166n66 for the concept of 'cover-text'.

incompatible with the search for the truth. Thus, the concept of 'rhetorical historiography' not only hides the real nature of Ephorus' and Theopompus' historiography (see below), but prevents us from understanding Isocrates in a more constructive way: as an intellectual who participated in the debates on the meaning and utility of history (an abiding interest for every intellectual in the fourth century, and not for historians alone). Similarly, modern critics tend to apply misleading labels to Xenophon and his works. Accordingly, they fail to understand that he, like Isocrates, was an experimenter in various prose genres, and did not feel compelled to conform to pre-existing models, but rather changed them, freely moving from one genre to another within a single work.

Once we become aware of the pitfalls outlined above, new and more constructive avenues of interpretation open up. Indeed, the last point indicates a fundamental feature of the fourth century. It seems that intellectuals of this period—historians, orators, and philosophers alike—looked for new modes of writing, deliberately crossing the boundaries between genres. Perhaps because the boundaries of prose genres were yet to be clearly defined (as in the case of historiography, see below), and also because intellectuals did not think that knowledge was the prerogative of a particular discipline, they could afford to move freely across generic boundaries on the basis of particular goals. This was an age for experimenters and innovators, an age for polymaths. Unsurprisingly, the fourth century was the time when philosophers such as Aristotle were able, when necessary, to practice history with a high degree of methodological awareness, clearly inspired by the method of Thucydides (Bertelli, this volume).

Certainly, the fourth century was also the time when historiography, by distinguishing itself from other disciplines, became a literary genre (*genos historikon*) with precise methods and aims. One may say that defining and crossing boundaries are two closely connected activities, and in this respect, Theopompus of Chios' contribution was decisive (Vattuone, this volume). One of the most complex and important intellectuals of the fourth century—on a par with Isocrates, Xenophon, and Aristotle—the historian Theopompus is often remembered as *philalethes* by ancient authors. Indeed, he never disavowed Thucydides' historical credo, but rather extended the purview of historical inquiry, by insisting that the practice of historiography was not a *parergon*, something to be carried out on the side, but rather required a specific method of research, i.e. a thoughtful use of the sources.

On this, a comparative look at other fourth-century historians may be instructive. Xenophon, in his *Hellenica*, appears to have been less interested in documents than Thucydides had been. Nonetheless, his use of documents seems consistent with his predecessor's, with documents serving historiographical and not merely decorative purposes (Bearzot, this volume). Ephorus of Cyme drew upon comedy not as an authority to be blindly followed, as scholars have sometimes thought, but as evidence demonstrating that Pericles' responsibility for the outbreak of the Peloponnesian War was publicly debated by contemporaries and that his rhetorical strength was a decisive factor in initiating the war (Parmeggiani, this volume). Ephorus thus evinces a sophisticated approach to historical evidence. In this respect, we have every reason to conclude that fourth-century historians succeeded in maintaining the high standards of their fifth-century predecessors, and may even have surpassed them.

Concepts of continuity and development actually describe the relationship between fifth- and fourth-century historiography better than discontinuity and regression. Theopompus expanded the field of *aitiai*: alongside the causes of events, he studied the reasons for men's actions, their aims, plans, wishes, and passions. The Thucydidean aetiology of *aphanes*—i.e. the historical practice of revealing the most hidden causes of events and actions—was, in this way, strengthened. A similar claim can be advanced for Ephorus. His version of the causes of the Peloponnesian War testifies to how his consideration of new data and his disclosure of Pericles' thoughts and aims extended Thucydides' point of view on the causes of the war to give a different and, above all, a more complete picture. Ephorus treated Pericles' personal affairs, the internal politics of Athens, the politics of the Delian League, and the relationship between Athens and Sparta as interwoven problems (Parmeggiani, this volume). The increased attention devoted to historical causation is visible also in the fact that even fourth-century writers of *Persica*, a genre that bordered on ethnography, paid greater attention to explanation than did their fifth-century predecessors (Lenfant, this volume).

Clearly there is much more at stake than the simple 'praise and blame' that modern critics usually ascribe to Ephorus and Theopompus—and to various other historians—as if it were the only cause and purpose of their works. If the paradigmatic vision of history was crucial for some authors who, like Xenophon, did not feel compelled to adhere to the boundaries of *genos historikon*, the same cannot be said for others, such as Ephorus and Theopompus, who worked on the contrary to define these boundaries. Once again, we see that the concept of 'rhetorical historiography' does not adequately define Ephorus' and Theopompus' work and historiographical practice. We may also observe this in other respects. According to the traditional view of the fourth century, the collapse of the *polis* system gave rise to a new historiography, whose interest was mainly in ethics and literature, and not in politics (this being an effect of the 'corruption' of historiography by rhetoric). But far from being out of sight, politics were in fact crucial in the works of Ephorus and Theopompus. This is suggested by, for example, the choice by Ephorus of the Return of the Heraclidae as the starting point for his *Histories*. In the age of Philip II of Macedon, the Return appears to have played a prominent role in political debates, to the point that no writer of an history of Greece could ignore it. The very choice of such a beginning, then, confirms that Ephorus' approach to history was informed by his awareness of contemporary politics (Luraghi, this volume). The attention Ephorus paid to Spartan history as a central theme in his work points to a similar conclusion (Tully, this volume, discussing whether 'Universal History' is a legitimate label for Ephorus' *Histories*).

Ephorus is another major piece in the complicated puzzle of the fourth-century intellectual milieu.[6] But let us briefly consider, beyond the central figures we have already mentioned, the complexity of the historical frame. In the same way as the boundaries between disciplines were not clearly defined, or were in the process of being defined, so the wider Greek political situation in the period 404–323 BCE was in flux and susceptible to radical change. Since the last years of the Peloponnesian War (from 412 BCE), the Athenians had progressively lost their empire, while the Persians again played an active, indeed even dominant role in Greek politics. In order to understand the implications of this more clearly, we need to perform a mental experiment of sorts, thinking ourselves into the years between the King's Peace and the Sacred War, a time when everybody thought the Achaemenid Empire was there to stay (as impressively shown by Tuplin, this volume). Fourth-century writers of *Persica* focused their attention on the Persian king and his court, and in so doing, gave rise to a kind of 'political ethnography' that makes sense only in this political context (Lenfant, this volume). Finally, from the middle of the fourth century onward, the rise of Macedon had a deep impact on historiography: Theopompus subsumed the entire history of Greece under the deeds of Philip II (Vattuone, this volume), focusing his attention on the Macedonian king and his court.

Both these facts are testimony to the persistent centrality of politics within fourth-century historiography, despite the claims of many modern critics, who prefer to depict fourth-century historiography as a mere reaction to the literary tradition. After Aegospotami (405 BCE), the Spartans failed to replace the Athenians in the Aegean, both politically and culturally, and the cities of Asia Minor filled this cultural vacuum by each reasserting their own political and cultural identity, by recording local deeds, traditions—even if mutually conflicting—and monuments (Thomas, this volume). Something similar happened, one may observe, with the outstanding individuals of the age, who crafted their uniqueness before the public through statues, monuments and

---

[6] For a new and comprehensive examination of the existing evidence on Ephorus, presenting a reconstruction of the contents of his *Histories* and a definition of his historical aims and method of research, see Parmeggiani 2011.

historical works (Ferrario, this volume): memory was the battleground for identity, for individuals and communities alike. The flourishing of local/*polis* histories in the fourth century, especially in the Ionian *poleis*, seems better explained as a consequence of the need for political and cultural self-assertion against the hegemonic claims of Athens and Persia, than as a literary reaction—as Jacoby maintained—to the "grand history" of the struggle between Persians and Greeks (Thomas, this volume). Once again, we must conclude, the variety of forms of fourth-century historiography seems to find its roots in politics, and not in the inner dynamics of a literary tradition supposedly disconnected from politics.

A better understanding of fourth-century historiography and of fourth-century literature that dealt more generally with the past becomes possible when we put these writings into context, i.e. when we pay attention to their period and its historical specificity. When we put aside the preconceived notions that have long influenced modern critics, the fourth century appears in its full light as a period of innovations, problematic but stimulating, and in no way inferior to the fifth. The editor and the scholars who have contributed to the present volume will be satisfied if the collected papers provoke the reader to rethink, as now seems necessary, this complex of problems.

Bibliography

Bloch, H., ed. 1956. *Abhandlungen zur griechischen Geschichtschreibung von Felix Jacoby zu seinem achtzigsten Geburtstag am 19 März 1956*. Leiden.

Jacoby, F. 1909. "Über die Entwicklung der griechischen Historiographie und den Plan einer neuen Sammlung der griechischen Historikerfragmente." *Klio* 9:80–123. (= Bloch 1956:16–64)

———. 1926. "Griechische Geschichtschreibung." *Die Antike* 2:1–29. (= Bloch 1956:73–99)

Lenfant, D., ed. 2007. *Athénée et les fragments d'historiens, Actes du colloque de Strasbourg, 16–18 juin 2005*. Paris.

Parmeggiani, G. 2011. *Eforo di Cuma. Studi di storiografia greca*. Bologna.

Schepens, G. 1997. "Jacoby's FGrHist: Problems, Methods, Prospects." In *Collecting Fragments. Fragmente sammeln*, ed. G. W. Most, 144–172. Göttingen.

Schepens, G., and Bollansée, J., eds. 2005. *The Shadow of Polybius. Intertextuality as a Research Tool in Greek Historiography. Proceedings of the International Colloquium (Leuven, 21–22 September 2001)*. Leuven.

Strasburger, H. 1977. "Umblick im Trümmerfeld der griechischen Geschichtsschreibung." In *Historiographia antiqua. Commentationes Lovanienses in honorem W. Peremans septuagenarii editae*, ed. T. Reekmans et al., 3–52. Leuven.

2

Looking for the Invisible
Theopompus and the Roots of Historiography

RICCARDO VATTUONE

1. Theopompus and the Historiography of the IVth Century BCE

IT IS NOT ONLY the fragmentary nature of his work that hinders a critical evaluation of Theopompus. The idiosyncratic interests of one of his most important witnesses, Athenaeus, and the deep-seated ambiguity of Polybius' interpretation have done much to affect modern judgement, which oscillates between negative and positive assessments, between attempts to categorize Theopompus as a proponent of so-called 'rhetorical historiography' and balanced appreciations that take stock of the writer's broad cultural interests. Apart from the 'moralism' of Athenaeus' interpretation, we must also come to terms with the shadow of Polybius, which is so often cast over earlier historiography, although in this case its impact may be beneficial, in a sense, considering that Book 12 of Polybius' *Histories* is to a remarkable degree pervaded by reflections on fourth-century historiography.[1]

Just as has been the case with Ephorus, modern criticism has generally avoided addressing Theopompus as a whole.[2] In part, this is because fourth-century Greek historiography is burdened not only by Polybius' judgment

---

[1] Schepens and Bollansée 2005; Walbank 2005; Chávez Reino 2005 (on the relationship between Polybius and Ephorus); Bearzot 2005 (on Polybius and Theopompus).

[2] While the accounts of Pédech 1989 and Shrimpton 1991 are specifically descriptive, the studies of Connor 1968 and Flower 1994 deal with important themes: political history in the fifth century observed from a fourth-century point of view, the biographical and rhetorical tradition of the work, but they do not attempt to confront the problem in all its complexity. The same 'censorship' has affected Ephorus, to whom only one twentieth-century study has been devoted, and an incomplete and superficial one at that (Barber 1935).

but also by the nineteenth-century philological prejudice, according to which Thucydides stands alone among the scientific historians, with his successors attacked as mere elaborators of an established tradition.[3] This position, we should note, attracts supporters even today.[4] But the problem does not, in fact, involve only fourth-century historiography; there is a need, by extension, for a balanced evaluation of earlier historiography. Our interpretation of Thucydides, for example, would certainly benefit from rejecting the implausible description of him as a 'scientific' historian, a historian, that is to say, *ante litteram*.

The difficulty in evaluating Theopompus lies essentially in pulling together the contradictory assessments of ancient authors and the controversial or negative tradition that underlies much modern appreciation. Guido Schepens and John Marincola have made considerable progress to this end, the one emphasizing Theopompus' acumen in interpreting events that took place after the Peloponnesian War, the other insisting on the broadness of his compass in his "contemporary universal history": a history, that is to say, that is spatially universal but fundamentally contemporary, interwoven though it is with elaborate digressions.[5] But rehabilitation need not be the aim of a new edition of Theopompus' fragments or interpretation of what remains of his work and personality. As Dino Ambaglio has said about Diodorus Siculus, the process of looking beyond established prejudices does not *ipso facto* mean recognizing in an ancient author a new grandeur and stature.[6] The point is not to rehabilitate a controversial text and its author, but to study it as fruitfully as possible.[7]

A balanced examination of the works of Ephorus and Theopompus would, I think, permit us to write different pages not only of Greek historiography but also of Greek and even general history. The fourth-century perspective on events central to the fifth century, e.g. the 'Pentecontaetia' and the 'Peloponnesian War', is not less reliable through being farther removed from the events. Such

---

[3]   Wachsmuth 1895:501f.; Schwartz 1907:7f.; Laqueur 1911; Jacoby 1926a:1f.; see Fornara 1983:42. A close examination of the problem can now be found in Parmeggiani 2011:9–25.

[4]   To get a sense of the point of view of Wilamowitz and his school it is sufficient to read the central chapter, devoted to Ephorus, of Frances Pownall's recent book (Pownall 2004:113-142), beginning with the assumption contained in the work's subtitle: *The Moral Use of History in Fourth Century Prose*. Bruno Bleckmann's judgement on fourth-century historiography (1998) and on the anonymous author of the *Hellenica Oxyrhynchia* (2006) is similarly oriented, although with more originality. But it seems to me that Bleckmann deals with classical Greek historiography with the same schemas that he has applied to the late Empire, with some exegetical risk.

[5]   Schepens 1993:169f.; Marincola 2007b (esp. 175). I dealt with Theopompus' historiography in the Greek *Universalgeschichte* in Vattuone 1998:84f.

[6]   Ambaglio 1995:17.

[7]   A new edition with commentary on Theopompus by G. Ottone and A. Chávez Reino is forthcoming in the series *I frammenti degli storici greci*, edited by E. Lanzillotta. Several interpretative guidelines can be found in Ottone 2004:129f., and in Gazzano et al. 2009:73–212.

an erroneous assumption stems from naïveté, since a contemporary perspective is by no means better informed or less biased and, therefore, no more accurate or less corrupt. The Isocratean critique of *opsis* and *akoe* assumes that the critical examination of the sources is, like a special *gnome*, at the very centre of the critical thinking of the fourth century.[8] I would not lightly commit myself to Polybius' critique of Timaeus, that of *bibliake hexis*: we all work like Timaeus.

That is to say, a careful examination of Theopompus, rather than a rehabilitation, offers historical alternatives. It is possible to choose not to read Athenian history along the lines of the excursus in Book 10 of the *Philippica*; nevertheless such a long-term perspective can free our interpretation of Athenian democracy after the Persian Wars not only from Isocrates' *Panathenaicus* but also from Thucydides' encomium of Pericles and the notion of a decline that sets in after Pericles' death. Theopompus' point of view certainly revolved around Eubulus and his political activity (FF 99–100), but for this very reason we can situate Cimon and Pericles in a wider frame that spans the sixth to the fourth century (FF 88–89). We tend to think that what is left of fifth-century Greek historiography is pure, pristine, and original, while we ought to admit that it is only an interpretation of complex and debated themes of that time. Theopompus' reaction to the series of Philathenian epideictic flourishes also touches on events of the fifth century, peace treaties proved wrong by a meticulous epigraphical study (F 154).[9] Athenians lie about their past: Theopompus revises the Athenian *vulgata* of the fifth century along the lines of what Thucydides purports to be doing in 1.20, where he is faced with a tradition that is as firmly entrenched as it is false.[10] That Theopompus' interpretation of the previous century was informed by the events of his own day should not surprise or shock us, in the name of a

---

[8] Nicolai 2004:74f. (see esp. 77–78 on Isocrates *Panathenaicus* 149f.). The mistake is usually to think that Isocrates' ideas are passed on to his disciples as tasks to be fulfilled.

[9] Theopompus notoriously criticizes the reliability of the συνθῆκαι written in Ionic script that were set up by the Athenians against the Persians, pointing out that it was only during the archonship of Euclides (403/2) that they began to use that alphabet (cf. F 155). It is not stated in the text which treaties are concerned, and so it is not certain that Theopompus is here talking about the Peace of Callias (Pédech 1989:115f.). The occasion for this remark is also unclear: it may be a critique of the Athenian pride in having forced the Persians to agree to unfavorable terms with them. Perhaps the context is a critique of the "Cimonian" treaty (Plutarch *Cimon* 13), which was considered false by Callisthenes too (13.4 = FGH 124 F 16).

[10] The Athenians are accused of falsifying the oath taken by the Greeks before the battle of Plataea and for the excessive magnification of the battle of Marathon, which did not take place as described in hymns devoted to it. The accusation concerning the falsification of history is more general: καὶ ὅσα ἄλλα . . . ἡ Ἀθηναίων πόλις ἀλαζονεύεται καὶ παρακρούεται τοὺς Ἕλληνας (FGH 115 F 153). On the basis of F 156, where we find an excursus on the Sacred War of 448–446 BCE, Connor 1968:94f. argues that this polemic was aimed at demonstrating the duplicity of Athens, touched upon by Plutarch *Pericles* 21 in a discussion of Athenian interests in central Greece (Shrimpton 1991:79–80).

peculiar kind of 'classicism' whereby everything that belongs to the fifth century is authentic and still uncontaminated, while later revisions (in fact new interpretations based on critical reflection) would be distortions and therefore rhetorical.[11] If there is any doubt about the consistency of the praise that Dionysius of Halicarnassus bestowed on Theopompus (T 20a), it is worth remembering that the burden of proof, here and elsewhere, lies on the claimant, the incredulous.

For Theopompus, beginning the *Hellenica* where Thucydides left off was not an attempt to pay homage to the historiographical tradition or to the authority of a prematurely interrupted source, but a way to undermine the meaning of 404 BCE as a historical threshold. As a writer of Greek History, he saw in Lysander's victory a concise and clear beginning that extended the war in the following decade up to Sparta's eventual defeat. Only someone who had seen Philip II at Corinth in 337/6 BCE could take such a long-term view and give a different interpretation not only to the fifth century and the relationships between Greece and Persia but also to the eastern perspective of Agesilaus and Lysander. The choice of embedding his Greek History into the events of Philip's times, a choice that would displease Polybius (T 19; F 27), was a profound statement about the autonomy of the *polis* and the new era that had begun, rather than a sign of regret of the sort that lies behind the event (i.e. the Battle of Mantinea) that Xenophon used to close and contain the narrative of his *Hellenica*.

It seems obvious—although if it is, it is generally to the displeasure of my contemporaries—that Theopompus read his own time against a background (between Herodotus and the battle of Cnidus in 394 BCE) that had certainly undergone a 'deformation' but had also experienced an enrichment of perspective, meaning, and value. Schwartz's lashing judgement on Ephorus (or, in more recent times, that of Bleckmann on the anonymous author of the *Hellenica Oxyrhynchia*) stems from the assumption that 'Isocratean' historians were in fact practicing another craft, and that their 'history' was in fact a long and tedious epideictic oration. A look at the *proemia* of these works, however, explicitly contradicts this view. We may in the end still distrust each of these preambles and consider them to be insincere or empty, but such an interpretation must be proven and not simply stated. In fact, for Ephorus, quite the opposite

---

[11] It is possible that Theopompus relied in his epigraphical research a little too faithfully on the information about the initiative of Archinus in 403/2 BCE (Pédech 1989:114–115n128). But we should not, at any rate, doubt the seriousness of his method. Theopompus certainly took into account the polemic against Athens' hypocrisy regarding its interests in Greece and in the Aegean sea, but this does not mean that his reconstruction is rhetorical, in the pejorative sense of the term, that is was based only on reversing other opinions or was devoid of any historiographical content.

conclusion was reached after a careful examination of each fragment;[12] and a renewed investigation of Ephorus calls for a similar course for Theopompus.[13] As it is, alas, our best handbooks are written as if Theopompus and Ephorus did not exist at all.

2. History as *Techne*: The Birth of a 'Genre'

It is Athenaeus who is most responsible for our image of Theopompus: a judge and a merciless moralist, who eulogized Alcibiades but struck down the indecent *mores* of the barbarians and Philip and the Macedonian court.[14] This is the Theopompus known also to Nepos, Cicero, Dionysius of Halicarnassus, and, as we shall see, to Lucian, who warns historians not to incur the same charge as the historian of Chios, who "aggressively attacks many people and makes a profession of it, with the result that he accuses rather than recounts the facts."[15] The charge that Theopompus turned the field of history into a tribunal does not exclude the fact that he narrated the facts, nor does Lucian mean this when he says "with the result that he accuses rather than recounts the facts" (ὡς κατηγορεῖν, μᾶλλον ἢ ἱστορεῖν τὰ πεπραγμένα). Tradition defines Theopompus

---

[12] Parmeggiani 2011:704f., 718f., and passim.

[13] See *supra*, n7. We must first consider what is meant by a fragment, the significance of the citations, and the importance of the context of the citing sources. We often think, with some hermeneutic naiveté, that Jacoby's *Fragmente* are indeed what survives of a lost work, without the input of the commentary that can render them as such (Vattuone 1991:12f.).

[14] On the nature of the tradition of Athenaeus, see *infra* section 5 (esp. 28–31). Nepos is surprised by the praise accorded to Alcibiades by Thucydides, Timaeus, and Theopompus, particularly because of the concordance between these last two in praising him beyond all others (*nescio quomodo in illo uno laudando consenserunt*: Alcibiades 11 = FGH 115 F 288; FGH 566 F 99). It is not clear from Nepos whether Timaeus and Theopompus, who are usually in disagreement, do in fact praise Alcibiades in the same way or whether they both praise him to the exclusion of anyone else. The second alternative is in fact impossible, since we know that, according to Polybius, Timaeus' encomium of Timoleon was no less exaggerated. Nepos goes on to say that the *duo maledicentissimi* agree *only* on the praise of Alcibiades, that they disagree, then, on all the rest of their judgements. We know that Timaeus distanced himself from Theopompus at least with regard to the tradition about Timoleon, both before and after his arrival in Sicily (FGH 566 F 116 vs FGH 115 F 334; FGH 566 F 117 vs FGH 115 F 341); on this, see Vattuone 1991:95f. Another problem is whether the common praise extended also to Alcibiades' adaptability to foreign *mores*, which is what we read in Nepos, but cautiously published by Jacoby in a smaller typeface. Such an ethical-political re-evaluation of Alcibiades' eclecticism would certainly not be out of line with Theopompus' historical sensibilities (Pédech 1989:233).

[15] Lucian *Quomodo historia conscribenda sit* 59 (FGH 115 T 25a). Lucian refers to the accusation against Theopompus as traditional (καὶ τὴν αὐτὴν Θεοπόμπῳ αἰτίαν ἕξεις . . .). When Lucian is writing, then, this is already a stereotype, which is only acknowledged and emphasized by the author, albeit paradoxically (. . . ὡς κατηγορεῖν, μᾶλλον ἢ ἱστορεῖν τὰ πεπραγμένα). It certainly does not indicate that Theopompus renounced writing up facts for the sake of moralism in and of itself. Lucian's criticism is directed towards the excessive use of certain categories, even if it was accepted as legitimate for historiography. There are useful insights in Shrimpton 1991:23f.

as φιλαλήθης, which indicates a love both for the truth of what happened and for scrupulous exactness and completeness (ἀκρίβεια: T 28a; F 181a).[16] The greatest admirer of Theopompus is without a doubt Dionysius of Halicarnassus. In a famous passage at *ad Pompeium Geminum* 6, after stating that Theopompus was the most famous of Isocrates' pupils and making reference to his rhetorical works, Dionysius adds that he wrote books of history worthy of praise (ἱστορίαν πραγματευμένος, ἄξιος ἐπαινεῖσθαι), in particular because of his choice of subjects (the end of the Peloponnesian War and the history of Philip's times); the clarity with which he presents his material (οἰκονομία); and, most of all, his dedication to the toils of writing (ἐπιμελείας καὶ φιλοπονία τῆς κατὰ τὴν συγγραφήν).[17] Dionysius has Theopompus' books in front of him as he writes, open to the pages of the *proemium*, which were perhaps a little longer than we would have liked.[18] But despite his predecessor's verbosity, Dionysius can appreciate his critical engagement. Had Jacoby been less cautious in isolating Theopompus' words from Dionysius' comments, everybody would agree that Dionysius' praise was based on the *proemium* to the *Philippica*, where Theopompus stated the difficulties of his research, the expenses involved, and the effort of assembling the material (παρασκευή) necessary for constructing the work.[19] There was no need—so, I think, Dionysius means to say—for Theopompus to

---

[16] Athenaeus' judgement (3.85a–b = FGH 115 T 28a) clearly relies on this passage from Dionysius' *ad Pompeium Geminum* (6.2 = FGH 115 T 20a). The ἀνδρὸς φιλαλήθους καὶ πολλὰ χρήματα καταναλώσαντος εἰς τὴν περὶ τῆς ἱστορίας ἐξέτασιν ἀκριβῆ, described in F 181a, is the synthesis of Dionysius' praise of Theopompus: μάλιστα δὲ τῆς ἐπιμελείας τε καὶ φιλοπονίας τῆς κατὰ τὴν συγγραφήν, also recalled by Suda s.v. Ἔφορος (E 3953 Adler = FGH 115 T 28b = FGH 70 T 28a; see Chávez Reino 2010:262f.). An analysis of F 181a allows us to understand how the account of events tied to individuals and to *poleis* or *ethne* far from the Greek motherland was likely approached by way of the ethnographical method, i.e. with a narration of the events enriched with scholarly explanations and etiology, in the style of Hecataeus. Shrimpton 1991:86-87 believes that the story of Clearchus was inserted into the excursus on the Pontus Euxinus. On ἀκρίβεια, see Fantasia 2004:41f.

[17] Dionysius of Halicarnassus *ad Pompeium Geminum* 6.2 = FGH 115 T 20a. Dionysius' text 'contains' several fragments from, and *testimonia* about Theopompus: this is once again proof that studying a fragmentary author is no more or no less than studying the traditions which preserved his work.

[18] Dionysius of Halicarnassus *Roman Antiquities* 1.1.1 = FGH 115 F 24; Shrimpton 1991:63-64; Santi Amantini 2009:75f.

[19] Dionysius of Halicarnassus *ad Pompeium Geminum* 6.2 = FGH 115 T 20a = FGH 115 F 26. Jacoby cautiously published the text in a smaller typeface because of a textual problem (εἰ καὶ † μηδὲν ἔγραψε). Aujac 1992:97 does not even mention this problem in the apparatus, overlooking Radermacher and Heller's efforts, and solving the problem with two soothing commas. He was clearly more convinced than his illustrious predecessors that Theopompus—as Dionysius attests—had spoken too much of his achievements and could have refrained from wordiness without precluding the positive judgement of posterity ("even if he had written *nothing*"). Notwithstanding Aujac's *souplesse*, Dionysius' text is difficult to untangle and would merit from critical suggestions. This does not keep us from understanding the general topic expressed by Theopompus in his *proemium* (Vattuone 1997:88f.).

insist too much on the merits of his own writing; the reader was in a position easily to appreciate the quality of the effort the historian had made and the validity of his sources of information.

In the statement of purpose that Dionysius reads in Theopompus' introduction there is a point of particular importance that recalls another famous fragment from the *proemium*, which has been preserved by Photius (F 25), in which Theopompus declares the superiority of himself and his contemporaries over earlier historians.[20] Photius expresses surprise and incredulity; he cannot understand whether the historian is measuring himself against Herodotus and Thucydides, against only Hellanicus and Philistus, or indeed whether his words actually refer to the famous orators, Gorgias or Lysias. Photius' difficulty, I think, arises from his inability to successfully resolve the ambiguity of the expression ἐν λόγοις/λόγων, which lies at the heart of the comparison. What should be evident to all—as the historian from Chios thought at any rate—was that the lofty culture and critical awareness of his own time was superior to that of earlier historians (πολλὴν γὰρ τοιαύτην παίδευσιν ἐπίδοσιν λαβεῖν κατὰ τὴν αὐτοῦ ἡλικίαν).

Dionysius, read against the background of Polybius (12.27.8–9), makes us well understand this point, so important for the foundation of the Greek historical consciousness. After describing the vastness of Theopompus' sources of information, Dionysius says (T 20a): "he did not consider history, as others did, to be a subsidiary activity to life, but rather the most necessary and useful action of all" (οὐ γὰρ ὥσπερ τινὲς πάρεργον τοῦ βίου τὴν ἀναγραφὴν τῆς ἱστορίας ἐποιήσατο, ἔργον δὲ τὸ πάντων ἀναγκαιότατον). This claim, which Dionysius read in the lengthy *proemium*, does not merely underline the fact that in the ancient world historiography was considered inferior to action. (Plutarch, for his part, understood not only that many historians wrote their works in exile but also that the brilliant exploits of the Athenians certainly exceeded in fame and glory the writers who tried to narrate them.)[21] In his examination of the *proemium* of the *Philippica*, Dionysius had come upon something more important that had to do with the nature of the historian's critical undertaking.

Dionysius' discussion of Theopompus' prologue (*ad Pompeium Geminum* 6.3 = T 20a) directly references a passage from Thucydides, in the first speech of

---

[20] On F 25, see Flower 1994:13f., 155f.; Vattuone 1997:88–92. In F 25, it is clear that Theopompus did not consider himself to be a disciple of Isocrates, but, if anything, his contemporary and rival.

[21] Plutarch *De gloria Atheniensium* 346f–347c: inasmuch as they are both mimetic activities, historiography and painting cannot compete with the protagonists of events. We have no evidence that Plutarch is here referring to Theopompus' proud claims; nevertheless his defense of history as a *techne* that, like other *technai*, deserves complete commitment, as Polybius well knew, could be considered a manifesto of a program that did not attract many followers in antiquity. The title of Plutarch's work itself (πότερον Ἀθηναῖοι κατὰ πόλεμον ἢ κατὰ σοφίαν ἐνδοξότεροι) clearly indicates which tradition prevailed up to the end of the Roman Empire and beyond.

Pericles (1.142.9), where the *strategos* highlights Athenian naval superiority in comparison with Sparta's inexperience, which it would be impossible to improve in a short amount of time. The conclusion that Pericles reaches is significant: "navigation is a technical skill, like any other, and so it cannot be practiced here and there or on the side [. . .]" (τὸ δὲ ναυτικὸν τέχνης ἐστίν, ὥσπερ καὶ ἄλλο τι, καὶ οὐκ ἐνδέχεται, ὅταν τύχῃ, ἐκ παρέργου μελετᾶσθαι, ἀλλὰ μᾶλλον μηδὲν ἐκείνῳ πάρεργον ἄλλο γίγνεσθαι).[22] The close relationship between τέχνη 'technical skill' and πάρεργον 'subsidiary activity' in Theopompus, following the example of Thucydides, is further underscored by a passage from Polybius (12.27.8–9), in which the Achaean historian uses Theopompus to define his own critical method. While Timaeus used only books to write his work, Polybius insists that research, although it requires rather more effort and expense, is in fact the most important part of *historia* (12.27.6). The reference to Theopompus F 26, i.e. the testimony of Dionysius with which we have been dealing, is clear, and this is made explicit immediately afterwards: Ephorus declares that the best way to acquire knowledge was through autopsy, although this was impossible in a *Universalgeschichte* (FGH 70 F 110),[23] and Theopompus says that: "He is best in matters of war who has been involved in the most dangers; he is most powerful in words who has taken part in the most political disputes. And the same thing applies to medicine and navigation."[24] In light of this passage from Polybius (which is for us also FGH 115 F 342), it seems that in Theopompus' *proemium*, οὐ . . . πάρεργον τοῦ βίου 'not a mere accessory of life' in the context of history claimed for συγγραφή 'written composition' a technical dimension that had not before been an object of reflection. The presumption of Theopompus that so irritates Photius in F 25 must be, on the authority of Polybius, who takes it over as his own, his meditation on the boundaries of history in a time when the cultural conflict between history and oratory was particularly marked. According to Photius, the *proemia* of Ephorus and Theopompus were very similar to one

[22] The meaning of πάρεργον as a 'subsidiary activity, subordinate element' can be found in Euripides *Hercules Furens* 340, Plato *Republic* 2.370c, and Thucydides 6.69.3. In Thucydides 7.27, the war that Agis conducts from Decelaia in Attica is waged οὐκ ἐκ παρέργου, i.e. not superficially, not lightly. Theopompus takes the image of the steersman from the Periclean *logos*, assigning it a methodological use.

[23] In Ephorus F 110, following a tradition with roots already in Thucydides 1.22.3, the limits of autopsy certainly do not lead to a devaluation of one's own direct experience, or that of others, but they do open up the possibility of a history not strictly (and not only) contemporary, following a method that, once again, is already present in Thucydides' archaeology (cf. Parmeggiani 2011:114f.).

[24] Polybius 12.27.8–9: τοῦτον μὲν ἄριστον ἐν τοῖς πολεμικοῖς τὸν πλείστοις κινδύνοις παρατετευχότα, τοῦτον δὲ δυνατώτατον ἐν λόγῳ τὸν πλείστων μετεσχηκότα πολιτικῶν ἀγώνων. Τὸν αὐτὸν δὲ τρόπον συμβαίνειν ἐπ'ἰατρικῆς καὶ κυβερνητικῆς.

another:[25] readers of Ephorus know also that his decision to write about a past no longer verifiable by autopsy (FGH 70 F 9) meant that his historical method would be defined precisely through a contrast with epideictic rhetoric.[26] The discussion was to be resumed by Timaeus and others and would be at the center of historical reflection in the Hellenistic age.[27]

Greek historiography acquired the features of a specific genre through a deepening of its technical characteristics and a corresponding need for an all-abiding commitment. Theopompus was not arguing against Thucydides (or Herodotus); he was trying, rather, to 'assimilate' them. His claim about the primacy of the fourth century, which astonishes Photius, has to do in fact with the extension of the field of research, the vastness of the civilized world, and the obligation to draw on disparate sources. And this expansion of the field of history stems from the dilation of the inhabited Greek world. I shall not address here whether or not Ephorus and Theopompus did in fact accomplish their task, but the significance of Theopompus' proemial claims should not be ascribed only to his colossal self-esteem. Dionysius considers Theopompus to have been verbose, but he never accuses him of promising to do more than he actually did. The supremacy (προτεύειν) that Theopompus so exalted, referred, of course, to a primacy ἐν λόγοις, in rhetorical ability, but above all to cultural primacy: as we saw above in the passage from Photius' *Bibliotheca*, "in philosophy and knowledge" (ἐν τῷ φιλοσοφεῖν καὶ φιλομαθεῖν). History becomes a genre among others through the enunciation and the defense of its own technical skills.

3. Hidden Causes

The variety of historical interests that we can observe in Theopompus is not, according to Dionysius, a result of his erudition in and of itself, although, I believe, Theopompus himself claimed this as an innovation and virtue of his enterprise, a sort of *prokatalepsis* against accusations often directed toward those, like himself, who possessed lively intellectual curiosity. The accusation that seems to have been leveled at Theopompus, namely that his use of digressions was excessive, seemed inconsistent in the eyes of his major critic, since the boundless diversity (ἀφθονία) of Theopompus' research actually was not simply superimposed on, or appended to the historical narrative: it was woven into the

---

[25] Photius *Bibliotheca* 176.121a = FGH 70 F 7, which Jacoby does not consider to belong with the other proemial fragments of Theopompus, as he should have done (Vattuone 1997); cf. Parmeggiani 2011:34f.

[26] Vattuone 1998:183f.; Parmeggiani 2011:38f., 99f., and passim.

[27] Polybius 12.28.8 = FGH 566 F 7; Vattuone 1991:22f.

very fabric of the action (*ad Pompeium Geminum* 6.4–6 = T 20a).[28] In accordance with the tastes of his time, Dionysius noted the presence of an interesting philosophical perspective in the wealth of information and data, an observation that may also belong to the encomium that Theopompus addressed to the culture of his own age.[29] Jacoby, for what it is worth, does not take a clear or bold stance on the boundaries of the fragment in the long citation assigned to T 20a.

The best-known part of Dionysius' appraisal of Theopompus is the passage that immediately follows:

τελευταῖόν ἐστι τῶν ἔργων αὐτοῦ καὶ χαρακτηρικώτατον, ὃ παρ' οὐδενὶ τῶν ἄλλων συγγραφέων οὕτως ἀκριβῶς ἐξείργασται καὶ δυνατῶς οὔτε τῶν πρεσβυτέρων οὔτε τῶν νεωτέρων. τί δὲ τοῦτο ἐστί; τὸ καθ' ἑκάστην πρᾶξιν μὴ μόνον τὰ φανερὰ τοῖς πολλοῖς ὁρᾶν καὶ λέγειν, ἀλλ' ἐξετάζειν καὶ τὰς ἀφανεῖς αἰτίας τῶν πράξεων καὶ τῶν πραξάντων αὐτὰς καὶ τὰ πάθη τῆς ψυχῆς, ἃ μὴ ῥάιδια τοῖς πολλοῖς εἰδέναι, καὶ πάντα ἐκκαλύπτειν τὰ μυστήρια τῆς τε δοκούσης ἀρετῆς καὶ τῆς ἀγνοουμένης κακίας.

There remains his crowning and most characteristic quality, one which is found developed with equal care and effect in no other writer, whether of the older or the younger generation. And what is this quality? It is the gift of seeing and stating in each case not only what is obvious to the multitude, but of examining even the hidden motives of actions and actors and the feelings of the soul (things not easily discerned by the crowd), and of laying bare all the mysteries of seeming virtue and undiscovered vice. (Translation by W. R. Roberts)

Dionysius of Halicarnassus *ad Pompeium Geminum* 6.7

---

[28] Theopompus' variety of interests (people, foundations, kings, customs, καὶ εἴ τι θαυμαστὸν ἢ παράδοξον ἑκάστη γῆ καὶ θάλασσα φέρει), was probably an object of Theopompus' self-pride in the long *proemium* of his *Philippica*. It did not, however, aim only to delight, nor did it serve only as a digression, since the richness of material is integrated into the narration of *pragmata* (συμπεριείληφεν [ἐν] τῇ πραγματείᾳ). Strabo reminds us that, unlike others, Theopompus thought ὅτι καὶ μύθους ἐν ταῖς ἱστορίαις ἐρεῖ κρεῖττον ἢ ὡς Ἡρόδοτος καὶ Κτησίας καὶ Ἑλλάνικος καὶ οἱ τὰ Ἰνδικὰ συγγράψαντες (1.2.35 = FGH 115 F 381), i.e. he wanted to narrate *even* mythical tales *within* his historical work, and he wanted to do it better than his predecessors, Herodotus, Ctesias, and Hellanicus. We usually attribute to simple haughtiness any comparison with illustrious ancestors, but the most important aspect here is that Theopompus consciously realizes that he is employing different literary forms within his *pragmata*. The hypothesis that Dionysius' *ad Pompeium Geminum* 6.4 is itself an important testimony to Theopompus' *proemium* finds here one more supporting argument.

[29] The passage immediately following F 381 (see previous note) is a defence of the philosophical utility of the historian's *polymathie* in open contrast with the critics, here again in the form of a *prokatalepsis* (FGH 115 T 20a4–5: καὶ μηδεὶς ὑπολάβῃ ψυχαγωγίαν ταῦτ' εἶναι μόνον—οὐ γὰρ οὕτως ἔχει—ἀλλὰ πᾶσαν ὡς ἔπος εἰπεῖν ὠφέλειαν περιέχει). Aujac 1992:166 (Strabo 1.2.23).

Dionysius may not be an enthusiast of Thucydides, but he knows him well and is certainly aware of the refined reflection on the causes of the Peloponnesian War that opens the first book of the *Histories* and in fact infuses the entire work. Theopompus, then, is not the first to assert the necessity of going beyond an understanding of events based only upon unquestioned tradition (cf. Thucydides 1.20.3: τὰ ἑτοῖμα), which renders the search for truth, inasmuch as it is superficial, too easy. This is not the place to discuss in detail the fact that Thucydides' decision to look beyond appearances necessitates the distinction of various levels of causation. The events that took place in Greece between 436 and 431 BCE were among the causes of the great *kinesis*, but, to take a long-term view that 'justifies' the digression termed the 'Pentecontaetia' (1.89–117), it was above all Spartan fear in the face of Athenian power (1.23.6). For the Athenian historian, it would have been too easy (and perhaps unfair) to blame Pericles for the final disaster, as his contemporaries probably did.[30] The cause that was not evident for the majority was embedded in a process that nobody could stop, but that Pericles, more than anyone else, could have controlled.

Dionysius certainly knows this page of fifth-century history and uses it to define Theopompus' innovation: we have no proof that Theopompus himself explicitly professed this innovation with respect to his predecessors, but attentive readers of Dionysius' minor works should not be surprised by this possibility. As Dionysius attests, the major characteristic of Theopompus' work (τῶν ἔργων αὐτοῦ καὶ χαρακτηρικώτατον) is that he explored the hidden causes of events and the motivations of his protagonists. With respect to Thucydides, then, his approach is novel in that it does not focus only on the hidden causes of actions (τὰς ἀφανεῖς αἰτίας τῶν πράξεων) but takes into consideration also the hidden motives of the actors (τὰς ἀφανεῖς αἰτίας τῶν πραξάντων αὐτὰς), which most people did not perceive.

If we consider how Ephorus, in a similar cultural milieu, deals with the causes of the Peloponnesian War (in conjunction with Diodorus 12.39–41, of course), we can better understand the significance of the amplification about which Dionysius, and likely Theopompus as well, speaks regarding those unseen

---

[30] This problem is clearly described by Cawkwell 1997:20f.; see also Connor 1984:21f.; Rood 1998:208f.; and Foster 2010:183f. The charges come from comedy and from rhetoric, and Thucydides seems to react to a common notion (as he says in 1.20.3) when he states that the war was inevitable (1.139.4, 140.4–5; 2.59.1) and, therefore, not to be blamed on Pericles (Plutarch *Nicias* 9.8-9; *Alcibiades* 14.1f.). Fourth-century historiography does not accept Thucydides' 'silence' on internal politics: Diodorus 12.39-41—which is not to be taken as a mirror for Ephorus FGH 70 F 196—retains a complex tradition that cannot be reduced to *gossip* (Jacoby 1926b:93). See Parmeggiani 2011:354f., 417f.

causes/reasons.[31] We are not dealing here, as Jacoby thinks, with a historiography reduced to gossip and divorced from the scientific rigor of Thucydides. What Theopompus advocates is an interpretation of events that goes beyond the inevitability of historical causation as seen by Thucydides, itself a function of the immutability of human nature. For Theopompus, the category ἀφανές includes also the intentions, plans, desires, and even the private passions of the protagonists.[32]

Readers of this *testimonium* in Jacoby's collection, or rather the section of Dionysius' *ad Pompeium Geminum* to which it corresponds, usually focus on the end of the sentence, "and to reveal all the secrets of what appears to be virtue and what is not recognized as vice" (καὶ πάντα ἐκκαλύπτειν τὰ μυστήρια τῆς τε δοκούσης ἀρετῆς καὶ τῆς ἀγνοουμένης κακίας), as if this expression synthesized everything that was said before it. It is more likely, however, that this was for Theopompus an additional element, not in any way meant to cover the entire category of hidden causes (ἀφανεῖς αἰτίαι), which Dionysius is clearly presenting progressively, in a list in which the last one is by no means the most important. The merciless moralist in Lucian is evident even in Dionysius, a sort of judge of Hades, who condemns and (less frequently) absolves, at times going too far with observations not pertinent to the main narrative. Theopompus, the *maledicentissimus*, gets carried away: but Dionysius certainly does not reduce the causal perspective of the *Philippica* to this tribunal activity. We cannot overlook the structure of the passage and its articulation. The ἀφανές in Theopompus is not simply the accumulation of vices and alleged virtues that underlie the historical process, hiding from the gaze of those who are not in a position to see them; it is above all what moves a man to make decisions, to act, and to think about accomplishing enterprises, without neglecting, as many modern readers of Theopompus have assumed, the events themselves and the inextricable network that makes them seem uncontrollable. Ephorus did not believe that the most dramatic war fought among the Greeks depended on such inherent reasons

---

[31] This passage from Diodorus contains traces of Ephorus' version that points not only to the chronological time span (from mid-fifth century to the end of the fourth), but also and in particular to the dynamics of domestic affairs and their effects on the relationship between Athens and the Peloponnesian League, all of which serves to demonstrate political initiative and decisions that lead to the war. Diodorus does not cite Ephorus *ad litteram*, but it is possible that he cites him to show where the Cumaean differed from his predecessor, using Herodotean models. See Parmeggiani 2011:354f., 417f., and also in this volume, 115f. Diodorus' citation of comic sources here is not in itself a trivialization of the causes, but a way to show how the decisions of Pericles were received and contested (cf. Thucydides 1.140–144). Ephorus F 196 is very helpful in enabling us to understand the value of Dionysius' discussion of Theopompus, which comes, it seems to me, from the explicit declaration of Theopompus himself.

[32] Vattuone 2007:151–152.

as *arche* or the laws of nature to which it was bound. Along these lines, even if we know very little of Theopompus' theory, we should consider the writer of the *Philippica*. It was the very threatening force of this individual, Philip, that clarifies (if any clarification is needed) the role that decisions, choices, and human emotions played in the shaping of events.

To go beyond appearances, viz., the understanding of οἱ πολλοί, in order to understand events is the mental attitude out of which *historie* developed in Greece: Herodotus and Thucydides are aware of Xerxes' ambition and the impetuous behavior of Alcibiades, but they both think (in different ways and from different points of view) that the actions of those characters belong to a dynamic that is to a great extent out of their grasp. During the fourth century, however, alongside an interpretation of facts and their connections there prevails an attention to a different sort of anthropology, one that was considered much less as a constant that could render all events foreseeable and universal, but rather much more contingent on its own dynamics, tied to individual and well-defined personalities, who created unexpected innovation and discontinuity in the course of history. If the point of view of fourth-century historiography was richer, as Theopompus thought, it owed this expansion of its horizons to the advent of a new era, whose meaning was not easy to understand.

4. Philip and 'Universal' History

Polybius is a valuable witness for reading what remains of Theopompus' work. In our discussion of F 26, we have already alluded to the debt that the Achaean historian owes to his fourth-century predecessors in the way that he defines his method by way of a polemic against Timaeus. It will be enough here to look carefully at 12.27–28, in order to see the ways in which he assimilates concepts, images, and structures from his colleagues whom he criticizes for their narrative faults, but never accuses of embodying the limitations attributed to them by modern philology. Polybius does not think of Ephorus and Theopompus as orators who dabbled in history, interested only in vacuously amplifying sequences described by others.[33] The image of Theopompus as φιλαλήθης 'a lover of truth' derives not only from Athenaeus but also from Polybius' independent interpretation, later reiterated by Dionysius. By φιλαλήθης, Polybius means the same characteristic that he recognizes, in spite of all his faults, even

---

[33] The structure of Polybius' criticism against Timaeus is based on images and thoughts found in Ephorus and Theopompus. It is enough to read Polybius 12.27–28 to verify this. The critique of the predecessors touches their technical ability in describing military events, but nowhere their identity as historians. Walbank 1967:409; Pédech 1989:146; Vattuone 1997:100f.; Bearzot 2005:64f.

in Timaeus, namely the quality of being accurate in every page of his research.[34] And it is important to keep in mind that our use of the term 'rhetorical historiography' does not take into account the judgment, elsewhere considered authoritative, of authors who were very aware and critical of their colleagues, and who were certainly closer to their predecessors and in a position to read their works.

Unlike Dionysius, Polybius does not praise Theopompus' *hypotheseis*; that is to say, he does not appreciate his decision to abandon the *Hellenica* in order to write about Philip (8.11.3 = T 19). Polybius makes this claim, alongside other observations about Theopompus, in the context of polemic, where he finds fault with those historians who through cowardice and fear either said nothing about or else falsified the violent capture of Messene by Philip V in 213 BCE.[35] Polybius' criticism of these omissions and distortions raises, by way of analogy, the theme of the relationship between Theopompus and Philip II. The series of chapters that follows serves to clarify the reasons for Polybius' strong disapproval: why abandon the history of Greek *poleis* to write about a man and the events of his time? As we shall see, Polybius also does not tolerate the αἰσχρολογία 'harsh criticism' that Theopompus inflicts on Philip and his court, but he is unable to understand the reason why his predecessor, after having decided to continue Thucydides' work, "as he approached the events around Leuctra and the most famous deeds of the Greeks, right in the middle, threw aside Greece and the things happening there, to change topics and write about Philip's deeds."[36] According to Polybius, it would have been much better to include such matters in the *Hellenica* rather than incorporate the *Hellenica* into the account of an individual's actions (ἥπερ ἐν τῇ Φιλίππου τὰ τῆς Ἑλλάδος), however important he may have been. From this clue, we understand first of all that Theopompus' *Philippica* was not a biography but the history of events that occurred in Greece at the time of Philip, a history that had as a unifying element the affairs of Philip and Macedon. That is to say, Theopompus chose a specific *cheirismos* to give an account of Greek events during the time of the Macedonian king (ἐν τῇ Φιλίππου τὰ τῆς Ἑλλάδος). What irritated the Achaean historian, who was himself certainly linked to the period of the *polis* and the autonomy of the Greek leagues, is precisely the fact that his predecessor had written Greek history by employing what he considered to be a objectionable structure, even though he

---

[34] Polybius 12.11.1-2 (FGH 566 T 10. See also F 12) is about the critical accuracy of Timaeus, unintentionally highlighted by showing how, in the case of Locris, Timaeus had intentionally overlooked, omitted, or modified information which he had included. Vattuone 1991:49f.

[35] Walbank 1967:78.

[36] συνεγγίσας τοῖς Λευκτρικοῖς καιροῖς καὶ τοῖς ἐπιφανεστάτοις τῶν Ἑλληνικῶν ἔργων, τὴν μὲν Ἑλλάδα μεταξὺ καὶ τὰς ταύτης ἐπιβολὰς ἀπέρριψε, μεταλαβὼν δὲ τὴν ὑπόθεσιν τὰς Φιλίππου πράξεις προὔθετο γράφειν.

had at his disposal the glorious times of Leuctra and, above all, those of the foundation of Megalopolis wherein lay the roots of the Achaean League.[37]

Polybius' judgment may be clear enough in substance but not in the way in which it is expressed: what does he mean, for example, by "as he approached the events around Leuctra and the most famous deeds of the Greeks" (συνεγγίσας τοῖς Λευκτρικοῖς καιροῖς καὶ τοῖς ἐπιφανεστάτοις τῶν Ἑλληνικῶν ἔργων)? The twelve books of the *Hellenica* close at 394 BCE: the criticism of Polybius, then, is that Theopompus chose to end his Greek History with a Spartan date, inadequate inasmuch as it preceded a decadence that had yet to reveal the age that emerged from the end of the Spartan hegemony, well beyond the brief period of Theban glory. In other words, the events around Leuctra were glorious because Sparta's fall could be considered as the beginning of a new, Achaean, history. But Polybius' expression in itself can only be understood if we assume that he had before him the very passage in which Theopompus had justified his narrative choice. In 12.27, as we have already seen, Polybius is reading Theopompus. And it is typical of the Achaean historian to use the words of fellow historians when addressing the limits and faults of their works; his critique of Timaeus is a case in point, particularly when he criticizes Timaeus' bookish approach to historiography by way of a captious exegesis of his *proemium*.[38] Timaeus, for what it is worth, had for his part treated Aristotle along very similar lines, scornfully judging him an immoderate glutton for his culinary interests.[39] Polybius' phrase, "as he approached the events around Leuctra and the most famous deeds of the Greeks," makes sense only if it is, in fact, an expression taken directly from Theopompus' lengthy introduction to his work, about which Dionysius of Halicarnassus spoke. That said, we can infer that the historian, when confronted with what was happening during his own day—with the period, we might say, in which he had begun work on his history, a period adjacent to the final days of the Spartan hegemony (370–360 BCE)— understood that the end of the Greek *polis* could not be represented by the dramatic events of the Theban invasion of the Peloponnesus but could only be described within the history of Philip and Macedon's ascent. The fact that the phrase "as he approached the events around Leuctra and the most famous deeds of the Greeks" comes directly from Theopompus seems also demonstrated by the comment that Polybius appends to his critique of Theopompus. While Theopompus, he says, would not have been able to defend himself before the charge of having unjustly employed *aischrologia*, he might nevertheless have done so regarding his change of *hypothesis*. Thus, Polybius writes: "As to this deviation from the right path however,

[37] Walbank 1962:2.
[38] Polybius 12.25h1 = FGH 566 F 34; Polybius 12.25d1 = FGH 566 T 4c; Vattuone 2002:182f.
[39] Polybius 12.8.4 = FGH 566 F 156; Düring 1957:385; Vattuone 1991:36.

which made him change the theme of his history, he might perhaps have had something to say, if any one had questioned him about it" (οὐ μὴν ἀλλὰ πρὸς μὲν ταύτην τὴν ἁμαρτίαν, καθὸ μετέβαλε τὴν ὑπόθεσιν, ἴσως ἂν εἶχέ τι λέγειν, εἴ τις αὐτὸν ἤρετο, 8.11.7).[40] What Theopompus might have said in his defense (ἴσως ἂν εἶχέ τι λέγειν) is exactly what he wrote, and exactly what Polybius asked him (εἴ τις αὐτὸν ἤρετο) while he read, a procedure typical of Hellenistic exegesis. With the expression, "as he approached the events around Leuctra and the most famous deeds of the Greeks," then, a quotation that Polybius took directly from Theopompus, the historian from Chios justified his choice of immersing his Greek History into a wider setting. It is this awareness of new historical horizons that will reinforce the enterprise of *Universalgeschichte*.

Our exegesis of T 19 once again demonstrates how ambiguous and inadequate is Jacoby's distinction between 'Testimonia' and 'Fragments'.[41] Polybius 8.11 'contains', I believe, not only a *testimonium* about Theopompus (T 19) but also a fragment from his *proemium*,[42] another remarkable aspect of that critical awareness that pushed Theopompus to consider Cnidus the end of Spartan hegemony and the essential vitality of the Greek *polis*, well before Sparta's humiliation at Leuctra; in addition, it led him to consider all of fourth-century history to have been inexorably linked to the Macedonian hegemony and the imposing, grandiose figure of Philip II.

The greater charge that Polybius makes against Theopompus—quite apart from his cultural debt toward him—was that of furnishing an incoherent image of Philip II. The context for this criticism is, as was the case for T 19, his reproach of historians' silence in the face of the brutal conduct of Philip V towards Messenia at the end of the third century BCE. For Polybius, Philip V ought to have been condemned for his actions, and instead his flatterers dedicated to him an encomium that naturally omitted any reference to his misdeeds. Indeed, it would have been enough for them not to omit anything, or rather to avoid giving false praise and false blame (λοιδορεῖν ψευδῶς . . . τοὺς μονάρχους οὔτ' ἐγκωμιάζειν):

---

[40] Translated by E. S. Shuckburgh.

[41] Schepens 1997:71f. discusses this problem. Normally the *aporia* is resolved by returning to the text of the *testimonium* and approaching the problem on a thematic level. We should abandon the persistent idea that there is a rigid distinction between *testimonia* and *fragmenta*, that is, that the fragment of an historian can exist without a commentary. On this problem, see Parmeggiani 2011:32f.

[42] The study of Dionysius' text—from which comes our FGH 115 T 20a—allows us to better understand that the so-called 'fragments' from Theopompus' *proemium* are far more numerous than Jacoby's collection leads us to believe. Better would be to say: the topics treated by Theopompus in his *proemium* are much broader than what we read in Jacoby. There is nothing wrong with continuing to speak about fragments and *testimonia*, using the classical definition, as long as we remember that it is a choice of convenience only, which often does not correspond to sound hermeneutic principles nor to the very nature of the passages under discussion.

it is not that Polybius rejects all judgments on the behavior of great individuals, but rather demands they be consistent with the developing narrative and appropriate for the character of each (ἀκόλουθον δὲ τοῖς προγεγραμμένοις ἀεὶ καὶ τὸν πρέποντα ταῖς ἑκάστων προαιρέσεσι λόγον ἐφαρμόζειν) (8.8.6–7). Theopompus' work is the clearest example, in Polybius' eyes, of the incorrect employment of historical judgment, inasmuch as it violates both of these requirements: his censure of the Macedonian king is both inconsistent with and ill-suited to the ethos of the character. Polybius' accusations, we should note, stem from historiographic principles, not only from a cumbersome moralism:[43] the description of facts and characters must abide by a linearity of assessment that does not admit contradictions and subtleties. If the decision to write about Philip came from his conviction that "Europe had never before borne a man such as Philip, the son of Amyntas" (μηδέποτε τὴν Εὐρώπην ἐνηνοχέναι τοιοῦτον ἄνδρα παράπαν οἷον τὸν Ἀμύντου Φίλιππον), then it would not have been possible for Theopompus to describe the king, either in the *proemium* or in any other part of the work, as squandering his family possessions through his immoderate passion for women, as unfaithful and violent against Greek *poleis* that had already been subjugated to his will, or as a drunkard, intoxicated on almost every page. Polybius' assessment of Theopompus' Philip is analogous to that of the Sicilian tyrants described by Timaeus.[44] Just as the Timaean Agathocles has no place in Polybius' rigid deontology that can neither tolerate the use of comic sources to discredit the tyrant in his early childhood nor admit his *aischrologia*,[45] so too the Philip of Theopompus, his court of generals, and his soldiers, who are given over to baseness of every kind, are intolerable.[46] The τοιοῦτον ἄνδρα

---

[43] Polybius' unease towards Theopompus is meaningful only if he distinguished *in rebus* very different aspects of Philip's representation (cf. Momigliano 1975). Although well grounded in his cultural amnesia, the idea that Polybius did not understand the irony of his predecessor in calling Philip II a "great man" (Shrimpton 1977:123f.; 1991:22, 162–163) does not take into account the complexity of critical judgement on the Macedonian, as well as on other figures, like Lysander and Agesilaus. Polybius is well aware of the distinction between history and encomium (10.21.8), since it "touches" also his beloved Philopoemen.

[44] In Timaeus, Agathocles is the threatening, but great character who aspired to kingship, although he was only a tyrant. The *incipit* of Diodorus' Book 19, which is devoted to Agathocles' career, looks inconsistent even to modern readers, who are compelled to separate 'favorable' from 'unfavorable' sources, where the traces of Timaeus absorbed into the *Library* reflect only a dark, complex evaluation of this character (cf. Vattuone 2005:321f.).

[45] Polybius 8.11.5–13 (FGH 115 F 225a and the parallel F 225b = Athenaeus 6.260d–261a); Pédech 1989:214f.

[46] This is the famous case of the *pais* Agathocles (Polybius 12.15 = FGH 566 F 124b), for whom Timaeus used "inappropriate sources" (such as comedy) to cover both the boy and the adult with outrageous jests. As Walbank records (1962:2), the charge of *aischrologia* raised against Theopompus becomes in Dionysius a reason to praise his manifest freedom of judgment. Also well known is the fact that Theopompus' contradictions in his depiction of Philip, inasmuch as they are without logic, annoy Polybius much more than those of Timaeus on Agathocles: if

in F 27 has been discussed at length, too much perhaps and with contradictory results.[47] Here—just as with the events around Leuctra (Λευκτρικοὶ καιροί)—the τοιοῦτον must represent an emphasis that Polybius put on Theopompus' text in order to highlight the grandiose figure of Philip II and his impressive historical role, not to mention the vicious aspects of his behavior. In reading the interminable *proemium*, Polybius considers his predecessor's choice unacceptable.

Quite apart from his critical choices, Polybius' viewpoint is telling: Theopompus certainly was violent in his attack of Philip II, but the problem, for Polybius, was not his use of categories such as blame or encomium, nor his narration of historical events. What is stressed in F 27 is that the historian from Chios justified his decision to abandon the *Hellenica* and saw Philip II as a grandiose, but also a dark and threatening presence in Greek history—a man displaying the customs typical of barbarians, in a moral climate that is completely detached from that aristocratic ethic on which the *polis* had been based. Polybius' historiographical principles prevent him from accepting that *in rebus* Philip's time and Philip himself are inherently contradictory. In any case, in his opinion *aischrologia* should never have been used, since it suits neither the 'genre', nor the figure against whom it is aimed. It is not accidental that some time later, and with substantial accuracy, the long tale of excesses at the Macedonian court is taken up again by Athenaeus (6.260d-261a = FGH 115 F 225b) in his description of the harmful effects on kings and governors of *kolakeia*.

According to Polybius, Ephorus was "the first and only one to have undertaken a universal history" (5.33.2 = FGH 70 T 7), an assertion that Diodorus will later echo (4.1.2; 16.76.5); this assertion has been coolly greeted by modern scholars,[48] who prefer to connect, by now almost as an historiographical tic, Ephorus' 'generality' to Isocratean Panhellenism.[49] On the other hand, contemporary historians and philologists consider that the most appropriate way to understand *koinai praxeis* (or rather τὰ καθόλου) is precisely by defining it by way of Ephorus' own schema, namely as a history that embraces all the known and inhabited world both spatially and chronologically.[50] Polybius, for his part,

---

nature had given these gifts to the Macedonian, it would be possible to show immediately afterwards his corrupt customs, even if they were hidden (8.10.12f.).

[47] The expression, although ambiguous (Connor 1968:137f.) and clearly *not* ironical (*pace* Shrimpton 1991), should not reveal more than the stature of a character who deeply influenced an entire historical epoch. Flower (1994:98f.) is right when he sees in Polybius' interpretation a grave misunderstanding, because what he considers to be a contradiction is the very essence of the judgment on his character. Pédech (1989:247f.) complains that there are not sufficient arguments to back up this interpretation, which seems to him at most a possibility. Parmeggiani (2011:616) rightly stresses Theopompus' freedom of judgment.

[48] Marincola 2007b:172–174; Parmeggiani 2011:711f.

[49] Momigliano 1975:697f.; Roveri 1964:58f.; Burde 1974:17f.; Alonso Núñez 2002:39f.

[50] Alonso Núñez 2002:117; Marincola 2007b:171.

aspired to write a 'universal history' without going back to the remotest past but instead by demonstrating the extraordinary convergence of all history under the aegis of Rome in the short time span of fifty years (1.3.1–4.1): it is the incredible trajectory of an extraordinary historical subject that allows events hitherto disparate and disjoined to be assembled into a significant unity.[51] Ephorus, then, is a strange ancestor of Polybius. Polybius' admiration, which stems perhaps from Timaeus' anti-Ephoran polemic, reveals in fact just how different was his own project, focused as it was on a short period, no longer than a century, from his predecessor's *Universalgeschichte*, which reached all the way from the Heraclids to the present day. Polybius is not deluded: it was possible, then, to undertake τὰ καθόλου in space and in time, as Ephorus did, or to limit oneself to a contemporary perspective, focusing on one historical element at the center of the narrative, and making it universal *in rebus*.[52] Polybius could not ignore that the *Histories* of both Herodotus (revolving around the theme of the *Persica*) or in fact of Thucydides (focused on the no less general theme of the war between the Athenians and the Peloponnesians) had the writing and the economy that aspired to go beyond the fragmentary dimension of the events. It is not a paradox that Thucydides insists in the first line of his work that the conflict at the center of his account was "global" and "general".[53] Polybius knows this, and if he considered Ephorus, and not Herodotus, Thucydides, or another historian, to have been the first writer of *Universalgeshichte*, we must look elsewhere for the reason.[54]

If we look again at Polybius' criticism of Theopompus' decision to move from the *Hellenica* to the *Philippica*, we are able to observe that Polybius' negative evaluation is based not only on the underestimation of the so-called Λευκτρικοὶ καιροὶ καὶ τὰ ἐπιφανέστατα τῶν Ἑλληνικῶν ἔργα: the *proemium* of the *Philippica*, in which we know that Theopompus justified his choice, must have contained

---

[51] Pelling 2007:245f.

[52] Marincola 2007b:171.

[53] In the first *proemium*, the sentence used to define the disruption caused by the 'great war' (1.1.2: κίνησις γὰρ αὕτη μεγίστη δὴ <u>τοῖς Ἕλλησιν</u> ἐγένετο καὶ <u>μέρει τινὶ τῶν βαρβάρων, ὡς δὲ εἰπεῖν καὶ ἐπὶ πλεῖστον ἀνθρώπων</u>) signifies a broad and 'general' dimension of the conflict. It is not so strange to point out that Greek historiography, beyond the chronological limits of past/present, aims to a *universal dimension*. Vattuone 1998:75f.

[54] The conclusions of Parmeggiani 2011:726f. clarify the complexity of Polybius' judgment on the previous historiography. It is from the critique of Theopompus' Philip that we are able to understand why the Achaean historian recognizes in Ephorus and not in Theopompus the primogeniture of this writing model; the fact that Ephorus kept a coherent form with his tidy and precise work lies behind Polybius' evaluation. Nevertheless, this may not be enough. I think that Polybius' choice, very close to those of Theopompus and even Timaeus, prompts in him the encomium of Ephorus and the despise for the excessive variety of themes in Theopompus' work. See *infra*.

both the declaration of the threatening grandeur of Philip and the reason why Greek history was immersed in and contained by the affairs of the Macedonian king (συμπεριλαβεῖν . . . ἐν τῇ Φιλίππου τὰ τῆς Ἑλλάδος : Polybius 8.11.4). The independence of Greek history of "the times of Leuctra" and the true significance of this period for the birth of the Achaean League, an epochal event in the context of the third to second centuries BCE, were considered in Theopompus' prologue to be less important than the convergence of all the most significant events in the unifying ascent of Philip and Macedon. The inclusion of Greek history in the *Philippica* does not merely serve as a superficial organizational principle (*cheirismos*); it gives the work meaning and direction. For Theopompus, τὰ περὶ Φιλίππου embraces both the crucial battle of Cnidus and the dramatic break constituted by the fall of Sparta's naval power. Theopompus' perspective (and it could not be otherwise) is oriented towards the great Asian campaign, which the Greek *polis*, precisely at Cnidus with the end of Spartan thalassocracy, had lost. Not only does this explain Theopompus' praise of Lysander, but it also clarifies that the structure of the *Philippica* is an explicit declaration of a universal perspective, whose characterizing element has to do with its subject and its spatial extent, not its chronological completeness. Polybius' irritation (perhaps even excessive) at this decision is just what he felt for Timaeus who, in wanting to make Sicily, which was only a tea cup, into the centre of the world, could claim to be the author of a universal history (Polybius 12.23.4–7 = FGH 566 F 119a); placing Timoleon "over the most splendid heroes" and Sicily, which had been liberated by Timoleon, at the pivot of the entire history, "he, who had written only about Italy and Sicily, considered it natural to be worthy of comparison with writers of universal history" (12.23.7: αὐτὸς ὑπὲρ Ἰταλίας μόνον καὶ Σικελίας πραγματευόμενος εἰκότως παραβολῆς ἀξιωθῆναι τοῖς ὑπὲρ τῆς οἰκουμένης καὶ τῶν καθόλου πράξεων πεποιημένοις τὰς συντάξεις). This charge against Timaeus is crucial for our understanding of Polybius' reaction to the *Philippica's proemium*; for Polybius completely and disdainfully denies what both Timaeus and Theopompus had claimed by the extent of their interests and the choices they made.

Polybius' encomium and acknowledgement of Ephorus, as well as his criticism of the *proemium* of the *Philippica*, finds its justification in one idea: Ephorus was the first to write a spatially and chronologically 'universal history', just as Polybius was the first to conceive a *Universalgeschichte* that certainly comprised all known space but is limited in time to the rise of Rome, an event that absorbs all other history within itself. Polybius grants Ephorus a primacy that he denies, in order to confer it on himself, Theopompus, Timaeus, and even on Herodotus and Thucydides, who had been epitomized or resumed by Theopompus. That is to say, and this is the paradox in T 19 and F 27, Theopompus made a choice that paralleled that of the Achaean critic: to subsume Greek history within τὰ Φιλίππου, because only so powerful an individual, of so dark and grand stature, could give a meaning to, indeed a way of reading, a series of events that would otherwise have been scattered in the fundamental crisis of the *poleis*.

5. The Judge and the Historian. Observations on the Tradition of Theopompus' Fragments.

It is common practice in studies of Greek historiography—but also in different fields—to assign to those dealing with τὰ γεγενημένα ("past events") a philosophical foundation or to make them disciples of somebody in order to justify their framework, the profound reasons behind their research. For instance, Hecataeus is linked to Ionic philosophy; Herodotus and Thucydides to the sophists; Ephorus and Theopompus, of course, to Isocratean rhetoric, and so on to, limiting ourselves to only a few examples, the 'Aristotelian' Duris and the Stoics, Polybius and Posidonius. Although it is certainly hard to deny that an author, an intellectual, is influenced by the culture of his own time, and that, in turn, his culture is somehow affected by him, I do not believe that philosophical thinking determined the orientation and choices of these historians. In any case, the subordination of *historia* to *philosophia* is more appropriate to the age of Hegel, Collingwood, or Croce than to the fourth-century Greece of Isocrates, Plato and Aristotle. Even if we admit that Theopompus was a disciple of Isocrates, we should not, at any rate, believe that the works of the former are the necessary and inevitable development of the broad, and not always coherent, ideology of the latter.[55] The Isocratean Theopompus was unable to free himself from further debts. The merciless judge depicted in the critique of Polybius (and of Dionysius, too), *maledicentissimus*, as tradition records, must have been motivated to engage in this censorial activity by some cultural tradition. And it is in this way that a 'cynical' matrix has been granted to Theopompus, without adding or detracting from his image as orator and historian.[56] As for Ephorus, I think that Theopompus, too, is far more linked to the tradition of the 'genre' inaugurated by him as a *techne* than dependent upon any cultural stream: that

---

[55] Flower 1994:42f.

[56] Murray's thesis (1946) has often been recycled, without search for further proof. Pédech 1989:233f. highlights the relationships between the *maledicentissimus* and the thinking of Antisthenes, i.e. a philosophical approach which tends to go beyond superficial causes looking for a greater depth. Pédech is the first one to question this approach at the end of his work (235f.).

is, Theopompus is more a student of Herodotus, Philistus, or Thucydides than of Isocrates.[57]

To gain a more balanced understanding of Theopompus' historiographical identity, it is not enough, of course, to analyze only the intentions he expresses in the *proemia* and elsewhere. We should read the fragments in their context, going beyond even the established interpretations. But first it will be necessary to take a preliminary look at the typology of the tradition that has preserved Theopompus and provided us with his prevailing image. The brief observations that follow, although limited, can, I think, serve as the basis for further investigation.

Athenaeus of Naucratis, along with his *Deipnosophists*, is the fullest and most descriptive conduit for the surviving traces of Theopompus' works.[58] As we have seen, Athenaeus defines the historian from Chios as *philalethes* (F 181a), recording here as a sort of *leitmotiv* that his love for truth expressed itself by way of the great expense he faced in order to obtain all the materials needed for a scrupulous work (πολλὰ χρήματα καταναλώσαντος εἰς τὴν περὶ τῆς ἱστορίας ἐξέτασιν ἀκριβῆ). The context of this fragment—a discussion of various miraculous herbs that can prevent the effects of hemlock and other poisons—is instructive in many ways. In Book 38, Athenaeus tells us, Theopompus speaks at length (διηγούμενος) about Clearchus, the tyrant of Pontic Herakleia, and the habitual use of the medicinal shrub rue by those participating in the tyrant's dangerous banquets. The tale was known to other sources, as well, and was at some stage even attributed to Euphorion. Athenaeus' text suggests here that the account of Clearchus, which earned his favorable judgment, is much longer and certainly not reducible to the boundaries of the citation. Theopompus is adduced here—and elsewhere in the *Deipnosophists*—because of his precision and reliability, to confirm a specific detail in the history of this tyrant and his cruelty. One may be *philalethes* even when speaking about miraculous events, as Theopompus did in his eighth book, in the context of a strange continent that Silenus describes to Midas in a fascinating dialogue (F 75a). Indeed, Aelian even describes him as a powerful mythologist, in reference to the same event (F 75c).

---

[57] Flower 1994:160f. The Herodotean Theopompus is not only the epitomator of the *Histories*, but also the heir to Herodotus' plurality of interests and pleasure in narrating. The fact that Theopompus aimed to continue Thucydides' work does not indicate a complete adherence to Thucydides' narrative choices, but rather Theopompus' desire to embrace two centuries (the 5th and the 4th) to understand the innovation of Philip II. Scholars have tended, however, to look for ideological connections where canonical connections are clear.

[58] As many as 73 out of 411 fragments (or 396, to exclude Jacoby's *Zweifelhaftes* FF 397–411) of Theopompus come from Athenaeus. This is a great number, and more than half of these quotations are 'direct'; however, the interests of Athenaeus are specific, and so strongly affect our view of Theopompus.

Theopompus' reputation as a 'lover of truth' is no different from what Polybius is forced to recognize in Timaeus and, for that matter, from the attitude that Thucydides claims against those whose superficiality makes them think that Hipparchus was tyrant at the time of his murder or that there was such a thing as a *lochos* of Pitane in the Spartan Army (1.20). Completeness and exactness are values embraced and suggested by ἀκρίβεια.[59] The Clearchus episode is exemplary: in Theopompus' history, it is likely that the history of the Herakleia and its 'tyrant' went hand in hand, written by way of anecdotes portraying the ethos of the individual. We cannot limit the richness of perspective to the interests of Athenaeus, who passes over the city to leave more space to Clearchus himself. It is unnecessary, I hope, to point out some of the reasons why a sophist would cut the narrative of the *Philippica* to suit the needs of a collection of symposial anecdotes. It is useful to remember, as a careful reading of the fragments in Athenaeus can show us, that Theopompus' account contains something else, although in the guise of moral judgment, stern and perhaps pedantic. The majority of the texts transmitted by the *Deipnosophists* deal with excesses of food, drink, and sex among barbarians or immoderate Greeks. The center of this picture is the dark figure of Philip in FF 224–225a/b. Alongside the Macedonian king, we encounter legendary figures, such as Cotys of Thrace, with his religious mania to marry Athena (F 31); Straton, King of Sidon, with his extravagant rivalry with Nicocles over luxury (F114); the Argive Nicostratus, immoderate in his flattery (F 124); Thys, king of Paphlagon, and the interminable food of his banquet (F 179), who approaches Niseus the Syracusan in immoderacy at the table, as if both ate nearly to the point of death (F 188). There are also entire populations, like the Athenians and the Etruscans, who spend in revelry far more than they spend for the public matters, devoting themselves to all kind of sexual extravagances (F 213; F 204). Above all, it is the barbarians (although also the Athenians or Thessalians) who seem to have borne the brunt of the bitterness that Polybius did not tolerate when aimed at Philip; but he took care not to consider it the predominate characteristic of Theopompus' historiography.[60]

It is possible, however, to go beyond Athenaeus, by using Athenaeus. In F 121 (10.444e–445a), Hegesilochus is depicted as overcome with alcohol and food and deprived of the esteem of the Rhodians; but, before describing his

---

[59] Fantasia 2004:51f.

[60] It is not legitimate to get any idea about the complex work of Theopompus from these fragments of *débauche*. So many scholars agree, from Wilamowitz to Murray, followed by Connor 1968:12 ". . . but certainly the entire *Philippica* was not such a compilation of exotic sensuality"); Reed 1976:52f.; Shrimpton 1991:28; Flower 1994:8 ("the result is that our impression of Theopompus is necessarily distorted"); Chávez Reino and Ottone 2007:146f.

sexual excesses, Athenaeus clearly gives a summary of what he will not retain from Theopompus' account: the expression, "speaking about the oligarchic regime established by Hegesilochus and his friends in Rhodes" (λέγων περὶ τῆς ὀλιγαρχίας ἣν κατεστήσατο μετὰ τῶν φίλων), synthesizes the broader context in which the citations about his *mores* should be inserted; it is, of course, on these *mores* that Athenaeus focuses, and not on the political situation of the island in the mid-fourth century. Theopompus' judgment on Hegesilochus is political; in any case, it aims to reveal that the tyrant wanted his countrymen to consider him worthy of governing the city, adducing as evidence a relatively unknown piece of evidence. That is to say, the tale about Rhodes contains the actions of Hegesilochus and reveals unknown sides of his personality, just as Dionysius indicates in the *ad Pompeium Geminum*. It seems reasonable, then, that here too Theopompus did not confine himself to mere moral judgment.[61]

We note something similar in F 135, a part of Theopompus' excursus on the Adriatic sea in Book 21[62]—in the text of Athenaeus, this precedes the citation of F 89 from Book 10. Here, the *mores* of Pisistratus (who is self-controlled and *sophron*) are seen in relationship to his sensitive policy towards the demes and the *chora*, and his demagogic policy is not presented in as negative a light as we would expect; and the analogy (perhaps already present in the text of Book 21) is with the figure of Cimon, who claimed Pisistratus as his model. Here, too, the political and moral judgments are clearly connected, within Theopompus' partial but very important reinterpretation of fifth-century Athenian history, which lumped Pericles together with his degenerate successors, *pace* Thucydides.[63] F 143, a description of the corrupted *mores* of Charidemus of Oreus, is also clearly linked to Athenian politics and to their tendency to grant citizenship too readily.[64]

We may continue to read Athenaeus in this way. Even the most 'scandalous' of the fragments (224 and 225 a/b) allow us to suppose that the political judgment and the historical narrative were not limited to the grotesque. In the synthesis with which he closes the citation from Theopompus, Athenaeus calls the Macedonians plunderers (*lestai*) and this proves their lack of *paideia*. The narrative of historical events is appropriately (not speciously or falsely) interwoven with the digressions, ethical evaluations, and the elaboration of causes. It was possible to be violent, a lush without scruples, but nevertheless efficient

---

[61] Shrimpton 1991:122-123. Pédech 1989:207f. prefers to point out the 'psychological' aspect of Theopompus' ethics. The so-called moralism of Theopompus seems very well integrated into the historiographical perspective of Dionysius of Halicarnassus' *ad Pompeium Geminum* 6.5 (FGH 115 T 20a) where philosophical value and political judgement are attributed to his sentences.

[62] Vattuone 2000:11f.

[63] Connor 1968:19f.

[64] Shrimpton 1991:140.

and attentive to politics; this is, in fact, explicitly stated about Callistratus, the son of Callicrates, in F 97, a fragment from Book 10. What for Polybius seemed an irreconcilable contradiction with reference to Philip—to repeat the short-sighted judgment already applied to Timaeus' Agathocles—is perfectly consistent with Theopompus' view. The citation from Timaeus is instructive since it allows us to see that for both historians Athenaeus provides the same *leitmotiv*: the *tryphe* of money weakens *mores* and infects neighbors. This is the case with the numerous Timaean fragments that deal with the Achaean cities of Italy, and, in the same way, with Theopompus regarding the fatal contact between the democracies in Byzantium and Chalcedon (F 63).[65] Both historians clearly have a viewpoint that is bitter and moralistic, sometimes even cynical, but their narration cannot be reduced to this trait. What I have demonstrated with regard to Timaeus, I think, also applies to Theopompus.[66]

It is also possible to go beyond Athenaeus by using other sorts of citations, above all other sources, in particular the commentaries to Demosthenes (Didymus *in primis*), but also Strabo and Plutarch. F 307, for example, preserves a segment of narrative about King Cotys of Thrace and his offspring that is quite full, although synthesized for the purposes of the lexicon entry that preserves it. Thrace had become a focus of interest for the Greeks from before its final annexation by Philip II in 343 BCE. Philochorus had dealt with Thrace in his *Atthis*, on account of the good relationship between Athens and Cotys.[67] In connection to the events that begin his work, Theopompus provides an extensive history of Thrace, and it is here that we find the admittedly tangential account of Cotys, with his immoderate appetite and his profound love for Athena. Modern scholars compare Herodotus to Theopompus, who declared himself capable of writing better *fabulae* than his famous predecessor (FGH 115 F 381). His delight in extravagant digressions and titillating anecdotes was not to the detriment of patient, detailed reconstruction of broad historical events.[68]

The two *logoi* of Philocrates and Aristophon (F 164; F 166), retained by Didymus, are full of historical judgments on the situation in Athens in 347/6

[65] Shrimpton 1991:150f. The conclusion by Pédech 1989:240–241 on his "Théopompe méconnu," starting from the moralizing imprint of his work, is unacceptable: "Expliquer les événements par un enchaînement logique à la façon de Thucydide ne paraît pas avoir été le souci de Théopompe." In Dionysius, moralism, mythological taste and *mirabilia* constitute the character of Theopompus' tale, well inserted in the *pragmata*. They become here a means of distinguishing between scientific historiography and rhetorical and novelistic historiography, going against Thucydides as well.

[66] Vattuone 1991:319f.

[67] FGH 115 F 307 (Lex. in Demosthenes *Aristocrates*, fr. A1) = FGH 328 F 42. See Costa 2007, 292f.

[68] Jacoby 1913:510; Bruce 1970:96f. Dionysius' judgement (*ad Pompeium Geminum* 6.4–6) is considered to be decisive by Flower 1994:161f. in confirming the link between the historian and the epitomizer on the level of the narration, the excursus, and the choice of subjects.

BCE, in particular Aristophon's summary of the financial situation in the city on the eve of the Peace of Philocrates. The account of Hermias of Atarneus in Didymus (F 291) helps not only to clarify the tone of Theopompus' entire account—his harsh judgment, for example, on the money-changer, who was immoral and violent and only by chance in a position of power—but also reveals that he covered Hermias' attempt to reestablish the city's ancient constitution after he came to power in Atarneus. The events of 341, followed by the death of the tyrant, surely left room for a more extensive history only alluded to in the *Deipnosophists.*

We can observe similar attention to the broader background in the fragments in Strabo and Plutarch. In the *Geography*, the texts of the citations—we think, perhaps, of the excursus on the Adriatic (F 129f.), the Peloponnesus (F 383), Epirus (F 382), Boeotia (F 385), Mariandynians (F 388), the Hellespont, and Sestus (F 390)—are articulated according to the ethnographic approach of Hecataeus, a tendency echoed both by Ephorus and Timaeus in their description of *topoi* that have to do with local traditions that were not widely known. Here, the citations from Theopompus define unknown terms or provide a story that is unique, miraculous, or unattested elsewhere. Strabo says that Theopompus aimed to narrate myths better then Herodotus, Ctesias, Hellanicus, and the authors of *Indica* (F 381). In fact, what Theopompus actually said was that he would tell "even myths better than Herodotus, Ctesias, Hellanicus, and the authors of *Indica*" (φήσας ὅτι καὶ μύθους ἐν ταῖς ἱστορίαις ἐρεῖ, κρεῖττον ἢ ὡς Ἡρόδοτος καὶ Κτησίας καὶ Ἑλλάνικος καὶ οἱ τὰ Ἰνδικὰ συγγράψαντες), emphasizing a superiority in comparison to his predecessors of the sort that is contained in Photius' version of his *proemium* (F 25).

In Plutarch, too, we can see that the exclusively moralistic quotations that predominate in Athenaeus are but one aspect of Theopompus' research. The figure of Agesilaus is illustrative of the relationship between Theopompus' narration of events and his historical judgment. In the central section of Plutarch's *bios*, we find several fragments of an account characterized by evaluations similar to those that assail Philip. According to Theopompus, it was agreed that Agesilaus, who was the only one to receive the command of land and sea troops during the war in Asia Minor, was "the greatest . . . and the most prominent of those then living" (μέγιστος . . . καὶ τῶν τότε ζώντων ἐπιφανέστατος), although "he was prouder of his virtue than he was of his power" (*Agesilaus* 10.9-10 = FGH 115 F 321). Nevertheless, there are some cracks, here and elsewhere, resulting in a more nuanced picture. Entrusting Pisander with the fleet was clearly a mistake not only because, despite his courage, Pisander had no experience (Xenophon *Hellenica* 3.4.27–29), but also because Agesilaus privileged the interests of his family over those of the state. Agesilaus' virtue, of which he was so proud, clearly had limits, and Theopompus was not prepared to gloss over them in order to paint an idealized portrait of him. The king's valor is not at stake, and he very realistically seems to want to prevent the Spartans from facing Epaminondas' army during the Theban invasion, "against so great, as Theopompus says, a river and wave of war" (πρὸς τοσοῦτον, ὥς φησι Θεόπομπος, ῥεῦμα καὶ κλύδωνα πολέμου); and because of the part he played in causing the invasion, Agesilaus was forced to bend his virtue to mere calculations and to tolerate offenses. It is quite probable that the greatness and limitations of Agesilaus, according to Theopompus' portrayal of him, were that of a king who recognized the splendor of his city at the time of the expedition to Asia, but was forced to humiliating terms not long afterward. The lofty figure of F 321 does not only try to limit damages, but he incautiously pushes away the invaders with an offer of money, useless inasmuch as they were already in the process of leaving Laconia (*Agesilaus* 32.13–33.2 = FGH 115 F 323). Plutarch wonders why it is only Theopompus who remembers this detail, which is ignored by all others (*Agesilaus* 33.1). Agesilaus' mistake, namely his responsibility for the invasion of Peloponnesus, did not contradict the fact that the Spartans owed the salvation of their city—and on this all were agreed—to Agesilaus, through his wise renouncing of his personal ambitions. It is unclear whether we should also ascribe to Theopompus Plutarch's discussion of the causes of Sparta's fall just after this passage (*Agesilaus* 33.4), in which Plutarch blames Sparta's downfall on the introduction of a perverse taste for power and supremacy. Agesilaus' cautiousness, in any case, was not able to revive Sparta: it was a single error, as Plutarch says just after F 323, that drove the *polis* to its end, just as in the case of an otherwise healthy body infected by disease.

Theopompus' depiction of Agesilaus, as preserved in Plutarch, is a privileged means, in my opinion, to understand the complexity of his historical judgment about contemporary events. As Plutarch's *Agesilaus* shows, Theopompus analyzed contemporary events in detail, corrected the tradition regarding them, and discussed them from a long-term perspective that allowed for a more complex understanding of their causes. Agesilaus is not a character from an encomium, but a multifaceted politician, just as happens in the vivid action of events and not in the assemblies where things are described and said in order to persuade. In Theopompus' description, Agesilaus' errors and virtues are intertwined without malice, reflecting Theopompus' interest in going beyond mere celebration. In the same way, Theopompus' complex and articulate evaluation of Demosthenes (F 328), softened in a way that displeases Plutarch (he was not "moody and flighty": F 326), takes into account a variety of actions and, most of all, the *dynamis* of an orator who forces Philip to peace. The focus is here on the strength of *logos* in driving events, of a politician who controls situations through his words. The positive portrait of Lysander (F 332) is also not merely a rhetorical encomium but is subjected to the critical meticulousness that the Greeks call *akribeia*. The subversive, innovative character of his politics that could have saved the *polis* from the Persian threat, was rejected, just as in the case of Alcibiades.

What is striking in Plutarch's citations of Theopompus is the latter's innovative and idiosyncratic narrative. The account of Timoleon in Greece, namely the assassination of Timophanes, before his successful invasion of Sicily is an item that Timaeus will pick up again in the context of a polemic against Theopompus.[69] Here, we can perhaps better understand what Dionysius meant when he highlighted Theopompus' interest in ἀφανές; this is not simply a matter of vices and virtues sought at the level of gossip. Theopompus extends the account of the Corinthian leader beyond the bounds of the period of Timoleon's life usually discussed, to reveal what lies behind the tale of a Corinthian condottiere who abandons his homeland to try his luck elsewhere. The reasons behind his expedition to free Syracuse from tyranny, then, become at least also about domestic affairs, about his motherland, in a perspective pursued by Ephorus to describe the events that lead up to the Peloponnesian War and had been overlooked by Thucydides. It was not enough to celebrate Timoleon as a heroic liberator: the episode of Timophanes' homicide did not detract from his successful western campaign, but rather provided a balanced discussion of the causes and motivations.

These observations—and there are many others that ought to be added—enable, I think, a more satisfactory reading of Theopompus' work. This *deinos* mythologist is an author, punctilious, comprehensive, and meticulous. He narrates broad historical developments, ably interspersing his narrative with digressions of every sort; he attacks opponents so as to include both praise and blame in his account. Quite apart from Athenaeus' charge of a rhetorical and epideictic moralism, Theopompus seems to be an historian in the full meaning of the term and certainly to have been influenced more by Thucydides and Herodotus than by his putative teacher, Isocrates.

[69] FGH 115 F 334, Shrimpton 1991:92. See Plutarch *Timoleon* 4.5 = FGH 566 F 116 = FGH 70 F 221. See Diodorus 16.65.5; Nepos *Timoleon* 1.3–6; Talbert 1974:36f.; Sordi 1983:263; Vattuone 1991:94.

Bibliography

Alonso Núñez, J. M. 2002. *The Idea of Universal History in Greece from Herodotus to the Age of Augustus.* Amsterdam.

Ambaglio, D. 1995. *La Biblioteca storica di Diodoro siculo: problemi e metodo.* Como.

Aujac, G., ed. 1992. *Denys d'Halicarnasse. Opuscules rhétoriques.V., texte établi et trad. par G. Aujac.* Paris.

Barber, G. 1935. *The Historian Ephorus.* Cambridge.

Bearzot, C. 2005. "Polibio e Teopompo. Osservazioni di metodo e giudizio morale." In Schepens and Bollansée 2005:56–71.

Bleckmann, B. 1998. *Athens Weg in die Niederlage. Die letzten Jahre des peloponnesischen Krieges.* Stuttgart.

———. 2006. *Fiktion als Geschichte. Neue Studien zum Autor der Hellenika Oxyrhynchia und zur Historiographie des vierten vorchristlichen Jahrhunderts.* Göttingen.

Bloch, H., ed. 1956. *Abhandlungen zur griechischen Geschichtschreibung von Felix Jacoby zu seinem achtzigsten Geburtstag am 19 März 1956.* Leiden.

Bruce, I. A. F. 1970. "Theopompus and Classical Greek Historiography." *History and Theory* 9:86–109.

Burde, P. 1974. *Untersuchungen zur antiken Universalgeschichtsschreibung.* Diss., Munich.

Cawkwell, G. 1997. *Thucydides and the Peloponnesian War.* London.

Chávez Reino, A. 2005. "Los claroscuros del Éforo de Polibio." In Schepens and Bollansée 2005:19–54.

———. 2010. "Echos de Theopompo en la Suda." In *Il Lessico Suda e gli storici greci in frammenti. Atti dell'incontro internazionale (Vercelli, 6-7 novembre 2008)*, ed. G. Vanotti, 207–266. Rome.

Chávez Reino, A. and Ottone, G. 2007. "Les fragments de Théopompe chez Athénée. Un aperçu général." In *Athénée et les fragments d'historiens, Actes du colloque de Strasbourg (16-18 juin 2005)*, ed. D. Lenfant, 139–174. Paris.

Connor, W. R. 1968. *Theopompus and Fifth-Century Athens.* Washington.

———. 1984. *Thucydides.* Princeton.

Costa, V., ed. 2007. *Filocoro di Atene. I. Testimonianze e frammenti dell'Atthis, a cura di V. Costa.* Rome.

Düring, I. 1957. *Aristotle in the Ancient Biographical Tradition.* Göteborg.

Fantasia, U. 2004. "ἀκριβής." In *Lexicon historiographicum graecum et latinum* 1, ed. C. Ampolo et al., 36b–66a. Pisa.

Flower, M. A. 1994. *Theopompus of Chios. History and Rhetoric in the Fourth Century BC.* Oxford.

Fornara, C. W. 1983. *The Nature of History in Ancient Greece and Rome.* Berkeley.

Foster, E. 2010. *Thucydides, Pericles, and Periclean Imperialism.* Cambridge.

Gazzano, F., et al., eds. 2009. Ingenia asiatica. *Fortuna e tradizione di storici d'Asia Minore, Atti della prima giornata di studio sulla storiografia greca frammentaria (Genova, 31 maggio 2007)*. Rome.

Jacoby, F. 1913. "Herodotos." *RE* Suppl. II. 205–520.

———. 1926a. "Griechische Geschichtschreibung." *Die Antike* 2:1–29. (= Bloch 1956:73–99)

———. 1926b. *Die Fragmente der griechischen Historiker.Zweiter Teil: Zeitgeschichte. C. Kommentar zu Nr. 64–105.* Berlin.

Laqueur, R. 1911. "Ephoros. 1. Die Proömien." *Hermes* 46:161–206.

Marincola, J., ed. 2007a. *A Companion to Greek and Roman Historiography*, I. Malden.

———. 2007b. "Universal History from Ephorus to Diodorus." In Marincola 2007a:171–179.

Momigliano, A. 1975. "La Storia di Eforo e le Elleniche di Teopompo." In *Quinto Contributo alla storia degli studi classici e del mondo antico*, II, 683–706. Rome. (= *Rivista di filologia e di istruzione classica* 13:180–204 [1935].)

Murray, G. 1946. "Theopompus: Or the Cynic as Historian." In *Greek Studies*, 149–170. Oxford.

Nicolai, R. 2004. *Studi su Isocrate. La comunicazione letteraria nel IV sec. a.C. e i nuovi generi della prosa.* Rome.

Ottone, G. 2004. "Per una nuova edizione dei frammenti di Teopompo di Chio: riflessioni su alcune problematiche teoriche e metodologiche." *Ktema* 29:129–143.

Parmeggiani, G. 2011. *Eforo di Cuma. Studi di storiografia greca.* Bologna.

Pédech, P. 1989. *Trois historiens méconnus: Théopompe, Duris, Phylarque.* Paris.

Pelling, C. 2007. "The Greek Historians of Rome." In Marincola 2007a:244–258.

Pownall, F. 2004. *Lessons from the Past. The Moral Use of History in Fourth-Century Prose.* Ann Arbor.

Reed, K. 1976. *Theopompus of Chios: History and Oratory in the Fourth Century.* PhD diss., University of California, Berkeley.

Rood, T. 1998. *Thucydides. Narrative and Explanation.* Oxford.

Roveri, A. 1964. *Studi su Polibio.* Bologna.

Santi Amantini, L. 2009. "Testimonianze su Teopompo nei fragmenta jacobiani." In Gazzano 2009:73–87.

Schepens, G. 1993. "L'apogée de l'archè spartiate comme époque historique dans l'historiographie grecque du début du IVe s. av. J.-C." *Ancient Society* 24:169–203.

———. 1997. "Timaeus FGrHist 566 F 28 Revisited: Fragmenta or Testimonia?" *Simblos* 2:71–83.

Schepens, G., and Bollansée, J., eds. 2005. *The Shadow of Polybius. Intertextuality as a Research Tool in Greek Historiography. Proceedings of the International Colloquium (Leuven, 21-22 September 2001)*. Leuven.

Schwartz, E. 1907. "Ephoros (1)." *RE* VI 1:1–16.

Shrimpton, G. S. 1977. "Theopompus' Treatment of Philip in the *Philippica*." *Phoenix* 31:123–144.

———. 1991. *Theopompus the Historian*. Montreal.

Sordi, M. 1983. *La Sicilia dal 368/7 al 337/6*. Rome.

Talbert, R. J. A. 1974. *Timoleon and the Revival of Greek Sicily 344-327 B.C.* Cambridge.

Vattuone, R. 1991. *Sapienza d'Occidente. Il pensiero storico di Timeo di Tauromenio*. Bologna.

———. 1997. "Una testimonianza dimenticata di Teopompo (Phot., Bibl., 176, P. 121 A, 30–34). Note sul proemio dei Philippika." *Simblos* 2:85–106.

———. 1998. "Koinai Praxeis. Le dimensioni 'universali' della storiografia greca fra Erodoto e Teopompo." In *L'ecumenismo politico nella coscienza dell'Occidente (Bergamo, 18-21 settembre 1995)*, ed. L. Aigner Foresti, et al., 57–96. Rome.

———. 2000. "Teopompo e l'Adriatico. Ricerche sui frammenti del libro XXI delle Filippiche (FGrHist 115 FF 128–136)." *Hesperia* 10:11–38.

———. 2002. "Timeo di Tauromenio." In *Storici greci d'occidente*, 177–232. Bologna.

———. 2005. "Timeo, Polibio e la storiografia greca d'Occidente." In Schepens and Bollansée 2005:89–122.

———. 2007. "ἀφανής." In *Lexicon historiographicum graecum et latinum* 2, ed. C. Ampolo et al., 146a–152b. Pisa.

Wachsmuth, C. 1895. *Einleitung in das Studium der alten Geschichte*. Leipzig.

Walbank, F. W. 1962. "Polemic in Polybius." *Journal of Hellenic Studies* 52:1–12.

———. 1967. *A Historical Commentary on Polybius* II. Oxford.

———. 2005. "The Two-way Shadow. Polybius among the Fragments." In Schepens and Bollansée 2005:1–18.

3

Rethinking Isocrates and Historiography[1]

JOHN MARINCOLA

1.

IT IS A TRUISM often expressed when studying classical historiography
that we are hampered by an absence of theoretical writings on the subject.
Although we know the names of several works written "On History" in
antiquity,[2] only three essays have come down to us with any claim to be theoretical in orientation, and each of the three, in different ways, is something of
an embarrassment. Perhaps the least problematic one, Lucian's *How to Write
History*, has been held to give some useful advice on the writing of history in a
Thucydidean mode, but even this work has come under fire: Moses Finley long
ago called it "a shallow and essentially worthless pot-boiler,"[3] and more recently

---

[1] This paper was originally delivered at Harvard University in February 2007; I thank Nino Luraghi
and Riccardo Vattuone for the kind invitation to participate in the conference they had organized. I received helpful comments there from Michael Flower, Nino Luraghi, Roberto Nicolai,
Guido Schepens, and Pietro Vannicelli. None of them necessarily agrees with what is stated here.
A fuller version was delivered as the Second Annual T. B. L. Webster Classics Graduate Student
Lecture at Stanford University in February 2011, and I am grateful to the graduate students there
for the kind invitation to speak, and for the very helpful discussion that followed my presentation. It must be emphasized that this paper represents only a first attempt at sorting out the
place of Isocrates in historiographical thought, and tries to suggest some broader outlines in
considering his work and its influence. It does not pretend to any kind of comprehensiveness
(for one important omission, see below, n49) but I hope in due course to provide a full study of
Isocrates within the context of fourth-century historiography. The text of Isocrates used here
is that of B. G. Mandilaras (Teubner, 3 vols. 2003); translations are those of D. C. Mirhady and Y.
L. Too, *Isocrates* I and T. L. Papillon, *Isocrates* II (Austin 2000 and 2004, respectively), sometimes
slightly modified.

[2] Works on history are attested for Theophrastus (Diogenes Laertius 5.47), Praxiphanes
(Marcellinus *Vita Thucydidis* 29), Metrodorus of Scepsis (FGH 184 F 2), Caecilius of Caleacte (FGH
183 F 2), Theodorus of Gadara (FGH 850 T 1), and the third-century CE sophist, Tiberius (Suda s.v.
Τιβέριος [T 550 Adler]); on the Latin side, there is Varro's *Sisenna uel de historia* (Gellius 16.9.5).
The Lamprias catalogue of Plutarch's works mentions "How We Discern the True History" (No.
124), and a four-volume "On Neglected History" (No. 54), but nothing is known of either.

[3] Finley 1971:12.

A. J. Woodman has argued that the work is mainly concerned with praise and blame and the attendant dangers thereon, rather than with any actual theoretical approach to inquiring about the past.[4] And indeed, there is but one chapter in the whole work that deals with inquiry (47), and it is hardly enlightening or encouraging. For the two others, alas, the verdict is even more dire: Dionysius of Halicarnassus' essay *On Thucydides* seems perfectly happy not to consider any of the ways in which Thucydides gathered and processed his information, and is mainly concerned with the word choice, arrangement, and stylistic adornment that is proper to writing history; while Plutarch's *On the Malice of Herodotus* seems to many simplistic in the extreme, envisioning history as nothing other than a series of noble deeds performed with the highest motives in mind.[5]

It is perhaps not surprising, then, that historiographers look everywhere to find any theoretical exposition in any genre that will help us to understand the ancients' approaches to writing history. And in our search we have often been led to two writers whose cultural and literary importance and influence seem undeniable. So the remarks made by Cicero in Book 2 of his *De Oratore* have been combed repeatedly to find out how he thought history should be written—even though the work is not mainly, or even largely, concerned with that topic. And on the Greek side scholars have looked to Isocrates, one of the cardinal figures of the fourth century, to shed some light on the writing of history in his own time and beyond. And the result is that even though neither Cicero nor Isocrates ever wrote a history proper,[6] they have acquired great importance for modern scholars as historiographical theorists, and they have come to serve in modern studies of classical historiography as spokesmen for certain ways of treating the past.

Isocrates has been considered an influential figure in studies of ancient historiography not only because he was an important teacher in general but also because the style of historiography which he supposedly bequeathed to subsequent generations—rhetorical historiography—had a long after-life for both Greek and Roman historians.[7] The term 'rhetorical history', as I have argued elsewhere, is an unfortunate one, since every narrative history is a rhetorical construct and there is no reason to oppose 'rhetoric' to 'research'.[8] Nonetheless,

---

[4] Woodman 1988:42, 68nn257–258.

[5] The latter work is nonetheless valuable for what it tells us about some important approaches to the writing of history in antiquity: see Marincola 1994:191-203; Pelling 2007:145–164.

[6] Cicero came close, with a ὑπόμνημα of his consulship (*ad Atticum* 2.1.2), a poem *De Consulatu Suo* (FF 6–11 Traglia) and one *De Temporibus Suis* (FF 12–17); cf. Büchner 1939:1245–1253. None of Cicero's 'historical' works was, strictly speaking, a narrative history.

[7] On Isocrates and history see: Blass 1892:48–50; Peter 1897:ii190–191; Bury 1909:160–170; Peter 1911:180–183; Scheller 1911; Kalischek 1913; Schmitz-Kahlmann 1939; Ullman 1942; Avenarius 1956:81–85 and *passim*; Welles 1966; Hamilton 1979; Nouhaud 1980; Nickel 1991; Flower 1994:42–62; Nicolai 2004:74–87; Fox and Livingstone 2007: 542–561, esp. 551–553; Parmeggiani 2011:34–38.

[8] Marincola 2001:111–112.

the term has entered scholarly discourse and continues to be used, and although not everyone uses it in the same way, there are a number of recurring character-istics that distinguish rhetorical historiography, including a serious concern with style and language (sometimes to the detriment of everything else), the composi-tion of speeches and even of actions based not on any historical record but on the criteria of probability and appropriateness, and finally a concern with pleasure rather than instruction.[9] Much, if not all, of this has been laid at Isocrates' door. In this paper I would like to reconsider how much of it is deserved.

To begin with the obvious, Isocrates never wrote history, and in the proem to the *Panathenaicus* he states clearly that although histories are justly praised he did not use his talents in that direction:

νεώτερος μὲν ὢν προηρούμην γράφειν τῶν λόγων οὐ τοὺς μυθώδεις οὐδὲ τοὺς τερατείας καὶ ψευδολογίας μεστούς, οἷς οἱ πολλοὶ μᾶλλον χαίρουσιν ἢ τοῖς περὶ τῆς αὐτῶν σωτηρίας λεγομένοις, οὐδὲ τοὺς τὰς παλαιὰς πράξεις καὶ τοὺς πολέμους τοὺς Ἑλληνικοὺς ἐξηγουμένους, καίπερ εἰδὼς δικαίως αὐτοὺς ἐπαινουμένους, οὐδ' αὖ τοὺς ἁπλῶς δοκοῦντας εἰρῆσθαι καὶ μηδεμιᾶς κοσμιότητος μετέχοντας, οὓς οἱ δεινοὶ περὶ τοὺς ἀγῶνας παραινοῦσι τοῖς νεωτέροις μελετᾶν, εἴπερ βούλονται πλέον ἔχειν τῶν ἀντιδίκων, ἀλλὰ πάντας τούτους ἐάσας περὶ ἐκείνους ἐπραγματευόμην τοὺς περὶ τῶν συμφερόντων τῇ τε πόλει καὶ τοῖς ἄλλοις Ἕλλησι συμβουλεύοντας, καὶ πολλῶν μὲν ἐνθυμημάτων γέμοντας, οὐκ ὀλίγων δ' ἀντιθέσεων καὶ παρισώσεων καὶ τῶν ἄλλων ἰδεῶν τῶν ἐν ταῖς ῥητορείαις διαλαμπουσῶν καὶ τοὺς ἀκούοντας ἐπισημαίνεσθαι καὶ θορυβεῖν ἀναγκαζουσῶν.

When I was younger, I chose not to write discourses that were mythic or full of wonders and fictions, the sort that the multitude enjoy more than those that concern their own security; I also avoided those that related the great deeds of the past and the wars fought by Greeks, although I knew that these were justly praised, and also those that when spoken seem simple and unadorned, such as people who are skillful in courts teach the young to practice if they want to have the advantage in litigation. I rejected all these and devoted myself to discourses that gave advice about what would be advantageous to Athens and the rest of the Greeks, and that were full of many ideas, with frequent antithesis and parisosis and other figures that make oratory shine and compel the audience to applaud and cause a stir.

Isocrates *Panathenaicus* 1–2

---

[9]   Parmeggiani 2011:37 observes that the term comprises at least six different concepts.

Nor can we find anywhere in his works theoretical writings on history, such that it is natural to ask how he became so influential a figure in the history of historiography. Here the link was long ago agreed to be the biographical testimonia from antiquity that claimed Ephorus and Theopompus to be his students.[10] Eduard Schwartz argued fiercely against the notion, and Jacoby agreed with him,[11] but scholars have continued to accept this datum. They must then, of course, draw conclusions backwards, so to speak, arguing that from Ephorus and Theopompus we can see what the tenets of Isocratean historiography really were. This all gets very tricky given that the histories of Ephorus and Theopompus don't actually survive, but no matter. J. B. Bury, for one, had no difficulty in asserting that Ephorus owed to Isocrates the moralizing platitudes, the elaborate speeches, and the conventional battle-scenes, all of which "conformed more or less to a model scheme" and "sacrifice[d] truth to effect."[12] Both Ephorus and Theopompus are also supposed to owe to Isocrates their panhellenic sentiments and the use of history as a source of moral edification.[13]

More recently, much of this prominent, indeed pre-eminent, role has been scaled back, and the question of Isocrates' importance for historiography has been seriously challenged. Michael Flower in his book on Theopompus questioned just how influential Isocrates could have been, given that he was not himself a historian, he wrote nothing on historiographical methodology, and his supposed students can be shown to have held views incompatible both with one another (thereby seriously questioning any uniform approach to be assumed from Isocrates) and with their teacher; and Giovanni Parmeggiani in his recent book on Ephorus expresses a similar skepticism.[14] To me this is a useful corrective, and an approach to which I am generally sympathetic. I think it may be worthwhile, nonetheless, to try to situate Isocrates more carefully in his fourth-century context, and to think again about the relationship of rhetoric and historiography.

2.

Although much has been claimed for the importance of Isocrates on the method of writing history, his influence, if we leave the details aside, is generally thought to revolve around three aspects: first, stylistic adornment; second, a particular

---

[10] FGH 70 TT 1–3; 115 TT 1, 2, 5a; older discussion in Kalischek 1913.
[11] Schwartz 1907:1–2; Jacoby 1926:22–23.
[12] Bury 1909:164; cf. Pownall 2004:133.
[13] Usher 1969:101–102.
[14] Flower 1994:42–62; Parmeggiani 2011:34–36.

methodological approach to the past; and third, a view of history as a collection of paradigms.

Let us take first stylistic adornment. Isocrates is often held responsible for the 'rhetoricization' of history, that is to say, for bequeathing to historiography an abiding, indeed overriding, concern with language and stylistic beauty. Now it can hardly be doubted that Isocrates cared greatly about style, and there are several passages in which he expresses his belief that great events and important matters need to be written in an elevated style; the opening of *Panathenaicus*, mentioned above, is one of the best known passages, as is the following:

εἰσὶ γάρ τινες, οἳ τῶν μὲν προειρημένων οὐκ ἀπείρως ἔχουσι, γράφειν δὲ προήρηνται λόγους, οὐ περὶ τῶν ὑμετέρων συμβολαίων, ἀλλ' Ἑλληνικοὺς καὶ πολιτικοὺς καὶ πανηγυρικούς, οὓς ἅπαντες ἂν φήσειαν ὁμοιοτέρους εἶναι τοῖς μετὰ μουσικῆς καὶ ῥυθμῶν πεποιημένοις ἢ τοῖς ἐν δικαστηρίῳ λεγομένοις. καὶ γὰρ τῇ λέξει ποιητικωτέρᾳ καὶ ποικιλωτέρᾳ τὰς πράξεις δηλοῦσι, καὶ τοῖς ἐνθυμήμασιν ὀγκωδεστέροις καὶ καινοτέροις χρῆσθαι ζητοῦσιν, ἔτι δὲ ταῖς ἄλλαις ἰδέαις ἐπιφανεστέραις καὶ πλείοσιν ὅλον τὸν λόγον διοικοῦσιν. ὧν ἅπαντες μὲν ἀκούοντες χαίρουσιν οὐδὲν ἧττον ἢ τῶν ἐν τοῖς μέτροις πεποιημένων, πολλοὶ δὲ καὶ μαθηταὶ γίγνεσθαι βούλονται, νομίζοντες τοὺς ἐν τούτοις πρωτεύοντας πολὺ σοφωτέρους καὶ βελτίους καὶ μᾶλλον ὠφελεῖν δυναμένους εἶναι τῶν τὰς δίκας εὖ λεγόντων.

Some people experienced in the forms I have mentioned did not choose to write speeches for private contract suits but ones of a political character pertaining to Hellas to be delivered in panegyric assemblies. Everyone would agree that these are more like musical and rhythmical compositions than those uttered in the law courts. They set out events with a more poetic and complex style and seek to employ grander and more original *enthymemes* [i.e. arguments], and in addition, they dress up the whole speech with many other eye-catching figures of speech. The whole audience enjoys when they hear these as much as poetic compositions, and many wish to study them, for they think that those who are at the forefront of this kind of competition are much wiser and better and can be more useful than those who are eloquent in legal matters.

Isocrates *Antidosis* 46-47

We need not doubt, therefore, that Isocrates thought elevated prose was an appropriate medium for his writings. Scholars of historiography, however, seem to equate a love of language with a disdain for (or, perhaps simply, a lack of concern with) the truth as if the two necessarily went hand in hand. By itself, however, style is not necessarily hostile to the discovery of the truth of what happened in the past: there are many well-regarded historians with a fine style: one thinks of Gibbon, or, more recently, Syme. Some have argued, of course, that it is not a simple matter to divorce words from things, and style is not so easily separated from substance;[15] but even so, style and truth need not be inimical. For that to happen, there has to be another aspect, namely that stylistic concern comes at the cost of accuracy: in other words a concern with style *replaces* a concern for accuracy or truth. (That plank of Isocratean historiography is supplied by another passage which we shall look at below, section 3.)

Now of course lurking behind all this is a kind of unspoken assumption that history before Isocrates was somehow *not* rhetorical, that historians of the fifth century were not concerned, or not much concerned, with language and style. While it might have been easier a generation or so ago to convince ourselves that neither Herodotus nor Thucydides paid much attention to rhetoric, it would be hard to find someone today who really thinks this is the case. Indeed some recent scholarship seems almost to suggest that if anyone should be held responsible for rhetorical historiography it might well be Thucydides himself.[16] And while that is perhaps somewhat too extreme, there are certainly troubling aspects of his work. He has a tendency, as has been frequently pointed out, to use superlatives throughout his work, claiming that his events are the 'biggest', 'most important', 'greatest', and so forth.[17] He may, of course, have genuinely believed this, but the effect upon the reader is nonetheless the same. In addition, one might look to the aggressively argumentative style of the 'Archaeology', where language, demonstration, and proof are all placed in the service of a particular argument that Thucydides wishes to advance, namely, that his war was the greatest of all wars (magnification again).[18] There is as well the highly artificial nature of the speeches, which are thoroughly rhetorical, carefully constructed and highly abstract, with echoes both within the pair of speeches and with other speeches scattered throughout the history.[19] If we are looking for a rhetorical historian, we need look no further. Yet to call Thucydides a rhetorical historian is, again, not saying much. So a preferable alternative would be to admit that historiography from its very beginnings was a literary art form, modeling itself on other art forms—epic especially—and, like them,

---

[15]   Moles 1993:114–115.
[16]   Woodman 1988:1–69; further references in Marincola 2001:98–103.
[17]   Grant 1974.
[18]   On the method of the 'Archaeology', see Connor 1984:20–32; Hornblower 1987:100–107.
[19]   No purpose would be served here by entering into the enormous bibliography on the speeches; some work before 2000 is surveyed in Marincola 2001:77–85; see also Scardino 2007; Rusten 2009:492–493.

seeking to establish itself as an elevated genre with an elevated language (not, for example, like comedy, lyric, or mime), and that Thucydides then took that interest in elevated language in a particular and rather idiosyncratic direction.

Although Thucydides' work was certainly known in the fourth century,[20] we need to remind ourselves that his history had not yet become canonical, but represented instead one particular approach to the past. We often seem to believe that later historians failed to grasp what Thucydides had tried to teach them, and that they failed to continue his noble achievement. Yet there is another way of looking at things that might bring us closer to understanding what we actually have from the fourth century. It is undeniable that the later ancient tradition saw Herodotus and Thucydides as founders of the genre; yet perhaps because of that, we tend, rather anachronistically, to see historiography as already fixed in their works and 'established' as a genre by the end of the fifth century. In doing so, we lose sight of, or devalue, the activity and contributions of the fourth century. Yet if we can look aside from what we think the fourth century *ought* to have learned from Thucydides, we might say that historians of the time *were* reacting to Thucydides, just not in the way that we might have expected them to.

To take one example, no one doubts that Xenophon knew Thucydides' work. But instead of assuming that Xenophon rejected the Thucydidean approach because he was too ignorant or parochial to understand it, we can just as easily postulate that he rejected Thucydidean style and arrangement because he thought they were inappropriate to how *he* envisioned the uses of history. So too the Oxyrhynchus historian, who followed Thucydides in terms of method and arrangement, writes in a style of Greek that is straightforward and bland, one that could hardly be more different from that of Thucydides.[21] In other words, both of these historians took some things from Thucydides and rejected others.

Nor is this surprising when we consider that one of the aspects that would have made Thucydides' history less appealing to fourth-century writers was the way in which it was conceived and structured, i.e. as a face-off between two competing and largely equal powers, who control a number of allies or subjects, such that everything tends towards a head-to-head conflict. It is true that the pronounced binary structure of the early books breaks down as the narrative goes on,[22] but even so, how useful in the fourth century would a focus such as Thucydides' have been? The fourth century was, after all, no longer a world of two superpowers, but rather of one, Persia—although she played an inconsistent hand while the other important powers, Athens, Sparta, and Thebes,

[20] Strebel 1935:7–19; Hornblower 1995:47–68.
[21] See Bruce 1967:18–20.
[22] Dewald 2005:144–154.

schemed to achieve hegemony, and worked now with, now against one another (and Persia). It is no wonder, then, that Xenophon abandoned the Thucydidean structure once he finished his treatment of the Peloponnesian War.

Let us suppose, then, that both Xenophon and the Oxyrhynchus historian wrote in a more straightforward style because they felt that such a style was more appropriate to history. In this way they actually employed far *less* rhetorical adornment than had Thucydides. And if that is the case, where might Isocrates' beliefs have fit in? We can almost certainly say that Isocrates was of the opinion that an approach such as that of Xenophon or the Oxyrhynchus historian towards history—using for the most part a simple and straightforward style—was unacceptable. Not because Isocrates ever expressed himself on Xenophon's work specifically, but because he emphasized again and again that for lofty and important subjects one needed a lofty and fine style. Isocrates' demand, therefore, reasserts the importance of a 'high' style for historiography, as in Thucydides, but not necessarily in the *manner* of Thucydides (whose style may already have seemed harsh in the fourth century). In other words, Isocrates or those influenced by him might have thought that Thucydides was right to compose history in a highly elaborate style, but that the particular style he chose was inappropriate.

I wish to emphasize that the *context* for such an approach as Isocrates' was not necessarily an attack on Thucydides, nor indeed on any kind of historiography in particular. We must recall that quite apart from narrative histories the ancients remembered their pasts through many media and in different genres, including law court speeches, the *epitaphios*, and non-verbal media. All of this would have engendered a larger discussion concerning the appropriate way to remember great deeds, and it is not to be expected that historians would have failed to see the relevance of these discussions to their own tasks.

So on the matter of style, it seems to me that we should see Isocrates as part of a larger debate in the fourth century about the way to commemorate great deeds, including those of the past. Through his school and his influence, Isocrates' beliefs would percolate through the on-going contemporary debate and might well have been taken up by would-be historians—although I wish to emphasize again that Isocrates himself was probably not concerned about *historiographical* style in particular. But any approach from an important teacher who said that great words are needed for great matters could not but influence a genre that always claimed the greatness of the subject as one of its justifications for existing.[23]

---

[23] On the greatness of the subject as a justification for writing history, see Marincola 1997:34–43.

3.

Let us turn now to methodology. Though not a historian, Isocrates' works are suffused with history both contemporary and non-contemporary.[24] Although there have been many analyses of Isocrates and his approach to history,[25] we still lack a thorough and comprehensive study of his attitude towards the past. It has been common, however, to select certain passages from his works as representative or indicative of his approach to history. One of the most frequently cited is *Panegyricus* 7–10. Here Isocrates says that he will give advice about the war against Persia and about Greek unity, a topic that is much worked but which he hopes to treat differently. It is a theme, he says, that is still appropriate for discussion:

πρὸς δὲ τούτοις εἰ μὲν μηδαμῶς ἄλλως οἷόν τ᾽ ἦν δηλοῦν τὰς αὐτὰς πράξεις, ἀλλ᾽ ἢ διὰ μιᾶς ἰδέας, εἶχεν ἄν τις ὑπολαβεῖν, ὡς περίεργόν ἐστι τὸν αὐτὸν τρόπον ἐκείνοις λέγοντα πάλιν ἐνοχλεῖν τοῖς ἀκούουσιν· ἐπειδὴ δ᾽ οἱ λόγοι τοιαύτην ἔχουσι τὴν φύσιν ὥσθ᾽ οἷόν τ᾽ εἶναι περὶ τῶν αὐτῶν πολλαχῶς ἐξηγήσασθαι καὶ τά τε μεγάλα ταπεινὰ ποιῆσαι καὶ τοῖς μικροῖς μέγεθος περιθεῖναι καὶ τὰ παλαιὰ καινῶς διελθεῖν καὶ περὶ τῶν νεωστὶ γεγενημένων ἀρχαίως εἰπεῖν, οὐκέτι φευκτέον ταῦτ᾽ ἐστί, περὶ ὧν ἕτεροι πρότερον εἰρήκασιν, ἀλλ᾽ ἄμεινον ἐκείνων εἰπεῖν πειρατέον . . . ἡγοῦμαι δ᾽ οὕτως ἂν μεγίστην ἐπίδοσιν λαμβάνειν καὶ τὰς ἄλλας τέχνας καὶ τὴν περὶ τοὺς λόγους φιλοσοφίαν, εἴ τις θαυμάζοι καὶ τιμῴη μὴ τοὺς πρώτους τῶν ἔργων ἀρχομένους, ἀλλὰ τοὺς ἄρισθ᾽ ἕκαστον αὐτῶν ἐξεργαζομένους, μηδὲ τοὺς περὶ τούτων ζητοῦντας λέγειν, περὶ ὧν μηδεὶς πρότερον εἴρηκεν, ἀλλὰ τοὺς οὕτως ἐπισταμένους εἰπεῖν ὡς οὐδεὶς ἂν ἄλλος δύναιτο.

In addition, if it were not possible to reveal the same actions in only one way, one could suppose that it is superfluous for one speaking the same as those [sc. who have already spoken] to annoy the audience again. But since words have such a nature that it is possible to discourse on the same things in many ways, and make great things lowly or give size to small things, or to go through the things of old in a new way or to speak about things that have recently happened in an old style, so one must not avoid those topics on which others have spoken, but one must try to speak better than they . . . And I think that both the other arts and philosophic rhetoric would make the greatest advance if one marveled at and honored not the ones who first began these works, but

---

[24] See especially Schmitz-Kahlmann 1939.
[25] See above, n7.

the ones who made each of them their best, and not the ones who want to speak about those things that no one has ever spoken about before, but those who know how to speak in a way that no one else can.

Isocrates *Panegyricus* 7–10

This passage has been thought to demonstrate Isocrates' concern to rhetoricize history.[26] Some years ago I argued that what we have here is a traditional praise of the powers of oratory, which *could* be seen as a plea for stylistic excellence, although the context suggests that what Isocrates means by speaking "in a way no one has before" concerns the *content* of the advice which will be based on the *proper use* of the *exempla* which history provides. Isocrates does indeed go on to vaunt his own powers, but he is not divorcing style and content, and it is clear that the excellence of his speech is a result of the excellence of his advice, that is, again, its content.[27] Could one take this statement out of context and use it to justify the re-working of non-contemporary history? Certainly; but it is clear that scholars who want to use this passage as a theoretical basis for Isocratean historiography are building on shaky foundations. The other passage, *Panathenaicus* 149–150, may seem to offer more. This passage is a digression that is itself a comment on the narrative of great deeds in Athenian history just given by the orator. Isocrates has been speaking on early Athenian history, starting from before a time when words such as "oligarchy" and "democracy" even existed, then treating certain aspects of the early king Theseus and his followers, and, after a brief interruption, returning to the democracy and its excellences. Then Isocrates continues:

τάχ' οὖν ἄν τινες ἄτοπον εἶναί με φήσειαν (οὐδὲν γὰρ κωλύει διαλαβεῖν τὸν λόγον) ὅτι τολμῶ λέγειν ὡς ἀκριβῶς εἰδὼς περὶ πραγμάτων οἷς οὐ παρῆν πραττομένοις. ἐγὼ δ' οὐδὲν τούτων ἄλογον οἶμαι ποιεῖν. εἰ μὲν γὰρ μόνος ἐπίστευον τοῖς τε λεγομένοις περὶ τῶν παλαιῶν καὶ τοῖς γράμμασι τοῖς ἐξ ἐκείνου τοῦ χρόνου παραδεδομένοις ἡμῖν, εἰκότως ἂν ἐπετιμώμην· νῦν δὲ πολλοὶ καὶ νοῦν ἔχοντες ταὐτὸν ἐμοὶ φανεῖεν ἂν πεπονθότες. χωρὶς δὲ τούτων, εἰ κατασταίην εἰς ἔλεγχον καὶ λόγον, δυνηθείην ἂν ἐπιδεῖξαι πάντας ἀνθρώπους πλείους ἐπιστήμας ἔχοντας διὰ τῆς ἀκοῆς ἢ τῆς ὄψεως, καὶ μείζους πράξεις καὶ καλλίους εἰδότας ἃς παρ' ἑτέρων ἀκηκόασιν ἢ 'κείνας, αἷς αὐτοὶ παραγεγενημένοι τυγχάνουσιν.

Some perhaps might say—since nothing prevents me from interrupting my speech—that I am unusual in daring to say that I know accurately

[26] See Scheller 1911:65f.; Peter 1897:ii190; idem 1911:180–183; Avenarius 1956:81–83.
[27] Marincola 1997:276–277, which ought to have cited Usher 1990:150–151.

about affairs at which I was not present when they occurred. But I think I am doing nothing illogical. For if I alone trusted to the traditions and records about things of long ago which have come down to us from that time, then reasonably I would be censured. But as it is, even many intelligent men would seem to have the same experience as I. And apart from this, if I were put to the test and proof, I could demonstrate that all men have greater knowledge from oral tradition than from autopsy and know greater and finer deeds having heard them from others rather than from events at which they themselves happened to be present.

Isocrates Panathenaicus 149–150

Some scholars have seen here an inversion by Isocrates of the typical relationship between eyes and ears in the historiographical tradition, in which autopsy is always superior to oral report.[28] And so once autopsy was devalued, it became easier for historians to disavow research. Yet here again this seems to be misreading what Isocrates actually says. Isocrates is saying no more than that men rarely witness great deeds, and that their main source of information about them is not their own experience but tradition, however they receive this; this is especially true, of course, when the deeds are very ancient.[29]

Isocrates first claims as one of the proofs for his accurate knowledge of the past the fact that tradition has recorded the events he narrates. That might seem a slim thread by which to hang such a narrative, but Isocrates elsewhere also expresses his belief that the traditions of events are what give them their believability. In *Panegyricus* 69, Isocrates is speaking of the attacks made on Athens in early times by the Thracians, Scythians, and Amazons. He notes that although these peoples thought they could easily defeat the Athenians, they were utterly destroyed, and then remarks:

> δῆλον δὲ τὸ μέγεθος τῶν κακῶν τῶν γενομένων ἐκείνοις· οὐ γὰρ ἂν ποθ' οἱ λόγοι περὶ αὐτῶν τοσοῦτον χρόνον διέμειναν, εἰ μὴ καὶ τὰ πραχθέντα πολὺ τῶν ἄλλων διήνεγκεν.

> The magnitude of the troubles they encountered is clear, for the reports about them would not have lasted so long if these events were not far more important than others.

Isocrates Panegyricus 69

---

[28] Avenarius 1956:82; Nickel 1991:235; Roth 2003 *ad loc.*
[29] I reprise here the remarks made in Marincola 1997:277–278.

What is interesting is that in both of these passages Isocrates feels compelled to explain to his audience how he knows about these events. This means that he is aware that he is treading on ground that some would not consider secure and that some in his audience would be hesitant to accord belief to such early events. His approach here seems largely 'passive', and his reliance on tradition, on what has been handed down, might strike us as naive. But we would do well to remember that even Thucydides in the 'Archaeology', for all the critical spirit with which he invests his work, had at bottom to rely on the traditions about the Trojan War and the early Greek migrations and those about Minos and his empire. The difference is not about tradition; it is one of approach, and one's approach was dependent on how one wished to use the past. (I shall come back to this.)

Another passage often cited to illuminate Isocrates' historical method is *Panegyricus* 28–31, where Isocrates is speaking of Demeter:

πρῶτον μὲν τοίνυν, οὗ πρῶτον ἡ φύσις ἡμῶν ἐδεήθη, διὰ τῆς πόλεως τῆς ἡμετέρας ἐπορίσθη· καὶ γὰρ εἰ μυθώδης ὁ λόγος γέγονεν, ὅμως αὐτῷ καὶ νῦν ῥηθῆναι προσήκει. Δήμητρος γὰρ ἀφικομένης εἰς τὴν χώραν ἡμῶν, ὅτ’ ἐπλανήθη τῆς Κόρης ἁρπασθείσης, καὶ πρὸς τοὺς προγόνους ἡμῶν εὐμενῶς διατεθείσης ἐκ τῶν εὐεργεσιῶν, ἃς οὐχ οἷόν τ’ ἄλλοις ἢ τοῖς μεμυημένοις ἀκούειν, καὶ δούσης δωρεὰς διττάς, αἵπερ μέγισται τυγχάνουσιν οὖσαι, τούς τε καρπούς, οἳ τοῦ μὴ θηριωδῶς ζῆν ἡμᾶς αἴτιοι γεγόνασι, καὶ τὴν τελετήν, ἧς οἱ μετέχοντες περί τε τῆς τοῦ βίου τελευτῆς καὶ τοῦ σύμπαντος αἰῶνος ἡδίους τὰς ἐλπίδας ἔχουσιν, οὕτως ἡ πόλις ἡμῶν οὐ μόνον θεοφιλῶς, ἀλλὰ καὶ φιλανθρώπως ἔσχεν, ὥστε κυρία γενομένη τοσούτων ἀγαθῶν οὐκ ἐφθόνησε τοῖς ἄλλοις, ἀλλ’ ὧν ἔλαβεν, ἅπασι μετέδωκεν. καὶ τὰ μὲν ἔτι καὶ νῦν καθ’ ἕκαστον τὸν ἐνιαυτὸν δείκνυμεν, τῶν δὲ συλλήβδην τάς τε χρείας καὶ τὰς ἐργασίας καὶ τὰς ὠφελείας τὰς ἀπ’ αὐτῶν γιγνομένας ἐδίδαξεν. καὶ τούτοις ἀπιστεῖν μικρῶν ἔτι προστιθέντων οὐδεὶς ἂν ἀξιώσειεν.

πρῶτον μὲν γὰρ ἐξ ὧν ἄν τις καταφρονήσειε τῶν λεγομένων ὡς ἀρχαίων ὄντων, ἐκ τῶν αὐτῶν τούτων εἰκότως ἂν καὶ τὰς πράξεις γεγενῆσθαι νομίσειεν· διὰ γὰρ τὸ πολλοὺς εἰρηκέναι καὶ πάντας ἀκηκοέναι προσήκει μὴ καινὰ μέν, πιστὰ δὲ δοκεῖν εἶναι τὰ λεγόμενα περὶ αὐτῶν. ἔπειτ’ οὐ μόνον ἐνταῦθα καταφυγεῖν ἔχομεν, ὅτι τὸν λόγον καὶ τὴν φήμην ἐκ πολλοῦ παρειλήφαμεν, ἀλλὰ καὶ σημείοις μείζοσιν ἢ τούτοις ἔστιν ἡμῖν χρήσασθαι περὶ αὐτῶν. αἱ μὲν γὰρ πλεῖσται τῶν πόλεων ὑπόμνημα τῆς παλαιᾶς εὐεργεσίας ἀπαρχὰς τοῦ σίτου καθ’ ἕκαστον ἐνιαυτὸν ὡς ἡμᾶς ἀποπέμπουσι, ταῖς δ’ ἐκλειπούσαις πολλάκις ἡ Πυθία προσέταξεν ἀποφέρειν τὰ μέρη τῶν καρπῶν καὶ ποιεῖν πρὸς τὴν πόλιν τὴν ἡμετέραν τὰ πάτρια. καίτοι περὶ τίνων χρὴ μᾶλλον πιστεύειν ἢ περὶ ὧν ὅ τε θεὸς ἀναιρεῖ καὶ πολλοῖς τῶν Ἑλλήνων συνδοκεῖ καὶ τά τε πάλαι ῥηθέντα τοῖς παροῦσιν ἔργοις συμμαρτυρεῖ καὶ τὰ νῦν γιγνόμενα τοῖς ὑπ' ἐκείνων εἰρημένοις ὁμολογεῖ;

First of all then, that which our nature first needed was provided by our city. For even if the account has become mythical, nevertheless it should be told even now. Demeter once came to our land, wandering about after her daughter Kore was kidnapped, and since she looked favorably on our ancestors because of their kindness—which no one other than the initiates is allowed to hear—she gave two gifts to Athens that are, in fact, our two most important possessions: the fruits of the earth that have allowed us to live civilized lives and the celebration of the mystery rites that grant to those who share in them glad hopes about the end of their life and about eternity. As a result, our city was not only loved by the gods but also was considerate of other people so much that when it gained such great goods, it did not begrudge these gifts to others but shared what it had with everyone else. Even now, we still share the mystery rites every year, and we have taught others about the use, the care, and the benefits coming from the fruits of the earth. And if I add a bit more detail, no one would disbelieve this.

First, the reason one might scorn this story—because it is ancient—might also make someone accept that the events probably happened. Since many have told the story, and everyone has heard it, it is right to consider the story not something recent but nonetheless trustworthy. Second, we not only have recourse to the argument that we received the fabled story a long time ago, but can use even greater proofs than this. To commemorate our ancient gift, most cities send the first part of their offerings to us each year; and those who do not are often ordered by the Pythia to bring a portion of their crop and perform the ancestral duties toward our city. Furthermore, what should we trust more than something ordered by the god and approved by most Greeks, where the ancient reports agree with current practice, and current practice agrees with what was spoken by the ancients?

Isocrates *Panegyricus* 28–31

Of particular interest here is the remark that the λόγος has become μυθώδης. Isocrates elsewhere uses the terms μῦθος, μυθολογέω, and μυθώδης in several ways: to mark a contrast between present and early times;[30] to designate the activity of early writers;[31] and to designate stories that concern the gods.[32] The 'mythic' is allied with sensationalism and falsehood,[33] and is contrasted with both 'the useful' and 'the truth'.[34] There is no reason, therefore, to posit Isocrates' meaning here as in any way different from how he uses these terms elsewhere.[35] Indeed, his usage has much in common with how the historians themselves treat the 'mythic': for them, μῦθοι frequently have an exaggerative or not wholly trustworthy aspect, and stories of the gods are particularly prone to becoming μυθώδεις because they occur in a realm in which demonstration is mostly impossible.[36] So too here, it is precisely in telling the story of divine activity that Isocrates realizes that he must be careful and not assume the kind of accuracy one finds in later events. Indeed, Isocrates recognizes that the story is not of the same nature as an account of contemporary history (that is what καινά must refer to: recent events), but he argues, perhaps somewhat surprisingly, that the very fact of the story's antiquity is a guarantee of its trustworthiness. Towards the end of the speech, he invokes the god Apollo and this has been thought to be irrelevant to historical proof. Yet the appeal to the oracle of Apollo, like the fact of the story's antiquity, is only part of a larger argument. The main point that strengthens trust in the story, as Isocrates details it here, is that still today other Greek cities send Athens their first-fruits, and thus "present events tally with the statements which have come down from the men of old." In other words, an enduring custom confirms a literary account.

Although this might certainly seem to lack the kind of historical rigor that we might like, how different is it from what historians in the fifth and fourth centuries were doing? To be sure, the question of historical methodology is not an easy one. That the ancients established a hierarchy of historical investigation

---

[30] *Evagoras* 36: τῶν παλαιῶν; *Panegyricus* 158: Τὰ Τρωϊκά and Τὰ Περσικά.

[31] *To Nicocles* 49: ὁ μὲν [sc. Ὅμηρος] γὰρ τοὺς ἀγῶνας καὶ τοὺς πολέμους τοὺς τῶν ἡμιθέων ἐμυθολόγησεν, οἱ δὲ [sc. οἱ πρῶτοι εὑρόντες τραγῳδίαν] τοὺς μύθους εἰς ἀγῶνας καὶ πράξεις κατέστησαν.

[32] *To Demonicus* 50: Zeus sired Heracles and Tantalus ὡς οἱ μῦθοι λέγουσι.

[33] *Panegyricus* 1: νεώτερος μὲν ὢν προῃρούμην γράφειν τῶν λόγων οὐ τοὺς μυθώδεις οὐδὲ τοὺς τερατείας καὶ ψευδολογίας μεστούς, οἷς οἱ πολλοὶ μᾶλλον χαίρουσιν.

[34] *To Nicocles* 48: δεῖ τοὺς βουλομένους ἢ ποιεῖν ἢ γράφειν τι κεχαρισμένον τοῖς πολλοῖς μὴ τοὺς ὠφελιμωτάτους τῶν λόγων ζητεῖν, ἀλλὰ τοὺς μυθωδεστάτους (commentators have noted there seems to be an echo of Thucydides 1.22.4 at the beginning of this passage, with the distinction between what is μυθῶδες and what is useful). *Evagoras* 66: εἰ τοὺς μύθους ἀφέντες τὴν ἀλήθειαν σκοποῦμεν.

[35] Hamilton 1979:293–294 says that the term here does not have to do with the story's veracity but denotes rather "a story which has come to have a special fame and function in Greek tradition," but this is special pleading and unconvincing, given that, as Hamilton himself notes, Isocrates elsewhere distinguishes μῦθοι from truth.

[36] See Marincola 1997:117–126; Meijering 1987:78–82.

is hardly to be doubted, but the extent to which it actually contributed to the real knowledge of the past is more uncertain. For contemporary history autopsy was paramount and was followed by personal inquiry of those who were themselves eyewitnesses.[37] For non-contemporary history there was no unanimity, and one was forced to rely on the tradition. If we look at Thucydides in the 'Archaeology', we find that he, like Isocrates, uses the evidence of present-day customs to confirm the truth of his reconstructive account: for example, the fact that the people of Ozolian Locris, Aetolia, and Acarnania in Thucydides' day still carried weapons was a result of the fact that in earlier days they had been raiders of other people's goods (1.5.3). Or again he sees no reason to discount the fact that Mycenae was a great city "as tradition maintains" simply because in his own day it was a small place (1.10.1).[38] And elsewhere in his history, when he is treating events earlier than the Peloponnesian War—Themistocles and Pausanias, Harmodius and Aristogeiton, the Sicilian archaeology—Thucydides resorts to the same mixture of inference, bald assertion, and acquiescence in or contradiction of the tradition; and it is questionable whether he had the intellectual tools to do otherwise.[39]

Indeed, the question of how to deal with what tradition had handed down was a difficult one, and no historian in antiquity at any point really had much idea of how to actually *research* the past. Tradition could not be ignored; too often it was all that one had. And if one chose not to treat contemporary history— as many did—it was necessary to come up with some way of understanding or explicating the past. The realm of non-contemporary history was never subject to a single methodology: as we have said, certainty about the distant past could never be equal to that of the present or more recent times, but since no one could come up with a formula for extracting a certain percentage of truth from tradition, the main contestation revolved around *how much* credence ought to be given to accounts of past events.[40] This in turn might depend on what you were using the past for: if you want to devalue the past to the advantage of the present, you attack the tradition if it presents greatness (as does Thucydides); if, on the other hand, you want to use the past to admonish the present to maintain its standards, you emphasize its greatness (as does Isocrates). Naturally, a modern historian might find fault with Isocrates for concentrating on the past

---

[37] Marincola 1997:63–86.

[38] On the methodological importance of the 'Archaeology', see de Romilly 1956:240–298; Connor 1984:20–32; Allison 1989:11–27; Ellis 1991; Pothou 2009:126–133.

[39] On Themistocles and Pausanias, see Hornblower 1991:211–225, esp. 211: "the general handling recalls . . . Herodotus"; on the Sicilian archaeology, idem 2008:259–299; on Harmodius and Aristogeiton, ibid. 434–440.

[40] On the different methodologies for non-contemporary history see Schepens 1975 (now in slightly revised form in Marincola 2011:100–118); Marincola 1997:63–86, 95–117; Bosworth 2003.

rather than the present, but at the same time a fifth- or fourth-century historian would have had no difficulty in seeing the methods used by Isocrates as akin to his own. Isocrates' reliance on tradition is not absurd, nor indeed even intellectually worthless, given that without it, he and others would have had virtually *nothing* to say about their early history.

4.

And that brings us finally to Isocrates and παραδείγματα or *exempla*. It is often assumed that Isocrates developed an approach to history that saw events as paradigms that could be manipulated by the speaker, and that this was something that contributed to the devaluation of actual history: in other words, the repeated use of *exempla* in a manner that removed them from their chronological context contributed to an ahistorical way of looking at the past.[41] Here again a particular passage is brought forward:

αἱ μὲν γὰρ πράξεις αἱ προγεγενημέναι κοιναὶ πᾶσιν ἡμῖν κατελείφθησαν,
τὸ δ' ἐν καιρῷ ταύταις καταχρήσασθαι καὶ τὰ προσήκοντα περὶ ἑκάστης
ἐνθυμηθῆναι καὶ τοῖς ὀνόμασιν εὖ διαθέσθαι τῶν εὖ φρονούντων ἴδιόν
ἐστιν.

For past deeds we hold in common, but the use of these at the proper time and the consideration of what is appropriate for each, and the good arrangement of words belong to those who think rightly.

Isocrates *Panegyricus* 9

That Isocrates here approves of *exempla* is undeniable: but to what extent is this inimical to history? And where does such a viewpoint fit in with what actual historians had been doing?

It has often been pointed out that *exempla* are as old as Greek literature itself, already present in Homer.[42] *Exempla* are already visible in Herodotus' history, used by speakers as a way of forming judgments about the future or persuading their addressees to adopt a particular course of action.[43] The characters in

---

[41] See e.g. Schmitz-Kahlmann 1939:v–xi. I treat the fourth-century interest in *exempla* more fully in a forthcoming study.

[42] *Exempla* in the *Iliad*: Nestor: 1.260–273; Phoenix tells the story of Meleager: 9.529–605; Achilles uses the example of Niobe: 24.602–620. On Homeric heroes and the past, Grethlein 2006.

[43] Solon invokes Tellus and Cleobis and Biton as *exempla*: Herodotus 1.30–31; Croesus uses himself as an *exemplum*: 1.207; So(si)clees on Corinthian tyranny: 5.92–93; Xerxes and his predecessors: 7.8. Inferences from *exempla* are not, however, straightforward and unproblematic: see Pelling 2006.

Thucydides' work do not use historical *exempla* very often, preferring instead to argue from universally held principles, although there are still a few quite important instances.[44] In the fourth century, the use of *exempla* was continued and extended and really came into its own. By the early fourth century, the Greeks had nearly a hundred years of fairly reliable historical narrative that detailed the doings of their city-states both individually and in conflict with one another. So perhaps it was only to be expected that whereas earlier writers and speakers would have employed events that we might think of as mythological, writers in the fourth century now had a large supply of more securely attested 'historical' actions. We can see the speakers in Xenophon's *Hellenica*, for example, bringing forward historical *paradeigmata*.[45] The orators, too, refer to the value of *exempla*: in the *To Demonicus*, Isocrates says that Demonicus, when deliberating with himself, should make past events the παραδείγματα of what will occur, for the unseen is most quickly comprehended by the seen, and there are a series of remarks in other orators that parallel this one.[46] We see here, of course, a close relationship to the kinds of claims made about history in general, and this is one of those areas in which history and rhetoric shared some common ground: it is not so much that history was 'rhetoricized', as that the speakers in historiographical works operated in the same way that speakers in the real world did.

---

[44] Typical is Pericles' tactic in the Funeral Oration not to rehearse the deeds of the Athenians' ancestors, but instead to concentrate on the here and now (Thucydides 2.36). There are, however, a few noteworthy instances of the employment of historical *exempla*. Hermocrates successfully uses the example of Athenian action in the Persian War, when the Athenians were compelled to become accomplished sailors by the Persian threat, to motivate his own Syracusans to practice their skill and not lose heart in the face of earlier Athenian victories (7.21). Alcibiades, at the beginning of Book 6, very similarly to Xerxes in Herodotus, uses the example of past Athenian actions and character to urge the Athenian assembly to vote for the Sicilian expedition (6.17–18, with Raaflaub 2002 for the similarity to Herodotus' Xerxes). Perhaps the most significant use of history in Thucydides is the Plataean defense before the Spartans where the Plataeans remind the Spartans of Plataea's efforts in the Persian Wars and the role they played in defending Greece (3.54, 58). Again, this use of historical *exempla* is not necessarily straightforward: the Spartan decision not to be swayed by the Plataeans' invocation of history is put down by the historian to the fact that in the moment the Thebans were more useful to the Spartans than were the Plataeans (3.68.4).

[45] Although, as with Herodotus (above, n42), the *exempla* are not straightforward and easily interpreted: see Marincola 2010:269–279, where I argue that the historical *exempla* attributed by Xenophon to a series of speakers in Books 6 and 7 contain a metahistorical critique, possibly a quite pessimistic one, of the value of history itself.

[46] Isocrates *To Demonicus* 34: βουλευόμενος παραδείγματα ποιοῦ τὰ παρεληλυθότα τῶν μελλόντων· τὸ γὰρ ἀφανὲς ἐκ τοῦ φανεροῦ ταχίστην ἔχει τὴν διάγνωσιν. Cf. Lysias 25.23: χρὴ τοίνυν, ὦ ἄνδρες δικασταί, τοῖς πρότερον γεγενημένοις παραδείγμασι χρωμένους βουλεύεσθαι περὶ τῶν μελλόντων ἔσεσθαι; Andocides *De Pace* 32: τὰ γὰρ παραδείγματα τὰ γεγενημένα τῶν ἁμαρτημάτων ἱκανὰ τοῖς σώφροσι τῶν ἀνθρώπων ὥστε μηκέτι ἁμαρτάνειν.

And this may be linked to a larger societal context, for the belief that the future will be much like the past is quite common in a traditional society.

It is important to emphasize that *exempla* do not necessarily have only one function; in fact, they work differently given their context. They can be used as tools for education or as devices of persuasion, or as evidence or elements of proof in epideictic oratory. Much of the study of the use of *exempla* by the Attic orators has focused on the question of their historical reliability, and scholars often speak of historical 'deformation' or an 'unscrupulous' use of historical events by the orators in order to make a point.[47] I, on the other hand, would like to make three points that I think are insufficiently appreciated and that offer a more positive evaluation of *exempla*.

First, the profusion of historical *exempla* in the fourth century is evidence of the importance of the past and of history to the Greeks at that time. I think it no exaggeration to say that fourth-century Greeks were constantly thinking about the past and its relevance to their own situation. Second, since historical *exempla* in oratory are used in a certain way, as a tool in argumentation designed to guide the audience to a particular conclusion, we should not fail to perceive that how the speaker uses an *exemplum* will depend on his interpretation of the event and its importance. The use of historical *exempla*, therefore, is an implicit contestation over the *meaning* of history. If correct, this would suggest that the use of *exempla* by writers was always a dynamic, rather than a static, process. Although certain examples might be used again and again to make a particular point, the interpretation of each *exemplum* was not carved in stone: as a tool of argumentation and proof, the *exemplum* was subject to examination and challenge, and could be accepted, emended, or discarded. And that is what I think Isocrates is getting at in *Panegyricus* 9. His remark indicates that the past, far from being dead or univocal, was a protean thing, capable of being examined and used from a variety of viewpoints, and not limited in its meaning or applicability. Third and finally, the recourse by scholars to labelling the use of historical *exempla* as inaccurate or as a deformation assumes a wholly passive audience. It presumes that the listeners were completely or largely unaware of what orators were doing, or that they failed to recognize conventions that they heard almost every day of their lives. To take but one example, the topics and arrangement of the *epitaphios* were well known—so well known that they could be easily mocked by Plato in the *Menexenus*.[48] Yet it would be foolish to follow Plato in assuming a

---

[47] *Exempla* in oratory: Jost 1936; Pearson 1941; Perlman 1961; Loraux 1981; Nouhaud 1980; Worthington 1991; id. 1994; Pownall 2004.

[48] The classic study of the *epitaphios* is that of Loraux 1981; on Plato's *Menexenus*, see Henderson 1975; Pownall 2004:38–64.

wholly gullible audience, listening to the rehearsal of Athenian deeds as if they were gospel. On the contrary, the different ways in which the orators would have approached the timeless themes of Athenian myth and history would have fostered a much more critical spirit than we are sometimes willing to grant the everyday Athenian. Perhaps we find it hard to imagine that the Athenians in attendance at the funeral oration might not have *expected* to hear historical truth nor have looked for that; rather, they may have wished to hear the orator discharge his task with skill and appropriateness, while being simultaneously (mildly) innovative and investing the occasion with deep emotion. Context, here as elsewhere, determines the conventions.

So in sum I believe that there is no reason to consider the use of historical *exempla* in and of itself hostile to history. On the contrary, the recourse to the past meant that the orator was in a constant state of examining the lessons of history, and in a constant struggle to understand the meaning of history.

5.

Let me now try to sum up some of what I have been saying. In this paper I am aware that I have not been advancing a particular thesis about Isocrates but rather offering a series of observations about his relationship to the historiography of the fifth and fourth centuries. It is singularly unfortunate that the historians of the fourth century are so often condemned in the standard handbooks and faulted for their inferiority to their great predecessors of the fifth century. By contrast, I would see the fourth century as a time of impressive innovation where generic boundaries were not yet fixed and policed. Rather than pass judgment about the merits of the fourth century, however, it seems to me more worthwhile to try to understand what the role of history was in the fourth century and beyond, and rather than view this later historiography as something 'corrupted' by rhetoric, we would do well to attend to how and why the use of history remained so important.

If we do not wish to assign Isocrates a place of cardinal importance in the development of historiographical theory—and I believe that we should not— neither is it fair to write him out of the picture altogether. That he was not a historian and had no methodology for the writing of history he himself makes clear, and we can see that his main interest is in playing an important role as advocate in the present by encouraging his fellow Athenians and fellow Greeks to do great deeds. Yet one cannot help noticing the large and consistent role that history plays across the whole vast oeuvre of Isocrates, where the past is never far from view, and can be employed either as a yardstick by which to measure the inadequacy of the present, or as a spur to contemporaries to achieve deeds equal to or greater than their ancestors. Nor can it be coincidence, I think, that Isocrates was engaged with some of the same issues that the fourth-century historians were: the struggle for hegemony; the role that Athens and Sparta should play in contemporary history; the power and influence of Persia; and the rising star to the north in Macedon. Although Isocrates does not develop it specifically, his remark at *Panegyricus* 9 that the past belongs to us all, but that its elucidation is a matter for the well educated, places history in a central role in his vision of education.[49] Even if Isocrates was not the proponent of any historiographical program, he was, whether deliberately or fortuitously, an important participant in the fourth-century discussions of what history meant, and how it was or was not useful. And given that he lived in an era of generic innovation—for which his own discourses, among other things, serve as evidence[50]—it was inevitable that the debates about history would not and could not be confined to those who actually wrote narrative histories. History, we might say, was too important to be left to the historians.

Bibliography

Allison, J. 1989. *Power and Preparedness in Thucydides*. Atlanta.

Avenarius, G. 1956. *Lukians Schrift zur Geschichtsschreibung*. Meisenheim am Glan.

Blass, F. 1892. *Die attische Beredsamkeit ii*. Leipzig.

Bosworth, A. B. 2003. "Plus ça change . . . Ancient Historians and their Sources." *Classical Antiquity* 22:167–198.

Bruce, I. A. F. 1967. *An Historical Commentary on the Hellenica Oxyrhynchia*. Cambridge.

Büchner, K. 1939. "M. Tullius Cicero (29)." *RE* VII A1:827–1274.

Bury, J. B. 1909. *The Ancient Greek Historians*. London.

Connor, W. R. 1984. *Thucydides*. Princeton.

Dewald, C. J. 2005. *Thucydides' War Narrative: A Structural Study*. Berkeley.

Ellis, J. R. 1991. "The Structure and Argument of Thucydides' Archaeology." *Classical Antiquity* 10:344–380.

Finley, M. I. 1971. "Myth, Memory and History." In *The Use and Abuse of History*, 11–33. New York.

Flower, M. A. 1994. *Theopompus of Chios: History and Rhetoric in the Fourth Century B.C.* Oxford.

---

[49] I have not here dealt with Isocrates' role as teacher, though it is important if we are to come to a more complete understanding of his interest in history. For Isocrates as teacher, see Finley 1971; Too 1995:151–232; Poulakis 1997; Ober 2001; Poulakis and Depew 2004.

[50] On Isocrates' discourses as generically innovative see Papillon 2001:73–76.

Fox, M. and Livingstone, N. 2007. "Rhetoric and Historiography." In *A Companion to Greek Rhetoric*, ed. I. Worthington, 542–561. Malden, MA.

Grant, J. R. 1974. "Toward Knowing Thucydides." *Phoenix* 28:81–94.

Grethlein, J. 2006. *Das Geschichtsbild der Ilias: eine Untersuchung aus phänomenologischer und narratologischer Perspektive.* Göttingen.

Hamilton, C. D. 1979. "Greek Rhetoric and History: The Case of Isocrates." In *Arktouros: Studies presented to B. M. W. Knox.*, ed. G. W. Bowersock et al., 290–298. Berlin and New York.

Henderson, M. M. 1975. "Plato's Menexenus and the Distortion of History." *Acta Classica* 18:25–46.

Hornblower, S. 1987. *Thucydides.* London.

———. 1991. *A Commentary on Thucydides I: Books I-III.* Oxford.

———. 1995. "The Fourth Century and Hellenistic Reception of Thucydides." *Journal of Hellenic Studies* 115:47–68.

———. 2008. *A Commentary on Thucydides III: Books 5.25–8.109.* Oxford.

Jacoby, F. 1926. *Die Fragmente der griechischen Historiker. Zweiter Teil: Zeitgeschichte. C. Kommentar zu Nr. 64–105. Berlin.*

Jost, K. 1936. *Das Beispiel und Vorbild der Vorfahren bei den antiken Rednern und Geschichtschreibern bis Demosthenes.* Rhetorische Studien 19. Paderborn.

Kalischek, A. E. 1913. *De Ephoro et Theopompo Isocratis Discipulis.* Diss., Münster.

Loraux, N. 1981. *L'invention d'Athènes: histoire de l'oraison funèbre dans la 'cité classique'.* Paris. Also pub. as *The Invention of Athens: the Funeral Oration in the Classical City*, trans. A. Sheridan. Cambridge, MA, 1986.

Marincola, J. 1994. "Plutarch's Refutation of Herodotus." *Ancient World* 20:191–203.

———. 1997. *Authority and Tradition in Ancient Historiography.* Cambridge.

———. 2001. *Greek Historians. Greece & Rome* New Surveys in the Classics 31. Oxford.

———. 2010. "The 'Rhetoric' of History: Allusion, Intertextuality, and Exemplarity in Historiographical Speeches." In *Stimmen der Geschichte: Funktionen von Reden in der antiken Historiographie*, ed. D. Pausch, 259–289. Berlin.

———. 2011. *Greek and Roman Historiography.* Oxford Readings in Classical Studies. Oxford.

Meijering, R. 1987. *Literary and Rhetorical Theories in Greek Scholia.* Groningen.

Moles, J. L. 1993. "Truth, and Untruth in Herodotus and Thucydides." In *Lies and Fiction in the Ancient World*, ed. C. Gill and T. P. Wiseman, 88–121. Exeter.

Nickel, D. 1991. "Isokrates und die Geschichtsschreibung des 4. Jahrhunderts v. Chr." *Philologus* 135:233–239.

Nicolai, R. 2004. *Studi su Isocrate. La comunicazione letteraria nel IV sec. a. C. e i nuovi generi della prosa.* Rome.

Nouhaud, M. 1980. *L'utilisation de l'histoire par les orateurs attiques.* Paris.

Ober, J. 2001. "The Debate over Civic Education in Classical Athens." In *Education in Greek and Roman Antiquity*, ed. Y. L. Too, 175–208. Leiden.

Papillon, T. L. 2001. "Rhetoric, Art and Myth: Isocrates and Busiris." In *The Orator in Action and in Theory in Greece and Rome: Essays in Honor of G. A. Kennedy*, ed. C. Wooten, 73–93. Leiden.

Parmeggiani, G. 2011. *Eforo di Cuma. Studi di storiografia greca.* Bologna.

Pearson, L. 1941. "Historical Allusions in the Attic Orators." *Classical Philology* 36:209–229, reprinted in *Selected Papers*, ed. D. Lateiner and S. Stephens, 190–210. Atlanta, 1983.

Pelling, C. B. R. 2006. "Speech and Narrative in the Histories." In *Cambridge Companion to Herodotus*, ed. C. Dewald, and J. Marincola, 103–121. Cambridge.

———. 2007. "De Malignitate Plutarchi." In *Cultural Responses to the Persian Wars: Antiquity to the Third Millenium*, ed. E. Bridges et al., 145–164. Oxford.

Perlman, S. 1961. "The Historical Example: Its Use and Importance as Political Propaganda in the Attic Orators." *Scripta Hierosolymitana* 7:150–166.

Peter, H. 1897. *Die geschichtliche Literatur über die römische Kaiserzeit bis Theodosius I und ihre Quellen I-II.* Berlin.

———. 1911. *Wahrheit und Kunst.* Leipzig.

Pothou, V. 2009. *La place et le rôle de la digression dans l'œuvre de Thucydide.* Historia Einzelschrift 203. Stuttgart.

Pownall, F. 2004. *Lessons from the Past: The Moral Use of History in Fourth-Century Prose.* Ann Arbor.

Poulakis, T. 1997. *Speaking for the Polis: Isocrates' Rhetorical Education.* Columbia, SC.

Poulakis T., and Depew, D., eds. 2004. *Isocrates and Civic Education.* Austin.

Raaflaub, K. A. 2002. "Herodot und Thukydides: Persischer Imperialismus im Lichte der athenischen Sizilienpolitik." In *Widerstand - Anpassung - Integration: die Griechische Staatenwelt und Rom, Festschrift für Jurgen Deininger zum 65. Geburtstag*, ed. L. M. Günther and N. Ehrhardt, 11–40. Stuttgart.

de Romilly, J. 1956. *Histoire et raison chez Thucydide.* Paris.

Roth, P. 2003. *Der Panathenaikos des Isokrates: Übersetzung und Kommentar.* Berlin.

Rusten, J. S., ed. 2009. *Thucydides.* Oxford Readings in Classical Studies. Oxford.

Scardino, C. 2007. *Gestaltung und Funktion der Reden bei Herodot und Thukydides.* Berlin.

Scheller, P. 1911. *De hellenistica historiae conscribendae arte.* Diss., Leipzig.

Schepens, G. 1975. "Some Aspects of Source Theory in Greek Historiography." *Ancient Society* 6:257–274. Reprinted in Marincola 2001:100–118.

Schmitz-Kahlmann, G. 1939. *Das Beispiel der Geschichte im politischen Denken des Isokrates.* Philologus Suppl. xxxi, Heft 4. Leipzig.

Schwartz, E. 1907. "Ephoros (1)." *RE* VI 1:1–16.

Strebel, H. G. 1935. *Wertung und Wirkung des thukydideischen Geschichtswerkes in der griechisch-römischen Literatur.* Diss., Munich.

Too, Y. L. 1995. *The Rhetoric of Identity in Isocrates.* Cambridge.

Ullman, B. L. 1942. "History and Tragedy." *Transactions of the American Philological Association* 73:25–53.

Usher, S. 1969. *The Historians of Greece and Rome.* London.

———. 1990. *Isocrates: Panegyricus and To Nicocles.* Greek Orators III. Warminster.

Welles, C. B. 1966. "Isocrates' View of History." In *The Classical Tradition: Literary and Historical Studies in Honor of Harry Caplan*, ed. L. Wallach, 3–25. Ithaca.

Woodman, A. J. 1988. *Rhetoric in Classical Historiography: Four Studies.* London.

Worthington, I. 1991. "Greek Oratory, Revision of Speeches, and the Problem of Historical Reliability." *Classica et Mediaevalia* 42:55–74.

———. 1994. "History and Oratorical Exploitation." In *Persuasion: Greek Rhetoric in Action*, 109–129. London.

4

At the Boundary of Historiography
Xenophon and his Corpus

Roberto Nicolai

1. Historians and Sophists

THE TERMS sophist and sophistic are commonly applied to a diverse group of people, united by a broad range of interests, areas of expertise, and a preference for disseminating their works by way of public recitations (ἀκροάσεις).[1] If to an Athenian of the fifth century BCE, Socrates was a sophist (Aristophanes *Clouds*),[2] the same must have been true for Herodotus and, to some degree, for Thucydides as well.[3] Thucydides, however, explicitly takes a stand against creating a piece meant simply to display his rhetorical skills (1.22.4); instead, he made a τέχνη of political-military history, which he addresses to those who, through his history, would be capable of understanding the dynamics of politics and war. Thucydides' polemic against the logographers (1.21.1) anticipated that of Plato against the sophists, which endowed the term, sophist, with a negative connotation.[4] In the cases of both Thucydides and Plato, the issue at stake was the control of the education of the ruling classes.

Current scholarly consensus distinguishes historians from philosophers, relegating the so-called sophists to the latter category and thereby disregarding their contribution to the study of the past. But we can note general historical interests, looking only at the *Vorsokratiker*, in the work of Democritus,[5]

---

[1] Nicolai 2004c.
[2] Segoloni 1994.
[3] Thomas 2000.
[4] On the implications of the term λογογράφος for the way in which the work was published, see Ferrucci 2001.
[5] Diogenes Laertius 9.49: Περὶ τῶν ἐν Βαβυλῶνι ἱερῶν γραμμάτων, Περὶ τῶν ἐν Μερόῃ, Περὶ ἱστορίης, Χαλδαϊκὸς λόγος, Φρύγιος λόγος, Νομικὰ αἴτια.

Protagoras,[6] Hippias (in the description of his interests in Plato *Hippias maior* 285d), and Critias (πολιτεῖαι). At the same time, the history of historiography has privileged the strand of so-called 'Great' historiography, which treats the history of the Greeks and the majority of the Barbarians, to paraphrase Thucydides' *incipit*. In so doing, it has marginalized inquiries into the distant past (ἀρχαιολογία), as well as the various forms of local and regional historiography and the political treatment of history in the epitaphs, to say nothing of poetic works with historical content: epic, narrative elegy, tragedy (e.g. Phrynichus' *Miletou Alosis*; Aeschylus' *Persae*), and dithyrambs (Timotheus' *Persae*). The history of historiography, then, has become a history less of a literary genre than of a method, teleologically projected towards the achievements of modern historical science. The loss not only of the sophists' works, which had been condemned by Plato's judgment and by Aristotle's doxographies, but also of what are classified as minor branches of historiography has contributed to the emergence of a particular picture of the development of historiography that takes us, after the first uneasy steps, to the wide-ranging ἱστορίη of Herodotus and the mature historical analysis of Thucydides, only to decay afterwards into rhetorical or moralistic historiographical forms, or those designed to achieve dramatic effects. In recent years, this reconstruction of the history of historiography has been challenged on many fronts.[7]

The aim of this contribution is a thorough revaluation of Xenophon's work, particularly in relation to that of another great experimenter of various prose genres, Isocrates. Xenophon and Isocrates share paideutic aspirations, a freedom to move among preexisting literary genres and the ability to change them from within, and the tendency to assign a demonstrative and exemplary function to historical matter.

2. A Necessary Revisionism

In a famous article from 1935, Arnaldo Momigliano wrote: "Senofonte è tra gli scrittori greci uno di quelli che hanno più urgente bisogno di essere riesaminati nel loro complesso. La sua singolare e un poco ambigua personalità, ricca di motivi e di problemi quale pochi, ma incapace di fonderli in modo che essi diventino un sistema e perciò un programma, ha una perfetta aderenza alle condizioni spirituali del quarantennio 390-350 a.C., il quale dà una impressione di vita intensa, ma dispersa."[8] In the seventy years since Momigliano's

---

6   Diogenes Laertius 9.55: Περὶ πολιτείας, Περὶ τῶν οὐκ ὀρθῶς τοῖς ἀνθρώποις πρασσομένων, Περὶ τῆς ἐν ἀρχῇ καταστάσεως.

7   Nicolai 2006 and Schepens 2006.

8   Momigliano 1935:208.

pronouncement, some progress has been made towards a reappraisal of Xenophon's work, but more work still needs to be done. In fact, if Xenophon requires a general reexamination, we cannot today avoid feeling the need also to revise the interpretation of Xenophon given by Momigliano and successive critics.[9] In recent literature on Xenophon, one tendency is clear: often very early on in the introductory chapters, we find a discussion of the literary genre to which the work in question belongs. This phenomenon is particularly evident in criticism of the *Cyropaedia*, which some scholars actually describe as a collection of different literary genres,[10] sometimes even resorting to such blatant anachronisms as calling the work a pedagogical or historical novel, or a fictionalized biography. But the difficulties we have in defining the *Cyropaedia* (along with much of Xenophon's work), derives from a faulty approach to the problem of genres and models: Xenophon created literary products that were completely disconnected from any specific occasions of publication, and he used generic strategies appropriate for preexisting literary genres that he adapted to his own aims.[11] In this regard, Xenophon is not very different from Isocrates, except for the fact that the latter, as a teacher of rhetoric, explicitly thought about the choices he made, turning his reflections into tools for teaching rhetoric.[12]

Another frequently emphasized feature of Xenophon's work is what seems to be an unusual integration of literature and politics.[13] Once again, our categories of what is 'political' and what is 'literary' are inadequate. And, once again, the comparison with Isocrates is instructive. Just like Xenophon, Isocrates did not intend to influence the decision-making process: for this, he would have used different tools. Being political for him, in fact, meant inserting traditional political themes into speeches devised for didactic purposes, teaching politics through political discourse.

Finally, to complete the picture, Xenophon is often depicted as a split personality, a historian with modest capabilities and an aspiring philosopher

---

[9] A very useful overview of Xenophontic scholarship in the last thirty years of the twentieth century can be found in Vela Tejada 1998.

[10] See e.g. Tatum 1989:xv; Levine Gera 1993:1; Azoulay 2004:x, who speaks of a "*monstrum* littéraire."

[11] The experimental nature of Xenophon's works has made it difficult to classify them by genre: for example, according to Tatum 1989:35, Xenophon appears to us as a novelist but maintains a vague profile in terms of literary genre. The comparison with the novel is actually unhelpful, and it even causes problems on the level of literary system and functions of the various genres. Tatum 1989:40f., also states that Xenophon had a "protean imagination," which led him to work simultaneously on what we now regard as different literary forms.

[12] On Isocrates, see Nicolai 2004a. My research on the literary genres used by Isocrates has its roots in, and originates from, Rossi 1971 and Rossi 2000.

[13] Tatum 1989:xiv speaks of "political uses of fiction."

of little talent.[14] It is doubtful that the label 'philosopher', as we understand it, can be applied before Aristotle—and, in some respects, the same can be said for 'historian', too—but, more to the point, Xenophon's works elude even such an elementary distinction as this: historical material is as present in his *corpus* as is philosophical speculation. In order better to understand Xenophon, we must change our perspective and explore not the contents of the various works of the *corpus* but their function with respect to their reception.

3. Historical Matter in Xenophon's Corpus

The *Hellenika*, inasmuch as it is closest to our standards of historical writing, serves as a good point of entry for our exploration of Xenophon's approach to historical matter. The *Hellenika* covers only a segment of the past, with a beginning arbitrarily determined by the abrupt conclusion of Thucydides' work.[15] I do not want to resume the debate about the original shape of the work: whether, for example, the so-called *paralipomena* was meant to constitute a unity with Thucydides; nor do I believe that the different stages of its redaction can be reconstructed with any reasonable certainty—indeed, this is in many ways a false problem, stemming from our own publication practices and positivist obsessions with questions of origin and evolution.[16] Without venturing into indemonstrable hypotheses, we may note only that Xenophon's narrative is continuous; that is to say, there are no *proemia* or introductions to particular sections, nor general remarks on the history he is narrating.[17] The only exception is the conclusion: the *Hellenika* is not itself a work that is open to continuation, unless, that is, someone should take up the challenge of the final provocation.[18] The historical events narrated in the *Hellenika* as a whole can only be paradigms of

---

[14] On the tendency to separate the historian from the philosopher, see Dillery 1995:7, including n5 (with his example of the *Cambridge History of Classical Literature*); some negative opinions about Xenophon can be found in the examples suggested at 255n6. On Xenophon as a second-class author, a pale imitator of Thucydides, and an unimpressive copier of Plato, see Azoulay 2004:x.

[15] For a cogent analysis of passages that attest an awareness in Xenophon of Thucydides' work, on both a thematic and verbal level, see Rood 2004. On the complex relationship between the *Hellenika* and Herodotus and Thucydides, see Tamiolaki 2008. Important contributions to the reinterpretation of the Peloponnesian War by fourth-century historians can be found in Schepens 2007.

[16] On this issue, note the balanced position of Dillery 1995:12–15.

[17] Dillery 1995:10 deals with the absence of a *proemium* and concludes (11): "Xenophon may have deliberately avoided an introduction, inasmuch as it would have demanded, among other things, that he explains what was important about the recent past and how it explained the present and future, something he may well have been unable to do."

[18] The conclusion of the *Hellenika* does not allow us to consider it as incomplete: so Tatum 1989:50; see also 46 on the difficulties of trying to develop a consistent theme and building a coherent literary genre. The conclusion of the *Hellenika* with the battle of Mantinea, which did not

crisis and confusion, as Xenophon points out in the conclusion, where the battle of Mantinea becomes the metaphor of a Greece without stable hegemonies; but various other clearly marked paradigms are also introduced in the course of the narrative.[19] The structure of the *Hellenika* is not consistently annalistic, nor does it follow the Herodotean model.[20] Rather, Xenophon selects what he considers the central themes and facts and uses them to search for a behavioral model that is different not only from the political-military one employed by Thucydides but also from the ethical perspective of later biography.[21]

The *Anabasis*, which delineates the ideal military commander (Xenophon himself), also treats only a segment of history—in fact, Xenophon equates it directly with the *Hellenika* (see *Hellenika* 3.1.2: "As to how Cyrus collected an army and with this army made the march up country against his brother, how the battle was fought, how Cyrus was slain, and how after that the Greeks effected their return in safety to the sea—all this has been written by Themistogenes the Syracusan.")[22] Both works, moreover, correspond to contemporary definitions of the historical genre.[23] Xenophon's central role and the exemplarity of his behavior in the *Anabasis* in some respects allow the work to be compared to the *Cyropaedia* and the *Agesilaus*, as well as to Isocrates' Cypriot speeches.[24] That it is a new and innovative genre is uncontested, but similarities with later literary genres certainly should not imply that the *Anabasis* can be defined as a *commentarius* or a novel. The innovation consists in the fact that it recounts, in the style of a Thucydidean monograph (i.e. with narration and speeches),

---

prove to be as crucial as Xenophon had expected, is the object of important remarks by Dillery 1995:17–38.

[19] Nicolai 2006:700–702. On the conclusion, see 702f. Paradigms related to individuals and communities are analysed in Dillery 1995:123–176, especially in part IV, *Ideal Community, Ideal Leader: Paradigm as History*.

[20] See e.g. Dillery 1995:4.

[21] See Nicolai 2006:695–706, for a definition of the genre of the *Hellenika* and the function of this work, with a discussion of recent bibliography. On Xenophon's project, see Dillery 1995, especially the conclusion, 241–254.

[22] ὡς μὲν οὖν Κῦρος στράτευμά τε συνέλεξε καὶ τοῦτ᾽ ἔχων ἀνέβη ἐπὶ τὸν ἀδελφόν, καὶ ὡς ἡ μάχη ἐγένετο, καὶ ὡς ἀπέθανε, καὶ ὡς ἐκ τούτου ἀπεσώθησαν οἱ Ἕλληνες ἐπὶ θάλατταν, Θεμιστογένει τῷ Συρακοσίῳ γέγραπται. (Translation by C. L. Brownson) This passage in the *Hellenika* shares some features of the summaries at the beginning of Books 2, 3, 4, 5 and 7, which are not generally accepted by editors. For a different position, see Canfora 1970:26, with earlier bibliography.

[23] Isocrates *Antidosis* 45 ἕτεροι δὲ τὰς πράξεις τὰς ἐν τοῖς πολέμοις συναγαγεῖν ἐβουλήθησαν, *Panathenaicus* 1 τοὺς [sc. τῶν λόγων] τὰς παλαιὰς πράξεις καὶ τοὺς πολέμους τοὺς Ἑλληνικοὺς ἐξηγουμένους, Aristotle *Rhetoric* 1.4.1360a36-37 αἱ τῶν περὶ τὰς πράξεις γραφόντων ἱστορίαι. Hornblower 2007:30, compares the *Anabasis* to Caesar's *Commentarii* and stresses that both works are deeply apologetic. I shall not consider the details that this comparison entails, but I doubt that the apologetic aim prevails in Xenophon.

[24] Tatum 1989:5 states that the *Cyropaedia* is comparable to Isocrates' Cypriot speeches, if not for its literary type, at least as far as concerns it intentions.

an event in which the author acts as the main character and becomes himself a paradigm of behavior. Like the *Hellenika*, the *Anabasis* conspicuously lacks a *proemium*; but whereas this absence presents the *Hellenika* as a continuation of Thucydides, the *Anabasis* opens as an autonomous segment of history, beginning with the death of Darius. There is a further difference between the two works: the *Anabasis*, even without a *proemium*, nevertheless has a beginning (which provides background information), but it lacks an explicit conclusion or any remarks that could lend an overall meaning to the work, or at any rate a key to reading it. Perhaps the meaning of the *Anabasis* is clear enough from the narrative itself, while the intricate affairs recounted in the *Hellenika* close with a battle in which everybody is a winner and a loser at the same time. Xenophon's use of a pseudonym in the *Anabasis*, we should note, sheds some light on the manner of its publication; Xenophon clearly wanted to disseminate the work as if the enterprise had been recorded by a neutral narrator.[25] This would lend the description of Xenophon's exemplary behavior some credibility, a τέχνη inside the work, we might say, in the same way that the speeches can be defined as a τέχνη, albeit in this case a rhetorical one.[26]

The *Agesilaus* begins with a clear and unequivocal statement of genre, which apparently distinguishes it from historiography:

Οἶδα μὲν ὅτι τῆς Ἀγησιλάου ἀρετῆς τε καὶ δόξης οὐ ῥᾴδιον ἄξιον ἔπαινον γράψαι, ὅμως δ' ἐγχειρητέον. Οὐ γὰρ ἂν καλῶς ἔχοι εἰ ὅτι τελέως ἀνὴρ ἀγαθὸς ἐγένετο, διὰ τοῦτο οὐδὲ μειόνων ἂν τυγχάνοι ἐπαίνων.

I know how difficult it is to write an appreciation of Agesilaus that shall be worthy of his virtue and glory. Nevertheless the attempt must be made. For it would not be seemly that so good a man, just because of his perfection, should receive no tributes of praise, however inadequate. (Translation by E. C. Marchant)

Xenophon *Agesilaus* 1.1

But after a canonical introduction dedicated to the family and country of the *laudandus*, the work takes a different turn:

Ὅσα γε μὴν ἐν τῇ βασιλείᾳ διεπράξατο νῦν ἤδη διηγήσομαι· ἀπὸ γὰρ τῶν ἔργων καὶ τοὺς τρόπους αὐτοῦ κάλλιστα νομίζω καταδήλους ἔσεσθαι.

---

[25] According to Tatum 1989:12, the detachment of the author/narrator is a rhetorical strategy borrowed from Thucydides.

[26] For this interpretation of speeches in historiography, with particular attention to Thucydides, see Cole 1986 and 1991 and Nicolai 1992:63–69.

I will now give an account of the achievements of his reign, for I believe that his deeds will throw the clearest light on his qualities. (Translation by E. C. Marchant)

Xenophon *Agesilaus* 1.6

The verb διηγήσομαι is less a marker of genre than the phrase Ὅσα γε μὴν ἐν τῇ βασιλείᾳ διεπράξατο, which is explained by ἀπὸ ... τῶν ἔργων. The emphasis on τρόποι, a characteristic of the encomium, is substantiated in the historical account of Agesilaus' deeds, which occupies the central part of the work (1.6 to 2.31) and which itself concludes with clear indications of genre:

Καὶ ταῦτα μὲν δὴ εἴρηται ὅσα τῶν ἐκείνου ἔργων μετὰ πλείστων μαρτύρων ἐπράχθη. τὰ γὰρ τοιαῦτα οὐ τεκμηρίων προσδεῖται, ἀλλ᾽ ἀναμνῆσαι μόνον ἀρκεῖ καὶ εὐθὺς πιστεύεται.

Such, then, is the record of my hero's deeds, so far as they were done before a crowd of witnesses. Actions like these need no proofs; the mere mention of them is enough and they command belief immediately. (Translation by E. C. Marchant)

Xenophon *Agesilaus* 3.1

In addition to the recurrence of the term, ἔργα, we should note the distinction between μάρτυρες and τεκμήρια, which, aside from confirming the narrative as true, emphasizes the exemplary character of the recent and well-known facts the narrative describes. This distinction further recalls, although with different terminology, that made by Thucydides between ancient history, reconstructed ἐκ τῶν ἐπιφανεστάτων σημείων ("from the clearest signs," 1.21.1), and contemporary history, which is based upon eyewitnesses (1.22.2 f.). This historical section, which can be compared with the sections in the *Hellenika* devoted to Agesilaus, is followed by another one devoted to "the virtue in his soul" (ἐν τῇ ψυχῇ αὐτοῦ ἀρετή), echoed in summary in chapter 11. Exceptionally, just before this passage, Xenophon discusses the genre of the *Agesilaus*:

ἀλλὰ γὰρ μὴ ὅτι τετελευτηκὼς ἐπαινεῖται τούτου ἕνεκα θρῆνόν τις τοῦτον τὸν λόγον νομισάτω, ἀλλὰ πολὺ μᾶλλον ἐγκώμιον. πρῶτον μὲν γὰρ ἅπερ ζῶν ἤκουε ταῦτα καὶ νῦν λέγεται περὶ αὐτοῦ· ἔπειτα δὲ τί καὶ πλέον θρήνου ἄπεστιν ἢ βίος τε εὐκλεὴς καὶ θάνατος ὡραῖος; ἐγκωμίων δὲ τί ἀξιώτερον ἢ νῖκαί τε αἱ κάλλισται καὶ ἔργα τὰ πλείστου ἄξια;

However, let it not be thought, because one whose life is ended is the theme of my praise, that these words are meant for a funeral dirge.

They are far more truly the language of eulogy. In the first place the words now applied to him are the very same that he heard in his lifetime. And, in the second place, what theme is less appropriate to a dirge than a life of fame and a death well-timed? What more worthy of eulogies than victories most glorious and deeds of sovereign worth? (Translation by E. C. Marchant)

Xenophon *Agesilaus* 10.3

He emphasizes that this work belongs to the genre of the encomium—distinguishing it from the θρῆνος (lament)—and this is the opposite of what Isocrates did in his *Panegyricus*, where a panegyric discourse is combined with themes more appropriate to epitaphs:[27]

καίτοι μ' οὐ λέληθεν ὅτι χαλεπόν ἐστιν ὕστατον ἐπελθόντα λέγειν περὶ πραγμάτων πάλαι προκατειλημμένων, καὶ περὶ ὧν οἱ μάλιστα δυνηθέντες τῶν πολιτῶν εἰπεῖν ἐπὶ τοῖς δημοσίᾳ θαπτομένοις πολλάκις εἰρήκασιν· ἀνάγκη γὰρ τὰ μὲν μέγιστ' αὐτῶν ἤδη κατακεχρῆσθαι, μικρὰ δ' ἔτι παραλελεῖφθαι. ὅμως δ' ἐκ τῶν ὑπολοίπων, ἐπειδὴ συμφέρει τοῖς πράγμασιν, οὐκ ὀκνητέον μνησθῆναι περὶ αὐτῶν.

And yet I have not failed to appreciate the fact that it is difficult to come forward last and speak upon a subject which has long been appropriated, and upon which the very ablest speakers among our citizens have many times addressed you at the public funerals; for, naturally, the most important topics have already been exhausted, while only unimportant topics have been left for later speakers. Nevertheless, since they are apposite to the matter in hand, I must not shirk the duty of taking up the points which remain and of recalling them to your memory. (Translation by George Norlin)

Isocrates *Panegyricus* 74

Xenophon's argumentation here is consistent with the ennobling aims of encomia, yet his explicit reflections on literary genres and codes are characteristic of the fictional speeches of the Isocratean type. It may be instructive, then, to think of the *Agesilaus*, like Isocrates' speeches, as a literary encomium, not

---

[27] Cuniberti 2007:385, highlights the way in which Xenophon willingly stresses "la natura pubblica della *laudatio* del re Agesilao." As Cuniberti later says, "Senofonte propone così un encomio di fronte a tutti, una sorta di panegirico, rivolto, come quello di Isocrate, a tutti i Greci e finalizzato a celebrare il re spartano, per il quale è inutile chiedere onori, perché gli sono già attribuiti dalla legge di Licurgo, che lo innalza ad eroe, ma è necessario perpetuarne la memoria."

connected with any specific occasion; as far as we can tell, it lacks only one of the features inherent in Isocrates' work: it was not meant for school use.

In the fourth chapter of Xenophon's Socratic dialogue, the *Oeconomicus*, we find a brief outline of the τέχναι (arts) that should be practiced, with the King of Persia held up as example—that he is here a paradigm is clear from Socrates' words, "should we be ashamed of imitating the King of the Persians?" (Ἆρ(α) . . . μὴ αἰσχυνθῶμεν τὸν Περσῶν βασιλέα μιμήσασθαι; 4.4) The τέχναι practiced by the King of Persia are agriculture and the art of war: the King takes care of the needs of the army, inspects troops, and rewards with gifts and promotions the most efficient commanders and administrators, while punishing the corrupt and inefficient (see especially 4.7-9). Already in these first paragraphs, it is evident that the King of Persia in question is either the Cyrus of the *Cyropaedia* himself or his homonymous descendent, Cyrus the Younger, the protagonist of the *Anabasis*.[28] In fact, this section of the *Oeconomicus* can be considered to be a variation of the theme of the *Cyropaedia*, here realized through the technique of the Socratic dialogue. So too, the theme of *paradeisoi* (4.13f.), used here as evidence of the King's commitment to agriculture, finds a parallel in *Anabasis* 1.2.7 and in the many references to *paradeisoi* in the *Cyropaedia*. In the *Oeconomicus*, the anecdote at 4.16 refers clearly to Cyrus the Elder, inasmuch as this Cyrus is defined as "the most well-esteemed king" (εὐδοκιμώτατος . . . βασιλεύς), but Cyrus the Younger appears immediately afterwards (4.18), in addition to (καὶ) his illustrious predecessor.[29] Cyrus' skills as a commander are not presented in detail but are rather summarized by way of a sort of *praeteritio* that refers to the theme of the *Anabasis*: "One of the many proofs that he has given of this is the fact that, when he was on his way to fight his brother for the throne . . ." (Translation by E. C. Marchant, 4.18–19).[30] Only two episodes are explicitly recorded: first, the fact that nobody abandoned Cyrus to join Artaxerxes—although many troops of the King defected to Cyrus—and, second, the death of all of Cyrus' φίλοι (except Arieus) atop his body at Cunaxa (4.18f.; cf. *Anabasis* 1.9.29 and 1.9.31, almost *ad litteram*). More space is devoted to a dialogue between Cyrus and Lysander (4.20–25), which Lysander related to a Megarian guest.[31] The dialogue, keeping with the theme of the *paradeisos* that had been in part cultivated by Cyrus himself, closes the entire section, with Lysander praising Cyrus as "happy" (εὐδαίμων) because he is "a good man" (ἀγαθὸς . . . ἀνήρ).

---

[28] For parallel passages, see *Anabasis* 1.9.14f., 1.9.19, 1.9.22–26 and *Cyropaedia* 8.2.8 and 8.6.11.

[29] See on this topic Pomeroy 1994:248: the confusion between Cyrus the Elder and Cyrus the Younger seems to be deliberate; Xenophon might have transferred the virtues of the Elder to his unlucky namesake.

[30] καὶ τούτου τεκμήρια ἄλλα τε πολλὰ παρέσχηται, καὶ ὁπότε περὶ τῆς βασιλείας τῷ ἀδελφῷ ἐπορεύετο μαχούμενος.

[31] Pomeroy 1994:251 hypothesizes that Xenophon used either Persian officials or Ctesias.

Another variation on the theme of the *Cyropaedia* (although connected also to the *Anabasis, Agesilaus,* and to the *Hiero* as well) emerges in the conclusion of the dialogue in a discussion devoted to τὸ ἀρχικὸν εἶναι (21.2):[32]

Νὴ Δί᾽, ἔφη ὁ Ἰσχόμαχος, ἀλλὰ τόδε τοι, ὦ Σώκρατες, τὸ πάσαις κοινὸν ταῖς πράξεσι καὶ γεωργικῇ καὶ πολιτικῇ καὶ οἰκονομικῇ καὶ πολεμικῇ τὸ ἀρχικὸν εἶναι, τοῦτο δὴ συνομολογῶ σοί ἐγὼ πολὺ διαφέρειν γνώμῃ τοὺς ἑτέρους τῶν ἑτέρων·

'Of course it is,' cried Ischomachus; 'but I grant you, Socrates, that in respect of aptitude for command, which is common to all forms of business alike—agriculture, politics, estate-management, warfare—in that respect the intelligence shown by different classes of men varies greatly.' (Translation by E. C. Marchant)

Xenophon Oeconomicus 21.2

That leadership skills are common not only to agriculture, the topic with which the discussion began, but also to politics, economy, property management, and the art of war confirms that this is a key theme in the *Oeconomicus,* intentionally placed in a significant position, as in the beginning of the *Cyropaedia.* Xenophon's use of the same historical examples in works of different literary genre, thus, illustrates the interconnections between his historical and philosophical works.

4. Cyrus: Between Xenophon and Plato

Already in antiquity an allusion to Xenophon's *Cyropaedia* was recognized in the third book of Plato's *Laws.*[33] The reference in Plato, which could be extended to other works (now lost) that revolved around Cyrus (I am thinking of Antisthenes), may shed some light on the discussion in which Xenophon took part, on his fellow debaters and possible opponents, and on the literary genres involved. The passage is usually read in isolation (694c or 694c–695b) but should be kept in the context of the argument. That said, we ought to begin from 693d5, where the Athenian interlocutor raises the question about the balance between τὸ μοναρχικόν (monarchy) and τὸ ἐλεύθερον (freedom). The example that he suggests immediately thereafter is that of the Persian empire under Cyrus (694a2f.). The Athenian poses a further problem: the crisis of the empire under

---

[32] I will not address here the problem of the stages of publication of the *Oeconomicus,* which primarily involves the passage quoted here. On this subject, see Roscalla 1991:21–25.

[33] Pomeroy 1994:26, and Corcella 2010:47.

Cambyses and its recovery under Darius. He will proceed in his inquiry, he says, by way of divination (694c2f. "Shall I use a kind of divination to picture this?"),[34] a claim to which we should pay particular attention, since it clearly indicates that the characters in the dialogue (and Plato himself) had no sources on which to rely and were obliged instead to resort to conjecture, or rather to mantic arts. The passage to which I refer is as follows:

μαντεύομαι δὴ νῦν περὶ γε Κύρου, τὰ μὲν ἄλλ' αὐτὸν στρατηγόν τε ἀγαθὸν εἶναι καὶ φιλόπολιν, παιδείας δὲ ὀρθῆς οὐχ ἧφθαι τὸ παράπαν, οἰκονομίᾳ τε οὐδὲν τὸν νοῦν προσεσχηκέναι.

What I now divine regarding Cyrus is this,—that, although otherwise a good and patriotic commander, he was entirely without a right education, and had paid no attention to household management. (Translation by R. G. Bury)

Plato *Laws* 694c5–8

The key to the passage lies in the proposition, παιδείας δὲ ὀρθῆς οὐχ ἧφθαι ("he was . . . without a right education"), which some scholars have erroneously interpreted as a reference to the education that Cyrus himself never received.[35] It is, in fact, clearly explained by what immediately follows: while Cyrus was busy with warfare and could not pay enough attention to the education of his children and to the administration of his own house, women and eunuchs took care of these affairs in accordance with the customs of the Medes but contrary to the very different educatory principles of the Persians (694e6–695b8). The verb ἅπτω here means "engage in, undertake" (LSJ s.v.).[36] Dorion, then, is right to change the terms of the problem: Plato agrees with Xenophon on the excellence of Persian education and on Cyrus' virtues, but he differs from him regarding one important point. For Xenophon, law by itself is not enough to produce good leaders, and the responsibility falls entirely on the men in power; for Plato, on the other hand, laws are the foundation for a proper education of those who will be in power (696a3–8).

It seems clear, then, that if there is indeed an allusion to the *Cyropaedia* in the *Laws*, the debate between Plato and Xenophon is not so much about the education of children (to which Xenophon only briefly refers at 7.5.86), but in fact involves a far more important theme, namely the foundation of power and the *paideia* from which that power derives: their disagreement, that is to say, is

---

[34] βούλεσθε οἷον μαντείᾳ διανοηθέντες χρώμεθα, translation by R. G. Bury.
[35] Dorion 2003.
[36] As in *Republic* 3.411c5: μουσικῆς δὲ καὶ φιλοσοφίας μὴ ἅπτηται.

about the very function and role of Law.[37] Cyrus remains a paradigm, therefore, but, like every paradigm, he can be manipulated to fulfil different functions. Antisthenes, according to Diogenes Laertius (6.2), used the example of Cyrus to demonstrate that hard work is something good (a frequent theme in the *Cyropaedia* and in chapter 4 of the *Oeconomicus* as well). We should note, however, that among Antisthenes' writings there are as many as three works dedicated to Cyrus, in the fourth, fifth, and tenth volumes of his collected works (6.16; 6.18); the treatise that Diogenes assigns to volume five, *Cyrus* or *On Kingship*, might in fact partly overlap with the contents of the *Cyropaedia*.

To conclude, the paradigm of Cyrus was used with particular frequency in works related to the genre of the *politeia*, owing its popularity both to general Greek interest in the Persians and to the diffusion of works specifically about Persia (Ctesias) or at any rate engaged in Persian history and customs (Herodotus).[38] That Plato belongs to this tradition is confirmed by *Laws* 695a2–5, a passage that seems to recall the final sentence of Herodotus' work, Cyrus' response to Artembares (9.122).[39] In Herodotus, as in Plato, it is the harsh soil of Persia that engenders strong warriors and future conquerors, with Plato specifying that Cambyses and Xerxes were products of a soft education entrusted to women and eunuchs in the luxury of the court. Herodotus himself seems to be one of the authors who has contributed most to the popularity of the paradigm.[40] Cyrus' paradigmatic function should make us rethink the aim of works that we are quick to classify either as historical or as philosophical and works on which we bestow anachronistic labels, as in the case of the *Cyropaedia*.

One last consideration regarding the origin of the Persian paradigm: as far as we know, it was first used not by a historian but by Aeschylus, who in his *Persae* exploited geographical and anthropological distance in order to endow with exemplary force an event that had occurred only eight years before.[41] Already in the *Persae* we can note the centrality of the theme of decadence resulting from the inappropriate use of power. In this regard, we should note that it is Darius and his successor, Xerxes, who are introduced in Plato's *Laws*

---

[37] Xenophon *Cyropaedia* 8.1.8: ὅταν μὲν ὁ ἐπιστάτης βελτίων γένηται, καθαρώτερον τὰ νόμιμα πράττεται· ὅταν δὲ χείρων, φαυλότερον.

[38] On the differing perceptions that the Greeks had of the Persians and their fortune in western culture, see Corcella 2007 and Corcella 2010, with bibliography.

[39] Flower 2006:287.

[40] See Flower 2006:282, according to whom Herodotus had enough cultural distance to give an impartial account of Cyrus' failures.

[41] On the *Persae* as a reflection on memory, open to interpretation on a meta-literary level; on the creation of identity through ethnic and chronological distance; and on the relation between past and present in tragedy, see Grethlein 2007.

directly after Cyrus and Cambyses as examples, respectively, of revival and decay (695c5–696a3).

5. The *Memorabilia* as a Genre.

In light of Tatum's observation that the *Memorabilia* begins as an apology and finishes as an encomium, we ought to reconsider this work with an eye toward generic markers.[42] We should first note that the apologetic opening statement uses the same words that Isocrates employs in his *Panegyricus* (Πολλάκις ἐθαύμασα). The apology proper finishes at 1.2.62–64, at which point Xenophon turns to the benefits of Socrates' activity, both in action and in speech:

Ὡς δὲ δὴ καὶ ὠφελεῖν ἐδόκει μοι τοὺς συνόντας τὰ μὲν ἔργῳ δεικνύων ἑαυτὸν οἷος ἦν, τὰ δὲ καὶ διαλεγόμενος, τούτων δὴ γράψω ὁπόσα ἂν διαμνημονεύσω.

In order to support my opinion that he benefited his companions, alike by actions that revealed his own character and by his conversation, I will set down what I recollect of these. (Translation by E. C. Marchant)

Xenophon *Memorabilia* 1.3.1

The conclusion of the *Memorabilia* refers precisely to this passage, thereby closing the extensive encomiastic component in a ring. It is worth pointing out that Xenophon, in this recapitulation of Socrates' virtues, emphasizes that the image he has drawn corresponds to the truth:

All who knew what manner of man Socrates was and who seek after virtue continue to this day to miss him beyond all others, as the chief of helpers in the quest of virtue. For myself, I have described him as he was: so religious that he did nothing without counsel from the gods; so just that he did no injury, however small, to any man, but conferred the greatest benefits on all who dealt with him; so self-controlled that he never chose the pleasanter rather than the better course; so wise that he was unerring in his judgment of the better and the worse, and needed no counsellor, but relied on himself for his knowledge of them; masterly in expounding and defining such things; no less masterly in putting others to the test, and convincing them of error and exhorting them to follow virtue and gentleness. To me then he seemed to be all that a truly good and happy man must be. But if there is any doubter,

---

[42] Tatum 1989:54.

let him set the character of other men beside these things; then let him judge. (Translation by E. C. Marchant)

Xenophon *Memorabilia* 4.8.11[43]

On closer inspection, we can see that we are faced here with a multilayered correspondence: through his actions, Socrates revealed the way he was (1.3.1 οἷος ἦν); Xenophon, who knew the way he was (οἷος ἦν), emphasizes the sorrow of those who aspire to virtue (4.8.11); the picture that Xenophon has drawn of Socrates matches precisely with what he was (ibid. τοιοῦτος ὢν οἷον ἐγὼ διήγημαι); and finally, in the final synthesis, Socrates seems to be like the man who excels in every virtue (ibid. ἐδόκει τοιοῦτος εἶναι οἷος ἂν εἴη ἄριστός τε ἀνὴρ καὶ εὐδαιμονέστατος). Again, the parallel with Isocrates is instructive. In the long *proemium* to the *Antidosis*, Isocrates reflects on the genre in which he has chosen to describe his thought and life. Isocrates represents himself as embittered by his fellow citizens' incorrect opinion of him and committed to finding a way of explaining to them and to posterity "the character that I have, the life I lead, and the education which I practice" (καὶ τὸν τρόπον ὃν ἔχω, καὶ τὸν βίον ὃν ζῶ, καὶ τὴν παιδείαν περὶ ἣν διατρίβω, 6). The best solution, it seems to him, is to write a speech that would be the very image of his thought and of his life.[44] In this way, he would be able to achieve his two main objectives: to let his fellow citizens know who he really is, and, at the same time, to leave a monument of himself.[45]

At this point (8), Isocrates pauses to reflect on literary genre, rejecting the encomium (ἐπαινεῖν) in favor of the judicial speech, in particular the *apologia*. In the same way, Xenophon opens his Socratic work with an articulate *apologia*. Both strategies, in fact, are designed to mask an encomium, implicitly in Xenophon, explicitly in Isocrates, whose intention, after all, is to use his speech for pedagogic purposes. What is denied, of course, is just what is actually done: in Isocrates' case, an elaborate encomium (a self-encomium, moreover), built into a mixed-genre speech, as the author himself admits (*Antidosis* 12, quoted *infra*).

---

43 τῶν δὲ Σωκράτην γιγνωσκόντων, οἷος ἦν, οἱ ἀρετῆς ἐφιέμενοι πάντες ἔτι καὶ νῦν διατελοῦσι πάντων μάλιστα ποθοῦντες ἐκεῖνον, ὡς ὠφελιμώτατον ὄντα πρὸς ἀρετῆς ἐπιμέλειαν. ἐμοὶ μὲν δή, τοιοῦτος ὢν οἷον ἐγὼ διήγημαι, εὐσεβὴς μὲν οὕτως ὥστε μηδὲν ἄνευ τῆς τῶν θεῶν γνώμης ποιεῖν, δίκαιος δὲ ὥστε βλάπτειν μὲν μηδὲ μικρὸν μηδένα, ὠφελεῖν δὲ τὰ μέγιστα τοὺς χρωμένους αὐτῷ, ἐγκρατὴς δὲ ὥστε μηδέποτε προαιρεῖσθαι τὸ ἥδιον ἀντὶ τοῦ βελτίονος, φρόνιμος δὲ ὥστε μὴ διαμαρτάνειν κρίνων τὰ βελτίω καὶ τὰ χείρω μηδὲ ἄλλου προσδεῖσθαι, ἀλλ᾽ αὐτάρκης εἶναι πρὸς τὴν τούτων γνῶσιν, ἱκανὸς δὲ καὶ λόγῳ εἰπεῖν τε καὶ διορίσασθαι τὰ τοιαῦτα, ἱκανὸς δὲ καὶ ἄλλως δοκιμάσαι τε καὶ ἁμαρτάνοντα ἐλέγξαι καὶ προτρέψασθαι ἐπ᾽ ἀρετὴν καὶ καλοκαγαθίαν, ἐδόκει τοιοῦτος εἶναι οἷος ἂν εἴη ἄριστός τε ἀνὴρ καὶ εὐδαιμονέστατος. εἰ δέ τῳ μὴ ἀρέσκει ταῦτα, παραβάλλων τὸ ἄλλων ἦθος πρὸς ταῦτα οὕτω κρινέτω.

44 *Antidosis* 7: λόγος ὥσπερ εἰκὼν τῆς ἐμῆς διανοίας καὶ τῶν ἄλλων τῶν [ἐμοὶ] βεβιωμένων.

45 Ibid.: μνεμεῖόν μου καταλειφθήσεσθαι πολὺ κάλλιον τῶν χαλκῶν ἀναθημάτων.

Isocrates' reflections on the genre of the encomium, however, are not unique to the *Antidosis*: in the *Helen* and *Busiris*, he deliberately straddles the line between encomium and *apologia*; in the *Evagoras*, moreover, he insists that it was his own innovation to have composed an encomium in prose, and he explores another boundary, this time between encomium and protreptic; finally, in many instances, like in the *Nicocles*, the *Panathenaicus*, and in the aforementioned *Antidosis*, Isocrates reflects on self-encomium.[46]

6. Xenophon, Isocrates and the genres of prose

Of the themes that Xenophon tends to privilege, I am most interested here in *paideia* and the exercise of power.[47] It is often in relation to these themes that Xenophon introduces historical matter into his various works, in some cases closer to the style of Thucydidean historiography (e.g. the so called *paralipomena* at the beginning of the *Hellenika*), in other cases rather farther from this model. The work that structurally most resembles the *Hellenika* is the *Anabasis*, to which Xenophon himself refers in the *Hellenika* ostensibly to avoid repeating a story. But the *Anabasis* introduces an important innovation: a clear protagonist, Xenophon himself, who speaks about himself in the third person. The role of Xenophon and also of Cyrus the Younger links the *Anabasis* to the *Cyropaedia*, and to the *Agesilaus* as well, a work that is formally an encomium and that outlines the characteristics of an ideal commander. Also present in the *Anabasis* is the theme of *paideia*, and not only in the passage that we might call the *Cyropaedia minor* (*Anabasis* 1.9): think, for example, of the profile of Proxenus, who believed himself ready for command because he had studied with Gorgias (2.6.16f.), and the entertaining dispute between Xenophon and Cheirisophus about κλέπτειν (stealing) in Spartan and Athenian education (4.6.15f.). One might ask why Xenophon does not speak about his own *paideia* in the *Anabasis* but appears there already perfectly ready for speech and action, a sort of Athena, who emerges fully armored from the head of Zeus. The answer lies in the different paradigms pursued in the *Cyropaedia* and in the *Anabasis*.

---

[46] Nicolai 2004a:87–99.

[47] See e.g. Tatum 1989:37, according to whom the largest part of Xenophon's career is dedicated to the theme of the 'ideal leader', a theme explored by way of different literary genres: philosophic dialogue, technical monograph, encomium, philosophical and military memoir, philosophy, and history. The enquiry into the true nature of power is a central theme in Mueller-Godingen 2007 analysis. See also Azoulay 2004:xiv, who deals with the quest for models of authority, investigated from different points of view.

At the centre of Xenophon's literary output we should place the *Cyropaedia*, which shares with the *Anabasis* the centrality of a character who embodies a political and paideutic ideal but is also in some parts openly sophistic, with dialogues quite in harmony with works labeled as 'philosophical'.[48] The other, so-called minor works, are deeply connected to the major ones: the *Hiero*, a philosophical dialogue on power,[49] a theme that frequently recurs in the *Memorabilia* as well; the *Oeconomicus*, another dialogue, this time on the theme of household administration, which differs only in scale from the government of a city, as Xenophon himself affirms[50]; the *Constitution of the Lacedaimonians*, which traces Sparta's success back to Lycurgus' laws and discusses the reasons for the recent crisis of the city;[51] the *Poroi*, on the revenues of the city of Athens; the *Cynegeticus*, a treaty on hunting as a form of education; the *On Horsemanship* and the *Hipparchicus*, which deal with the art of horsemanship from the private and public perspective respectively.[52] In this last work, too, there are allusions to the theme of *paideia*: see *Hipparchicus* 1.7 (the commander must make his men εὐπειθεῖς) and 6.1 (comparison of the cavalry commander with the potter molding his clay). More distinct, at least from a formal perspective, are the *Apologia*, *Memorabilia* and *Symposium*, which bear the signs of another codified genre, that of the λόγοι Σωκρατικοί. The very presence of Socrates as a central character in these works, of course, ensures here too the importance of the theme of education.

With respect to preexisting literary production, Xenophon behaves with the great freedom that is granted to prose, employing codes of pre-existing genres to change them from within: this is the case with Thucydidean historiography in the *Hellenika* and in the *Anabasis* and with technical treatises in the *Cynegeticus*, the *On Horsemanship*, and the *Hipparchicus*. The philosophical

---

[48] Levine Gera 1993:26–131.

[49] Gray 2007:36, observes that Simonides' aporetic style in the dialogue can be compared to that of Socrates in the *Memorabilia*. See also 2, where she emphasizes the difficulty of deciding whether Xenophon preferred the rule of the law (*Constitution of the Lacedaimonians*) or personal rule (*Hiero*). The fact, highlighted by Gray, that similar difficulties arise when comparing Plato's *Laws* and *Republic*, demonstrates that this is a false problem. Questions posed by different works are in part independent from each other, and the idea of constructing a systematic political philosophy, aside from being anachronistic, takes no account of the dynamics of the literary system. Other problematic combinations, related to law and personal power, are suggested by Gray 2007:12f.: *Cyropaedia* 8.1.24, *Oeconomicus* 12.20. On the *Hiero*, see also Sevieri 2004.

[50] *Memorabilia* 3.4.6 and 3.4.12. See Pomeroy 1994:241, in particular on the rewards to subordinates, common in Persian administration and used in housekeeping by Isomachus and his wife.

[51] See Gray 2007:39: Xenophon's innovation consists in ascribing Spartan success to the consistent plan of only one legislator. On the *Constitution of the Lacedaimonians* see Gianotti 1990; Rebenich 1998; and Lipka 2002. On the problematic chapter 14, see Meulder 1989; Bianco 1993; and Humble 2004.

[52] See Althoff 2002.

dialogue, too, is adapted to Xenophon's own interests (*Hiero*, *Oeconomicus*), as is the encomium (*Agesilaus*), a genre with a long poetic tradition but a much more limited history as a prose genre (Isocrates, as we recall, had claimed that his *Evagoras* was a complete innovation). We can think about the *Constitution of the Lacedaimonians* in the same way, a work that certainly invokes the genre of the πολιτεῖαι but intends to be neither an exhaustive exposition of Lycurgus' laws, nor a political reflection along the lines of Plato's *Republic* and *Laws*.[53] Any knowledge of sophistic prose, now only dimly graspable through bare titles and scanty fragments, would certainly enable us better to understand Xenophon's attitude towards preexisting prose genres.

We must not position Xenophon after Thucydides, as an inadequate continuator, or beside Plato, as a less perceptive disciple of Socrates, but rather beside Isocrates, the other great innovator and experimenter of Greek prose, who was, like Xenophon, committed to the themes of education and politics.[54] Isocrates considered the path of rhetoric to be the key to the proper formation of the citizen and the political man; Xenophon, on the other hand, aimed at teaching the technical skills required by the exercise of power and, on a reduced scale, in private life for the administration of one's own property. These skills, all of which fall within *paideia*, range from war to horsemanship, from hunting to economy, from constitutional theory to dialectic. Both Isocrates and Xenophon refused to consider philosophy as merely an abstract speculation, and both claimed to be representatives of the one philosophy that was truly useful, capable of shaping competent men and good citizens.[55] After listing some of Socrates' disciples, Xenophon explains what prompted them to follow their teacher: "not that they might shine in the courts or the assembly, but that they might become gentlemen, and be able to do their duty by house and household, and relatives and friends, and city and citizens.[56] And he adds: "Of these not one, in his youth or old age, did evil or incurred censure" (*Memorabilia* 1.2.48, translation by E. C. Marchant).[57] In his portrait of Agesilaus, where he focuses

---

[53] According to Gray 2007:40, the focus of the *Constitution of the Lacedaimonians* on education implies that it does not aim to be a complete catalogue of Sparta's laws.

[54] According to Tuplin 1997:66, "Education is a—perhaps the—great social or cultural issue of the later classical era," and the *Cyropaedia*, *Antidosis* and *Republic*, are contributions to the same debate.

[55] According to Gray 2007:3, Xenophon was a philosopher capable of contributing to political thought. The problem, of course, is what we mean by 'philosopher'. On the relationship of Xenophon to contemporary philosophical trends, see Eucken 1983.

[56] οὐχ ἵνα δημηγορικοὶ ἢ δικανικοὶ γένοιντο, ἀλλ᾽ ἵνα καλοί τε κἀγαθοὶ γενόμενοι καὶ οἴκῳ καὶ οἰκέταις καὶ οἰκείοις καὶ φίλοις καὶ πόλει καὶ πολίταις δύναιντο καλῶς χρῆσθαι. Isocrates also dismisses the charge that he gave instruction in writing judicial speeches: *Antidosis* 2, 30 and 228.

[57] καὶ τούτων οὐδεὶς οὔτε νεώτερος οὔτε πρεσβύτερος ὢν οὔτ᾽ ἐποίησε κακὸν οὐδὲν οὔτ᾽ αἰτίαν ἔσχεν.

on particular character traits, we find those same qualities described in greater detail:

> Another quality that should not go unrecorded is his urbanity. For although he held honour in fee, and had power at his beck, and to these added sovereignty—sovereignty not plotted against but regarded with affection—yet no traces of arrogance could have been detected in him, whereas signs of a fatherly affection and readiness to serve his friends, even if unsought, were evident. He delighted, moreover, to take his part in light talk, yet he showed an eager sympathy with friends in all their serious concerns. Thanks to his optimism, good humour, and cheerfulness he was a centre of attraction to many, who came not merely for purposes of business, but to pass the day more pleasantly. Little inclined to boastfulness himself, he heard without annoyance the self-praise of others, thinking that, by indulging in it, they did no harm and gave earnest of high endeavour. On the other hand, one must not omit a reference to the dignity that he showed on appropriate occasions. (Translation by E. C. Marchant)

Xenophon *Agesilaus* 8.1–3[58]

If we compare these passages with Isocrates' conception we find a number of convergences:

> Whom, then, do I call educated, since I exclude the arts and sciences and specialties? First, those who manage well the circumstances which they encounter day by day, and who possess a judgement which is accurate in meeting occasions as they arise and rarely misses the expedient course of action; next, those who are decent and honorable in their intercourse with all with whom they associate, tolerating easily and good-naturedly what is unpleasant or offensive in others and being themselves as agreeable and reasonable to their associates as it is possible to be; furthermore, those who hold their pleasures always under control and are not unduly overcome by their misfortunes,

---

[58] Ἀλλὰ μὴν ἄξιόν γε αὐτοῦ καὶ τὸ εὔχαρι μὴ σιωπᾶσθαι· ᾧ γε ὑπαρχούσης μὲν τιμῆς, παρούσης δὲ δυνάμεως, πρὸς δὲ τούτοις βασιλείας, καὶ ταύτης οὐκ ἐπιβουλευομένης ἀλλ' ἀγαπωμένης, τὸ μὲν μεγάλαυχον οὐκ εἶδέ τις, τὸ δὲ φιλόστοργον καὶ θεραπευτικὸν τῶν φίλων καὶ μὴ ζητῶν κατενόησεν ἄν. καὶ μὴν μετεῖχε μὲν ἥδιστα παιδικῶν λόγων, συνεσπούδαζε δὲ πᾶν ὅ τι δέοι φίλοις. διὰ δὲ τὸ εὔελπις καὶ εὔθυμος καὶ ἀεὶ ἱλαρὸς εἶναι πολλοὺς ἐποίει μὴ τοῦ διαπράξασθαί τι μόνον ἕνεκα πλησιάζειν, ἀλλὰ καὶ τοῦ ἥδιον διημερεύειν. ἥκιστα δ' ὢν οἷος μεγαληγορεῖν ὅμως τῶν ἐπαινούντων αὐτοὺς οὐ βαρέως ἤκουεν, ἡγούμενος βλάπτειν οὐδὲν αὐτούς, ὑπισχνεῖσθαι δὲ ἄνδρας ἀγαθοὺς ἔσεσθαι. ἀλλὰ μὴν καὶ τῇ μεγαλογνωμοσύνῃ γε ὡς εὐκαίρως ἐχρῆτο οὐ παραλειπτέον.

bearing up under them bravely and in a manner worthy of our common nature; finally, and most important of all, those who are not spoiled by successes and do not desert their true selves and become arrogant, but hold their ground steadfastly as intelligent men, not rejoicing in the good things which have come to them through chance rather than in those which through their own nature and intelligence are theirs from their birth. Those who have a character which is in accord, not with one of these things, but with all of them—these, I contend, are wise and complete men, possessed of all the virtues. (Translation by George Norlin)

Isocrates *Panathenaicus* 30–32[59]

Like Isocrates, Xenophon has been misunderstood: his works have been isolated from each other and evaluated on an essentially formal basis. Those works that were the pieces of a paideutic and political project have been reduced to pamphlets of interest only to the antiquarian or specialist in military and economic history. But like Isocrates, Xenophon was read in antiquity above all as a model of clear Attic prose.

On the subject of literary genres, leaving aside the *congeries* method employed by some scholars in order to describe the *Cyropaedia*, we must entertain the possibility that Xenophon deliberately practiced a kind of *Kreuzung der Gattungen*. This possibility was explicitly theorized by Christopher Tuplin, who situates the *Cyropaedia* "in a crosscut of four 'ordinary' genres": historiography, encomium, Socratic dialectic, and technical pamphlet.[60] Here, too, it may be helpful to think of Isocrates, who did not operate as a scientist in search of surprising intersections among different literary genres, but rather created new genres, completely unconnected with any specific occasion and relying instead

---

[59] Τίνας οὖν καλῶ πεπαιδευμένους, ἐπειδὴ τὰς τέχνας καὶ τὰς ἐπιστήμας καὶ τὰς δυνάμεις ἀποδοκιμάζω; Πρῶτον μὲν τοὺς καλῶς χρωμένους τοῖς πράγμασι τοῖς κατὰ τὴν ἡμέραν ἑκάστην προσπίπτουσι, καὶ τὴν δόξαν ἐπιτυχῆ τῶν καιρῶν ἔχοντας καὶ δυναμένην ὡς ἐπὶ τὸ πολὺ στοχάζεσθαι τοῦ συμφέροντος· ἔπειτα τοὺς πρεπόντως καὶ δικαίως ὁμιλοῦντας τοῖς ἀεὶ πλησιάζουσι, καὶ τὰς μὲν τῶν ἄλλων ἀηδίας καὶ βαρύτητας εὐκόλως καὶ ῥᾳδίως φέροντας, σφᾶς δ' αὐτοὺς ὡς δυνατὸν ἐλαφροτάτους καὶ μετριωτάτους τοῖς συνοῦσι παρέχοντας· ἔτι τοὺς τῶν μὲν ἡδονῶν ἀεὶ κρατοῦντας, τῶν δὲ συμφορῶν μὴ λίαν ἡττωμένους, ἀλλ' ἀνδρωδῶς ἐν αὐταῖς διακειμένους καὶ τῆς φύσεως ἀξίως ἧς μετέχοντες τυγχάνομεν· τέταρτον, ὅπερ μέγιστον, τοὺς μὴ διαφθειρομένους ὑπὸ τῶν εὐπραγιῶν μηδ' ἐξισταμένους αὑτῶν μηδ' ὑπερηφάνους γιγνομένους, ἀλλ' ἐμμένοντας τῇ τάξει τῇ τῶν εὖ φρονούντων καὶ μὴ μᾶλλον χαίροντας τοῖς διὰ τύχην ὑπάρξασιν ἀγαθοῖς ἢ τοῖς διὰ τὴν αὑτῶν φύσιν καὶ φρόνησιν ἐξ ἀρχῆς γιγνομένοις. Τοὺς δὲ μὴ μόνον πρὸς ἓν τούτων, ἀλλὰ καὶ πρὸς ἅπαντα ταῦτα τὴν ἕξιν τῆς ψυχῆς εὐάρμοστον ἔχοντας, τούτους φημὶ καὶ φρονίμους εἶναι καὶ τελέους ἄνδρας καὶ πάσας ἔχειν τὰς ἀρετάς.
[60] Tuplin 1997:67.

on written publication.[61] Such experimentation with literary genres allows him to use the codes and communicative strategies appropriate to these preexisting genres without the new work losing its own identity. Had Xenophon wanted to describe the genre of the *Cyropaedia*, he might have done so along the lines of Isocrates' definition of his *Antidosis* (10-12). Here, Isocrates first lists the different elements of the work: the judicial frame, the reflections on culture, the aspects useful for the education of the young, and citations from his previous works:

> For, I assure you, it has not been an easy nor a simple task, but one of great difficulty; for while some things in my discourse are appropriate to be spoken in a court-room, others are out of place amid such controversies, being frank discussions about philosophy and expositions of its power. There is in it, also, matter which it would be well for young men to hear before they set out to gain knowledge and an education; and there is much, besides, of what I have written in the past, inserted in the present discussion, not without reason nor without fitness, but with due appropriateness to the subject in hand. (Translation by George Norlin)

Isocrates Antidosis 10[62]

After emphasizing the difficulty of mastering the length of the speech and the variety of forms it contains,[63] Isocrates reaffirms his determination to complete it, in spite of his old age, strongly insisting on the veracity of the speech.[64] He concludes by advising future readers to take into account the fact that they are dealing with a mixed genre.[65]

The fictional juridical frame is of course absent from the *Cyropaedia*, which employs instead a historical frame according to which the material is arranged in chronological order. Also absent is one of the most extraordinary innovations

---

[61] Nicolai 2004a.

[62] Ἔστιν γὰρ τῶν γεγραμμένων ἔνια μὲν ἐν δικαστηρίῳ πρέποντα ῥηθῆναι, τὰ δὲ πρὸς μὲν τοὺς τοιούτους ἀγῶνας οὐχ ἁρμόττοντα, περὶ δὲ φιλοσοφίας πεπαρρησιασμένα καὶ δεδηλωκότα τὴν δύναμιν αὐτῆς· ἔστι δέ τι καὶ τοιοῦτον, ὃ τῶν νεωτέρων τοῖς ἐπὶ τὰ μαθήματα καὶ τὴν παιδείαν ὁρμῶσιν ἀκούσασιν ἂν συνενέγκοι, πολλὰ δὲ καὶ τῶν ὑπ' ἐμοῦ πάλαι γεγραμμένων ἐγκαταμεμιγμένα τοῖς νῦν λεγομένοις, οὐκ ἀλόγως οὐδ' ἀκαίρως, ἀλλὰ προσηκόντως τοῖς ὑποκειμένοις.

[63] *Antidosis* 11: Τοσοῦτον οὖν μῆκος λόγου συνιδεῖν καὶ τοσαύτας ἰδέας καὶ τοσοῦτον ἀλλήλων ἀφεστώσας συναρμόσαι καὶ συναγαγεῖν καὶ τὰς ἐπιφερομέναςτ οἰκειῶσαι ταῖς προειρημέναις καὶ πάσας ποιῆσαι σφίσιν αὐταῖς ὁμολογουμένας οὐ πάνυ μικρὸν ἦν ἔργον.

[64] *Antidosis* 11: μετὰ πολλῆς μὲν ἀληθείας εἰρημένον . . . .

[65] *Antidosis* 12: Χρὴ δὲ τοὺς διεξιόντας αὐτὸν πρῶτον μὲν ὡς ὄντος μικτοῦ τοῦ λόγου καὶ πρὸς ἁπάσας τὰς ὑποθέσεις ταύτας γεγραμμένου ποιεῖσθαι τὴν ἀκρόασιν.

in the *Antidosis*, namely the anthology of some passages by the author himself.[66] Broad philosophical reflections and considerations useful on the pedagogical level are, however, widely present in this work, as is the concept of ἀλήθεια, which is itself reinforced by the formally historical narrative. Although it is true that nowhere in Xenophon's work do we find any explicit guidelines for the reader, we should nevertheless be on the lookout for possible internal markers that refer to the recitation: this may well be the case with the brief summaries appended to the beginning of many books of the *Anabasis*.

It is also important to recall that, quite unlike other works of Xenophon, the *Cyropaedia* has a *proemium*, which contains a strong marker of genre: the definition of the theme, namely the correct exercise of power (1.1.3 τὸ ἀνθρώπων ἄρχειν ("to rule over men"); cf. 1.1.6) aimed at its own preservation. On this basis, Levine Gera maintains that the *proemium* is intended to ensure that the work has a place in the genre of the political pamphlet or 'πολιτεία literature'.[67]

In the position that I have tried to outline, it is no longer meaningful, in Tatum's words, to investigate the boundary between history and fiction.[68] Tatum maintains that "it was the generic flexibility of prose itself that enabled Xenophon to move so easily across the boundary between history and fiction" and that "like any prose writer, he was engaged in the invention of his own genre." We can agree with this formulation, except for the idea that a boundary did, in fact, exist: Xenophon was interested in establishing not so much the truth of his information as its exemplarity. The two categories of history and fiction belong to our literary and historiographical perception, not to that of an Athenian of the fourth century. Despite important and admirable attempts like those of Herodotus and Thucydides, very few were interested in investigating the reliability of an account of an event from the remote past, if it had some fundamental and paradigmatic value. At best, they tried to forward the most likely possibility. Similarly, the need to generate new paradigms took precedence over questions of *veritas*. Thucydides' genius lies in the fact that he linked exemplarity to the reliability of the reconstruction and that he highlighted the limits of his own work (and that of others): ancient history can only be sketched; speeches can not be precisely reported. The fact that after Thucydides the link between reliability and exemplarity was not consistently emphasized is due not the inferior caliber of later historians, but rather to their different aims. On this point, Tuplin has said that we cannot exclude the possibility that the *Cyropaedia*, from the point of view of its author, was essentially an historical

---

[66] Nicolai 2004b.
[67] Levine Gera 1993:11; see also 13: Xenophon insists that the *Cyropaedia* is not just a portrait of an ancient Persian King but his own contribution to contemporary political theory.
[68] Tatum 1989:57.

work.[69] More precisely, according to Tuplin, Xenophon would not have thought of the material in the *Cyropaedia* as non-historical, because Greek authors did not use as a factual framework for an historical discourse what they did not consider to be historical.[70] The *Cyropaedia*, Tuplin continues, is not fiction, and the analogy with Herodotus and Thucydides is actually inapplicable, as Xenophon is doing something different: he is using a version of the life of Cyrus to illustrate how power has to be exercised. On the basis of his didactic and ideological aims, Xenophon, according to this reading, made a selection from the Achaemenid historical tradition and from other information gathered directly and indirectly.[71] We cannot, then, speak of *fictionality*; we must rather question our own concept of history.

Xenophon experimented with several historiographical forms, some that are today canonical, others that are far from our models: his liminality (with respect to modern categories) has made him an atypical author. It is perhaps time to give him a more appropriate position, however, not only in the delicate transition between the aural and written diffusion of literature but also in the evolution of historical literature, which cannot be separated from the genres related to sophistic prose: πολιτεῖαι, encomia, technical treatises, and so forth. The whole of his *corpus* could be better understood in apposition to the polygraphia of other *corpora*, precisely those, now alas lost, of the sophists.[72]

Bibliography

Althoff, J. 2002. "Form und Funktion der beiden hippologischen Schriften Xenophons *Hipparchicus* und *De re equestri* (mit einem Blick auf Simon von Athen)." In *Antike Fachtexte*, ed. T. Fögen, 235–252. Berlin.

Azoulay, V. 2004. *Xénophon et les grâces du pouvoir. De la charis au charisme.* Paris.

Bianco, E. 1993. "Il capitolo XIV della *Lakedaimonion Politeia* attribuita a Senofonte." *Museum Helveticum* 53:12–24.

Canfora, L. 1970. *Tucidide continuato.* Padua.

Cole, T. 1986. "Le origini della retorica." *Quaderni Urbinati di Cultura Classica* 23:7–21.

———. 1991. *The Origins of Rhetoric in Ancient Greece.* Baltimore.

---

[69] Tuplin 1997:68.
[70] Tuplin 1997:96.
[71] Tuplin 1997:153.
[72] On Xenophon's polygraphia, see the effective definition in Azoulay 2004:xi: "S'en tenant aux seuls ouvrages parus dans la collection des universités de France, cette liste donne l'impression d'un inventaire à la Prévert, juxtaposant genres, thèmes et espaces sans nécessité apparente."

Corcella, A. 2007. "Immagini dei Persiani. Appunti su Peter Julius Junge." In *Con gli occhi degli antichi. Filologia e politica nelle stagioni della cultura europea, Atti del Convegno internazionale di studi, Palermo-Agrigento, 27-29 settembre 2006*, ed. G. Nuzzo, 243–278. Palermo.

———. 2010. "Pane, crescione e sale. La dieta dei Persiani tra Senofonte e Girolamo." *Quaderni di storia* 72:31–88.

Cuniberti, G. 2007. "Per chi scrive Senofonte? Il ruolo dei Lacedemoni nella produzione e ricezione dell'opera di Senofonte." *Ktema* 32:379–390.

Dillery, J. 1995. *Xenophon and the History of his Times.* London.

Dorion, L.-A. 2003. "Une allusion à la Cyropédie au livre III des Lois (694c)." In *Plato's Laws: From Theory into Practice*, ed. S. Scolnicov and L. Brisson, 281–285. Sankt Augustin.

Eucken, C. 1983. *Isokrates: seine Positionen in der Auseinandersetzung mit den zeitgenössischen Philosophen.* Berlin.

Ferrucci, S. 2001. "ἅπαξ λέγειν. Il λογογράφος tra storia e oratoria." *Seminari romani di cultura greca* 4:103–126.

Flower, M. 2006. "Herodotus and Persia." In *The Cambridge Companion to Herodotus*, ed. C. Dewald and J. Marincola, 274–289. Cambridge.

Gianotti, G. F. 1990. "Gli Eguali di Sparta." In *Senofonte. L'ordinamento politico degli Spartani*, 17–39. La città antica 5. Palermo.

Gray, V. J. 2007. *Xenophon on Government.* Cambridge.

Grethlein, J. 2007. "The Hermeneutics and Poetics of Memory in Aeschylus's *Persae.*" *Arethusa* 40:363–396.

Hornblower, S. 2007. "Warfare in Ancient Literature: the Paradox of War." In *The Cambridge History of Greek and Roman Warfare: Greece, the Hellenistic World and the Rise of Rome*, ed. P. Sabin et al., 22–53. Cambridge.

Humble, N. 2004. "The Author, Date and Purpose of Chapter 14 of the *Lakedaimonion Politeia.*" In Tuplin 2004:215–228.

Levine Gera, D. 1993. *Xenophon's Cyropaedia. Style, Genre and Literary Technique.* Oxford.

Lipka, M. 2002. *Xenophon's Spartan Constitution. Introduction, Text, Commentary.* Berlin.

Meulder, M. 1989. "La date et la cohérence de la *République des Lacédémoniens* de Xénophon." *L'Antiquité classique* 58:71–87.

Momigliano, A. 1935. "L'egemonia tebana in Senofonte e in Eforo." *Atene e Roma* 3.2:101–117 = A. Momigliano 1982. *La storiografia greca.* Turin. 204–224.

Mueller-Goldingen, C. 2007. *Xenophon. Philosophie und Geschichte.* Darmstadt.

Nicolai, R. 1992. *La storiografia nell'educazione antica.* Pisa

———. 2004a. *Studi su Isocrate. La comunicazione letteraria nel IV secolo a.C. e i nuovi generi della prosa.* Rome.

———. 2004b. "Isocrate e le nuove strategie della comunicazione letteraria: l'Antidosi come "antologia d'autore." In *La cultura ellenistica. L'opera letteraria e l'esegesi antica. Atti del Convegno, Università di Roma "Tor Vergata" 22-24 settembre 2003*, ed. R. Pretagostini and E. Dettori, 187–197. Rome.

———. 2004c. "ἀκρόασις." In *Lexicon Historiographicum Graecum et Latinum 1*, ed. C. Ampolo et al., 66–70. Pisa.

———. 2005. "Omero, Tucidide e Platone sulla preistoria dell'umanità e sulle fondazioni di città." *Seminari romani di cultura greca* 8:237–261.

———. 2006. "Thucydides continued." In *A Companion to Thucydides*, ed. A. Rengakos and A. Tsakmakis, 691–719. Leiden.

———. 2011. "Logos Didaskalos: Direct Speech as a Critical Tool in Thucydides." In *Thucydides—a Violent Teacher?*, ed. G. Rechenauer and V. Pothou, 159-169. Goettingen.

Pomeroy, S. B. 1994. *Xenophon. Oeconomicus, A Social and Historical Commentary.* Oxford.

Rebenich, S. 1998. *Xenophon. Die Verfassung der Spartaner.* Darmstadt.

Rood, T. 2004. "Xenophon and Diodorus: Continuing Thucydides." In Tuplin 2004:341–395.

Roscalla, F. 1991. *Senofonte. Economico, intr., trad. e note di F. R., con un saggio di D. Lanza.* Milano.

Rossi, L. E. 1971. "I generi letterari e le loro leggi scritte e non scritte nelle letterature classiche." *Bulletin of the Institute of Classical Studies* 18:69–94.

———. 2000. "La letteratura alessandrina e il rinnovamento dei generi letterari della tradizione." In *La letteratura ellenistica. Problemi e prospettive di ricerca. Atti del Colloquio internazionale Università di Roma "Tor Vergata", 29-30 aprile 1997*, ed. R. Pretagostini, 149–161. Rome.

Schepens, G. 2006. "Storiografia e letteratura antiquaria. Le scelte di Felix Jacoby." In *Aspetti dell'opera di Felix Jacoby, Seminari Arnaldo Momigliano, Scuola Normale Superiore di Pisa, 18-19 dicembre 2002*, ed. C. Ampolo, 149–171. Pisa.

———. 2007. "Tucidide 'in controluce'. La guerra del Peloponneso nella storiografia greca del IV secolo a.C." In *Il dopoguerra nel mondo greco. Politica, propaganda, storiografia*, ed. L. Santi Amantini, 57–99. Rome.

Segoloni, L. M. 1994. *Socrate a banchetto. Il Simposio di Platone e i Banchettanti di Aristofane.* Rome.

Sevieri, R. 2004. "The Imperfect Hero: Xenophon's *Hiero* as the (Self-)Taming of a Tyrant." In Tuplin 2004:277–287.

Tamiolaki, M. 2008. "Les *Hélleniques* entre tradition et innovation. Aspects de la relation intertextuelle de Xénophon avec Hérodote et Thucydide." *Cahiers des études anciennes* 45:15–52.

Tatum, J. 1989. *Xenophon's Imperial Fiction: On the Education of Cyrus.* Princeton.

Thomas, R. 2000. *Herodotus in Context.* Cambridge.

Tuplin, C. J. 1997. "Xenophon's *Cyropaedia*: Education and Fiction." In *Education in Greek Fiction*, ed. A. H. Sommerstein and C. Atherton, 65–162. Bari.

———, ed. 2004. *Xenophon and his World. Papers From a Conference Held in Liverpool 1999.* Stuttgart.

Vela Tejada, J. 1998. *Post H. R. Breitenbach: Tres decadas de estudios sobre Jenofonte, 1967-1997.* Zaragoza.

5

The Use of Documents in Xenophon's *Hellenica*

Cinzia Bearzot

THE CONFERENCE '*L'uso dei documenti nella storiografia antica*' (Gubbio 22–24 maggio 2001), which presented findings of research conducted under the direction of Paolo Desideri, and the proceedings of which were published in 2003, highlighted the fact that ancient historians, although well aware of the rhetorical nature of historical writing, actually privileged the role of documentary sources. This paper originates from those conclusions, more recently echoed in a conference held in Rome at the Istituto Italiano per la Storia Antica (November 2007).[1]

In the 2001 conference, I studied the use of documents in Thucydides.[2] Using the same methodological principles, and building on the results of that research, I intend to identify the types of documents used by Xenophon and then to comment on the way the historian cites or refers to these documents, on his sources of information, on the physical location of the documents, and finally on the type of subjects to which they refer.

1. Status quaestionis

Xenophon's use of documents (a topic that was not considered in the 2001 conference) has generally been disregarded by Xenophontic scholarship. J. K. Davies devotes some interesting pages to the use of documents in fourth-century historiography but does not refer to Xenophon.[3] P. J. Rhodes, who recently wrote on documents in the Greek historians, does briefly discuss Xenophon: he concludes that the historian's text is close to the original version of some treaties, but does not think that Xenophon was interested in assembling and

---

[1]   Moggi et al. 2007.
[2]   Bearzot 2003.
[3]   Davies 1996.

reproducing documentary texts in a systematic way.[4] C. Zizza, in an in-depth review of the proceedings of the 2001 conference, refers to his forthcoming essay on Xenophon's use of inscriptions, but limits his investigation to two passages from the *Anabasis* (5.3.5; 5.3.13) and one from the *Cyropaedia* (7.3.15–16), since Xenophon's *Hellenica* never refers to epigraphical documents.[5]

Despite the small number of studies on this topic, Xenophon is an important source, and an analysis of his approach is central to understanding the general use of documents in ancient historiography. In particular, I propose to compare his methodological principles to those of his predecessors, Herodotus and Thucydides, who were very interested in documents and who, unlike Xenophon, were investigated in several contributions to the 2001 conference.[6]

My paper is based on a catalogue of about 120 passages, and considers not only the documents fully or partially transcribed by Xenophon (cases of transcription are actually rare) but also "latent" documents, to which L. Canfora has drawn scholars' attention with regard to Thucydides.[7] This catalogue may perhaps be incomplete in terms of these "latent" documents, but I hope that my omissions are neither large nor serious.

2. Types of documents

My research on Thucydides highlighted the wide range of documents that the historian used: treaties, inscriptions, letters, laws and decrees, oracular responses, literary works, oaths, arbitrations, charters for the foundation of colonies, and lists of various kinds.

In Xenophon's *Hellenica* the range is less wide. The most commonly represented categories are treaties (49, of which nine are truces allowing for the collection of the dead); the rest are decrees (34, mostly Athenian), oaths (12), letters (6), lists (6), oracular responses (5), and laws (3). Xenophon refers to different types of documents (e.g. γνώμη, κήρυγμα), but inscriptions (24 in Herodotus, 8 in Thucydides)[8] and literary works are totally absent,[9] even though for these Xenophon could no doubt rely on a wider number of sources than his predecessors.

---

[4] Rhodes 2007:60–61.
[5] Zizza 2007:226–227n45; cf. Zizza 2012.
[6] On Herodotus, see Biraschi 2003, as well as the papers in Biraschi et al. 2003:153–263; on Thucydides, see, besides Bearzot 2003, Porciani 2003.
[7] See Canfora 1990:205–206.
[8] On Herodotus, see Fabiani 2003; on Thucydides, Zizza 1999; Bearzot 2003:291f.
[9] On considering literary works as "documents," see Nicolai 2003.

Treaties

International treaties are the prevailing type. Xenophon refers to them in specialized legal terminology: σπονδαί (truce, 13 references), εἰρήνη (peace, 12 references), συμμαχία (alliance, 6 references), συνθῆκαι (treaty, 4 references), φιλία (friendship, 2 references), ξύμβασις (agreement, 1 reference); εἰρήνη καὶ συμμαχία (peace and alliance, 1 reference); more rarely, verbs such as σπένδομαι (to conclude a truce, 2 references), διαλλάσσω (to bring about an agreement, 1 reference), συμμαχέω (to fight alongside someone, as someone's ally, 1 reference), συνχωρέω (to agree, to concede, 1 reference). In addition, Xenophon uses adjectival constructions, such as ὑπόσπονδος (under truce, 10 references) or σύμμαχος (ally, 2 references).[10] Due to the vast number of these documents, we shall consider only a selection.

First of all, it may be interesting to note that in two cases Xenophon refers to documents already mentioned by Thucydides. At 3.2.21 Xenophon mentions the alliance (συμμαχία) between Athens, Argos, Mantineia, and Elis of the year 420, which is fully transcribed by Thucydides (5.46.5–47);[11] and at 5.2.2 he refers to the expiration of the thirty-year truce concluded between the Lacedaemonians and Mantineans after the battle of Mantineia (418), mentioned briefly by Thucydides (5.81.1).

Unlike Thucydides, Xenophon rarely gives a full transcription of the text of the treaties; rather, he carefully paraphrases their clauses. These clauses are introduced by ἐφ' ᾧ, as in the following passage, regarding the peace treaty (εἰρήνη)[12] imposed by Sparta on Athens in 404:

> The Lacedaemonians . . . offered to make peace on these conditions (ἐποιοῦντο εἰρήνην ἐφ' ᾧ): that the Athenians should destroy the long walls and the walls of Piraeus, surrender all their ships except twelve, allow their exiles to return, count the same people friends and enemies as the Lacedaemonians did, and follow the Lacedaemonians both by land and by sea wherever they should lead the way.
>
> Xenophon *Hellenica* 2.2.20[13]

---

[10] For treaty-related terminology, see Santi Amantini 1979–1980, 1985, 1986, and 1996; for Xenophon in particular, see Santi Amantini 2000 (which looks at the semantic evolution of εἰρήνη, a term that acquires in Xenophon the meaning of 'peace treaty', in accordance with the general development of diplomatic language).

[11] His transcription can be compared with the original epigraphical text, cf. Tod 72 = IG I³.83.

[12] Cf. 2.2.19 (εἰρήνη; vb. σπένδομαι); 2.4.30 (παράσπονδον).

[13] All translations of Xenophon are taken from Brownson 1985–1986. Xenophon's information on the treaty of 404 must be compared with the rest of the tradition: see Bengtson 1962, no.

So, too, in his description of the reconciliation agreement (διαλλάσσω) between the Athenian democrats and the Three Thousand favored by King Pausanias in 403:

> And they effected a reconciliation on these terms (διήλλαξαν ἐφ' ᾧτε), that the two parties should be at peace with one another and that every man should depart to his home except the members of the Thirty, and of the Eleven, and of the Ten who had ruled in Piraeus. They also decided that if any of the men in the city were afraid, they should settle at Eleusis.[14]

Xenophon Hellenica 2.4.38

Other examples are provided at 3.2.20 (a draft of a treaty between Derkyllidas and Tissaphernes, dated to 397), 4.8.14 (a draft of a treaty between Sparta and the Persians, which was discussed during the negotiations of winter 392/1), 5.3.26 (a peace treaty between Sparta and Olynthos, dated to 379), and 7.4.6–11 (a peace treaty between Thebes, Corinth, and Phlius, dated to 365).

The most interesting documents, however, are the 'Common Peace' treaties, from the King's Peace to the Peace of Susa. Xenophon is the only author who fully transcribes the text of the King's Peace, or the 'Peace of Antalkidas', as he calls it at 5.1.36.[15] The document, in fact, displays traits of two different document types, since it is a letter of the King containing the text of the peace treaty (εἰρήνη; cf. 5.1.33 and 6.5.2, σπονδαί):

> So that when Tiribazus ordered those to be present who desired to give ear to the peace which the King had sent down, all speedily presented themselves. And when they had come together, Tiribazus showed them the King's seal (τὰ βασιλέως σημεῖα) and then read the writing (τὰ γεγραμμένα). It ran as follows (εἶχε δὲ ὧδε): "King Artaxerxes thinks it just that the cities in Asia should belong to him, as well as Clazomenae and Cyprus among the islands, and that the other Greek cities, both small and great, should be left independent, except Lemnos, Imbros,

---

211; Krentz 1989:185–186; Bearzot 1997:134f. In particular, it is noteworthy that Xenophon does not refer to the clause on πάτριος πολιτεία, mentioned by Aristotle (*Constitution of the Athenians* 34.2–3) and Diodorus (14.3.2). This is probably a deliberate choice, since the treaty would actually have employed the usual clause πολιτεύεσθαι κατὰ τὰ πάτρια, which simply indicated a non-interference warranty; this clause was consciously misinterpreted by oligarchical propaganda in order to convince the Athenian people that an oligarchical government, the πάτριος πολιτεία, had been imposed by the victorious Spartans on the defeated Athenians. Such propaganda, reflected in Aristotle and Diodorus, is ignored by Xenophon.

[14] See Bengtson 1962, no. 213; Bearzot 1997:15f.
[15] See Bengtson 1962, no. 242.

and Scyros; and these should belong, as of old, to the Athenians. But whichever of the two parties does not accept this peace (ταύτην τὴν εἰρήνην),[16] upon them I will make war, in company with those who desire this arrangement, both by land and by sea, with ships, and with money."

Xenophon Hellenica 5.1.30–31

In this passage, the historian emphasizes that he is citing a written document (τὰ γεγραμμένα); he refers to γράμματα again at 5.1.32, and at 6.5.3 he says that the King had put in writing (ἔγραψεν) his claim "that the Greek cities, both small and great, should be left independent." Furthermore, Xenophon mentions the seal of the royal letter (σημεῖα), which confirms its authenticity. Thus, he seems to be particularly interested in emphasizing the fact that his transcription refers to a written, certainly authentic document: he clearly ascribes to it a significant historiographical value.[17]

Xenophon makes a passing reference to the peace (εἰρήνη) of 375/4, which was immediately broken (6.2.1):[18] this reference, due to his particular interest in the relations between Athens and Sparta, is a significant piece of information, since Diodorus (15.38) seems to mistake the negotiations of 375/4 for those of 371 (cf. 15.50.4–6 and 51.4).[19]

Regarding the peace of Sparta in 371 (6.3.18, εἰρήνη; cf. 6.3.2 and 6.3.20; 6.3.19 σπονδαί),[20] Xenophon does not transcribe the text of the treaty but loosely paraphrases it, carefully enumerating its clauses:

> Since these men were adjudged to have spoken rightly, the Lacedaemonians voted to accept the peace, with the provision (ἐφ' ᾧ) that all should withdraw their governors from the cities, disband their armaments both on sea and on land, and leave the cities independent. And if any state should act in violation of this agreement, it was provided that any which so desired might aid the injured cities, but

---

[16] On the technical use of εἰρήνη as 'peace treaty' in this document, see Santi Amantini 2000:19. εἰρήνη is most often used by Xenophon to mean 'peace treaty'; the term occurs less frequently with the meaning of 'time or situation of peace' (in contrast to 'time or situation of war') or 'time or situation of peace' (as a consequence of a formal treaty) or, finally, 'peace negotiations' (see Santi Amantini 2000:21–22).

[17] On the correspondence between Xenophon's text and the original document (in comparison with Diodorus' paraphrase) and on the relation between the King's letter and the treaty signed by the Greeks, see Jehne 1994:36–37.

[18] See Bengtson 1962, no. 265.

[19] See Bearzot 2002:109f.; Bearzot 2004:97f.

[20] Bengtson 1962, no. 269.

that any which did not so desire was not under oath to be the ally of those who were injured.

Xenophon *Hellenica* 6.3.18

The written nature of the document emerges from 6.3.19, a passage that refers to the swearing of the treaty mentioned at 6.3.18 and alludes twice, by the verb ἀπογράφομαι, to the undersigning of the oath.[21]

As for the peace of Athens of 371/0 (6.5.1–3, εἰρήνη, cf. 6.5.37),[22] Xenophon partially paraphrases the treaty's content, which recalled the text of the King's Peace (σπονδαί); the only clause that he retains is the stipulation that "both small and great cities alike should be independent," just "as the King wrote." The historian does, however, fully transcribe the text of the oath sworn by the Greeks who signed the treaty:

The Athenians . . . invited to Athens all the cities which wished to participate in the peace which the King had sent down. And when they had come together, they passed a resolution to take the following oath (ὁμόσαι τόνδε τὸν ὅρκον), in company with such as desired to share in the peace: "I will abide by the treaty (σπονδαί) which the King sent down, and by the decrees (ψηφίσματα) of the Athenians and their allies. And if anybody takes the field against any one of the cities which have sworn this oath, I will come to her aid with all my strength." Now all the others were pleased with the oath; the Eleans only opposed it . . . But the Athenians and the others, after voting that both small and great cities alike should be independent, even as the King wrote, sent out the officers charged with administering the oath and directed them to administer it to the highest authorities in each city. And all took the oath except the Eleans.

Xenophon *Hellenica* 6.5.1–3

The transcription of the oath gives us a significant piece of information, found nowhere else; the oath requires the observance not only of the terms "sent down by the King" in the letter of 386 but also of the ψηφίσματα "of the Athenians and their allies," i.e. Aristotle's Decree and the subsequent δόγματα approved by the synedrion of the Second Athenian League. Thus, by the terms of the peace of 371/0, the Athenians successfully proposed to all Greeks the concept of autonomy that they had specified in Aristotle's Decree, taking advantage of the

---

[21] Xenophon's information on the Spartan peace congress of 371 might originate from Athenian ambassadors (cf. Riedinger 1993:539).

[22] Bengtson 1962, no. 270.

crisis of Sparta.[23] Xenophon's decision to transcribe not the text of the treaty, which was clearly identical to that of 386, but the text of the oath suggests that his intention was to select the most important information. It is remarkable, however, that the historian, who notes the significance of Aristotle's Decree for the history of the Common Peace, does not mention its ratification in 378/7.[24]

Finally, Xenophon gives a partial transcription of the Peace of Susa of 367,[25] reporting the clauses required by Pelopidas and granted by the King:

> Pelopidas was therefore asked by the King what he desired to have written (γραφῆναι) for him; he replied that Messene should be independent of the Lacedaemonians and that the Athenians should draw up their ships on the land; that if they refused obedience in these points, the contracting parties were to make an expedition against them; and that if any city refused to join in such expedition, they were to proceed first of all against that city.
>
> Xenophon Hellenica 7.1.36

It is noteworthy that at 7.1.37 another clause is mentioned, added (προσγεγραμμένα) because of the protestation of the Athenian ambassador, Leon. Moreover, this was probably not the only addition to the final text: in Plutarch's account (*Pelopidas* 30.7), Pelopidas himself is said to have required, in addition to the autonomy of the Greeks and the repopulation of Messene,[26] that "the Thebans should be regarded as the King's hereditary friends." The use of the verb, γραφῆναι (cf. also 7.1.37: γραφέντων δὲ τούτων), clearly indicates a written document, and this must be identified with the letter of the King (ἐπιστολή; τὰ γράμματα; τὰ γεγραμμένα) repeatedly mentioned at 7.1.39, with regard to the appeal for the Greeks to sign the peace:

> When the Thebans had called together representatives from all the cities to hear the letter (ἐπιστολῆς) from the King, and the Persian who bore the document (τὰ γράμματα), having shown the King's seal (τὴν βασιλέως σφραγῖδα), had read what was written therein (τὰ γεγραμμένα), although the Thebans directed those who desired to be friends of the King and themselves to swear to these provisions, the representatives from the cities replied that they had not been sent to

---

[23] Bearzot 2004:41f.

[24] On this much-debated omission, see Sordi 1951:286f. (according to Xenophon, the league already existed during the Corinthian War; thus, the historian did not identify a turning point in the year 378/7); Riedinger 1991:47f.; Daverio Rocchi 2002:38–39; Jehne 2004.

[25] See Bengtson 1962, no. 282.

[26] Mentioned also by Diodorus (15.81.3) in the context of his eulogy of Pelopidas.

give their oaths, but to listen; and if the Thebans had any desire for oaths, they bade them send to the cities.

. . .

Inasmuch as those who had come together refused to take the oath at Thebes, the Thebans sent ambassadors to the cities and directed them to swear that they would act in accordance with the King's letter (κατὰ τὰ βασιλέως γράμματα), believing that each one of the cities taken singly would hesitate to incur the hatred of themselves and the King at the same time. When, however, upon the arrival of the ambassadors at Corinth, their first stopping-place, the Corinthians resisted the proposal, and replied that they had no desire for oaths shared with the King, then other cities also followed suit, giving their answers in the same terms.

Xenophon *Hellenica* 7.1.39–40

Even in this case, it is noteworthy that Xenophon expressly underlines the written nature of the document and highlights its authenticity by mentioning its royal seal (σφραγίς).[27]

Thus, Xenophon seems to be particularly interested in the specific clauses of the 'Common Peace' treaties, which reflected the historical circumstances in which they had been ratified. In some cases he fully or partially transcribes the documents pertaining to these treaties, while in other cases he carefully paraphrases them; he frequently emphasizes that the document he refers to is written and authentic, even though he never explicitly reports the origin of his information (on which we can only speculate). P. J. Rhodes, who does not think that Xenophon was primarily interested in collecting and reproducing documentary texts, nevertheless admits with regard to some treaties (i.e. the peace between Athens and Sparta of 404; the King's Peace; the Peace of Sparta in 371; the Peace of Athens in 371/0) that "whether or not he has perfectly reproduced the document, his account seems at any rate to be closer to it than the corresponding account of Diodorus." Rhodes concludes that, even though the image of Xenophon as engaging in archival research is not persuasive, "what he obtained was or was close to the official text."[28] It is worth emphasizing that Xenophon's transcriptions of the text of the King's Peace and of the oath sworn

---

[27] Xenophon's information might come from the Athenian ambassador Leon, who was anti-Theban (cf. 7.1.33 and 7.1.37–38); cf. Bearzot 2012.

[28] Rhodes 2007:61.

for the Peace of Athens of 371/0 are significant contributions to our knowledge of the period.

Xenophon's particular interest in treaties certainly derives not only from his attention to the international balance of power in Greece but also from his political ideas, which were oriented towards the establishment of a stable international climate, based on diplomacy and law rather than on political and military might.[29]

Decrees

I have been able to identify 34 decrees in total, of which 19 are Athenian and three Spartan; the rest were approved by several political communities, by the Athenian or by the Peloponnesian League, for example, and even by members of illegal governments, such as the Thirty Tyrants or the Three Thousand. The terminology used by Xenophon privileges, instead of nouns of juridical nature, their corresponding verbs: ψήφισμα (6), δόγμα (3), γνώμη (2), but more often ψηφίζομαι and compounds (16), δοκέω and compounds (10), δίδωμι (1), and also expressions such as ψῆφον φέρειν (1) and ψῆφον δίδωμι (1).

The decrees included with other documents in Xenophon's account of the trial of the Arginousai *strategoi* (summer 406) in my opinion deserve particular attention (1.7).[30] The first "decree", the so-called γνώμη of Kallixenos, must be considered (strictly speaking) a προβούλευμα; Xenophon fully transcribes it:

> Then they called an Assembly, at which the Senate brought in its proposal (γνώμη), which Callixeinus had drafted in the following terms (εἰπόντος τήνδε): "Resolved, that since the Athenians have heard in the previous meeting of the Assembly both the accusers who brought charges against the generals and the generals speaking in their own defense, they do now one and all cast their votes by tribes; and that two urns be set at the voting-place of each tribe; and that in each tribe a herald proclaim that whoever adjudges the generals guilty, for not picking up the men who won the victory in the naval battle, shall cast his vote in the first urn, and whoever adjudges them not guilty, shall cast his vote in the second; and if they be adjudged guilty, that they

---

[29]   See Daverio Rocchi 2002:23f. On the terminology for diplomatic relations in Xenophon, see Orsi 2002; on the notion of "what is just" and "what is advantageous" in international relations, see Orsi 2004.

[30]   For bibliography on the Arginousai trial see Tuci 2002; see also Burckhardt 2000; Giovannini 2002.

be punished with death and handed over to the Eleven, and that their property be confiscated and the tenth thereof belong to the goddess."

Xenophon Hellenica 1.7.9–10

Kallixenos's γνώμη, to which Xenophon alludes in other passages (1.7.12–15; 1.7.26, where the procedure requiring a single vote for all *strategoi* is considered unconstitutional; and 1.7.34), is very important for understanding the legal aspects of this trial, to which Xenophon attributes a paradigmatic value.

The Arginousai trial also gives Xenophon the occasion to transcribe the decree (ψήφισμα) of Kannonos;[31] he is the sole author who refers to this document:[32]

> Now you all know, men of Athens, that the decree of Cannonus is exceedingly severe: it provides that if anyone shall wrong the people of Athens, he shall plead his case in fetters before the people, and if he be adjudged guilty, he shall be put to death by being cast into the pit, and his property shall be confiscated and the tenth part thereof shall belong to the goddess (εἶναι).[33]

Xenophon Hellenica 1.7.20

In his account of the trial, the historian mentions other documents in addition to Kallixenos's γνώμη and the ψήφισμα of Kannonos: the νόμος regarding traitors and the impious (1.7.22);[34] the γνώμη of Euryptolemos, which is a counter-proposal to Kallixenos's γνώμη (1.7.34); and two letters of the *strategoi* to the boule and to the assembly, one of which was actually sent (1.7.4), the other merely planned (1.7.17). Two other documents are also mentioned: the decree by which the assembly condemned the *strategoi* (1.7.34) and the decree containing προβολαί against the prosecutors of the *strategoi*, who were in turn charged with having "deceived the people" (1.7.35).

Xenophon's intention to reconstruct the unfolding of the trial to the best of his ability by highlighting its unconstitutional features and by underlining the demagogues' control over the Athenian assembly clearly led him to refer to a wide range of documents. But scholars have also emphasized Xenophon's inclination to associate crises of democracy with politically biased administration

---

[31] That this is in fact a partial transcription may be conjectured from the use of formulaic expressions.

[32] An allusion is in Aristophanes *Ecclesiazusae* 1089–1090; see Lévy 1990:153–154.

[33] Lavelle 1988.

[34] Mentioned also by [Plutarch] *Lives of the Ten Orators* 833e-f: τὸν νόμον, ὃς κεῖται περὶ τῶν προδόντων. cf. Harrison 2001:56–57.

of justice.[35] It cannot be overlooked that this relation was already present in Thucydides, on whose material Xenophon relied when writing the first part of the *Hellenica*.[36]

Particularly interesting is Xenophon's reference to Aristotle's Decree and to the δόγματα of the allies (ψηφίσματα) in the text of the oath sworn for the Peace of Athens in 371/0 mentioned above:

> I will abide by the treaty (σπονδαί) which the King sent down, and by the decrees (ψηφίσματα) of the Athenians and their allies.

Xenophon Hellenica 6.5.2

It is noteworthy that Xenophon refers to Aristotle's Decree (whose text was available in the corresponding inscription) in this passage only, only hinting at it by way of another document.

Xenophon also mentions other δόγματα by leagues, such as a δόγμα τῶν συμμάχων of the Peloponnesian League, which he partially paraphrases (5.4.37),[37] and the κοινὸν δόγμα of Thebes' allies, which was required for the return of an exile whose extradition had been requested in all allied cities (7.3.11); these δόγματα, like those of the Second Athenian League, seem to contribute to the definition of some aspects of Greek international law.

Oaths

Xenophon mentions 11 oaths, referring to them either by the noun ὅρκος or the verb ὄμνυμι. Most are connected with the undersigning of treaties (1.3.8–9; 3.4.6; 5.1.32; 5.3.26; 6.3.19; 6.5.1–3; 7.1.39–40; 7.4.6–11; and 7.4.36). In three cases, however, Xenophon refers to civic agreements: oaths sworn in Corinth in 393 (4.4.5), in Thespiae in 377 (5.4.55), and, most important, the oath of μὴ μνησικακήσειν, sworn in Athens in 403 (2.4.43),[38] to seal the reconciliation agreement favored by King Pausanias (cf. 2.4.38). But we should note that Xenophon is interested only in public, *polis*-wide oaths. Generally, the historian merely refers to the oath or briefly paraphrases it; he transcribes only the oath

---

[35] Lévy 1990:146f.; Daverio Rocchi 2002:34–35.

[36] See Sordi 1950:43f., who thinks that Xenophon's "documentary" precision could derive from Thucydidean material.

[37] "If any state undertook an expedition against any other while his army was in the field, he (Agesilaus) said that his first act would be to go against that state, in accordance with the resolution of the allies (κατὰ τὸ δόγμα τῶν συμμάχων)."

[38] The text is cited by Andocides *De Mysteriis* 90; cf. Aristotle *Constitution of the Athenians* 39.6.

sworn for the Peace of Athens of 371/0, most likely because of the important new clause that it adds to the oath formula of the King's Peace (see above).

Letters

Like Thucydides, Xenophon considers letters (ἐπιστολή (3), γράμματα (4), sometimes τὰ γράμματα (2) as a particularly interesting type of document: of the of six letters to which he refers, he provides a full transcription for two and a partial transcription for a third. At 1.1.23, the letter (γράμματα) of the Spartan Hippocrates, addressed to the Spartan government in the war season of 411 and intercepted by the Athenians, is transcribed in full:

> Meanwhile a letter (γράμματα) dispatched to Lacedaemon by Hippocrates, vice-admiral under Mindarus, was intercepted and taken to Athens; it ran as follows (λέγοντα τάδε): "The ships are gone. Mindarus is dead. The men are starving. We know not what to do."
>
> Xenophon *Hellenica* 1.1.23

Xenophon probably cites the letter, which had clearly been made public in Athens, in order to underline the striking situation at Sparta after the battle of Cizycus, which, according to Diodorus (13. 52–53), led the Spartans to ask for peace.[39]

In the account of the Arginousai trial, Xenophon mentions two letters. The first is the letter (ἐπιστολή), exploited by Theramenes during the trial, that had been sent by the *strategoi* in order to exculpate themselves for the abandonment of the fallen and the survivors. Xenophon alludes to it as follows:

> For as proof that the generals fastened the responsibility upon no person apart from themselves, Theramenes showed a letter which they had sent to the Senate and to the Assembly, in which they put the blame upon nothing but the storm.
>
> Xenophon *Hellenica* 1.7.4

The other letter mentioned during the trial is of a different nature. In his speech in defense of the *strategoi*, Euryptolemos recalls that they had intended to send a letter (γράμματα) to the Athenian government in order to lay the blame on the trierarchs, but were dissuaded from doing so by Pericles the Younger and Diomedon:

---

[39] For this and other sources, see Krentz 1989:101.

> I accuse them [Pericles and Diomedon], because they persuaded their colleagues to change their purpose when they wanted to send a letter to the Senate and to you, in which they stated that they assigned to Theramenes and Thrasybulus, with forty-seven triremes, the duty of picking up the shipwrecked, and that they failed to perform this duty.
>
> Xenophon *Hellenica* 1.7.17

This is no 'actual' letter but only a 'planned' one: a letter that could have been sent but never was. Evidently, this letter cannot correspond to the one exhibited by Theramenes, which blamed the storm after the battle and not the trierarchs; its contents, furthermore, are confirmed by the speech of the *strategoi*, reported by Xenophon at 1.7.5–6 in indirect form. Thus, it is noteworthy that Diodorus (13.101.2) writes that the letter that had actually been sent included charges made against the trierarchs: this was evidently the version promoted by Theramenes, as suggested by the speech that Xenophon ascribes to him at 2.3.35. We may, then, conclude that Xenophon's reference to this document attempts to identify Theramenes as the man behind the trial against the *strategoi*; the historian had perhaps found this reference in the material assembled by Thucydides, always inclined to reveal the duplicity of the *kothornos*. Xenophon's interest in the epistolary documents, in fact, seems connected with that of Thucydides, who cites 14 letters, eight of which are in the eighth book: O. Longo has appropriately emphasized the "prestige of the letter" in the Thucydidean work.[40]

Similar conclusions may be drawn from the interesting quotation of the letter of appointment (ἐπιστολή) given by King Darius II to Cyrus; Xenophon fully transcribes it:

> This Cyrus brought with him a letter, addressed to all the dwellers upon the sea and bearing the King's seal (τὸ βασίλειον σφράγισμα), which contained among other things these words (ἐν ᾗ ἐνῆν καὶ τάδε): "I send down Cyrus as karanus of those whose mustering-place is Castolus." The word karanus means 'lord'.
>
> Xenophon *Hellenica* 1.4.3

The transcription is probably partial (Xenophon expressly writes that the letter included something else: ἐν ᾗ ἐνῆν καὶ τάδε); a Greek version of the text (apart from the technical term *karanos*)[41] was in all likelihood available, since the letter was addressed to all the inhabitants of the Anatolian coast (τοῖς κάτω πᾶσι),

---

[40] Longo 1978:524f.
[41] Krentz 1989:126.

the Greeks included, in order to convince them to acknowledge the authority of the young prince. Xenophon emphasizes the authenticity of the document by mentioning the royal seal (σφράγισμα). The fact that the letter is cited in the part of the *Hellenica* that derives from Thucydidean material perhaps confirms Thucydides' thorough knowledge of Persian matters, especially evident in his eighth book.

But Xenophon's interest in epistolary documents is equally clear in later books of the *Hellenica*, where he mentions letters of the Persian King, including the clauses of the King's Peace and of the Peace of Susa. These two documents have already been discussed with regard to the corresponding peace treaties: here it should only be recalled that Xenophon fully transcribes the text of the first letter (5.1.30–31; he also alludes to it at 5.1.32 and at 6.5.2) while only referring to the second (7.1.39–40); in both cases, he stresses that the letter is read out and that it bears the royal seal in order to establish the authenticity of the document:

> So that when Tiribazus ordered those to be present who desired to give ear to the peace which the King had sent down, all speedily presented themselves. And when they had come together, Tiribazus showed them the King's seal and then read the writing. It ran as follows.
>
> Xenophon *Hellenica* 5.1.30

> When the Thebans had called together representatives from all the cities to hear the letter from the King, and the Persians who bore the document, having shown the King's seal, had read what was written therein, although the Thebans directed those who desired to be friends of the King and themselves to swear to these provisions.
>
> Xenophon *Hellenica* 7.1.39

Thus, just as with Thucydides, so too with Xenophon may we speak of the notable 'documentary' prestige of the letter, even though in the latter the range of documentary material is less wide. It is worth noting that the three letters of the Persian King are the sole documents whose authenticity is emphasized, although this may be a result of historical (rather than strictly historiographical) factors; that is to say, it is not (primarily) Xenophon who wants to assure his public that he is referring to authentic documents, but the King who wants to prove the authenticity of his message to the Greeks.

Oracular responses

Xenophon mentions five oracular responses, employing in two cases the term χρησμός; elsewhere he uses the verbs ἀποκρίνομαι (2) and σημαίνω (1). Three responses are uttered by Delphian Apollo, one by Olympian Zeus, and one by an unknown source. In comparison with Thucydides, who mentions 16 responses (mostly Delphic), Xenophon's attention for such phenomena is rather limited, despite his piety and his belief in divine intervention in history.[42]

At 3.3.3 Xenophon recalls Apollo's oracle (χρησμός)[43] on the χωλὴ βασιλεία 'lame kingship', regarding the accession to Agis' former throne, in dispute between Leotychidas and Agesilaus. The historian gives a brief paraphrase by way of Diopeithes the seer:

> But Diopeithes, a man very well versed in oracles, said in support of Leotychides that there was also an oracle of Apollo, which bade the Lacedaemonians beware of the lame kingship. Lysander, however, made reply to him, on behalf of Agesilaus, that he did not suppose the god was bidding them beware lest a king of theirs should get a sprain and become lame, but rather lest one who was not of the royal stock should become king. For the kingship would be lame in very truth when it was not the descendants of Herakles who were at the head of the state. After hearing such arguments from both claimants the state chose Agesilaus as king.
>
> Xenophon *Hellenica* 3.3.3

The text paraphrased here is fully quoted by Plutarch (*Agesilaus* 3.4; *Lysander* 22.5; *De Pythiae oraculis* 399b-c) and by Pausanias (3.8.9); some scholars have assumed that it in fact derives from a Spartan oracular collection.[44]

Xenophon mentions an oracle by Olympian Zeus for Agesipolis at 4.7.2. The response was uttered in the spring of 388 on the occasion of a military expedition against Argos; in the following paragraph the historian recalls the oracle of Delphic Apollo on the same issue, which he paraphrases as follows:

> Now when Agesipolis learned that he was to lead the ban, and when the sacrifices which he offered at the frontier proved favorable, he went to Olympia and consulted the oracle of the god, asking whether it would be consistent with piety if he did not acknowledge the holy truce

[42] For pertinent evidence, see Tuplin 1993:215; see also Sordi 1951:336f.; Dillery 1995:182f.

[43] Cf. Pausanias 3.8.9 and Justin 6.2.5, expressly speaking of Delphian Apollo.

[44] A variant is provided by the ἀρχαία μαντεία on the "lame kingship", mentioned by Diodorus 11.50.4; see Krentz 1995:177–178.

claimed by the Argives; for, he urged, it was not when the appointed time came, but when the Lacedaemonians were about to invade their territory, that they pleaded the sacred months. And the god signified (ἐπεσήμαινεν) to him that it was consistent with piety for him not to acknowledge a holy truce which was pleaded unjustly. Then Agesipolis proceeded straight from there to Delphi and asked Apollo in his turn whether he also held the same opinion as his father Zeus in regard to the truce. And Apollo answered (ἀπεκρίνατο) that he did hold quite the same opinion.

Xenophon Hellenica 4.7.2

It is worth noting that both responses seem to be contradicted by what follows. On entering Argolis, Agesipolis was welcomed by an earthquake, which he interpreted as a good omen (4.7.4); thereafter, his camp was struck by fatal lightning bolts, and sacrifices were unfavorable; in the end, the king abandoned his expedition.[45] Although Xenophon concludes that the campaign seriously damaged the Argives, one has the impression that the historian intends to emphasize the disjuncture between favorable responses and the actual results of the campaign;[46] this gap is rather striking, since even Thucydides, who at times challenges the reliability of oracles and alludes to their possible manipulation, never questions the prestige of the Delphic oracle.

Each of the three responses mentioned above concern Sparta, as does the oracle at 6.4.7, a χρησμός uttered by an unknown source; the response was favorable to the Thebans and was applied to the battle of Leuctra. Its content is paraphrased as follows:

Besides this, they were also somewhat encouraged by the oracle which was reported —that the Lacedaemonians were destined to be defeated at the spot where stood the monument of the virgins, who are said to have killed themselves because they had been violated by certain Lacedaemonians. The Thebans accordingly decorated this monument before the battle.

Xenophon Hellenica 6.4.7

It is noteworthy that in this context Xenophon, after mentioning other portents that took place in Thebes (such as the opening of the temple doors and the disappearance of the weapons from Herakles' temple), writes that "some, to be

---

[45] Bearzot 1993:113–114.
[46] Riedinger 1991:249.

sure, say that all these things were but devices (τεχνάσματα) of the leaders."[47] This episode, which also occurs in Diodorus' account (15.52.2f.), is particularly impressive in Xenophon. Although his intention to accuse the Theban leaders of deceiving the people is fully understandable, the passage reveals a mistrust in omens that clashes with Xenophon's general inclination to acknowledge divine intervention in history. For example, according to Xenophon, divine vengeance stemming from Sparta's violation of the oaths of the King's Peace in 382 causes the unexpected liberation of Thebes from Spartan occupation in 379 (5.4.1).[48] On the other hand, at 6.4.8 Xenophon writes that "in the battle, at any rate, everything turned out adversely for the Lacedaemonians, while for the other side everything went prosperously, even to the gifts of fortune": that is, above and beyond the manipulation by the Theban leaders, the oracle retains some value in Xenophon's eyes.

Finally, Xenophon paraphrases an oracle of Delphian Apollo about the sacred treasure in Delphi and its possible use by Jason, the tyrant of Pherae:

> What he intended, however, in regard to the sacred treasures, is even to this day uncertain; but it is said that when the Delphians asked the god what they should do if he tried to take any of his treasures, Apollo replied (ἀποκρίνασθαι τὸν θεὸν) that he would himself take care of the matter.

Xenophon Hellenica 6.4.30

On the whole, oracular documents in Xenophon seem to have a strictly political rather than religious value. This political interest is confirmed by 3.2.22, a passage in which Xenophon recalls that shortly after the Olympic crisis of 420[49] the Eleans prevented Agis from consulting the oracle of Olympian Zeus under the pretext that consulting on wars with the Greeks was forbidden. The passage does not refer to an oracular response (which was never in fact uttered), but underlines the interference between religion and politics.

Since Xenophon transcribes no oracular responses, it is unlikely that he derives such documents from an oracular collection, which has been proposed for the oracle on the χωλὴ βασιλεία. His sources are more probably oral witnesses, Spartan informants (perhaps Agesilaus himself for the oracle on the βασιλεία and for the two responses received by Agesipolis) or, for the oracle about Jason,

---

[47] Lanzillotta 1984; Bearzot 1993:106f. (with other sources on this episode).
[48] For other examples, see Riedinger 1991:250f.
[49] On the Olympic crisis of 420, see Bearzot 2013.

Polydamas of Pharsalus, Xenophon's informant on Thessalian affairs.[50] In this case, however, it is worth noting that the sentence is introduced by λέγεται. The so-called '*legetai* phrases' have been studied in Thucydides,[51] in whose work they reveal no consistent methodology; they can emphasize different issues, such as uncertainty of information, caution in the face of inexplicable events, or even the use of an oral or written source from which the author intends to keep some distance, since it provides unverifiable information. We may then wonder if in Xenophon the '*legetai* phrases' have a similar meaning, if the historian in these cases is suggesting that his information cannot be sufficiently verified.[52]

Lists

Xenophon refers to a few lists: the term κατάλογος occurs only once, while the verb γράφω, γράφομαι, and their compounds are used in most cases. The most interesting document is the list of the Thirty Tyrants, which is enclosed in their appointment decree (2.3.2); it is the only list that the historian fully transcribes, and it provides a key piece of information, even if some scholars consider it to be an interpolation.[53] Xenophon probably derives it from the original decree, and is the only source that provides complete prosopographical information about the Thirty (Aristotle's *Constitution of the Athenians* and the works of Lysias only sporadically mention the names of the Tyrants).[54] Other lists are merely alluded to by Xenophon: the κατάλογος of the Three Thousand drawn up by the Thirty Tyrants at the insistence of Theramenes (2.3.18; cf. also 2.3.51–52; 2.4.1; 2.4.9; and 2.4.28), which was created arbitrarily (2.3.51; Aristotle *Constitution of the Athenians* 37.1) and perhaps never published; the list of the Eleusinians also drawn up by the Thirty (2.4.8); the list of men to be arrested, which Kynadon communicated to the ephors by the so-called *skytale* (3.3.8–9); the list of Kynadon's accomplices (3.3.10–11); and the list of the signatories of the Peace of Sparta in 371 (6.3.19), for which the technical verb ἀπογράφομαι is used.

Another interesting document is the list of the Spartan ephors who served during the Peloponnesian War (2.3.9), which is fully transcribed: this list, however, is generally considered to have been interpolated, like the other chronological data from the two first books of the *Hellenica*.[55]

---

[50] Bearzot 2004:69–70. On the knowledge of Thessalian affairs by Xenophon, see Sordi 1988; Sordi 2001.
[51] Westlake 1977.
[52] Sordi 1951:282f.
[53] Krentz 1995:189f.; Rhodes 2007:61.
[54] Németh 2006:13f.,91f.
[55] Krentz 1989:192.

Laws

Xenophon mentions only three laws (νόμοι) in the *Hellenica*, two from Athens and one from Sparta: the Athenian law on traitors and the impious (1.7.22), partially transcribed in the account of the Arginousai trial; the Spartan law on navarchy and its annual rotation (2.1.7), whose content is summarized by the historian;[56] finally, the 'new laws' (καινοὶ νόμοι) passed by the Thirty Tyrants (2.3.51; cf. 2.3.52 and 54), which proclaimed, according to Xenophon's paraphrase, "that while no one of those who are on the roll of the Three Thousand may be put to death without your vote, the Thirty shall have power of life or death over those outside the roll."[57]

3. Subject matter of the documents

With regards to content, Thucydides and Xenophon are essentially interested in the same types of documents. Most of the documents cited have political relevance and refer to international relations; legal and religious documents are also well represented. Documents with administrative and economic interest, however, seem to be less relevant: we may recall in the former category the suspect list of the Thirty and the list of the ephors, probably interpolated; in the latter, the decree mentioned at 5.2.10, by which property was restored to those exiled from Phlius.

4. Form of citation

Xenophon's preferred methods of citation are references and paraphrase, although it is sometimes difficult to distinguish between the two (the use of technical, formulaic expressions speaks in favor of the latter). We find few cases of full or partial transcription, about half the number in Thucydides.

The five cases of full transcription are the letter of the Spartan Hippocrates intercepted by the Athenians in 411 (1.1.23), which is introduced by λέγοντα τάδε; the γνώμη of Kallixenos (1.7.9–10) introduced by εἰπόντος τήνδε (γνώμην); the list of the Thirty Tyrants (2.3.2), introduced by καὶ ᾑρέθησαν οἵδε; the text of the King's Peace (5.1.30–31), introduced by εἶχε δὲ ὧδε; and the oath of the Peace of Athens of 371/0 (6.5.1–3), introduced by τόνδε τὸν ὅρκον. To these documents we should add the (probably interpolated) list of the ephors mentioned above.

---

56 "And the Lacedaemonians granted them Lysander as vice-admiral, but made Aracus admiral; for it was contrary to their law for a man to hold the office of admiral twice." See Krentz 1989:134.
57 Krentz 1989:137, considers Aristotle *Constitution of the Athenians* 37.1 more accurate in referring to the text of the law, in accordance with the use of the term *autokrator* instead of *kyrios*.

Darius II's appointment letter for Cyrus (1.4.3), introduced by ἐν ᾗ ἐνῆν καὶ τάδε, is surely partially transcribed, since the καὶ reveals that the original text was longer. A partial transcription must be supposed in other cases too, despite the fact that a similar introduction to the text is lacking: for Kannonos' Decree (1.7.20), for the *nomos* on traitors and the impious (1.7.22), and also for the exchange of messages between Agesilaus and Tithraustes through ambassadors after the death of Tissaphernes in 395:

> When this battle took place Tissaphernes chanced to be at Sardis, so that the Persians charged him with having betrayed them. Furthermore, the Persian King himself concluded that Tissaphernes was responsible for the bad turn his affairs were taking, and accordingly sent down Tithraustes and cut off his head. After he had done this, Tithraustes sent ambassadors to Agesilaus with this message: "Agesilaus, the man who was responsible for the trouble in your eyes and ours has received his punishment; and the King deems it fitting that you should sail back home, and that the cities in Asia, retaining their independence, should render him the ancient tribute." When Agesilaus replied that he could not do this without the sanction of the authorities at home, Tithraustes said, "But at least, until you receive word from the city, go over into the territory of Pharnabazus, since it is I who have taken vengeance upon your enemy." "Then, until I go there," said Agesilaus, "give me provisions for the army." Tithraustes accordingly gave him thirty talents; and he took it and set out for Pharnabazus' province of Phrygia.
>
> Xenophon *Hellenica* 3.4.25–26

Xenophon's information about the content of these messages probably derives from Agesilaus, who was a protagonist in these events.[58] In addition, the text of the Peace of Susa (7.1.36), containing only the clauses that, according to Xenophon, had been required by Pelopidas, is probably also partially transcribed; indeed, we know that there were other clauses, such as the one about the eternal friendship between the King and the Thebans, also required by Pelopidas, to which Plutarch refers (*Pelopidas* 30.7), and the one that was added (προσγεγραμμένα), according to Xenophon (7.1.37), in response to the Athenian Leon.

On the whole, we may conclude that Xenophon is less interested than Thucydides in transcribing documents: yet the documents he does transcribe

---

[58] For other sources see Krentz 1995:192–193.

are often very important for our historical knowledge, such as the γνώμη of Kallixenos, the list of the Thirty Tyrants (if it is not interpolated), the text of the King's Peace, and the oath of the Peace of Athens of 371/0.

There are several reasons why Xenophon might have transcribed a document: his wish to clarify political or military events (the letter of Hippocrates) or trials (the γνώμη of Kallixenos) by citing documents that support his interpretation; his intention to furnish complete evidence (the list of the Thirty); his wish to emphasize the relevance of the κοινὴ εἰρήνη as a fundamental principle in fourth-century international law (the texts, fully or partially transcribed, of the common peaces); and, last, his interest in international relations, which also explains why treaties are the best attested type of document in the *Hellenica*.

5. Origins of information and authenticity of documents

Thucydides never states the origin of his information unless he cites a literary work (e.g. Homer and the ancient poets) or refers to inscriptions. In Xenophon, who cites neither epigraphical documents nor literary works in his *Hellenica*, such information about sources is almost completely lacking. There are cases of documents cited in speeches, however, such as the two decrees (of the Peloponnesian League and of the Thebans) mentioned by the Theban ambassadors who came to Athens in 395 (2.2.15) and the Olynthian decree on the alliance between Athens and Boeotia, recalled by Cleigenes of Acanthus in the Spartan speech of 382 (5.2.15). The word λέγεται, which introduces Xenophon's reference to the Delphic oracle about Jason of Pherae (6.4.30), also seems to refer to an oral tradition. Sometimes (especially in the case of lists, letters, treaties) the use of the verb γράφω, γράφομαι, and their compounds may imply the availability, even through a public reading, of a written document; in fact, a public reading is expressly mentioned with reference to the clauses of common peace treaties (cf. 5.1.30 for the King's Peace and 7.1.39 for the Peace of Susa). However, we can never exclude the mediation of eyewitnesses (Agesilaus or other Spartans; Athenian ambassadors).

Xenophon, like Thucydides, rarely emphasizes the authenticity of the documents he mentions: we can assume that he did not in general mistrust the documentary material he used. Xenophon's uncertainty about the oracle favorable to the Thebans mentioned (6.4.7) may be inferred from his reservations about the 'portents' which occurred before Leuctra and were considered as τεχνάσματα (devices) of the Theban leaders; the inconsistency between the favorable responses received by Agesipolis in 388 (4.7.2–3) and the negative outcome of the campaign in Xenophon's account is also worth noting. On the contrary, he does go out of his way to authenticate the three letters of the Persian King by invoking the royal seal (1.4.3; 5.1.30; 7.1.39).[59]

6. Location of documents

In Thucydides the physical location of documents is implicitly clear only for inscriptions and literary works. For other types of documents, except where the historian does provide explicit information, it is very difficult to form an opinion. In Xenophon, who never refers either to inscriptions or to literary works, information on the location of documents is lacking: we may only suppose that some documents come from archives (for example, in the case of the documentary material regarding the Arginousai trial).

7. Conclusions

As I emphasized in my paper from 2003, Thucydides is specifically interested in "documents", which he uses for historiographical and not merely decorative purposes. This historiographical interest is essentially confirmed in Xenophon, although the range of documents he considers is less broad than that of his predecessors, and he seems less inclined to transcribe documentary texts.

The prominence of international treaties and decrees, i.e. documents with political value, corresponds to the historiographical nature of the *Hellenica*; the treatment of other types of documents leads to the same conclusions (oaths mostly regard the undersigning of international treaties or civic agreements; all letters have an indisputable political value).

The lack of reference to inscriptions is worth noting, given the fact that much more epigraphical material was available in the fourth century than in the fifth (Xenophon does not even mention Aristotle's Decree, although he does hint at it in connection to the Peace of Athens of 371/0) and also that Xenophon cites inscriptions in other works, such as the *Anabasis*.[60] Also absent is any reference to literary works. Inscriptions and works such as archaic poetry are used by Thucydides in order to reconstruct non-contemporary history, for which there is a lack of eyewitnesses; we may wonder whether the lack of such material in the *Hellenica* is due to continuity with the Thucydidean method, since Xenophon writes contemporary history and as a consequence is able to have recourse to

---

[59] Krentz 1989:125.
[60] Zizza 2007:226–227n45; Zizza 2012.

eyewitnesses;[61] indeed, the use of inscriptions by historians is often connected with the reconstruction of non-contemporary history.[62]

Finally, the scanty interest in oracles shown by the 'pious' Xenophon is remarkable: Thucydides, who is not usually considered to have been particularly interested in religious matters, pays much more attention to oracular responses.

On the whole, Xenophon appears to be less interested in documents than his predecessors. He uses documents but not as widely as Herodotus and Thucydides, who consider them more methodologically relevant.[63] J. K. Davies has pointed out a rising interest in documents in fourth-century historiography, particularly in the Athenian context,[64] where they are favored for various reasons, such as the revision of the Athenian *corpus* of laws, the increasing tendency to draw up lists, the imitation of Herodotus and Thucydides, and the interest in working on documents regarding Athens' own past. Yet this does not seem to be the case in Xenophon. The corroboration of the historical narrative, which is typically the role of documents in Herodotus and Thucydides, depends in Xenophon on other methodological tools, such as authorial interventions and quotations of others' opinions, as pointed out by V. Gray: these 'tools' are parsimoniously inserted in Xenophon's work in compliance with programmatic and methodological principles, and are privileged over documents in order to increase the reliability of the historical reconstruction.[65] The special authoritativeness attributed to oral testimonies in comparison with written documents can probably be connected to the strictly contemporary nature of the *Hellenica*, since, as we have said, documents are more often used in the reconstruction of the distant past, while oral testimonies are preferred when reconstructing contemporary events.

Bibliography

Bearzot, C. 1993. "Mantica e condotta di guerra. Strateghi, soldati e indovini di fronte all'interpretazione dell'evento prodigioso." In *La profezia nel mondo antico*, ed. M. Sordi, 97–121. Contributi dell'Istituto de Storia Antica 19. Milan.

———. 1997. *Lisia e la tradizione su Teramene. Commento storico alle orazioni XII e XIII del corpus lysiacum*. Biblioteca di Aevum Antiquum 10. Milan.

---

[61] See Krentz 1989:6; Krentz 1995:5; Marincola 1997:69; Rhodes 2007:60. On the use of documents as methodological tools of non-contemporary history, see Marincola 1997:103f.

[62] Zizza 2007:229f.

[63] Cf. Thucydides 7.8.2, where the use of a written document—a letter—in its original form is considered a possible corrective for the limitations of oral testimonies, which are conditioned by witnesses' acuteness, memory and bias.

[64] Davies 1996:36–37.

[65] Gray 2003:111–123.

———. 2002. "Autonomia e federalismo nel contrasto fra Sparta e Tebe: la testimonianza di Senofonte." In *Atti della "Giornata tebana" (Milano, 18 aprile 2002)*, ed. F. Cordano, 79–118. Milan.

———. 2003. "L'uso dei documenti in Tucidide." In Biraschi et al. 2003:267–314.

———. 2004. *Federalismo e autonomia nelle Elleniche di Senofonte.* Milan.

———. 2012. "Xenophon on the Athenian Embassy to Susa (367 BC.)", *Historika. Studi di storia greca e romana* 1:21–37.

———. 2013. "The Relations between Argos and Sparta after the Peace of Nicias and the Olympic Crisis of the Year 420 BC." In *War, Peace, and the Panhellenic Games. Proceedings of the Colloquium, Olympia June 27rd–July 2rd, 2005*, ed. N. Birgalias et al., 279-298. Athens.

Bengtson, H. 1962. *Die Staatsverträge der griechisch-römischen Welt von 700 bis 338 v. Chr.* Munich.

Biraschi, A. M. et al., eds. 2003. *L'uso dei documenti nella storiografia antica (Atti del Convegno, Gubbio 22-24 maggio 2001).* Naples.

———. 2003. "Erodoto. Per una selezione e schedatura dei documenti." In Biraschi et al. 2003:153–160.

Brownson, C. L., ed. 1985–1986. *Xenophon, Hellenica, I-II.* Cambridge, MA.

Burckhardt, L. A. 2000. "Eine Demokratie wohl, aber kein Rechtsstaat? Der Arginusenprozess des Jahres 406 v. Chr." In *Grosse Prozesse im antiken Athen*, ed. L. Burckhardt and J. von Ungern-Sternberg, 128–143. Munich.

Canfora, L. 1990. "Trattati in Tucidide." In *I trattati nel mondo antico, Atti del Convegno di studi Roma 14-15 marzo 1986*, ed. L. Canfora et al., 193-216. Rome.

Ceva, M. 1996. *Senofonte, Elleniche.* Milan.

Daverio Rocchi, G. 1978. *Senofonte, Elleniche.* Milan. 2nd ed. 2002.

Davies, J. K. 1996. "Documents and "Documents" in Fourth-Century Historiography." In *Le IVe siècle av. J.-C. Approches historiographiques*, ed. P. Carlier, 29–39. Nancy.

Dillery, J. 1995. *Xenophon and the History of His Times.* London.

Fabiani, R. 2003. "Epigrafi in Erodoto." In Biraschi et al. 2003:161–185.

Giovannini, A. 2002. "Xenophon, der Arginusenprozess und die athenische Demokratie." *Chiron* 32:15–50.

Gray, V. 2003. "Interventions and Citations in Xenophon, Hellenica and Anabasis." *Classical Quarterly* 53:111–123.

Harrison A. R. W. 2001. *Il diritto ad Atene. II. La procedura.* Trans. P. C. Ghiggia. Alessandria. Orig. pub. 1971.

Jehne, M. 1994. *Koine eirene. Untersuchungen zu den Befriedungs- und Stabilisierungsbemühungen in der griechischen Poliswelt des 4. Jahrhundert v. Chr.* Hermes Einzelschriften 63. Stuttgart.

————. 2004. "Überlegungen zu den Auslassungen in Xenophons "Hellenica" am Beispiel der Gründung des Zweiten Athenische Seebunds." In Tuplin 2004:463–480.

Krentz, P. 1989. *Xenophon, Hellenica I-II.3.10.* Warminster.

————. 1995. *Xenophon, Hellenica II.3.11-IV.2.8.* Warminster.

Lanzillotta, E. 1984. "I prodigi per la battaglia di Leuttra." In *Problemi di storia e cultura spartana*, ed. E. Lanzillotta, 163–179. Rome.

Lavelle, B. M. 1988. "Adikia, the Decree of Kannonos, and the Trial of the Generals." *Classica et mediaevalia* 39:19–41.

Lévy, E. 1990. "L'art de la déformation historique dans les Helléniques de Xénophon." In *Purposes of History. Studies in Greek Historiography from the 4th to the 2nd Centuries B.C. (Proceedings of the International Colloquium, Leuven 24–26 May 1988)*, ed. G. Schepens, and R. E. de Keyser, 125–157. Studia Hellenistica 30. Louvain.

Longo, O. 1978. "Scrivere in Tucidide: comunicazione e ideologia." In *Studi in onore di Anthos Ardizzone* I, ed. E. Livrea and G. A. Privitera, 519–554. Rome.

Marincola, J. 1997. *Authority and Tradition in Ancient Historiography.* Cambridge.

Moggi, M. et al. 2007. "Documenti nella storiografia antica: prospettive informatiche." *Mediterraneo Antico* 10:161–252.

Németh, G. 2006. *Kritias und die Dreissig Tyrannen.* Habes 43. Stuttgart.

Nicolai, R. 2003. "La poesia epica come documento. L'esegesi di Omero da Ecateo a Tucidide." In Biraschi et al. 2003:79–109.

Orsi, D. P. 2002. "Trattative internazionali nelle "Elleniche" di Senofonte. Aspetti del lessico: i verbi della comunicazione." In *La retorica della diplomazia nella Grecia antica e a Bisanzio*, ed. L. R. Cresci et al., 71–109. Rome.

————. 2004. "Giustizia e "Realpolitik" nelle "Elleniche" di Senofonte." *Simblos* 4:77–104.

Porciani, L. 2003. "Logoi, erga, documenti. Il caso della tregua del 423 a.C. fra Atene e Sparta." In Biraschi et al. 2003:315–329.

Rhodes, P. J. 2007. "Documents and the Greek Historians." In *A Companion to Greek and Roman Historiography* I, ed. J. Marincola, 56–66. Malden.

Riedinger, J.-C. 1991. *Étude sur les Helléniques. Xénophon et l'histoire.* Paris.

————. 1993. "Un aspect de la méthode de Xénophon: l'origine des sources dans les Helleniques III-VII." *Athenaeum* 81:517–544.

Santi Amantini, L. 1979–1980. "Sulla terminologia relativa alla pace nelle epigrafi greche fino all'avvento della koinè eirene." *Atti dell'Istituto Veneto di Scienze, Lettere ed Arti* 188:467–495.

————. 1985. "Semantica storica dei termini greci relativi alla pace nelle epigrafi anteriori al 387/6 a. C." In *La pace nel mondo antico*, ed. M. Sordi, 45–68. Contributi dell'Istituto di storia antica 11. Milan.

———. 1986. "La terminologia degli accordi di pace nella tradizione letteraria greca fino alla conclusione delle guerre persiane." In *Serta historica antiqua*, I, 99–111. Rome.

———. 1996. "Il significato di eirene nelle "Storie" di Tucidide e nelle epigrafi contemporanee." In *Un incontro con la storia nel centenario della nascita di Luca De Regibus: 1895–1995 (Atti del pomeriggio di studio a Vogogna d'Ossola, 1° luglio 1995)*, ed. A. F. Bellezza, 155–164. Geneva.

———. 2000. "Voci di pace nella storiografia di Senofonte." *Rivista storica dell'Antichità* 30:9–26.

Sordi, M. 1950. "I caratteri dell'opera storiografica di Senofonte nelle Elleniche." *Athenaeum* 28:3–53.

———. 1951. "I caratteri dell'opera storiografica di Senofonte nelle Elleniche. 2." *Athenaeum* 29:273–348.

———. 1988. "Gli interessi geografici e topografici nelle Elleniche di Senofonte." In *Geografia e storiografia nel mondo classico*, 32–40. Contributi dell'Istituto di Storia antica 14. Milan.

———. 2001. "Le Elleniche di Senofonte e la storia locale tessala." In *Storiografia locale e storiografia universale. Forme di acquisizione del sapere storico nella cultura antica (Atti del Convegno di Bologna, 16-18 dicembre 1999)*, ed. C. Bearzot et al., 299–305. Como.

Tuci, P. A. 2002. "La boulé nel processo agli strateghi della battaglia delle Arginuse: questioni procedurali e tentativi di manipolazione." In Συγγραφή. *Materiali e appunti per lo studio della storia e della letteratura antica* 3, ed. D. Ambaglio, 51–85. Como.

Tuplin, C. J. 1993. *The Failings of Empire. A Reading of Xenophon Hellenica 2.3.11–7.5.27.* Historia Einzelschriften 76. Stuttgart.

———, ed. 2004. *Xenophon and his World. Papers from a Conference Held in Liverpool in July 1999.* Historia Einzelschriften 172. Stuttgart.

Westlake, H. D. 1977. "LEGETAI in Thucydides." *Mnemosyne* 30:345–362.

Zizza, C. 1999. "Tucidide e il tirannicidio: il buon uso del materiale epigrafico." *Annali della Facoltà di Lettere e Filosofia dell'Università di Siena* 20:1–22.

———. 2007. "I documenti nella storiografia antica. Alcune considerazioni a proposito di un libro recente." *Incidenza dell'antico* 5:209–234.

———. 2012. "Le iscrizioni nell'Anabasi di Senofonte." In *Il paesaggio e l'esperienza. Scritti di antichità offerti a Pierluigi Tozzi in occasione del suo 75° compleanno*, ed. R. Bargnesi and R. Scuderi, 189–211. Pavia.

6

The Causes of the Peloponnesian War
Ephorus, Thucydides and Their Critics

Giovanni Parmeggiani

THE CAUSES of the Peloponnesian War constitute such a persistent theme in discussions of fifth-century Greek history, in part because of the complexity of the aetiological view of our earliest source, Thucydides.

ἤρξαντο δὲ αὐτοῦ Ἀθηναῖοι καὶ Πελοποννήσιοι λύσαντες τὰς τριακοντούτεις σπονδὰς αἵ αὐτοῖς ἐγένοντο μετὰ Εὐβοίας ἅλωσιν. διότι δ' ἔλυσαν, τὰς αἰτίας προύγραψα πρῶτον καὶ τὰς διαφοράς, τοῦ μή τινα ζητῆσαί ποτε ἐξ ὅτου τοσοῦτος πόλεμος τοῖς Ἕλλησι κατέστη. τὴν μὲν γὰρ ἀληθεστάτην πρόφασιν, ἀφανεστάτην δὲ λόγῳ, τοὺς Ἀθηναίους ἡγοῦμαι μεγάλους γιγνομένους καὶ φόβον παρέχοντας τοῖς Λακεδαιμονίοις ἀναγκάσαι ἐς τὸ πολεμεῖν: αἱ δ' ἐς τὸ φανερὸν λεγόμεναι αἰτίαι αἵδ' ἦσαν ἑκατέρων, ἀφ' ὧν λύσαντες τὰς σπονδὰς ἐς τὸν πόλεμον κατέστησαν.

The Athenians and Peloponnesians began the war by breaking the Thirty Years Peace made after the conquest of Euboia. As for the reason why they broke the peace, I have written first the *aitiai* and differences, so that no one should ever have to enquire into the origin of so great a war for the Greeks. I regard the truest *prophasis*, which was least apparent in speech, as this: the Athenians, becoming great and arousing fear in the Spartans, made the war inevitable. The openly expressed *aitiai* on each side, however, on the basis of which they broke the peace and began to fight, were the following. (Translation by T. Rood, modified)

Thucydides 1.23.4–6

Critics tend to admire Thucydides' subtle distinction between *aitiai es to phaneron legomenai* and *alethestate prophasis*,[1] but they are generally less comfortable with his formulation of the two sets of causes: one consisting in individual episodes of tension between Athens and Sparta's allies, particularly Corinth, in the years leading up to the war (specifically the events of Corcyra and Potidaea); the other a process that followed immediately upon the end of Xerxes' expedition (the growing tension between the two leading Greek cities, Athens and Sparta).

By qualifying it as *alethestate*, Thucydides is clearly claiming that the *prophasis* is more important for a correct understanding of the origins of the war. In other words, he is asserting that a proper perception of the origins of the war depends upon a consideration of the previous fifty years as well as careful attention paid both to the *physis* of the Athenian *arche*, as an ever increasing force in Greek history, and to Sparta's *phobos*, as a reactive force in Greek history.

Thucydides never implies, however, that the *aitiai es to phaneron legomenai* are unconnected to the breakout of the war. As he himself observes: "As for the reason why they [sc. the Athenians and Lacedaemonians] broke the peace, I have written first the *aitiai* and the differences, so that no one should ever have to enquire into the origin of so great a war for the Greeks." (Thucydides 1.23.5, translation by T. Rood.) The meaning of this statement is clear: if there had been no Corcyra and Potidaea, there would have been no Peloponnesian War in 431 BCE. It is obvious, then, that the relationship between *aitiai es to phaneron* and *alethestate prophasis* cannot be presented as if it were a relationship between *false* and *true* causes.[2]

In recent years, Tim Rood has argued that the *aitiai es to phaneron* are deeply related to the *alethestate prophasis*, that they are, in fact, part of the same aetiological system.[3] Rood's remarks allow us to recover a unity of thought in Thucydides' interpretation of the origins of the war. Yet, the problem remains: why does Thucydides make a distinction between *aitiai es to phaneron* and

---

[1]   See for example Hornblower 2003:65, *ad loc.*: "The explicit formulation of a distinction between profound and superficial causes is arguably Th.'s greatest single contribution to later history-writing."

[2]   On the basis of Thucydides' account of the events, Kagan 1969:345-374 thinks that the tension between Athens and Corinth (i.e. the Thucydidean *aitiai*) was the main cause for the war and, inasmuch as this tension was not what Thucydides considered the *alethestate prophasis*, that Thucydides was in fact wrong in his interpretation of the origins of the war. But—I observe— Thucydides never denies the *aitiai es to phaneron* the status of real causes. Moreover, it is clear that the *aitiai es to phaneron* are not mere pretexts for going to war, as they have been interpreted, for example, by Dionysius of Halicarnassus (*On Thucydides* 10 on Athenian support of Corcyra as a cause οὐκ ἀληθῆ, i.e. fabricated by the Spartans) and, in modern times, by de Ste. Croix 1972:50–63.

[3]   Rood 1998:208-215, esp. 209n16.

alethestate prophasis? I would suggest that there is something more at stake than the opposition between 'superficial' and 'profound' causes.

In his disclosure of the *alethestate prophasis*, Thucydides brings into play the concept of *ananke*, which is entirely absent from his discussion of the *aitiai*.[4] In other words, he distinguishes between two sets of causes because there are two different kinds of problems to solve. The first is a problem of historical contingency and properly concerns the origin of the Peloponnesian War in 431 BCE. How did the war actually break out? This is the problem for which the *aitiai* are invoked. The second is a philosophical problem and concerns the nature of the war between Athens and Sparta. Was the war accidental or necessary? This is the problem for which the *alethestate prophasis* is invoked. Thucydides' answer, in short, is that the war was necessary: if there had been no Corcyra and Potidaea, there would have been no Peloponnesian War in 431 BCE; the war would instead have erupted at a different time. Without depriving the *aitiai* of their aetiological function, the concept of *alethestate prophasis* allows Thucydides to emphasize the inevitability of the war. With his *alethestate prophasis*, then, Thucydides tries to raise his reader's awareness and encourage an original, philosophical vision of history.

According to Thucydides, the inevitability of the war was not a concept that common people could easily grasp (ἀφανεστάτην δὲ λόγῳ). In fact, unlike the single events that he classifies as *aitiai es to phaneron*, the ongoing tension between Athens and Sparta was distant in time and more complex in form. Such a relationship, therefore, can only be revealed by a master of history and politics, whose insight is particularly canny. By insight I mean control of the facts from the distant past, knowledge of the *physis* of man and especially, of the *physis* of power. In two demonstrations of Book 1, the *Archaeologia* (1.2–19) and the *Pentecontaetia* (1.89–117), Thucydides gives a full display of this type of knowledge, which we may consider to be the theoretical backbone of his political science.

Naturally, we have the option of trusting Thucydides' mastery and thus gratefully accepting his lesson about the causes of the war and its historical necessity. However, some critics have noted that Thucydides does not inquire into important events that occurred in the years immediately before the war,

---

[4]   Thucydides 1.23.6 reads: ἀναγκάσαι ἐς τὸ πολεμεῖν. The subject of ἀναγκάσαι is the entire process (i.e. Athenian expansion, *auxesis,* together with Spartan fear, *phobos*). The object of ἀναγκάσαι is not explicitly stated, and this is not by chance, judging from schol. *ad loc.*: τὰ ὀνόματα ῥήματα ἐποίησεν· βούλεται γὰρ δηλοῦν ὅτι μεγάλοι γινόμενοι οἱ Ἀθηναῖοι ἀνάγκην παρέσχον τοῦ πολέμου. Critics have attempted without success to understand whether Thucydides puts the blame for the war on the Athenians or the Spartans. As Rood 1998:222–223 rightly points out, Thucydides is quite elusive on the issue of responsibility for the war.

such as the Megarian Decree.[5] Some have drawn our attention to the artful rhetorical construction of Book 1, or have disagreed with Thucydides' insistence that the war was unavoidable.[6] Some situate Thucydides' work within the context of contemporary political debates about the responsibility for the war, debates that were quite animated during and after the Peloponnesian War; in light of this, they find Thucydides' account unsatisfactory: in their opinion, Thucydides' explanation is defective and, even worse, biased.[7]

Among Thucydides' critics is Karl Julius Beloch, who notes that the difficulties experienced by Pericles and his party in the preceding years had a direct impact on the outbreak of war.[8] During this period, Pheidias, Anaxagoras, and Aspasia were all put on trial, incidents that are recorded by sources other than Thucydides, such as ancient comedy and—it is supposed—a pamphletistic tradition hostile to Pericles.[9] Indeed, this is at the core of Diodorus' account of the causes of the Peloponnesian War (12.38–41), the main source for which, Diodorus tells us, was the fourth-century historian Ephorus of Cyme (FGH 70 F 196).

Modern critics rarely praise Ephorus' historiography. If we look at F 196, the fragment on the causes of the Peloponnesian War, we can perhaps understand why. Here, besides a reference to Pericles' personal affairs, we find three citations from ancient comedy, apparently adduced by Ephorus as evidence. The first two, from Aristophanes' *Peace* and *Acharnians*, clearly assert Pericles' responsibility for initiating the war. If some critics believe that Thucydides defended Pericles too vehemently, many more contend that Ephorus preferred the silly inventions of poets and the vulgar insinuations of pamphleteers over Thucydides' trustworthy account and subtle aetiological analysis, and that he

---

[5]   See Meyer 1899:302–303.

[6]   See Schwartz 1919 and Kagan 1969:357-374 respectively.

[7]   See especially Badian 1993:125–162. Comparing Thucydides to a modern journalist, Badian asserts that the historian laid the blame for the war on Sparta in an attempt to obscure Pericles' personal responsibilities and defend him from the attacks of his contemporaries. In sum, Thucydides worked as an *apologist*, tendentious as a pamphletist.

[8]   Beloch 1914:294-298. In Beloch's view, Pericles desired war only to protect his position at home, and he succeeded by means of demagogy.

[9]   The exact chronology of the trials of Pericles' associates is controversial (see Podlecki 1998). But it is nevertheless worth stressing that scholium to Aristophanes *Peace*, line 605 (Philochorus FGH 328 F 121) provides us with no more than a *terminus post quem* for Pheidias' trial (438/7 BCE). From Plutarch *Pericles* 31–32 (surely the best account we have of the trials, together with Diodorus 12.39.1–2 [Ephorus F 196]), we learn of several public decrees before 431 BCE, all of them pertaining to Pericles and his associates. One in particular, that of Dracontides (Plutarch *Pericles* 32.3), was directed against Pericles' financial administration (see below, Diodorus 12.38.2–4 and 39.3 [Ephorus F 196]). It is also important to note that various sources, including Thucydides (2.65.3), tell us that Pericles was fined in 430 BCE and was not reconfirmed as *strategos* (see also Plato *Gorgias* 516a; Diodorus 12.45.4-5; Plutarch *Pericles* 35.4). Gomme 1956b:184, we may recall, considers Thucydides to be "deliberately silent" on this issue.

held only Pericles accountable for the war. Such a formulation has long formed the basis for Ephorus' supposed ignorance in historical matters.[10]

Among Ephorus' detractors is Felix Jacoby. In his view, Thucydides had unduly neglected Athenian internal politics, and so Ephorus would have written an account of the causes of the Peloponnesian War better than that of Thucydides had he both paid attention to Thucydides' text and at the same time examined Athenian internal politics without surrendering to the lethal seduction of comedy or pamphlets.[11] I would suggest instead that, as is evident from Thucydides' text, at the time when he was writing (after 431 BCE, at least), Pericles was commonly viewed as responsible for the war; Thucydides thus writes to counter this opinion.[12] With regard to Ephorus, we could ask Jacoby if it would have been possible or conceivable for a historian of the fourth century to examine the internal politics of fifth-century Athens without considering the comic tradition and, more generally, the literature of the time, which was an

---

[10] See especially Müller 1841:lxiiia–b (compare Creuzer 1845:325); Cauer 1847:60 with n1; Stelkens 1857:12–13, 25; Klügmann 1860:29; Matthiessen 1857–1860:878; Blass 1892:433; Endemann 1881:7–9; Vogel 1889:533; Meyer 1899:329-333; Busolt 1904:704; Schwartz 1903:680–681; Schwartz 1907:14; Peter 1911:172; Jacoby 1926b:93, *ad* FGH 70 F 196; Jacoby 1954:489–490, *ad* Philochorus FGH 328 F 121; Barber 1935:106–112; Momigliano 1975, esp. 700; Gomme 1956a:44–46, 69–70; Gomme 1956b:186; and many others, e.g. Dover 1988:50. One should also recall Plutarch *De Herodoti malignitate* 855f–856a on the tendentiousness of writers of ancient comedy in explaining the origins of the war by emphasizing the cases of Pheidias and Aspasia. But, apart from Ephorus' insistence on Pericles' private affairs and seemingly uncritical use of ancient comedy as a source, what has been often criticized in Ephorus is his presumed inability to comprehend the international dynamics that lead to war, on which, in contrast, Thucydides aptly focused his attention. See also Giuliani 1999, especially 37–40; Banfi 2003:180-183; Pownall 2004:133–134; Hose 2006:680. If they do not consider Thucydides' explanation of the war to be an *apologia* of Pericles, modern critics tend to view Ephorus' explanation as a historiographical collection of pamphlet/comic tradition against Pericles. If, on the other hand, they do suspect Thucydides' explanation of the war to be an *apologia* of Pericles, they still do not, curiously, try to re-evaluate Ephorus' explanation. Generally speaking, Ephorus' account is viewed by critics as a serious step backward from the high-standard account of Thucydides. Aside from Marx's and Vogel's attempts to defend Ephorus (see below, text and n20), notable exceptions to this widespread critical trend are found in the work of Connor and especially Schepens, cited below, n17 and n23.

[11] Jacoby 1926b:93, *ad* FGH 70 F 196: "das charakteristische für ihn (sc. Ephorus) ist gerade, daß er nicht vermocht hat, diese darstellung (i.e. the picture of the Athenian internal politics) in ihren berechtigten zügen mit der thukydideischen zu vereinigen und so ein vollbild der zum kriege treibenden strömungen zu zeichnen." Note the somewhat ambiguous way that Jacoby 1954:490, hints at Thucydides' faults, without acknowledging Ephorus' attention to Athenian internal politics and Pericles' affairs: "he (sc. Ephorus) was the first historian to collect the gossip, *which perhaps was not entirely gossip*, and which Thukydides passed over in a manner not altogether to be approved." (emphasis added)

[12] See especially Thucydides 1.139.4, 140.4–5; 2.59.1-2; Plutarch *Nicias* 9.9. Cf. *Alcibiades* 14.2. The Thucydidean thesis about the inevitability of the war is indeed a shield that defends Pericles from contemporary charges and challenges the widespread notion that Athens had entered the war for insignificant reasons (ἐπ' αἰτίαις μικραῖς).

Giovanni Parmeggiani

active part of the ongoing political debate. The answer, I maintain, would be no. For modern historians too, ancient comedy (when correctly used) is a documentary source. The question, then, becomes: does Ephorus make good or bad use of ancient comedy? But there is a second question also: does Ephorus, as has been suggested, simply lay blame for the war on Pericles, thereby neglecting the wider scenario of international politics, or is his aetiological view somewhat more subtle? To answer this, we must take a closer look at F 196, and the other texts apparently indebted to Ephorus for the causes of the Peloponnesian War.[13]

F 196 is a difficult text. Diodorus mentions Ephorus at the end of a long and seemingly lacunose account: αἰτίαι μὲν οὖν τοῦ Πελοποννησιακοῦ πολέμου τοιαῦταί τινες ὑπῆρξαν, ὡς Ἔφορος ἀνέγραψε ("Now the causes of the Peloponnesian War were in general what I have described, as Ephorus has recorded them." 12.41.1, translation by C. H. Oldfather). By his use of the term τινες Diodorus seems to be saying that this is approximately what Ephorus said about the causes of the Peloponnesian War.[14] But from F 196 we do learn of several matters: first, Pericles' difficulties in giving an account of his financial administration to the demos,[15] and his will to resolve such difficulties by means of a war (12.38.2–4);[16] second, the trials of his associates Pheidias (charged with embezzlement of public funds that had been allocated for Athena's statue) and Anaxagoras (12.39.1–3); third, Pericles' involvement in these charges, which in fact masked political attacks by his opponents, and his aim to resolve these troubles with a war (12.39.3); and finally, the existing problem of the Megarian Decree (12.39.4), and the consequent debate during which Pericles urged his

---

[13] It is not my main concern, in the present paper, to examine F 196 exhaustively. For a complete analysis of this important text and for what it suggests about Ephorus' methodology and view of fifth-century Athens, see Parmeggiani 2011:354, 417-458, 673-679.

[14] This was already clear in Vogel 1889:538: "Jedenfalls besitzen wir bei Diodor *nur einen Auszug* aus Ephoros." (emphasis added).

[15] Diodorus 12.38.2–4 (compare 39.3) says that Pericles had been officially requested to submit an ἀπολογισμός or περὶ τῶν χρημάτων ἀπολογία. It is highly likely, in my view, that this measure resulted directly from the famous decree of Dracontides, about which Plutarch speaks in *Pericles* 32.3–4 (δεχομένου δὲ τοῦ δήμου καὶ προσιεμένου τὰς διαβολάς, οὕτως ἤδη ψήφισμα κυροῦται Δρακοντίδου γράψαντος, ὅπως οἱ λόγοι τῶν χρημάτων ὑπὸ Περικλέους εἰς τοὺς πρυτάνεις ἀποτεθεῖεν, οἱ δὲ δικασταὶ τὴν ψῆφον ἀπὸ τοῦ βωμοῦ φέροντες ἐν τῇ πόλει κρίνοιεν. Ἅγνων δὲ τοῦτο μὲν ἀφεῖλε τοῦ ψηφίσματος, κρίνεσθαι δὲ τὴν δίκην ἔγραψεν ἐν δικασταῖς χιλίοις καὶ πεντακοσίοις, εἴτε κλοπῆς καὶ δώρων εἴτ' ἀδικίου βούλοιτό τις ὀνομάζειν τὴν δίωξιν). It is worth noting that both Diodorus 12.38.2-39.3 (Ephorus F 196) and Plutarch *Pericles* 31–32 put Pheidias' trial and Dracontides' Decree at about the same period (i.e. immediately before the war), but do not regard Dracontides' Decree as a consequence of Pheidias' trial.

[16] It has been argued that Diodorus 12.38.2–4 is not Ephoran in origin: see Vogel 1889: 532–539. Vogel's thesis was endorsed (with new arguments) by Busolt 1904:704n2, and by Jacoby 1926a:98–99; Jacoby 1926b:92–93 (*ad* FGH 70 F 196), 335 (*ad* Aristodemus FGH 104 F 1.16). Compare Barber 1935:107–108; Stylianou 1998:50; Hose 2006:678n55. I am persuaded, however, that Diodorus 12.38.2–4 does indeed derive from Ephorus; see Parmeggiani 2011:417–419, with notes.

fellow citizens not to surrender to Sparta's ultimatum (12.39.5–40.6). At the end of this account, as we have seen, the reader encounters the term τινες, and is prompted to wonder whether Ephorus actually said all of this. If so, furthermore, can we assume that he said it in this form?

Scholars of the twentieth century generally agree that Diodorus' account is only an *imperfecta imago* of what Ephorus wrote about the causes of the war. In order to reconstruct what one might call 'Ephorus' version', then, Diodorus' supposed lacunae are often supplemented with information from Plutarch (*Pericles* 31–32), Aristodemus (FGH 104 F 1.16.1–4), and from scholia of late antiquity on the works of Thucydides, Aristophanes, and Hermogenes.[17] These texts, considered together, constitute the so-called 'Ephorus tradition'; here, we find both more detailed information than Diodorus alone provides about the cases of Pericles' associates (Aspasia in particular, notably absent from Diodorus' account), and more extensive quotations from Aristophanes' *Peace* and *Acharnians*.[18]

Nevertheless, when we look for Ephorus in works other than that of Diodorus, a new question arises. In reading Aristodemus, we find not only information about Pericles' private affairs, Pheidias' trial, the Megarian Decree, and extensive quotations from Aristophanes, but also other data, including the affairs of Corcyra and Potidaea and—last but not least—the Thucydidean *alethestate prophasis*, here defined as *aitia alethestate*.[19] Is Ephorus, then, the source only for the causes that implicate Pericles, or for all the causes named by Aristodemus? Is it possible, perhaps, that Ephorus is simultaneously considering different versions of the causes of the war, not in fact neglecting Thucydides' version but—as is evident in Aristodemus' account—redefining it?

---

[17] On these scholia, see especially Connor 1961:1–81.

[18] It will suffice to recall that Aristodemus quotes from *Acharnians* verses 524–534, whereas Diodorus cites only verses 530–531. But note that Diodorus quotes Eupolis' fr. 102 K.A., which Aristodemus does not. As we will see, Eupolis' fr. 102 K.A. was in Ephorus' original account.

[19] More specifically, in reading Aristodemus, we are dealing with consistent aetiological material organized into four different sets of causes: 1) chapter 16 includes the narrative about Pericles, his intention to go to war because of Pheidias' trial, and his proposal of the Megarian Decree (paragraph 1). This information is complemented by extensive quotations from Aristophanes' *Peace* and *Acharnians* (paragraphs 2–3), and by an anecdote (paragraph 4: Alcibiades suggests to Pericles that he find a way to not give any financial account to the *demos*. This version is shorter than that of Diodorus [12.38.3–4]); 2) chapter 17 presents the affairs of Corcyra; 3) chapter 18 presents the affairs of Potidaea; 4) chapter 19 includes what seems very likely to be an abridged version of the Thucydidean *alethestate prophasis* but with a notable shift in perspective: in Thucydides' *alethestate prophasis* the Athenian *auxesis* compels Sparta to *phobos*, and the combination of *auxesis* and *phobos* compels, by necessity, the two city-states to war; in Aristodemus' *aitia alethestate*, the initiative comes clearly from Sparta reaction to the Athenian *auxesis*, whose features are expressly defined (i.e. "increasing number of boats, money, allies . . ."); the text ends here.

This solution actually has a longer history than might appear at first sight. Meier Marx, the very first editor of Ephorus' fragments in 1815, conjectured that Ephorus might very well have included in his history as a vulgate tradition the information about Pericles' personal affairs that we find in Diodorus.[20] Eduard Schwartz suspected that Diodorus rearranged various tales that Ephorus had collected.[21] Robert Connor's idea was in some way similar: Ephorus, in a Herodotean manner, might have collected different versions of the origins of the war, without necessarily preferring one over the others.[22] If this were true, Ephorus would approximate the author about whom Jacoby had dreamt, a historian who could present his reader with a complete aetiological picture of the problems connected with the origins of the Peloponnesian War.[23]

But before we draw any conclusions from Aristodemus' text alone, we need to take a closer look at Diodorus' account (F 196), for it is the only one in which the name of Ephorus is expressly mentioned. As we shall see, it seems possible to reach, through Diodorus, a different conclusion about Ephorus' view of the causes of the Peloponnesian War.

The quotations from the comic poets appear only at the end of the fragment, immediately before the concluding mention of Ephorus. Here we find, together with the two quotations from Aristophanes (*Peace* 603-606, 609-611 and *Acharnians* 530-531), a quotation from Eupolis' *Demoi* (fr. 102 K.A.). This quotation does not concern Pericles' personal affairs, Aspasia, Anaxagoras, Pheidias, or the Megarian Decree, but rather his rhetorical ability:

> "One might say Persuasion rested on his [Pericles'] lips; such charm he'd bring, and alone of all the speakers in his list'ners left his sting." (Translation by C. H. Oldfather)

> Eupolis *Demoi* fr. 102 K.A. (Diodorus 12.40.6)

---

[20] Marx 1815:231, *ad* fr. 119 (= F 196): "Sed Ephori nostri ut vindicemus integritatem et probitatem, nihil fere restat, nisi ut plures, quarum notitiam acceperit, belli caussas ab eo, ut historico, proditas fuisse statuamus, deteriorem vero a Diodoro, non acerrimi iudicii homine, electam." Note Marx's remark on Diodorus' uninspired selection of Ephoran materials. Marx's apology of Ephorus did not win the approval of many nineteenth-century critics (see Müller 1841:lxiiib; Stelkens 1857:25n1; Klügmann 1860:29n3; Endemann 1881:9n5; *pro*-Marx's thesis Vogel 1889:538).

[21] Schwartz 1903:680.

[22] Connor 1961:76-78.

[23] Schepens 2007:88-90, with n75, has recently argued that Aristodemus' sets of causes of the Peloponnesian War (FGH 104 F 1.16-19) reflect Ephorus' original account: Ephorus, on this model, would have classified four causes in order of growing importance, from the first and least important, namely Pericles' private affairs (chapter 16), to the fourth and most important one, that is, Spartan *phobos* of the Athenian *auxesis* (chapter 19).

In editing F 196, Jacoby chose to expunge the Eupolis quotation, believing it to be irrelevant to the problem of the causes of the war.[24] Even if this were the case, it is not reason enough to reject it: we cannot ignore that it is in Diodorus' text, that it appears immediately before Ephorus' name, and finally, that it is not the only instance in the fragment that emphasizes Pericles' rhetorical ability.[25] Given that this quotation could be part of Ephorus' original account of the causes, it would be better to take it into careful consideration.

At first sight, it would seem that by quoting all the poetic evidence at the end of his account, Diodorus gathered together miscellaneous information, thereby confusing the evidence that Ephorus had originally organized in an ordered manner. But things are probably otherwise. The three quotations from ancient comedy are introduced in this way:

> Having said all of this and having urged his fellow citizens to war, Pericles persuaded [ἔπεισε] the *demos* not to submit to the Lacedaemonians. This he easily accomplished through the effectiveness of his words [ταῦτα δὲ ῥᾳδίως συνετέλεσε διὰ τὴν δεινότητα τοῦ λόγου], for which he had the nickname of 'Olympios'. (My translation)
>
> Diodorus 12.40.5

As we can see, the quotations from ancient comedy are introduced collectively with a formula that once again underscores Pericles' rhetorical strength.

The mention of Pheidias' trial and the Megarian Decree in the verses of Aristophanes' *Peace* quoted by Diodorus (verses 603–606, 609–611) obviously draws attention to the fact that, for Ephorus, Aristophanes was a primary source of information regarding Pericles' private affairs.[26] But the short quotation from the *Acharnians* (verses 530–531), with its link to Eupolis' *Demoi*, also clearly comments on the rhetorical power of Pericles *Olympios*.[27] We should

---

[24] See Jacoby 1926a:101; Jacoby 1926b:95, *ad* FGH 70 F 196.

[25] Pericles' rhetorical ability is a leitmotif in F 196 (see Diodorus 12.38.2, 39.5, 40.5, and also *infra*).

[26] Although he was not the only one. It must be stressed that Ephorus could not derive all the details we read in Diodorus 12.38.2–39.3, about Pericles' private affairs and the trials of his associates, from ancient comedy's vague allusions. Furthermore, it is highly probable that Ephorus in fact diverged from Aristophanes on important issues. See below, text and n28.

[27] The two quotations appear together under the name of Eupolis alone (Diodorus 12.40.5). Diodoran manuscripts read: καὶ πάλιν ἐν ἄλλοις Εὔπολις ὁ ποιητής Περικλέης οὐλύμπιος ἤστραπτεν, ἐβρόντα, συνεκύκα τὴν Ἑλλάδα. Πειθώ τις ἐπεκάθιζεν ἐπὶ τοῖς χείλεσιν· οὕτως ἐκήλει καὶ μόνος τῶν ῥητόρων τὸ κέντρον ἐγκατέλειπε τοῖς ἀκρωμένοις. Is this an error only in Ephorus' manuscripts from the first century BCE (compare Cicero *ad Atticum* 12.6a.1 and *Orator* 29, where Aristophanes *Acharnians*, verses 530–531, are attributed to Eupolis)? See Vogel 1889:533n1; Schwartz 1907:14; Mesturini 1983. The possibility exists that Ephorus intentionally intertwined Aristophanes' and Eupolis' verses in order to describe Pericles as a formidable demagogue, a speaking Zeus among orators.

therefore conclude that Ephorus' primary concern was not to quote the comic poets merely to substantiate the veracity of what had been said about Pericles' personal responsibilities but, rather, to demonstrate that Pericles' responsibility was publicly debated by his contemporaries and that the effectiveness of Pericles' rhetorical strength, which was recognized by his contemporaries, was a decisive factor in initiating the war.

Pericles' rhetorical strength was surely central to Ephorus' view of the causes of the Peloponnesian War. We infer this not from Aristodemus or from other texts of the 'Ephorus tradition' but, again, from Diodorus. In the section of F 196 that precedes Aristophanes' and Eupolis' quotations, Diodorus relates—extensively and in indirect form—Pericles' oration on the advantages of not abrogating the Megarian Decree (12.39.5–40.5). What interests us here is not the content of the oration itself but the way in which the oration is first introduced, after a brief allusion to Sparta's ultimatum to Athens:

> At the meeting of the assembly to discuss such matters [the Megarian Decree and the ultimatum from Sparta] Pericles, by far the most eloquent of all the citizens [δεινότητι λόγου πολὺ διαφέρων ἀπάντων τῶν πολιτῶν], persuaded [ἔπεισε] the Athenians not to abrogate the decree, saying that ... (My translation)

> Diodorus 12.39.5

We have to link this *incipit* (12.39.5) to the *explicit* (12.40.5), which—as we have just seen—introduces the quotations from ancient comedy. The entire passage reads as follows:

> At the meeting of the assembly to discuss such matters Pericles, by far the most eloquent of all the citizens, persuaded the Athenians not to abrogate the decree, saying that [the content of Pericles' oration follows]... Having said all this, and having urged his fellow citizens to war, Pericles persuaded the *demos* not to submit to the Lacedaemonians. This he easily obtained by the effectiveness of his words, for which he had the nickname of 'Olympios' [Aristophanes' and Eupolis' quotations follow]. (My translation)

> Diodorus 12.39.5–40.5

This 'ring composition' emphasizes the underlying message: Pericles wanted the war, and he succeeded in pursuing it largely because of the rhetorical prowess that he exercised over the masses. Since Ephorus is mentioned at the end of

Diodorus' account, we must conclude that Pericles's rhetorical effectiveness was a major point in Ephorus' original view.

Obviously, Pericles would have had no opportunity to realize his plan had there not been an ultimatum from Sparta and, consequently, a public debate on the Megarian Decree. This consideration leads us to understand a second underlying message: Pericles wanted the war, and he succeeded in pursuing it because of pre-existing tension between Athens and Sparta.

From this second point a new question arises: did Ephorus, as Aristophanes before him (*Peace*, verses 603–611), think that Pericles proposed the Megarian Decree with the aim of provoking the war and thereby escaping the current attacks on his associate Pheidias and on himself? That is to say, did Ephorus describe the tension between Athens and Sparta as depending exclusively upon Pericles' will to defend himself from the Pheidias affair? I would like to make two observations to address these questions. First, according to Aristodemus' version (FGH 104 F 1.16.1), Pericles proposed the Megarian Decree with the aim of causing the war, thus saving himself from the Pheidias scandal in Athens. But this is not what Diodorus, citing Ephorus, claims. It is worth noting that Diodorus does not connect Pericles' private affairs (12.38.2–39.3) with the Megarian Decree (12.39.4). After describing Pheidias' and Anaxagoras' trials and recalling Pericles' intention to promote the war, Diodorus notes:

> Because there was a decree passed by the Athenians [ὄντος δὲ ψηφίσματος παρὰ τοῖς Ἀθηναίοις], by which the Megarians were prevented from accessing the agora and the harbours... (My translation)

> Diodorus 12.39.4

If Ephorus, on the basis of Aristophanes' *Peace*, had emphasized the Periclean authorship of the Megarian Decree as an intentional weapon for provoking the war, we would expect Diodorus' text to read somewhat differently. Ephorus may in fact have corrected Aristophanes' view: Pericles proposed the Megarian Decree and this action was surely a decisive step toward war, but he did not intend to solve, by way of this decree, his personal troubles.[28] My second observation is that Sparta's ultimatum, as it is represented by Diodorus (12.39.4), seems to be such an aggressive measure against Athens that it is inexplicable as a simple reply to the Megarian Decree. It is clear that Ephorus said much

---

[28] Diodorus' text suggests that Ephorus had a careful approach to the information provided by ancient comedy. It is worth stressing that, while Aristophanes regards Pheidias as guilty of misappropriation of public funds (*Peace* 605: πράξας κακῶς), Ephorus regards him as a victim of a scheme devised by Pericles' opponents (see Diodorus 12.39.1–2; cf. Plutarch *Pericles* 31.2). This is indeed another difference—and not a minor one—between the versions of Aristophanes and Ephorus.

more than what Diodorus tells us about the increasing political tension between Athens and Sparta. We must conclude, therefore, that Ephorus did not link this tension exclusively to Pericles' intention to defend himself from the Pheidias affair but that he took into consideration broader political circumstances, which Diodorus does not choose to include.[29]

Although an *imperfecta imago* and far from complete, Diodorus' account does allow us to observe a coherence in Ephorus' original vision. We have thus far distinguished two different aetiological streams: one concerning Pericles' political situation at Athens, the other the official relationship between Athens and Sparta in the years before the war. Briefly put, the Peloponnesian War was, on the one hand, provoked by Pericles' resolution to put an end to personal attacks on himself and his associates through war and to hamper a public inquiry into his financial administration, and, on the other hand, by a pre-existing tension between Athens and Sparta.

The debate on the Megarian Decree that had been going on in Athens since Sparta's ultimatum clearly marks the confluence of these two streams; at this convergence, the war was decided, and it was decided by rhetoric. Curiously enough, Ephorus—the historian who has been universally credited as having made History the servant of Rhetoric—gives us one of the clearest statements in historiography on the dramatic damages that can result when rhetorical persuasiveness and demagogy enter into politics. It will suffice to recall Ephorus F 207 on Lysander's revolutionary *logos*, περὶ τῆς πολιτείας, which was "written," as we read in the fragment, "in so persuasive a way."[30] From this fragment we understand that Ephorus' interest in demagogy and rhetorical persuasiveness was not circumstantial but rather essential to his approach to the internal dynamics of the Greek states.

I think that we have come a long way from traditional views about Ephorus. We understand that Ephorus not only sheds light on Pericles' responsibilities for the war by pointing out the problematic impact of demagogy on internal politics, but also that he did not ignore the political situation outside Athens, the aetiological stream in Ephorus' original account that Diodorus chose not to develop. Furthermore, Ephorus' use of information drawn from ancient comedy was subtler than it is usually considered to be.[31] Ephorus did not employ

---

[29] In Ephorus' view the cases of international politics after 460 BCE were aetiologically decisive. Diodorus, on the other hand, doesn't care for them; for he wants to show the differences between Ephorus and Thucydides, he only emphasizes Pericles' private affairs. See Parmeggiani 2011:354.

[30] Plutarch *Lysander* 30.5.

[31] See also above, 125 and n28.

Aristophanes' and Eupolis' texts as *pisteis* in the strict sense of the word.[32] Comic poets witnessed both the political debate on the responsibilities of the war and Pericles' rhetorical strength; as witnesses they recorded instances that a scrupulous historian should never ignore,[33] in part because Pericles' contribution to the Athenian debate on the Megarian Decree was deemed by almost every historian (Thucydides included) to have been decisive for the war.

Ephorus did not express the same view as Thucydides about the Peloponnesian War; contrary to Thucydides, he believed that the war could have been avoided, and he investigated the issue of Pericles' responsibility for the war, his desire for war for personal reasons, and his success through rhetoric and demagogy. Furthermore, Ephorus showed how all these instances worked in the context of the growing political tension between Athens and Sparta. But we can go even further and note, thanks again to Diodorus' account, that Ephorus began his analysis of Pericles' situation by focusing on neither polemical passages in the comic poetic tradition nor the aggressive speculations of pamphlets, but rather on an historical event that is not reported by Thucydides in his *Pentecontaetia* (1.89–117), namely the transfer of the Delian League's treasure from Delos to Athens in the mid-fifth century. Scholars regard this event as one of the key moments of fifth-century Greek history. The passage reads:

> The Athenians, being fond of hegemony on the sea [τῆς κατὰ θάλατταν ἡγεμονίας ἀντεχόμενοι], transferred the common treasure from Delos—ca. 8,000 talents—to Athens and gave it to Pericles to administer. He [Pericles] was by far the first citizen, for his nobility, prestige, and rhetorical effectiveness [λόγου δεινότητι]. (My translation)

> Diodorus 12.38.2

The presence of this last detail no longer takes us by surprise. All the facts concerning Pericles that we find described later in the fragment (i.e. his financial administration, the trials of his associates, and his oration at the debate on the Megarian Decree) derive from this piece of information, which marks the beginning of the entire aetiological report on the origins of the war. Ephorus seems to find the roots of the Peloponnesian War in this historical context. The Athenians' attitude to thalassocracy looks like an 'original sin', in which all the citizens of Athens, including Pericles, shared responsibility. The difficult

---

[32] The verb διαπιστοῦται in Aristodemus (FGH 104 F 1.16.2) is misleading, and may reflect an oversimplification of Ephorus' original setting.

[33] See, for example, Diodorus 12.40.6: μέμνηται δὲ τούτων καὶ Ἀριστοφάνης . . . γεγονὼς κατὰ τὴν τοῦ Περικλέους ἡλικίαν, "Mention has been made of this even by Aristophanes. . ., who lived in the period of Pericles." (Translation by C. H. Oldfather)

situation in which Pericles was to be involved, after some years of autocratic and certainly flawed financial politics, was intriguing to Ephorus not because of his hunger for scandals. On the contrary, Ephorus was keenly aware that the Athenians' original ambitions for thalassocracy would and did have a negative impact on the politics of the Delian League. This view is deeply historical and has nothing to do with the supposed fiction or exaggerations on the part of the Athenian comedy or the pamphletistic tradition. Here we touch upon a historical situation to which Ephorus was quite sensitive, and in which he contextualized Pericles' affairs—quite a different circumstance from what we see in comedy or pamphlets.

In the *Life of Pericles* 12, Plutarch tells us that opponents of the oligarchic party often attacked Pericles at the assembly for his building projects on the Acropolis. They claimed that funds for this work came from the Delian treasure and that the projects themselves were too expensive. Pericles' use of the Delian League's treasure caused disaffection and open complaint from Athens' allies. In F 196, in his oration delivered during the Megarian Decree debate, Pericles alludes to Athena's statue and the expenses accrued from building the Propylaia and from the siege of Potidaea (40.2). His fiscal policy was a reality that Ephorus described more accurately and with more detail than Diodorus.[34] Pericles, then, was not only the object of Ephorus' observations, but also the means by which he explored the nature and the shortcoming of Athenian rule in the fifth century BCE. We should also note that the defects of Athenian imperialistic politics were another reason for the auto-critical meditation on the past by intellectuals in fourth-century Athens, and Ephorus worked in this specific context.[35]

I would like to conclude with a passage from Plutarch's *Life of Pericles*, which seems to me to retain the principal features of Ephorus' view of the causes of the Peloponnesian War. At 32.6 we find a curious new version of the metaphor of the fire employed by Aristophanes in his *Peace* 608–611:

ὡς δὲ διὰ Φειδίου προσέπταισε τῷ δήμῳ, φοβηθεὶς τὸ δικαστήριον μέλλοντα τὸν πόλεμον καὶ ὑποτυφόμενον ἐξέκαυσεν, ἐλπίζων διασκεδάσειν τὰ ἐγκλήματα καὶ ταπεινώσειν τὸν φθόνον, ἐν πράγμασι μεγάλοις καὶ κινδύνοις τῆς πόλεως ἐκείνῳ μόνῳ διὰ τὸ ἀξίωμα καὶ τὴν δύναμιν ἀναθείσης ἑαυτήν.[36]

---

[34] Compare 12.38.2, where Diodorus clearly condenses Ephorus' observations on the waste of public money on a personal initiative. That Ephorus analyzed Pericles' expensive fiscal policy in detail is also suggested by F 193.

[35] This self-criticism occurred especially during the years of the Social War (357–355 BCE).

[36] Note the similarities between our passage and Diodorus 12.39.3 (Ephorus F 196): ὁ δὲ Περικλῆς, εἰδὼς τὸν δῆμον ἐν μὲν τοῖς πολεμικοῖς ἔργοις θαυμάζοντα τοὺς ἀγαθοὺς ἄνδρας διὰ τὰς κατεπειγούσας χρείας, κατὰ δὲ τὴν εἰρήνην τοὺς αὐτοὺς συκοφαντοῦντα διὰ τὴν σχολὴν καὶ

And since in the case of Pheidias he had come into collision with the people, he feared a jury in his own case, and so kindled into flame the threatening and smouldering war, hoping thereby to dissipate the charges made against him and allay the people's jealousy, inasmuch as when great undertakings were on foot, and great perils threatened, the city entrusted herself to him and to him alone, by reason of his worth and power. (Translation by B. Perrin)

Plutarch *Pericles* 32.6

Whereas in Aristophanes' version, Pericles stirs up the fire of the war with the Megarian Decree (ἐξέφλεξε τὴν πόλιν / ἐμβαλὼν σπινθῆρα μικρὸν Μεγαρικοῦ ψηφίσματος· / κἀξεφύσησεν τοσοῦτον πόλεμον ὥστε τῷ καπνῷ / πάντας Ἕλληνας δακρῦσαι, τούς τ' ἐκεῖ τούς τ' ἐνθάδε, "he threw out that little spark, the Megarian Decree, set the city aflame, and blew up the conflagration with a hurricane of war, so that the smoke drew tears from all Greeks both here and over there." Translation by E. O'Neill Jr.), in Plutarch's narrative, Pericles is blowing on a fire already kindled (μέλλοντα τὸν πόλεμον καὶ ὑποτυφόμενον ἐξέκαυσεν, "he kindled into flame the threatening and smouldering war"). There is a slight difference between the two texts, and I am inclined to think that Plutarch's version reflects an important aspect of Ephorus' view. Pericles took advantage, for his own good, of pre-existing international tensions that would eventually lead to war regardless of Pheidias' trial and Pericles' own difficulties in Athens. The tragedy of the man who choses to save himself rather than his fellow citizens[37] was not disconnected from another great tragedy, that of the two leading cities of the Greek world on the brink of war. The picture we have, then, is perfectly congruent with the two aetiological streams that we have indentified in studying Ephorus F 196.

Plutarch's passage confirms our impression that Ephorus did not quote Aristophanes as an authority to be blindly followed. Ephorus felt free to craft new historical concepts by drawing on comedy's most evocative images. In Thucydides' view, if there had been no Corcyra or Potidaea, we would not have had the Peloponnesian War in 431 BCE. In Ephorus' view, if Pericles had not resolved to uphold the Megarian Decree, there would have been no war in 431 BCE. At that time, war was still avoidable, but it was only a matter of time before

---

φθόνον, ἔκρινε συμφέρειν αὑτῷ τὴν πόλιν ἐμβαλεῖν εἰς μέγαν πόλεμον, ὅπως χρείαν ἔχουσα τῆς Περικλέους ἀρετῆς καὶ στρατηγίας μὴ προσδέχηται τὰς κατ' αὐτοῦ διαβολάς, μηδ' ἔχῃ σχολὴν καὶ χρόνον ἐξετάζειν ἀκριβῶς τὸν περὶ τῶν χρημάτων λόγον. This too reveals the Ephoran origin of Plutarch *Pericles* 32.6.

37 See Diodorus 12.39.3 (F 196): ἔκρινε [Pericles] συμφέρειν αὑτῷ τὴν πόλιν ἐμβαλεῖν εἰς μέγαν πόλεμον.

tensions broke out between Sparta and Athens. Among the culprits behind the war of 431 BCE, Pericles was certainly predominant. But Sparta and Athens were both responsible for bad choices that they had previously made, when each willingly pursued political hegemony; their choices were going to be decisive. We can surmise from the reference in F 196 to the removal of the Delian League's treasure that Ephorus considered the collapse of the Panhellenic alliance between Athens and Sparta (ca. 462 BCE) to have been a negative turning point in the fifth century.[38]

Far from being a corrupter of the science of history, Ephorus of Cyme proves to be a very competent historian in matters of aetiology. Looking backward from the fourth century BCE, he did not believe the war of 431 was inevitable; he believed, like many modern historians, that Thucydides' thesis of *ananke* was unconvincing. When addressing the much-debated question of the causes of the Peloponnesian War, he chose to consider data that Thucydides had neglected. In so doing, Ephorus conformed to the fundamental methodological principle that he had proposed for his own research (διακριβοῦν εἰώθαμεν, ὅταν ἦι τι τῶν πραγμάτων ἢ παντελῶς ἀπορούμενον ἢ ψευδῆ δόξαν ἔχον, "I am accustomed to examine such matters as these with precision, whenever any matter is either altogether doubtful or falsely interpreted." Translation by H. L. Jones, modified).[39] Finally, he succeeded in forwarding a new aetiological scheme, which was wide and complete in all respects (he devoted attention to such matters as Athenian internal dynamics, the politics of the Delian League, and the relationship between Sparta and Athens, approaching them as reciprocally interwoven problems), and in fact more satisfying than the one Thucydides provided. A careful analysis of Ephorus' F 196 uncovers broader and more balanced insights into the origins of the Peloponnesian War and helps us see how, contrary to the *communis opinio*, fourth-century historiography is closer to the best examples of modern inquiry, both in its aetiological sensibility and its historical perspective.

Bibliography

Badian, E. 1993. *From Plataea to Potidaea. Studies in the History and Historiography of the Pentecontaetia.* Baltimore.

Banfi, A. 2003. *Il governo della città. Pericle nel pensiero antico.* Naples.

Barber, G. L. 1935. *The Historian Ephorus.* Cambridge.

Beloch, K. J. 1914. *Griechische Geschichte* II 1. Strasbourg.

---

[38] Compare Diodorus 11.64.3; Justin 3.6.1–4; see also Parmeggiani 2011:450-458. It is significant that, in Ephorus' view, the transfer of the public money from Delos to Athens dates back to this very period (see Robertson 1980:113–114), as does Cimon's ostracism.

[39] F 122 a.

Blass, F. 1892. *Die attische Beredsamkeit* II. Second edition. Leipzig.

Busolt, G. 1904. *Griechische Geschichte bis zur Schlacht bei Chaeroneia* III 2. Gotha.

Cauer, E. 1847. *Quaestionum de fontibus ad Agesilai historiam pertinentibus pars prior.* Vratislaviae.

Connor, W. R. 1961. *Studies in Ephoros and Other Sources for the Cause of the Peloponnesian War.* PhD diss., Princeton.

Creuzer, F. 1845. *Die historische Kunst der Griechen in ihrer Entstehung und Fortbildung.* Second edition. Leipzig.

Dover, K. J. 1988. "Anecdotes, Gossip and Scandal." In *The Greeks and Their Legacy. Collected Papers*, Vol. 2, 45–52. Oxford.

Endemann, K. 1881. *Beiträge zur Kritik des Ephorus.* Diss., Marburg.

Giuliani, A. 1999. "Riflessi storiografici dell'opposizione a Pericle allo scoppio della guerra del Peloponneso." In *Fazioni e congiure nel mondo antico,* ed. M. Sordi, 23–40. Contributi dell'Istituto di storia antica 25. Milan.

Gomme, A. W. 1956a. *A Historical Commentary on Thucydides* I. Oxford.

———. 1956b. *A Historical Commentary on Thucydides* II. Oxford.

Hornblower, S. 2003. *A Commentary on Thucydides* I. Oxford.

Hose, M. 2006. "The Peloponnesian War: Sources Other than Thucydides." In *Brill's Companion to Thucydides,* ed. A. Rengakos and A. Tsakmakis, 669–690. Leiden.

Jacoby, F. 1926a. *Die Fragmente der griechischen Historiker. Zweiter Teil: Zeitgeschichte. A. Universalgeschichte und Hellenika. Nr. 64–105.* Berlin.

———. 1926b. *Die Fragmente der griechischen Historiker. Zweiter Teil: Zeitgeschichte. C. Kommentar zu Nr. 64–105.* Berlin.

———. 1954. *Die Fragmente der griechischen Historiker. Dritter Teil: Geschichte von Städten und Völkern (Horographie und Ethnographie). b Supplement. A Commentary on the Ancient Historians of Athens (Nos. 323a–334). I. Text.* Leiden.

Kagan, D. 1969. *The Outbreak of the Peloponnesian War.* Ithaca.

Klügmann, J. A. 1860. *De Ephoro historico graeco.* Diss., Göttingen.

Marx, M. 1815. *Ephori Cumaei fragmenta.* Caroliruhae.

Matthiessen, C. 1857-1860. "Ein Beitrag zur Würdigung des Ephoros." *Jahrbücher für classische Philologie,* Suppl. III:875–894.

Mesturini, A. M. 1983. "Aristofane—Eupoli e Diodoro. A proposito di una citazione ciceroniana." *Maia* 35:195–204.

Meyer, E. 1899. *Forschungen zur alten Geschichte* II. Halle.

Momigliano, A. 1975. "La Storia di Eforo e le Elleniche di Teopompo." In *Quinto Contributo alla storia degli studi classici e del mondo antico* II, 683–706. Rome. (= *Rivista di filologia e di istruzione classica* 13:180–204 [1935].)

Müller, K. 1841. *Fragmenta historicorum graecorum* I. Paris.

Parmeggiani, G. 2011. *Eforo di Cuma. Studi di storiografia greca.* Bologna.

Giovanni Parmeggiani

Peter, H. 1911. *Wahrheit und Kunst. Geschichtschreibung und Plagiat in klassischen Altertum.* Leipzig.

Podlecki, A. J. 1998. *Perikles and His Circle.* London.

Pownall, F. 2004. *Lessons from the Past. The Moral Use of History in Fourth-Century Prose.* Ann Arbor.

Robertson, N. D. 1980. "The True Nature of the 'Delian League', 478-461 B.C." *American Journal of Ancient History* 5:64–96, 110–133.

Rood, T. 1998. *Thucydides. Narrative and Explanation.* Oxford.

Schepens, G. 2007. "Tucidide 'in controluce'. La guerra del Peloponneso nella storiografia greca del quarto secolo a.C." In *Il dopoguerra nel mondo greco. Politica, propaganda, storiografia,* ed. L. Santi Amantini, 57–99. Rome.

Schwartz, E. 1903. "Diodoros (38)." *RE* V 1:663–704.

———. 1907. "Ephoros (1)." *RE* VI 1:1–16.

———. 1919. *Das Geschichtswerk des Thukydides.* Bonn.

Ste. Croix, G. E. M. de. 1972. *The Origins of the Peloponnesian War.* Ithaca.

Stelkens, A. 1857. *De Ephori Cumaei fide atque auctoritate.* Diss., Monasterii.

Stylianou, P. J. 1998. *A Historical Commentary on Diodorus Siculus, Book 15.* Oxford.

Vogel, F. 1889. "Ephorus und Diodor über den Ausbruch des peloponnesischen Krieges." *Rheinisches Museum für Philologie* 44:532–539.

7

Ephorus in Context

The Return of the Heraclidae and Fourth-century Peloponnesian Politics[1]

Nino Luraghi

IN A FAMOUS PASSAGE at the beginning of Book 4, Diodorus discusses the difficulties facing the historian who wants to include in his work what Diodorus himself calls "the ancient *mythologiai*," i.e. the deeds of demigods, heroes, and great men of the most distant past. First of all, he says, there is no way of reconstructing a precise and reliable chronology. Second, the multitude of characters in action makes the narrative difficult to follow. Finally, there is the problem of inconsistencies among different mythic narratives. However, convinced that the deeds of these primordial figures are too important to be left aside, Diodorus decided to include them in his work, whatever the obstacles. His choice is all the bolder since, as he says, the most reputed among his predecessors had chosen to steer clear of the troubled waters of myth.[2] The first example of this omission that Diodorus brings up is his most important model, Ephorus of Cymae, who, according to Diodorus, left aside the old *mythologiai* and started his narrative with the return of the Heraclidae to the Peloponnesus. Ever since Jacoby, if not before, scholars have taken this passage as a reflection of Ephorus' ideas about the difficulty of reconstructing the past in an accurate and reliable way. Accordingly, it is generally assumed that Ephorus took the return of the Heraclidae as the upper boundary of the *spatium historicum*, a position that is compared to Herodotus' and Thucydides' views and interpreted in the

---

[1]   The present contribution was presented originally at the Harvard Workshop in 2006. The author wishes to thank warmly John Marincola for reading and commenting upon the final version (and for many years of scholarly friendship).

[2]   Diodorus 4.1.2–3. On this passage, and more generally on Diodorus' inclusion of myth within the scope of his work, see Marincola 1997:119–121.

framework of the separation of myth and history in Greek historiography.[3] More rarely Ephorus' choice of a starting point is seen as a skeptical reaction to the works of other fourth-century historians, such as Anaximenes of Lampsacus, who apparently went all the way back to the birth of the gods.[4]

The present paper will propose a different perspective on this passage. It will suggest that the exclusive emphasis on the return of the Heraclidae as a threshold of historical memory is not entirely justified by what we know about Ephorus' work. Judging by the evidence of the fragments, Ephorus may not have drawn as solid a line between *spatium mythicum* and *spatium historicum* as scholars have sometimes thought. On the other hand, the insistence on the return of the Heraclidae as a purely chronological threshold has diverted scholarly attention from other possible ways of understanding this aspect of Ephorus' work. Accordingly, it will be suggested that Ephorus' decision to begin the first book of his *Histories* with the return of the Heraclidae to the Peloponnesus is probably best understood in relation to its historical context, in particular to the extraordinary relevance assumed by the return of the Heraclidae in fourth-century Peloponnesian politics. The first point will be addressed rather briefly, building mostly upon a famous article by Guido Schepens and a more recent one by Giovanni Parmeggiani.[5] As for the main point, viz. the significance of the return of the Heraclidae in Ephorus' cultural and political world, a satisfactory discussion will require some more detail.

To begin with, however, it should be pointed out that the passage in which Diodorus refers to Ephorus' starting point objectively lends itself to the traditional interpretation.[6] Diodorus is indeed discussing here what we would call the extension of the *spatium historicum* and construing the return of the Heraclidae as the temporal threshold of Ephorus' *Histories*. However, we should be wary of taking for granted the fact that this passage accurately reflects Ephorus' own discussion of the upper chronological limit of history. Scholars have often assumed, explicitly or not, that the difficulties facing the historian who wants to include the old *mythologiai*, as outlined by Diodorus, actually go back to a discussion to the same effect in the proem of Ephorus' Book 1, with the difference

---

[3]   See e.g. Canfora 1999:26–41, Clarke 2008:99, and further bibliography in Parmeggiani 1999:109n7. According to the authoritative view of Jacoby 1926:25, Ephorus' choice of starting point is "not a consequence of Thucydides' criticism of the quality of older tradition but rather corresponds to the distinction, which was meanwhile generally accepted and had been already used in historiography by Herodotus, between a 'human' and a 'heroic' age of Greek history." Cf. the criticism of Schepens 1977:107n69. On Herodotus 3.122 as the first definition of the *spatium historicum*, see also Jacoby 1956:37–38 and n63. For a classic discussion of this concept, see von Leyden 1950.
[4]   See Schepens and Bollansée 2004:62–63 and Anaximenes FGH 72 T 14.
[5]   Respectively, Schepens 1977 and Parmeggiani 1999.
[6]   Parmeggiani 1999:109–110.

that Diodorus shows himself undaunted by the obstacles that had convinced Ephorus to leave out of the scope of his work that most distant portion of the past. And yet, in the same passage, Diodorus' off-hand reference to Callisthenes and Theopompus, two historians who are not known to have dealt with the distant past very much at all, should suggest caution. It should not be forgotten that what Diodorus is here really defining—and praising—is his own choice to include the tales of heroes and demigods in a work of history. In other words, the polemical tone of the passage recommends circumspection when drawing inferences. With his reference to Ephorus, Diodorus may well be pointing to a much simpler fact, namely, that the starting point of Ephorus' Book 1 was the return of the Heraclidae, which is not the same as saying that for Ephorus the return represented the upper chronological limit of a reliable historical narrative—far from it.[7]

Here, comparison especially with Thucydides' discussion of the possibility of reconstructing the past in a trustworthy way has impaired rather than aided interpretation of the passage, suggesting to scholars that the choice of the return of the Heraclidae as a starting point was the product of Ephorus' engaging in the same sort of argument, albeit rather more crudely and with different conclusions.[8] Now, it is certainly the case that, not unlike his predecessors Herodotus and Thucydides, Ephorus was alert to the difficulties of gaining reliable knowledge of the past. In a famous passage quoted in the *Lexicon of the Ten Orators*, which goes under the name of Harpocration, he expressed skepticism for detailed reports of events that were very far back in time. However, like his predecessors he seems to have thought in terms of greater or lesser reliability of stories and pieces of information regarding the distant past, not in terms of a sharp distinction between a mythic and a historical space.[9]

This point may be reinforced *e contrario* by pointing to the fact that Ephorus did indeed on occasion venture beyond the supposed threshold represented by the return of the Heraclidae. Quite apart from the fact that Book 1 clearly also

---

[7]   In any case, to say that for Ephorus the return of the Heraclidae was "the earliest securely datable historical event after the Sack of Troy" (Schepens and Bollansée 2004:61) is probably imprudent, since after all, Diodorus (16.76.5 = Ephorus FGH 70 T 10) says *almost* 750 years. Note the caution of Jacoby (1926:61), who points out that the exact year, 1069/8 BCE, was in all likelihood (actually, Jacoby has no doubt about this) calculated by later authors, while Ephorus gave only a number of generations, or a round number of years based on a calculation of generations; along the same lines is Laqueur 1911:324.

[8]   Almost inevitably, the comparison leads to the conclusion that Ephorus misunderstood Thucydides' methodological concerns; see Canfora 1999:28–29. Cf., however, Jacoby's view, above n2. This is not to deny the deep impact of Thucydides' *archaiologia* on later Greek historical thought, well outlined by Canfora 1999:30–38.

[9]   Ephorus FGH 70 F 9. See especially Schepens 1977:106–110; this is the main line of argument of Parmeggiani 1999.

included the prehistory, as it were, of the return, Schepens pointed to a number of fragments that deal with the time of the gods and heroes, and more recently Parmeggiani has drawn attention to the fact that, even there, Ephorus does not seem to have surrendered his critical attitude and renounced the possibility of distinguishing fact from fiction.[10] As an example, he discusses the famous passage on Apollo and the origins of the Delphic oracle, for which Ephorus was severely chastised by Strabo.[11] Like Diodorus, Strabo takes for granted a rigid divide between myth and history, which he accuses Ephorus of blurring. One of the points Strabo criticizes is the transformation of mythic creatures into human beings, a rationalization of myth that reminds one very much of Hecataeus and is typical of early Greek historiography. Of course, we would like to be able to appreciate more fully Ephorus' arguments and to understand how exactly he thought it possible to define in terms of truth or falsehood a narrative about the time of the gods: did he just get rid of the most obviously fantastic aspects? It would be particularly interesting to know what kind of evidence he accepted as reliable, when dealing with such early periods.[12]

The more we abandon the assumption that Diodorus' discussion of the difficulties of dealing with ancient *mythologiai* derives from Ephorus, the more his references to the return of the Heraclidae as the starting point of Ephorus' work[13] begin to resemble a kind of passage frequently met in Diodorus and in other authors, namely indications of the starting- and endpoints of previous historical works. In other words, these references to Ephorus may not be all that different from those devoted to Thucydides, whose work Diodorus says began with the year 432—not with the *archaiologia*, of course—or to Herodotus, whose *Histories* are said to start from the time before the Trojan War.[14] Similarly, Dionysius of Halicarnassus thought that Herodotus' work started with the beginning of the Mermnad dynasty[15]—although from the vantage point of the full preservation of Herodotus' *Histories*, most modern scholars would say that the really important historical threshold in Book 1 is Croesus, not Gyges. And of course, we all know that in Book 2, where Herodotus can rely on the solid base of Egyptian documentary tradition, both thresholds are gloriously trespassed

---

[10] Schepens 1977:106; Parmeggiani 1999:111–115; interesting observations on Ephorus' apparent departing from his normal views on historical reliability in Mazzarino 1966:336.

[11] Ephorus FGH 70 F 31b = Strabo 9.3.11–12. See the extensive discussion in Parmeggiani 2001, a contribution that repays a reader's patience.

[12] Parmeggiani 2001:183–188 points to Ephorus' scrutiny of rituals as clues in order to elucidate the origins of the cult.

[13] Besides Diodorus 4.1.3 (= Ephorus FGH 70 T 8), Diodorus 16.76.5 (= Ephorus FGH 70 T 10) should also be considered.

[14] Diodorus 12.37.2 and 13.42.5 on Thucydides and 11.37.6 on Herodotus.

[15] Dionysius of Halicarnassus *De Thucydide* 5.5, *ad Pompeium Geminum* 3.14.

upon.[16] The observable complexity of Herodotus' own ideas on the possibility of having reliable knowledge of the past is one more reason to be wary of drawing conclusions about Ephorus' definition of the *spatium historicum* from one sentence in Diodorus.[17] What would we think of Herodotus if all we had were these passages from Dionysius and Diodorus?

There is one further reason to be somewhat skeptical of the notion, based on Diodorus' passage, that the return of the Heraclidae represented for Ephorus the general threshold of historical memory. Even though details often elude us, it is clear that the thirty books of Ephorus' *Histories* were not arranged according to a strictly chronological sequence, but on the contrary, it appears that each book possessed some sort of thematic unity.[18] Books 4 and 5 appear to have constituted a sort of survey of political geography, with Book 4 dealing with Europe and, presumably, Book 5 with Asia, rounding off a first group of five books that seem to have functioned as an introduction of sorts to the whole work.[19] As for Books 1–3, things are less clear. Judging from the fragments, they may not have been arranged chronologically throughout, but rather according to a mixture of chronological and geographical criteria, with Book 2 dealing with Boeotia and Central Greece, and Book 3 with Attica and the Ionians of Asia Minor. It is unclear what their respective chronological starting points were.[20] Obviously, if this reconstruction of the contents of the three books is accepted, the role of the return of the Heraclidae as a chronological threshold ends up being strongly deemphasized.

In light of the considerations developed so far, there seems little to recommend the assumption that the return of the Heraclidae represented for Ephorus the farthest point in the past on which a historian could make confident

---

[16] Which is not to say that the generation of Croesus does not preserve the role of a qualitative threshold throughout the *Histories* (see especially Vannicelli 1993:13–18 and Rösler 2002:397–402). On Herodotus' attitude to Egypt's past and its relationship to his general views on the possibility of a reliable knowledge of the past, see Vannicelli 2001.

[17] All the more so, since according to Suda s.v. Ἔφιππος (E 3930 Adler = FGH 70 T 1), Ephorus started with the fall of Troy.

[18] On the arrangement of the matter in Ephorus, see Jacoby 1926:25–30 and the comprehensive discussion of Vannicelli 1987:166–182, with further bibliography.

[19] On the subject matter of Book 4, see FGH 70 F 42. For a recent discussion of the scope of Books 4 and 5 see Breglia 2001:147–162.

[20] All we can say is that Ephorus' version of the origin of the *Thebageneis*, FGH 70 F 21, from Book 2, appears to refer to a time before the return of the Heraclidae to the Peloponnesus (see Sordi 2002:275–279), but of course strictly speaking we cannot exclude the possibility that it came from a retrospective excursus of some sort; the same could in theory be true of Ephorus' Boeotian *archaiologia* in FGH 70 F 119 (without book number). For the geographic arrangement of Books 1–3, see among others Andrewes 1951:42 and Breglia 2005:298. But cf. Jacoby 1926:47 "hat E buch I–III als einheit behandelt, wie doch sicher IV–V?" Vannicelli 1987:170, the first three books "dovevano costituire una compatta unità," quoting Jacoby.

statements based on reliable evidence. Quite apart from the fact that we have no idea how many qualifiers accompanied his narrative of this early age, the evidence does not support the conclusion that the return of the Heraclidae was seen by him as the threshold separating the *spatium mythicum* from the *spatium historicum*. Such a negative conclusion opens the way to the possibility of looking elsewhere for an explanation of the starting point of Ephorus' Book 1. Considerations of a different order may explain how and why, in the course of the fourth century, the return came to be seen as a turning point in the history of the Peloponnesus, one that a historian could hardly afford to neglect.

The starting point of my discussion will be provided by an episode that took place probably in the spring of 337 BCE, and in any case soon after the battle of Chaeronea.[21] Various sources refer, separately, to Philip the Second granting portions of the territory of Sparta to Argos, Megalopolis, Tegea, and Messene, but there is only one reference that shows that we are actually looking at partial accounts of one and the same episode. Polybius relates a debate that took place at Sparta during the First Macedonian War, in the spring of 210 BCE, as ambassadors from Aetolia and Acarnania were trying to draw the Spartans into the Roman-Aetolian and Macedonian camp respectively. In order to convince the Spartans that the Macedonians were their traditional enemies, the Aetolian envoy Chlaeneas reminded them, among other things, that Philip the Second had curtailed their territory, turning parts of it over to their enemies, that is, to the Messenians, Argives, Tegeans, and Megalopolitans. The Acarnanian Lyciscus replied that Philip had really acted as a buffer in the conflict between Sparta and its enemies, restraining both parties and turning the judgment over to a common court formed by all the Greeks.[22] Needless to say, each party was depicting the episode in the way that best suited its argument, but both clearly viewed Philip's intervention as a single episode. Piecing together the whole dossier, it appears that Philip had marched into the Peloponnesus immediately after Chaeronea, in the fall of 338 or the spring of 337 BCE. There, he must have been welcomed by his former allies, the Argives and Arcadians, but in detail his movements are not entirely clear. He may have invaded Laconia already at this point, or he may only have sent an ultimatum to King Agis III, fresh on the Eurypontid throne after the death of Archidamus II. In any case, a Panhellenic jury, probably in the framework of the newly founded League of Corinth, sanctioned Philip's decisions, and possibly only at this point did Philip

---

[21] For what follows, see especially Piérart 2001 and Roebuck 1948:84–92.

[22] Polybius 9.28.7 and 9.33.11 respectively (date according to Walbank 1967:163); for Polybius' own views on the episode, see Polybius 18.14.7.

invade Laconia in order to compel the Spartans to comply.[23] The final result was that a number of territories located on the borders between Sparta and its neighbors changed hands. For most of them, it was not the first time that this had happened, and for none of them was it the last.

The punishment of Sparta may seem surprising, since the Spartans had not joined the Theban-Athenian alliance against Philip, but upon closer consideration, it is perfectly understandable. Ever since the forties of the fourth century, Philip had basically taken up the role of Thebes in Peloponnesian politics, offering alliance and support to the traditional enemies of Sparta, so his decision now was but the logical continuation of a well-established policy.[24] Furthermore, considering that the king of Macedon was about to embark on his expedition against the Persian Empire, it is easy to imagine that he wanted to make sure that no trouble would be stirred while he was away from Greece. The Spartan insurrection against Alexander in 331 BCE shows that Philip' caution was justified.[25]

All the territories that changed hands at this point had been the objects of dispute before, some for a very long time, and the disputes would flare up again and again until the Roman conquest of the Peloponnesus and beyond. Needless to say, in all cases the rights of possession on the territories supposedly went back to the most ancient times.[26] In reference to the Thyreatis, disputed between Argives and Spartans, Pausanias says that Philip, by giving it to the Argives, compelled the Spartans to remain inside the borders of their territory that had been established in the beginning.[27] Precisely what this meant is probably revealed by the claim of the Messenians in front of the Roman Senate in 25 CE: the Dentheliatis, disputed between them and the Spartans, had been theirs since the time of the return of the Heraclidae.[28] That this is no mere literary motif is confirmed by an inscription from Olympia that refers to a judgment over the territories of Aigytis and Skiritis, in favor of Megalopolis and against Sparta, soon after 164 BCE. The inscription refers to one or more previous adjudications of the same controversy, where apparently the decisive criterion had been the fact that the two territories had belonged to the Arcadians ever since

---

[23] This reconstruction is suggested by Piérart 2001:28 and 33. On the role of the League of Corinth, see also Magnetto 1994 and already Roebuck 1948:91–92.

[24] For the continuity between Philip's and Epaminondas' politics in the Peloponnesus, see Roebuck 1948:88. Hamilton 1982:69–79 offers a clear and perceptive reconstruction of the early stages of Philip's relationship to Sparta and his involvement in Peloponnesian politics.

[25] The preemptive nature of Philip's action is underscored by Ellis 1976:204.

[26] See the synopsis in Piérart 2001:33.

[27] Pausanias 2.20.1.

[28] Tacitus *Annals* 4.43.1-3. On the dispute over the Dentheliatis, see Luraghi 2008:16–27.

the Heraclidae had returned to the Peloponnesus.[29] In other words, the borders supposedly established at the time of the return of the Heraclidae were seen as an actual benchmark for territorial disputes from the late third century at the latest, and probably, as we will see, from well before that.

This observation should give us pause. It is one thing for envoys from a Greek city claiming portions of land of another city to say that that land had belonged to their city ever since mythical times; it is a rather different thing for a mythic episode to be acknowledged as a standard for actual political decision. For one thing, one wonders how the parties involved could figure out what had been the borders between Argos, Sparta, Arcadia and Messenia at the time of the return of the Heraclidae. Here, ancient evidence comes to the rescue of the puzzled historian. Sparse references document the existence of a work by Aristotle called something like "The Claims of the Greek Cities," and according to a *Life of Aristotle* Philip made use of it in order to solve the disputes between the Greeks. Proud of his achievement, Philip supposedly boasted of having "given borders to the land of Pelops." In other words, Aristotle's work seems to have found immediate application precisely in the region from which come the references to the borders set at the time of the return of the Heraclidae.[30] Clearly, a work of erudition prepared by the Lyceum is exactly what was needed. Sure enough, Aristotle's knowledge and authority would have weighed very little if Philip had not stood behind them. But a scenario in which "the borders of the return of the Heraclidae" had been worked out by way of erudite research and then used as alleged foundation for the curtailment of Sparta's territory in 337 BCE would make the later history of these border disputes much less puzzling. The judgment of the Panhellenic court convened by Philip could have been construed, in the Hellenistic period and later, as the first intervention of a third party in the controversies between Sparta and its neighbors, and this could explain why the borders established and implemented then remained so authoritative[31] afterwards, and also why they were so surprisingly definite—

---

[29] Syll.³ 665; for the text of the inscription and the context of the arbitration, see Harter-Uibopuu 1998:80–97. The reference to the return of the Heraclidae comes in lines 34–36, within a long reference to one or more previous judgments (lines 22–38). It is not certain whether lines 34–36 refer to Philip's judgment, as Harter-Uibopuu, following the traditional view, thinks, or to a later time, possibly 222 BCE after the defeat of Sparta at Sellasia by Antigonus Doson, as suggested by Piérart 2001:32–33.

[30] *Vita Aristotelis Marciana* 28–32 Gigon, on which see Düring 1957:107–108 and Gigon 1962:39. On the Δικαιώματα τῶν Ἑλληνίδων πόλεων and their use by Philip, see Jehne 1994:147–148 with references and Piérart 2001:33–34. On the *Vita Marciana*, dating back to the fifth century CE, and its sources, see Düring 1957:469–472, and Haake 2006:338–340 with further references.

[31] Authoritative from the point of view of Sparta's enemies, that is. It is striking that, from the fourth century onwards, the return of the Heraclidae appears never to have been used by the Spartans to support their territorial claims—striking, but not surprising: a cornerstone of the

myth does not normally tend to map onto territory in the precise and tidy way required by border disputes.

Whether or not we accept this fascinating scenario in all its details, Philip's decision to (re)instate the 'Heraclid' borders in the Peloponnesus, with or without Aristotle's advice, must have been a plausible act for the parties involved. It appears that the time of the return of the Heraclidae was seen as the most valid foundation for legitimate territorial claims. It clearly represented a pristine situation, carrying the powerful claim to legitimacy that belongs to the time of origins. The borders established then could be construed as based on hereditary rights in the cases of Messenia, Laconia, the Argolis, and Elis, and on autochthony in the case of Arcadia.[32] On top of this, Piérart rightly notes that the notion of reinstating the borders originally drawn by the descendants of Heracles must have been particularly appealing to Philip, since the Argeads were themselves considered descendants of Temenos, i.e. of the Argive branch of the Heraclid family.[33]

Earlier evidence, fragmentary though it is, gives the impression that Philip's intervention was the culmination of a process that had started earlier and had turned the return of the Heraclidae into the potential touchstone of almost any territorial claim in the region. The roots of the process lay almost certainly in Argos, probably sometime in the first half of the fifth century, around the time of the Persian Wars or soon thereafter.[34] Myths narrating the return of various descendants of Heracles to various parts of the Peloponnesus do not seem to have been particularly popular during the archaic age, but sparse attestations

---

story of the return was the division of the Peloponnesus, which implied the original existence of a Messenian kingdom in a region that the Spartans continued to claim as their own for decades after losing it in 369 BCE (see Jehne 1994:84–90).

[32] An excellent discussion of Heraclid rights over Messenia and Laconia, with attention to their legal aspects in the framework of classical Greek law, is found in Natoli 2004:68–73. The Argolid, of course, was Heracles' own fatherland. Elis was attributed to Oxylus by the Heraclidae as a reward for his help, but at the same time, Oxylus also had ancestral claims over the region and his, too, was a return (see Ephorus FGH 70 F 115 and Prinz 1979:307). Arcadia was left alone because its king Cypselus had concluded an alliance with the Heraclidae before they invaded the Peloponnesus (Pausanias 8.5.6) or because he had outsmarted the Heraclidae (Polyaenus 1.7), but, in any case, the Arcadians' right to their land was based on having always been there, as everybody admitted since the fifth century at the latest (see Herodotus 2.171.3). For reflections of fourth-century politics in these versions of Elean and Arcadian *archaiologia*, see below.

[33] Piérart 2001:37. On the Heraclid pedigree of the Argeads and on Philip's interest in it, see Huttner 1997:65–85. On the letter of Speusippus to Philip, where Heracles' deeds provide multiple justifications for Philip's expansionism, see now Natoli 2004 (favoring its authenticity).

[34] On the development of the myth of the return of the Heraclidae, I recapitulate here the conclusions formulated in Luraghi 2008:48–61. The author should warn the reader that scholarly consensus places the origins of the myth of the division among the Heraclidae rather earlier, sometime between the second half of the seventh century and the sixth; but see Luraghi 2008:59–60 and below in the text.

allow us to trace them back to the seventh century BCE.[35] Most prominent is a
famous elegy of Tyrtaeus, quoted by Strabo, which told of how the ancestors
of the Spartans, clearly Dorians, had been led to Laconia by the Heraclidae,
from whom their two kings descended.[36] What is missing from the record is any
indication of the existence in archaic literature of a story of the return that
involved more than one *polis* or region of the Peloponnesus, offering the kind
of coordinated foundation myth that we are familiar with from the later tradition, a myth that, in its simplest form, included the division of the southern and
eastern Peloponnesus into three parts and the creation of Dorian kingdoms in
Messenia, Laconia, and the Argolid. The first attestation of the myth of the division of the Peloponnesus among the Heraclidae does not appear until 462 BCE,
when Pindar attributes to Apollo the decision that in Argos, Lacedaemon, and
Pylos, descendants of Heracles and Aegimius should rule.[37]

In political terms, a myth that depicted as an originally independent
kingdom a region that was now part of Sparta was hardly neutral, and it is
unlikely to be an accident that the first observable traces of sustained interest
in this myth come from Athens, at a time when the Messenians, installed in
Naupactus, were strategically precious allies of the Athenians. Euripides appears
to have devoted at least three tragedies to the early stages of the return of the
Heraclidae: *Cresphontes*, *Temenus*, and *Temenidae*. *Cresphontes*, generally dated no
later than 425 BCE, is probably the earliest of the three and shows clear signs that
the soon-to-become-canonical story of the division of the Peloponnesus among
the Heraclidae was still in the process of coagulation. The eponymous character
is a son of the Heraclid king of Messenia, also called Cresphontes, and the plot
revolves around the vengeance he takes on his paternal uncle, Polyphontes, for
the murder of his father. Like Cresphontes Junior, Polyphontes appears to have
been introduced by Euripides, and shows up only very rarely in later sources.[38]
Euripides' other two Heraclid tragedies apparently dealt with the division of
the Peloponnesus among the sons of Aristomachus, focusing especially on
the Argive branch that sprang from Temenus. They are difficult to date, and

---

[35] For a comprehensive presentation of the evidence, see Prinz 1979:206–313, to be supplemented
with the new evidence on Euripides' Heraclid tragedies mentioned below. The extent to which
any of these stories conveys any amount of reliable historical information is irrelevant here; for
some orientation on the matter see Vanschoonwinkel 1991:331–366 and especially Eder 1998.

[36] Tyrtaeus fr. 2 West².

[37] Pindar *Pythian* 5.69–72. For the equivalence of Nestor's kingdom and Messenia, see also Pindar
6.35 (490 BCE).

[38] On Euripides' *Cresphontes*, see especially Harder 1985; further bibliography in Biagetti 2009:423.
Note that Euripides' Polyphontes, in spite of being Cresphontes Senior's brother, is never
mentioned as one of the sons of Aristomachus, Cresphontes' father; see Luraghi 2008:61n50 and
Biagetti 2009:439n93. On Polyphontes, see also Harder 1985:9–11.

a connection with the political scenario after the Peace of Nicias, when Argos and Athens became closely entangled, cannot be more than a very attractive and reasonable hypothesis.[39] In any case, and keeping in mind the complexities of the relationship between tragedy and politics, the return of the Heraclidae appears to have been singularly popular on the Athenian stage in years when both Argives and Messenians were playing an important role in Athenian foreign politics. Enduring interest in this myth on the side of the Argives is confirmed by Thucydides' rendering of the speech of the Argive general before the battle of Mantinea in 418 BCE: the Argives should fight against the Spartans to reestablish the equal subdivision of the Peloponnesus.[40]

With the first half of the fourth century, the division of the Peloponnesus among the Heraclidae started to become facts on the ground. We cannot tell with any confidence what role, if any, the myth played in the conflicts between Elis and its former dependencies, who went on to constitute the Triphylians and the Pisatans,[41] but with Epaminondas' invasion of Laconia in 369 BCE the lot of Cresphontes became an independent political entity, under the name of Messene. Unsurprisingly, the Argives were involved: the Theban victory suddenly made it seem as if the balance of power in the Peloponnesus that they had dreamt of at the time of the battle of Mantinea was now within reach. Equally unsurprisingly, a number of indices suggest that the return of the Heraclidae and the division of the Peloponnesus among them was repeatedly invoked on both sides as a precedent of sorts, for or against the new order established by the Thebans.[42] The most striking evidence of this is provided by the names of the five tribes into which the citizen body of the new Messenian polity was divided: Hyllis, Cresphontis, Aristomachis, Daiphontis, and Kleolaia. They took their names, that is, from the first Heraclid king of Messenia, and from his three direct ancestors, all the way back to Heracles' son Hyllos, and finally from the Argive Heraclid Daiphontes, son-in-law of Temenos.[43] At the same time, the Argives erected at Delphi, in a prominent position close to the sanctuary entrance, a semicircular monument on which bronze statues of their mythical

---

[39] On *Temenus* and *Temenidai*, see Harder 1991. Tentative dating not based on historical arguments points to the last two decades of the century. On the intricacies of Peloponnesian politics after the Peace of Nicias, Seager 1976 remains the best account.

[40] Thucydides 5.69.1; see Luraghi 2008: 56n34.

[41] See however below n42. On the origins of Pisatans and Triphylians, see Nafissi 2003:26–27 and respectively Giangiulio 2009 and Ruggeri 2009 with further references.

[42] More precisely, the Spartans seem to have invoked a version of early Heraclid-Dorian history in the Peloponnesus that made their conquest of Messenia legitimate—if Isocrates' *Archidamus* really reflects arguments used by the Spartans at this time; see below.

[43] On the Messenian tribes, attested at Ithome/Messene, Thouria, and Korone, see Luraghi 2008:230–231 with references to the evidence.

kings demonstrated a complete genealogical and dynastic line all the way from Danaus to Heracles, via Perseus—a most striking claim of their Heraclid heritage. According to Pausanias, the monument had been dedicated to celebrate their participation in the re-foundation of Messene by Epaminondas and the Thebans.[44]

Repercussions of this increase in the salience of the Heraclidae, and of the political developments that prompted and accompanied it, can be identified, with varying degrees of confidence, in the stories about other Peloponnesian states and their distant pasts. According to Euripides, Cresphontes' son (in his account, Cresphontes Junior) had been sent by his mother Meropes to a guest-friend in Aetolia. However, later sources, which appear to go back to fourth-century authors, inform us that the child had been saved by King Cypselus of Arcadia, who turns out to be Meropes' father and therefore the grandfather of the child, whose name has meanwhile become Aepytus. The connection with Arcadian support for the Messenians after 369 BCE is too obvious to require comment.[45] In the case of Elis, local foundation myths appear to have morphed under the influence of the return of the Heraclidae. The founding hero Oxylus, already responsible for the division of the land in Euripides' drama, turns out to be of Elean descent, and his migration to Elis could accordingly be recast as in fact a return to the land that belonged to his ancestors. This development can be dated with reasonable confidence to the early fourth century, based on a comprehensive study of Elean myths of origins.[46] The story found monumental expression in the form of a statue of Oxylus, erected in the agora of Elis and accompanied by an epigram that outlined his genealogy, including the migration of his ancestor Aetolus from Elis to Aetolia and Oxylus' return to the fatherland.[47]

The fact that the return of the Heraclidae had become a hot topic at this point is confirmed by its appearance in discussions of the legitimacy of the new political setup, such as Isocrates' *Archidamus*, which is set in the context of the

---

[44] Pausanias 10.10.5. Archaeological evidence and the political message of the monument are discussed in Salviat 1965.

[45] On the fate of Cresphontes' son in Euripides and in later sources, see now Biagetti 2009:439–450. Cypselus father of Meropes: Nicolaus of Damascus FGH 90 F 31 (generally taken to depend on Ephorus; Jacoby 1926:234–235 and 243) and Pausanias (8.5.6 et al.). Political meaning of the Arcadian connection: Luraghi 2008:62–63 with refs. (to which add now Biagetti 2009).

[46] On Oxylus' return to Elis see Ephorus FGH 70 F 115. On the development of Elean myth-history in the fourth century, see especially Sordi 1994 and Gehrke 2003:18–19. Oxylus in Euripides (*Temenus* or *Temenidae*): TGF (68)–(69) i = POxy 2455 fr. 9.

[47] The epigram is quoted by Ephorus, FGH 70 F 122a; for a date in the late fifth or early fourth century, see Jacoby 1926:4–5 and Sordi 1994:140–141. The connection between Aetolia and Elis was probably revamped in connection with the alliance at the time of the war between Sparta and Elis, but earlier versions of it appear to have existed, see Gehrke 2003:12–13.

negotiations between Thebes and Sparta in 366 BCE. Here, Isocrates reaffirms Spartan rights over Messenia, claiming that, after Cresphontes had been assassinated by his subjects, his sons had sought refuge at Sparta and had transferred to the Laconian branch of the Heraclidae their own land. Much in the same way, Tyndareus, in the absence of heirs after his two sons, the Dioscuri, had vanished from among mortals, had granted Laconia itself to Heracles, who had restored to him his kingdom. In both cases, Apollo had, as it were, confirmed the transaction, first by encouraging the Heraclidae to recover their ancestral land, and then by telling the Spartans to accept the suppliants, i.e. Cresphontes' sons, and their offer, i.e. possession of the lot of Cresphontes.[48] On other occasions, wearing his more usual Athenian hat, Isocrates could of course use the Heraclid myth against the Spartans. In the *Panegyricus*, around 380 BCE, he reproached them for being ungrateful to the Athenians who had saved the Heraclidae, the ancestors of their kings, while in the *Panathenaicus*, at the end of the 340s, he chastised their greed in not being content with the portion of the Peloponnesus that befell them at the time of the return of the Heraclidae and for having attacked and subjugated almost the entire region.[49]

By the mid-fourth century, the return of the Heraclidae appears to have become a convenient prism through which to observe contemporary Peloponnesian politics. This is shown most clearly by Plato's *Laws*, dating back to these very same years, where the early history of the Peloponnesus is structured by the Athenian speaker of the dialogue as a parallel history of the three Heraclid kingdoms of Sparta, Messene, and Argos. Interestingly, the *Laws* offer the only example of a pro-Spartan use of the return of the Heraclidae. Here, the common origins of the three kingdoms serve to emphasize the superiority of the Spartan constitution, thanks to which the Spartan monarchy was the only one of the three Heraclid monarchies to have survived degeneration, and Sparta the only one of the three to have fought against the barbarians in the Persian Wars, while the Argives had not participated in the defense of Greece and the Messenians had gone so far as to attack the Spartans in the very hour of Panhellenic danger.[50]

---

[48] Isocrates *Archidamus* 22–25. On the use of Isocrates' *Archidamus* as evidence, see Luraghi 2008:55n32.

[49] See Isocrates *Panegyricus* 61–63 and *Panathenaicus* 42–46. It may be significant that in the earlier speech Isocrates basically used the portion of the story of the Heraclidae that was commonly referred to in eulogies of Athens, i.e. the protection they were offered against Eurystheus by the Athenians (cf. Herodotus 9.27; on the topicality of this episode of Athenian myth-history, the illuminating observations in Canfora 1999:32–38), while in the later one he is more specifically referring to the stories associated with the final return of the Heraclidae to the Peloponnesus.

[50] Plato *Leges* 3.683c–693c; the supposed Messenian attack on Sparta is mentioned again in 3.698e. On the political message of Plato's depiction of Peloponnesian history, see Dušanić 1997. On

The interplay of political developments and mythic narratives is complex and dynamic, and therefore difficult to disentangle. Did the return of the Heraclidae acquire such a relevance because it made it possible to articulate in the same context the origins of all the Peloponnesians, or should we rather think that additional stories explaining the origins and whereabouts of non-Heraclid Peloponnesians, such as the Eleans, Arcadians, and Achaeans, were tied to the main story of the Heraclidae in order to create a comprehensive mythic template? To what extent did the emergence of new political entities and new systems of alliances prompt reformulations of the myths of origins, and to what extent were these new political realities formulated in terms of (partly preexisting) myths? One thing is certain: the volatile situation in the Peloponnesus in the first decades of the fourth century explains perfectly well the surge of interest in foundation stories that could help to make sense of the present political situation.

It may not be possible to tell precisely where Ephorus' Book 1 should be located in this historical context. The relatively abundant evidence, indirect and direct, for Ephorus' own narratives of the return and conquest of the Peloponnesus show with unmistakable clarity the signs of this very same political climate. Like Plato, Ephorus appears to have drawn a parallel history of the three Heraclid monarchies, to the advantage of Sparta, although unlike Plato he seems to have identified the root of the decadence of Argos and Messene in the way the kings had dealt with their subjects, and not in their arrogating of excessive powers.[51] They may be responding to one another, and in any case, they are both to some extent reacting to the same political situation. Plato left the *Laws* unfinished at the time of his death in 347 BCE. As for Ephorus, scholars have assigned tentative dates of composition to single books based on extremely uncertain indications contained in the fragments themselves. Jacoby thought that the first three books had appeared before 338 BCE, but Momigliano proposed an even earlier date of composition, around 350 BCE.[52] In all likelihood, Ephorus was writing Book 1 before Philip's intervention in the Peloponnesus came officially to confer on the return of the Heraclidae the status of ultimate touchstone of legitimate territorial claims in the region, although he certainly did not need Philip and Aristotle's Δικαιώματα to see the crucial importance acquired by this complex of stories. The return had played a very prominent

---

Plato's Messenian war, see Luraghi 2008:177–180.

[51] On this, see the perceptive observations of Andrewes 1951:41n3.

[52] See Jacoby 1926:24, based especially on FGH 70 F 121, where Naupactus, which Philip assigned to the Aetolians in 338 BCE, is said to be Locrian. Momigliano (1975:694–696) thought that Ephorus' remarks on Boeotia's favorable position for a maritime hegemony (FGH 70 F 119) could not have been formulated much later than 350 BCE.

role in debates and conflicts throughout the century. It is fair to say that the political history of fourth-century Greece could hardly be written in a meaningful way without reference to the return and related events.

In conclusion, one is reminded of Charles Fornara's witty remark that "no ancient writer could withstand the combined assaults of Wilamowitz, Schwartz, and Jacoby."[53] This is more than just a *bon mot*: the situation observed by Fornara goes a long way to explain some curious blindspots in modern research on Ephorus. The stereotype of the shortsighted armchair historian, out of touch with the world around him, has stuck to him very tenaciously. That he could not possibly be reacting in an intelligent way to historical developments has often been a silent presupposition in modern interpretations of his work. Related to this view is the readiness to regard Diodorus' discussion of the difficulties of dealing with the distant past as if it faithfully reflected Ephorus' thought, and accordingly to conclude that starting with the return of the Heraclidae was Ephorus' naïve response to better historians' concern for the possibility of reconstructing the distant past.

There is, however, another, more sympathetic way of reading Ephorus, the way pioneered by Guido Schepens and developed in recent years by Giovanni Parmeggiani, an approach whose trademark is an uncompromising shift in focus from passages of other authors, especially Diodorus, who were supposedly copying Ephorus, to the fragments themselves. The resulting image of Ephorus is rather different. The most important incunabula of this approach are represented by two articles by Arnaldo Momigliano from the mid-thirties of the last century, which were part of a broad reexamination of fourth-century historiography, left unfinished as a result of various circumstances, including a world war and, probably, changes in Momigliano's own research agenda.[54] For Momigliano, Ephorus had a specific vision of Greek history whose backbone was a succession of hegemonies and whose main focus was the causes and conditions that allowed one Greek city to become the leader of the Greek world. His reflections revolved around Sparta, Athens, and Thebes, whose respective strengths and weaknesses Ephorus analyzed, pointing to their historical development.[55] This way of seeing the history of the fourth century lies at the foundation of most modern conceptions thereof, and the historical concept of a Theban hegemony is ultimately a

---

[53] Fornara 1983:42n63. For Jacoby, Ephorus was "unworldly" ("weltfremd," Jacoby 1956:96) and his mentality was "shallow and petty-bourgeois" ("platt und spießbürgerlich," Jacoby 1926:23)

[54] See Momigliano 1966:347–365 and 1975:683–706 (both originally published in 1935). Insight in the purpose and logic of this part of Momigliano's research is provided by a letter of Momigliano to his teacher G. De Sanctis from 1930 published in Polverini 2006:15–16.

[55] Momigliano 1975:697–702.

product of Ephorus' historical thought.[56] His even-handed approach explains why scholars observing only a portion of the evidence could call Ephorus in turn pro-Theban, pro-Spartan, and pro-Athenian. Such a view of Greek history must have been one of the targets of Anaximenes' (or Theopompus'?) *Trikaranos* or 'the three-headed monster', a polemical pamphlet that lampooned Athens, Sparta, and Thebes for having mishandled the Greeks and thereby paved the way for Macedonian hegemony.[57] Seen from this perspective, the first three books of his *Histories* acquire a deeper meaning. By presenting in succession the origins of the three hegemonic *poleis* in their respective historical contexts,[58] they formed a veritable prologue for Ephorus' *Histories*.

As noted before, Ephorus was certainly interested in assessing the possibility of writing history of the distant past. He may well have chosen the return of the Heraclidae as the starting point of Book 1 for reasons that have to do with his views on how far back into the past a historian could go. Nevertheless, close consideration of the historical context in which Ephorus was writing suggests that in an important way his choice was dictated by historical circumstances that made it unthinkable, for whoever was going to write the history of Greece in the second half of the fourth century, to ignore the return of the Heraclidae.

Bibliography

Andrewes, A. 1951. "Ephoros Book I and the Kings of Argos." *Classical Quarterly* 1:39–45.

Bearzot, C. et al., eds. 2001. *Storiografia locale e storiografia universale. Forme di acquisizione del sapere storico nella cultura antica (Atti del Convegno di Bologna, 16-18 dicembre 1999)*. Como.

Biagetti, C. 2009. "La Messenia e gli Eraclidi." *La parola del passato* 64:411–451.

Breglia, L. 2001. "Storia universale e geografia in Eforo di Cuma." In Bearzot et al. 2001:139–164.

[56] On Ephorus' views on the Theban hegemony and on the reasons for its ultimate failure, see Momigliano 1966:361–365.

[57] On the *Trikaranos*, see Anaximenes FGH 72 T 6 (= Pausanias 6.18.5) and 72 F 20–21. According to Pausanias, Anaximenes composed the *Trikaranos* in the style of Theopompus, so that everybody in Greece believed Theopompus to be the author and hated him for that. The attribution to Anaximenes has generally been accepted in modern scholarship, but see Mazzarino 1966:384–388 for very perceptive arguments in favor of Theopompus. In any case, the work remains an important historical witness of the cultural and political context in which Ephorus wrote.

[58] It is only for Book 1 that this view be said to be really substantiated by the evidence; see the persuasive reconstruction of Andrewes 1951.

———. 2005. "Eforo e il modello erodoteo." In *Erodoto e il 'modello erodoteo.' Formazione e trasmissione delle tradizioni storiche in Grecia*, ed. M. Giangiulio, 277–314. Trento.

Canfora, L. 1999. *La storiografia greca*. Milan.

Clarke, K. 2008. *Making Time for the Past: Local History and the Polis*. Oxford.

Düring, I. 1957. *Aristotle in the Ancient Biographical Tradition*. Studia Graeca et Latina Gothoburgensia. Göteborg.

Dušanić, S. 1997. "Platon, la question messénienne et les guerres contre les Barbares." In *Esclavage, guerre, économie en Grèce ancienne: hommage à Yvon Garlan*, ed. P. Brulé and J. Oulhen, 75–86. Rennes.

Eder, B. 1998. *Argolis, Lakonien, Messenien. Vom Ende der mykenischen Palastzeit bis zur Einwanderung der Dorier*. Vienna.

Ellis, J. R. 1976. *Philip II and Macedonian Imperialism*. London.

Fornara, C. W. 1983. *The Nature of History in Ancient Greece and Rome*. Berkeley.

Funke, P., and Luraghi, N., eds. 2009. *The Politics of Ethnicity and the Crisis of the Peloponnesian League*. Hellenic Studies 32. Washington, DC.

Gehrke, H.-J. 2003. "Sull'etnicità elea." *Geographia antiqua* 12:5–22.

Gigon, O. 1962. *Vita Aristotelis Marciana herausgegeben und kommentiert von O.G.* Berlin.

Giangiulio, M. 2009. "The Emergence of Pisatis." In Funke and Luraghi 2009:65–85.

Haake, M. 2006. "Ein athenisches Ehrendekret für Aristoteles?" *Klio* 88:328–350.

Hamilton, C. D. 1982. "Philip II and Archidamus." In *Philip II, Alexander the Great and the Macedonian Heritage*, ed. W. L. Adams and E. N. Borza, 61–83. Lanham, MD.

Harder, A. 1985. *Euripides' Kresphontes and Archelaos: Introduction, Text and Commentary*. Leiden.

Harder, A. 1991 "Euripides' Temenos and Temenidai." In *Fragmenta dramatica. Beiträge zur Interpretation der griechischen Tragikerfragmente und ihrer Wirkungsgeschichte*, ed. H. Hofmann and A. Harder, 117–135. Göttingen.

Harter-Uibopuu, K. 1998. *Das zwischenstaatliche Schiedsverfahren im achäischen Koinon*. Vienna.

Huttner, U. 1997. *Die politische Rolle der Heraklesgestalt im griechischen Herrschertum*. Stuttgart.

Jacoby, F. 1926. *Die Fragmente der griechischen Historiker. Zweiter Teil: Zeitgeschichte. C. Kommentar zu Nr. 64–105*. Berlin.

———. 1956. *Abhandlungen zur griechischen Geschichtsschreibung*. Ed. H. Bloch. Leiden.

Jehne, M. 1994. *Koine Eirene. Untersuchungen zu den Befriedungs- und Stabilisierungsbemühungen in der griechischen Poliswelt des 4. Jhs. v. Chr.* Stuttgart.

Laqueur, R. 1911. "Ephoros." *Hermes* 46:161–206 and 321–354.

Leyden, W. von. 1950. "Spatium Historicum: The Historical Past as Viewed by Hecataeus, Herodotus, and Thucydides." *Durham University Journal* 42:89–104.

Luraghi, N. 2008. *The Ancient Messenians: Constructions of Ethnicity and Memory.* Cambridge.

Magnetto, A. 1994. "L'intervento di Filippo II nel Peloponneso e l'iscrizione Syll.³, 665." In Ἱστορίη. *Studi offerti dagli allievi a Giuseppe Nenci in occasione del suo settantesimo compleanno*, ed. S. Alessandrì, 283–308. Galatina.

Marincola, J. 1997. *Authority and Tradition in Ancient Historiography.* Cambridge.

Mazzarino, S. 1966. *Il pensiero storico classico* I. Rome.

Momigliano, A. 1966. *Terzo contributo alla storia degli studi classici e del mondo antico.* Rome.

———. 1975. *Quinto contributo alla storia degli studi classici e del mondo antico.* Rome.

Nafissi, M. 2003. "Elei e Pisati. Geografia, storia e istituzioni politiche della regione di Olimpia." *Geographia antiqua* 12:23–55.

Natoli, A. F. 2004. *The Letter of Speusippus to Philip. Introduction, Text, Translation and Commentary.* Stuttgart.

Parmeggiani, G. 1999. "Mito e spatium historicum nelle Storie di Eforo di Cuma (Note a Eph. FGrHist 70 T 8)." *Rivista storica dell'Antichità* 29:107–125.

———. 2001. "Eforo F 31b. L'indagine locale e l'autopsia archeologica." In Bearzot et al. 2001:165–197.

Piérart, M. 2001. "Argos, Philippe II et la Cynourie (Thyréatide): les frontières du partage des Héraclides." In *Recherches récentes sur le monde hellénistique. Acte du colloque en l'honneur de Pierre Ducrey*, ed. R. Frei-Stolba and K. Gex, 27–43. Bern.

Polverini, L. 2006. "Momigliano e De Sanctis." In *Arnaldo Momigliano nella storiografia del novecento*, ed. L. Polverini, 11–35. Rome.

Prinz, F. 1979. *Gründungsmythen und Sagenchronologie.* Göttingen.

Roebuck, C. 1948. "The Settlements of Philip II with the Greek States in 338 B.C." *Classical Philology* 43:73–92.

Rösler, W. 2002. "The Organization of Time in the *Histories*." In *Brill's Companion to Herodotus*, ed. E. J. Bakker et al., 387–412. Leiden.

Ruggeri, C. 2009. "Triphylia from Elis to Arcadia." In Funke and Luraghi 2009:49–64.

Salviat, F. 1965. "L'Offrande argienne de l'"hémicycle des rois' à Delphes et l'Héraclès béotien." *Bulletin de correspondance hellenique* 89:307–314.

Schepens, G. 1977. "Historiographical Problems in Ephorus." In *Historiographia antiqua. Commentationes Lovanienses in honorem W. Peremans septuagenarii editae*, 95–118. Leuven.

Schepens, G., and Bollansée, J. 2004. "Myths on the Origins of Peoples and the Birth of Universal History." In *Historia y mito: el pasado legendario como fuente de autoridad. Actas del simposio internacional celebrado en Sevilla, Valverde del Camino y Huelva entre el 22 y el 25 de abril de 2003*, ed. J. M. Candau Morón et al., 57-75. Malaga.

Seager, R. 1976. "After the Peace of Nicias: Diplomacy and Policy, 421-416 B.C." *Classical Quarterly* 26:249–269.

Sordi, M. 1994. "Strabone, Pausania e le vicende di Oxilo." In *Strabone e la Grecia*, ed. A. M. Biraschi, 137–144. Naples.

———. 2002. *Scritti di storia greca.* Milan.

Vannicelli, P. 1987. "L'economia delle Storie di Eforo." *Rivista di filologia e di istruzione classica* 115:165–191.

———. 1993. *Erodoto e la storia dell'alto e medio arcaismo (Sparta—Tessaglia—Cirene).* Rome.

———. 2001. "Herodotus' Egypt and the Foundations of Universal History." In *The Historian's Craft in the Age of Herodotus*, ed. N. Luraghi, 211–240. Oxford.

Vanschoonwinkel, J. 1991. *L'Egée et la Méditerranée orientale à la fin du deuxième millénaire. Témoignages archéologiques et sources écrites.* Louvain-la Neuve.

Walbank, F. 1967. *A Historical Commentary on Polybius* II. Oxford.

8

Ephorus, Polybius, and τὰ καθόλου γράφειν

Why and How to Read Ephorus and his Role in Greek Historiography without Reference to 'Universal History'[1]

JOHN TULLY

> I would be making the understatement of the century if I were to say that universal history has never been a clear notion.
>
> Momigliano 1982:533

> Ephorus, an utterly thoughtless writer, has at best the doubtful merit of having been the first to compose a Universal History [. . .].
>
> von Wilamowitz-Moellendorff 1908:10

MOMIGLIANO'S dry witticism remains all too apposite regarding 'Universal History' in general, but it should be qualified in one crucial respect. Modern analyses of Greek historiography, of Ephorus, and of 'Universal History' specifically in the context of Greek historiography, are (nearly) all clear that the concept of 'Universal History' is useful as a frame through which to understand the development of Greek historiography, and, particularly, Ephorus' role there.[2]

---

[1]   I should like to thank Nino Luraghi, Erich Gruen, Julia L Shear, Daniel Tober, and the fellow participants of the conference at l'Università di Bologna for their helpful comments; and the Department of Classics at the University of California, Berkeley, and Ulrich Gotter and the Seminar für Alte Geschichte, Universität Konstanz for their hospitality while working on this paper. For ease of reference, all translations are from the appropriate Loeb, except Polybius 5.33.5, which has been revised following Walbank 1956, 1967, 1979. Any infelicity that remains is, naturally, mine alone.
[2]   Nearly: one notable exception is Hornblower 1994a, who does not mention the concept of 'Universal History' at any point in his discussions of Ephorus, Polybius, or Diodorus; see

Recent scholars are occasionally more sympathetic to Ephorus than was the norm in the nineteenth and twentieth centuries, in part because of changing approaches to *Quellenforschung*, the analysis of indirect manuscript traditions such as that we possess for Ephorus.[3] Nevertheless, they still operate within this paradigm. They express the connection between Ephorus and 'Universal History' in different ways, depending on their immediate concern and methodology, but they still consider it meaningful to make one or both of the following two claims:

> (1) that Ephorus wrote 'Universal History', or, specifically, was the first so to do;[4]

especially 35–38. Otherwise, even work superficially more sceptical of the ancient tradition ultimately conforms to this paradigm. Thus, Alonso-Núñez traces 'Universal History' as a phenomenon back into the fifth century, and sees Ephorus, like Herodotus, as a precursor to 'Universal History' understood in a stricter sense than that favoured by Jacoby; see especially Alonso-Núñez 1999; Alonso-Núñez 2002; and the comparison of the definitions of 'Universal History' offered by Jacoby and Alonso-Núñez below, 157–160. Nevertheless, like other recent analyses, Alonso-Núñez's approach assumes evidence for breadth of coverage is evidence for attempted universality of coverage, and presupposes the validity of the notion of 'Universal History' as a hermeneutic tool to clarify the ancient discourse; compare Sacks 1981:96–121; Scafuro 1983:8–11, which are discussed below. Clarke 1999, Marincola 2007b, and now Pitcher 2009:113–120 are initially more cautious in their analysis, but confirm the traditional paradigm connecting Ephorus and 'Universal History' through their unwillingness to explore the ramifications of this caution in their broader discussion: on Clarke and Marincola, see n87 below; on Pitcher 2009:113–120, see n36 below.

3   Fornara 1983:42n63: "no ancient writer could withstand the combined assaults of Wilamowitz, Schwartz, and Jacoby, who made Ephorus the incarnation of all that was objectionable in Greek historiography." For an exposition of the contrary view ranging much more widely than the current focus on Ephorus' perceived connection with 'Universal History': Schepens 1977. Ephorus has not been well served by scholarship in the twentieth century, even compared to other fourth century historians, such as Theopompus and Hieronymus of Cardia, each of whom has been the subject of a recent book: Flower 1994, and Hornblower 1981 respectively. Nevertheless, Schepens, Vattuone, and Parmeggiani have done much to reframe the debate, and Parmeggiani in particular has cogently shown in a series of articles how modern views of Ephorus' attitude to the *spatium historicum*, and to autopsy, and regarding his lack of military competence have arisen from wide-spread misunderstandings of the ancient evidence. Parmeggiani 2011, which I have not seen, is the first book on Ephorus since Barber 1935.

4   Ephorus as the first (to attempt) a 'Universal History': Büdinger 1895:32 "Universalhistorie"; von Wilamowitz-Moellendorff 1908:10 "Universal History"; Jacoby 1909:87 "Universalgeschichte"; Jacoby 1926:25 "universalgeschichte"; Starr 1968:150 "Universal History"; Brown 1973:112 "World History"; Strasburger 1977:35 "Universalgeschichte"; Fornara 1983:42 "Universal History"; Alonso-Núñez 1990:177 "general history"; Meister 1990:89 "Universalhistoriker"; Luce 1997:109 "first 'universal' history of Greece"; Marincola 1997:69 "Universal History"; Marincola 2001:109 "'universal history'", 123; Chávez Reino 2005:50 "historia universal"; Walbank 2005:16 "Universal History"; Schepens 2007:50 "Universal History"; Engels 2009:187 "des Begründers der Gattung [sc. der Universalhistorie]". Ephorus as "Universal Historian": Lavagnini 1933:67 "una storia universale della Grecia"; Barber 1935:9 "world-history", 47 "Universal History"; Châtelet 1962:285 "histoire universelle"; Drews 1963:254 "Universal History"; Mazzarino

(2) that later Greek historiographers thought that Ephorus wrote 'Universal History', or, specifically, claimed that he was the first so to do.[5]

Here, I argue that these claims are flawed: no ancient author approached Ephorus as a practitioner of a specific sub-genre of History which they shared to the exclusion of other contemporary approaches to history, let alone as a 'Universal Historian' in any of the senses in which the phrase has been understood in modern scholarship. The innovative nature of Ephorus' history made him and it important in the later tradition, and encouraged later historiographers to express their own necessarily unique and superior historiographical purpose with reference to him and it. Ephorus was, however, but one of many foils to that end, including Herodotus, Timaeus, and many others. The surviving evidence does not justify the wide-spread modern suggestions that Ephorus was attempting 'Universal History' with its associated implication of rupture in the historiographical tradition between Ephorus and his predecessors. It instead confirms that Ephorus' work, like that of all Greek historiographers, offered a distinctive personal vision reflecting his time, and his interests, and that it

---

1966:1.482 "storia 'universale', 483 "universale storia di Greci e barbari"; Strasburger 1966:14 "Universalhistoriker"; Usher 1969:108 "Universal History"; Walbank 1972:66 "Universal History"; Roussel 1973:125 "grande histoire générale"; Burde 1974:21 "Universalhistoriker; Lehmann 1974:157 "Universalgeschichte"; Vannicelli 1987:183 "storia universale"; Meister 1990:66, 86 "Universalgeschichte"; Grant 1995:108 "Universal History"; Breglia Pulci Doria 1996:55 "storia universale"; Mortley 1996:40 "Universal History"; Schepens 1997:145 "Universal History"; Shrimpton and Gillis 1997:106, 121 "Universal History"; Flower 1998:365 "Universal History"; Vattuone 1998b:194 "«storia universale»"; Clarke 1999:255 "universal historian"; Breglia Pulci Doria 2001:149, 164 "storia universale"; Alonso-Núñez 2002:38 "general history"; Hose 2006:677 "Universal History"; Levene 2007:287 "'universal history'"; Marincola 2007b:171 "Universal History"; Nicolai 2007:22 "Universal History"; Timpe 2007:26 "Universalgeschichte"; Tuplin 2007:160 "so-called 'universal history'"; Engels 2008:149 "universal histories"; Cornell 2010: "universal historian"; Engels 2010:74 "universal histories".

[5]   Ephorus as perceived by Polybius as the first "Universal Historian": Büdinger 1895:23 "storia universale", 35 "Universalgeschichte"; Barber 1935:17 "Universal History"; Pédech 1964:496 "histoire universelle"; Momigliano 1972:285 "universal historian"; Walbank 1972:3, 42 "Universal History"; Brown 1973:112 "World History"; Roussel 1973:125 "histoire «universelle»"; Lehmann 1974:157–158 "Universalgeschichte"; Meister 1975:67 "Universalgeschichte"; Schepens 1977:95 "general history"; Momigliano 1978:11 "Universal History"; Sacks 1981:102 "Universal History"; Vannicelli 1987:183 "storia universale"; Alonso-Núñez 1990:175 "world history"; Meister 1990:85 "Universalhistoriker"; Lendle 1992:137 "Universalgeschichte"; Vattuone 1998a:61 "Universalgeschichte"; Rood 2007:149 "general history"; Clarke 2008:96 "'general history'"; Engels 2008:148 "Universal History"; Cornell 2010: "universal historian"; Sheridan 2010:47 "universal historian". Ephorus as perceived by Polybius as a "Universal Historian": Grant 1970:138 "a universal history of Greece"; Schepens 1977:95 "general history"; Fornara 1983:42 "universal [history]"; Marincola 1997:37 "Universal History"; Alonso-Núñez 2002:38; Timpe 2007:44 "Universalhistoriker".

was predicated, as all Greek historiography was, on a rich engagement with his predecessors.

My initial step is to review the terms of the scholarly debate. First, I illustrate how competing definitions of 'Universal History' have caused confusion, in particular because the definition central to Ephorus' status as *first* 'Universal Historian' involves a highly unusual understanding of the concept of 'Universal History'. Next, I briefly consider the nature of the fragmentary evidence for Ephorus' history, and outline how shifts in scholarly approaches to *Quellenforschung* have changed the strength and the nature of the claims that are made based on the surviving indirect tradition. Hence, I argue that past readings of Polybius 5.33.1-5, the single passage that has been interpreted as stating that Ephorus was (thought to be) the *first* (and only) to write 'Universal History' (τὸν πρῶτον καὶ μόνον ἐπιβεβλημένον τὰ καθόλου γράφειν) are unjustified,[6] and that recent attempts to preserve a generic reading by positing either confusion or conscious redefinition of the genre by Polybius are misguided.

As this passage is so central to the historiographical debate, I do not immediately offer a fresh interpretation. Instead, I analyse other important passages, principally from Diodorus, and argue that these approach Ephorus' history as part of a broad tradition, not as a point of rupture and generic innovation. Only then do I reanalyse Polybius 5.33.1-5. I first argue that Polybius' concern here was perspective as revealed by a work's structure, not coverage, and that such a reading is more consistent with Polybius' approach elsewhere. I next demonstrate that τὰ καθόλου γράφειν does not represent an independent genre for Polybius, let alone his historiographical ideal. Instead, it refers to but one of many skills required of the model historiographer. This analysis cumulatively confirms that there was no place for 'Universal History' in ancient historiographical analysis of Ephorus.

In the next section, I illustrate the advantages of this alternative approach to Ephorus without reference to 'Universal History' and the inherent presupposition of rupture between the fifth-century and the fourth-century historiographers. In particular, I support suggestions that Ephorus' history was meaningfully structured around the Return of Heraclidae. This conclusion calls into question earlier depictions of Ephorus as a detached 'armchair historian'. More critically in this context, however, it also explains without reference to generic similarity or to 'Universal History' why Polybius chose Ephorus as the

---

[6] And only: Schepens 1977:95 glosses that Ephorus was *at that time* the only writer to have written 'Universal History'; more often, Ephorus' uniqueness is elided in discussions, and Ephorus is presented purely as the *first* 'Universal Historian'. This reading is perhaps required for a generic understanding of this passage, but still significantly underplays its rhetorical context, discussed below, p. 178.

historiographer who came closest to Polybius' own perfection, specifically with regard to his ability τὰ καθόλου γράφειν. On this analysis, Polybius 5.33.1–5 and Polybius' relationship to Ephorus become another powerful example of the importance of Polybius' own Achaean heritage to his historiographical analysis and judgment. They tells us nothing, however, about Ephorus' generic innovation relative to his predecessors.

In concluding, I briefly turn to those later historiographers, such as Diodorus, who can justifiably be considered as writing something approximating to the modern concept of 'Universal History'. I consider how this reinterpretation of Ephorus' connection with 'Universal History', and of the role of genre more generally, affects scholars' approaches to those historiographers, and argue that it supports recent positive reappraisals of their work: all histories reflected unique combinations of political and social realities of their day, and the particular interests and approaches of the historiographers involved, just as the histories of the fifth century have long been recognized to have done. With the more open perspective advocated here, scholars can better appreciate this diversity, not least though greater awareness of the continuities, as well as the differences, between fifth- and fourth-century historiography.

1. 'Universal History' in Greek Historiography

The underlying tensions inherent in discussions of 'Universal History' with regard to Ephorus are evident in the general scholarly unwillingness to make explicit the definition involved when referring to Ephorus' history as a 'Universal History'. Where any elucidation is offered, it is normally in the form of a description of the bounds of Ephorus' work, as though such an explanation renders the concept of 'Universal History' self-evident. The ultimate source of these tensions is, however, more basic: the deep division between the definition that the phrase 'Universal History' would superficially seem to imply, and the way in which it has more commonly been deployed in Greek historiographical analysis.[7]

What might be termed 'strict definitions' insisting on both geographical and chronological universality are offered by Burde and Alonso-Núñez. For Burde, it should include "the historical events among all peoples of the then known world" ("die geschichtlichen Ereignisse bei allen Völkern der damals bekannten Welt"); for Alonso-Núñez, "Universal historians" should discuss "the

---

[7]   A second source of unease may be felt by many at the explicit aim of 'Universal History': Momigliano 1982:31: "Taken literally, the idea of universal history verges on absurdity. Who can tell everything that has happened? And who would like to listen if he were told?"; Clarke 1999:250: "A more preposterous aim could scarcely be imagined."

history of mankind from the earliest times and in all parts of the world known to them."[8] These are definitions in keeping with the use of the phrase outside scholarship on Greek historiography, with reference to such works as Toynbee's *Study of History*, or Kant's *Idee zu einer allgemeinen Geschichte in weltbürgerlicher Absicht*.[9]

Such definitions have not been the norm, however, in large part owing to the continuing influence of Jacoby's monumental *Fragmente der griechischen Historiker* (FGH).[10] For Jacoby, Ephorus' work was "the first real 'Universal History'" ("die erste wirkliche universalgeschichte"), precisely because he discussed the internal and external history of the Greek people as a whole in the motherland and the colonies. Ephorus did, in addition, deal with non-Greeks in so far as they came into contact with the Greeks, but Jacoby was explicit that he did not understand Ephorus as examining non-Greeks in their own right:[11] Ephorus' history was 'universal' because it covered all of Greece, rather than only one part, and not because it was global, as opposed perhaps to 'national'. Jacoby's discussion of Ephorus' history makes it clear, moreover, how he envisaged Ephorus' history differing from those of Herodotus and Thucydides. Jacoby recognised that Herodotus and Thucydides discussed events ranging across the Greek world and beyond, and events throughout history, but these descriptions were always subordinate to their primary narratives, which were the invasions of Darius and Xerxes, and the Peloponnesian War: Herodotus may have written six books of Persian history, but these were only the introduction to his description of the Persian War.[12] Ephorus' structure was quite different, narrating a chronologically and geographically broader range of events in the main narrative.

This view was not irrational. There is ancient evidence suggesting significant innovation by Ephorus relative to his predecessors: for example, according

---

[8] Burde 1974:6; Alonso-Núñez 2002:11.

[9] Kant 1874; Toynbee 1934–1961.

[10] Jacoby 1923–1958. For analysis of the merits and presuppositions of Jacoby's approach to Greek historiography: Strasburger 1977; Fowler 1996, especially 68; Humphreys 1997; Marincola 1999. For discussion of the merits of a continuation of FGH: Schepens 1997.

[11] Jacoby 1926:25: "[d]en *inhalt* der Ἰστορίαι, als der ersten wirklichen universalgeschichte . . . bildete die gesamte innere und äußere geschichte des griechischen volkes im mutterlande und den kolonien; dazu die der barbaren im osten und westen, soweit sie mit den Griechen in berührung kamen. um ihrer selbst willen sind die barbarenvölker nicht behandelt; denn die geographischen und naturwissenschaftlichen interessen der Ionier fehlen E[phorus] ebenso vollständig wie das verständnis für die naturhafte bedingtheit der menschen." By extension, Ephorus' history can be understood as having been panhellenic, rather than intrinsically *polis*-focussed; this would fit the tradition (cogently doubted by Jacoby, see below, p. 161) connecting Ephorus with Isocrates, but is not essential for Jacoby's analysis.

[12] Jacoby 1909:102.

to Diodorus, he organised the events of his books κατὰ γένος,[13] and he wrote thirty books, attaching to each one a preface.[14] Quite why Jacoby felt these hints implied that Ephorus' history was "Universal History," however, and, even more so, that it was "the first real Universal History," is less clear, although this view was certainly in keeping with contemporary scholarly notions envisaging the fourth century as a time of increased panhellenic awareness, leading to the 'decline of the *polis*' and expansion of the Greek world under and after Alexander.[15] What matters here is that this conclusion allowed Jacoby to create a hermeneutic connection with Polybius' statement that Ephorus was the first τὰ καθόλου γράφειν, and with other passages making use of the many other varied phrases used by ancient authors that have been adduced in this context.[16] Since Jacoby maintained that such phrases were referring to something close to his own concept of 'Universal History', their evidence became available for a much richer picture of the development of Greek historiography.

Despite its problems, Jacoby's circumscribed definition of 'Universal History', and his attempt to equate it to terms involved in ancient historiographical discourse have been fundamental to most interpretations attempted during the past one hundred years. The ongoing dominance of Jacoby's definition and work clarifies why some scholars still feel justified in referring to Ephorus as a 'Universal Historian' without further explanation, or with reference purely to the chronological bounds of his history. The power and range of Jacoby's argument regarding the equation of the modern and ancient historiographical discourses similarly explains why even recent scholars with very different methodological approaches from Jacoby choose to sidestep his generic equation by reference to 'general history' without addressing the more fundamental paradox involved in Jacoby's view, or feel it meaningful to use such oxymoronic phrases as 'universal history of the Mediterranean' or 'universal history of Greece'. There is widespread awareness of the difficulties involved in equating our modern views of 'Universal History' with the ancient discussions regarding τὰ καθόλου γράφειν, τὰς κοινὰς πράξεις, and other similar phrases.[17]

---

[13] Diodorus 5.1.4 = FGH 70 T 11: τῶν γὰρ βίβλων ἑκάστην πεποίηκε περιέχειν κατὰ γένος τὰς πράξεις; for varying interpretations of this phrase, see the discussions at Drews 1963; Vannicelli 1987 and below, p. 183.

[14] Diodorus 16.76.5 = FGH 70 T 10: βίβλους γέγραφε τριάκοντα, προοίμιον ἑκάστηι προθείς.

[15] For continuing reference to such societal factors in explaining the rise of 'Universal History', see below, p. 187, esp. n83.

[16] Burde 1974:6 offers τὰ καθόλου γράφειν, τὰ δὲ παρὰ πᾶσι γεγονότα and αἱ κοιναὶ τῆς οἰκουμένης πράξεις as examples of how Greek authors referred to 'Universal History'; Sacks 1981:101 suggests τὰ καθόλου γράφειν, τὰς κοινὰς πράξεις, οἰκουμένη, τὰ δὲ παρὰ πᾶσι γεγονότα, "and possibly" οἰκονομία, all specifically from Polybius.

[17] Burde 1974; Sacks 1981:96–121; Scafuro 1983; Clarke 1999; Marincola 2007b; Clarke 2008:97; see n5.

Nevertheless, in the end, the validity of our modern generic concerns in understanding the ancient discourse is not questioned: that it is meaningful, under some definition of 'Universal History', to call Ephorus a 'Universal Historian', or to state that Ephorus was perceived by later Greek historians to have been the first to attempt to write 'Universal History', has been the common presupposition of work on Greek historiography for more than a century, even though our methodological approaches to Ephorus and other fragmentary historians have radically shifted.

2. Ephorus and his 'Cover-Texts'

As with most ancient Greek historians, we do not possess a direct manuscript tradition for Ephorus' history. Instead, our evidence is indirect, through 'cover-texts' in authors referring to Ephorus, which have been traditionally divided into *testimonia* and *fragmenta*.[18] Many decades of *Quellenforschung* have been devoted to identifying these 'cover-texts', to analysing the nature of the relationship between the authors involved, and to drawing conclusions about the nature of Ephorus' life and his works. More recent work, however, tends to shy away from some of the more confident conclusions drawn in the past. The problematic and multifaceted nature of the relationships underlying 'cover-texts' is instead now emphasised. In particular, earlier notions of later authors mindlessly copying out extensive sections of the work of their sources have largely been abandoned.[19] Not only is there ever increasing emphasis on the partial and potentially misleading nature of even the shortest 'cover-text',[20] but more sophisticated analyses of ancient rhetorical and historiographical practices have reduced the willingness of scholars to take the statements offered as part

[18] 'Cover-texts': Schepens 1997:166n66; Brunt 1980:477, following Peters in his *Historicorum Romanorum Reliquiae*, offered *reliquiae* for similar reasons. These 'cover-texts' were successively collected for Ephorus by Marx 1815; Müller 1841; Jacoby 1923–1958. It has proved difficult to identify physical papyrus fragments of Ephorus. Early suggestions that he was the author of the *Hellenica Oxyrhynchia* are no longer accepted; for a recent discussion: Behrwald 2005, especially 9–13 for an overview of the vexed question of its authorship.

[19] For an early cautionary note regarding the use of Diodorus to reconstruct the historians of earlier historiographers, notably Ephorus: Drews 1962. For two recent contrasting views of the relationship between Diodorus and Ephorus: Stylianou 1998; Green 2006.

[20] See the seminal articles by Strasburger 1977; Brunt 1980. For an illustration of these difficulties through an investigation into the image of Herodotus to be gained from our 'cover-texts': Lenfant 1999. For a cogent discussion of the difficulties of using Polybius as a source for the previous historiographical tradition, see Pitcher 2009:113–120. Specifically on Polybius as a source for Ephorus, see Chávez Reino 2005, especially 19: "Las noticias de Polibio sobre Éforo no conforman un conunto de datos transparentes y coherentes que puedan traducirse en una imagen perfecta del historiador de Cime, de asimilación inmediata y susceptible de contrastarse con los conocimientos sobre este autor procedentes de otras fuentes."

of ancient discourses at face value.[21] Thus, the tradition connecting Ephorus and Theopompus with Isocrates is now more commonly understood as arising out of perceived stylistic similarities rather than an actual biographical link.[22] As a result, however, both the sheer quantity of individual fragmentary authors' works known to modern scholarship, and the extent of our knowledge of those works have, paradoxically, not grown, but shrunk.

These developments are particularly relevant to Ephorus' status as a 'Universal Historian'. For all Ephorus' prominence in diachronic narratives of Greek historiography, and the scholarly unanimity noted above regarding his connection with 'Universal History', no extant statement of his historical intent directly survives, let alone a prologue, such as for Herodotus or Thucydides. We can be confident in classifying Diodorus as a 'Universal Historian' in the stricter sense advocated by Alonso-Núñez and Burde, not so much from the surviving sections, as from Diodorus' own clear declaration that he believed that the most useful history was one that involved writing, to the best of his ability, a history of the entire world as though it were a single city from the most ancient times to his own day, in so far as it had been handed down, and from his claim that this was precisely what he had done.[23] We have no such direct evidence for Ephorus.

Ephorus' connection with 'Universal History' has instead to be established through other authors' analyses of his work, the very 'cover-texts' whose status is now in general perceived as so problematic. An awareness of this increased complexity is, however, only slowly reaching scholarship on Ephorus. Instead, the academic substructure on which current opinion is based essentially pre-dates these multiple revolutions in scholarship. Analysis of Ephorus continues to assume the hermeneutic value of 'Universal History' as a concept: when our various 'cover-texts' refer, for example, to τὰ καθόλου γράφειν or τὰς κοινὰς πράξεις, they are ultimately referring to something close to the modern concept of 'Universal History'. The nature of the discourse may need clarifying, and stripping of its rhetorical and polemical character, but no more. This presupposition is rather surprising, not least, as has often been noted, because of the lack of theoretical discussion about the nature of 'Universal History' among ancient historiographers.[24] Nevertheless, it has remained strong, in spite of the significant difficulties that have been encountered in attempting to maintain this connection.

---

[21] Marincola 1997.
[22] Already Schwartz 1907:1–2, 9 = Schwartz 1957:3–4, 15; Jacoby 1926:23; more recently: Flower 1994:42–62. This tradition is first attested in the first century BCE, but presumably is older: FGH 70 T 1–5, T 8, T 27–28.
[23] Diodorus 1.3–4, especially 3.6 and 4.6.
[24] Burde 1974:6; Sacks 1981:100, 102; Scafuro 1983:116.

3. 'Universal History' Deconstructed

The difficulties of insisting on 'Universal History' as an active generic concept with regard to Ephorus are clear in the analysis of a passage either explicitly cited or closely paraphrased in all the discussions above mentioned. It is the only passage considered to support an awareness of Ephorus as the first 'Universal Historian'. This passage is Polybius' statement involving Ephorus being τὸν πρῶτον καὶ μόνον ἐπιβεβλημένον τὰ καθόλου γράφειν.

Καίτοι γ' οὐκ ἀγνοῶ διότι καὶ πλείους ἕτεροι τῶν συγγραφέων τὴν αὐτὴν ἐμοὶ προεῖνται φωνήν, φάσκοντες τὰ καθόλου γράφειν καὶ μεγίστην τῶν προγεγονότων ἐπιβεβλῆσθαι πραγματείαν• (2) περὶ ὧν ἐγώ, παραιτησάμενος Ἔφορον τὸν πρῶτον καὶ μόνον ἐπιβεβλημένον τὰ καθόλου γράφειν, τὸ μὲν πλείω λέγειν ἢ μνημονεύειν τινὸς τῶν ἄλλων ἐπ'ὀνόματος παρήσω, (3) μέχρι δὲ τούτου μνησθήσομαι, διότι τῶν καθ' ἡμᾶς τινες γραφόντων ἱστορίαν ἐν τρισὶν ἢ τέτταρσιν ἐξηγησάμενοι σελίσιν ἡμῖν τὸν Ῥωμαίων καὶ Καρχηδονίων πόλεμον φασὶ τὰ καθόλου γράφειν. (4) καίτοι διότι πλεῖσται μὲν καὶ μέγισται τότε περί τε τὴν Ἰβηρίαν καὶ Λιβύην, ἔτι δὲ τὴν Σικελίαν καὶ Ἰταλίαν ἐπετελέσθησαν πράξεις, ἐπιφανέστατος δὲ καὶ πολυχρονιώτατος ὁ κατ' Ἀννίβαν πόλεμος γέγονε πλὴν τοῦ περὶ Σικελίαν, πάντες δ'ἠναγκάσθημεν πρὸς αὐτὸν ἀποβλέπειν διὰ τὸ μέγεθος, δεδιότες τὴν συντέλειαν τῶν ἀποβησομένων, τίς οὕτως ἐστὶν ἀδαὴς ὃς οὐκ οἶδεν; (5) ἀλλ' ἔνιοι τῶν πραγματευομένων οὐδ' ἐφ' ὅσον οἱ τὰ κατὰ καιροὺς ἐν ταῖς χρονογραφίαις ὑπομνηματιζόμενοι πολιτικῶς εἰς τοὺς τοίχους, οὐδ' ἐπὶ τοσοῦτο μνησθέντες, πάσας φασὶ τὰς κατὰ τὴν Ἑλλάδα καὶ βάρβαρον περιειληφέναι πράξεις.

I am not indeed unaware that several other writers make the same boast as myself, that they write general history (τὰ καθόλου γράφειν) and have undertaken a vaster task than any predecessor. (2) Now, while paying all due deference to Ephorus, the first and only writer who really undertook a general history, I will avoid criticizing at length or mentioning by name any of the others, (3) and will simply say this much, that certain writers of history in my own times after giving an account of the war between Rome and Carthage in three or four pages, maintain that they write universal history. (4) Yet no one is so ignorant as not to know that many actions of the highest importance were accomplished then in Spain, Africa, Italy, and Sicily, that the war with Hannibal was the most celebrated and longest of wars if we except that for Sicily, and that we in Greece were all obliged to fix our eyes on it, dreading the results that would follow. (5) But some of those who treat of it, after giving a slighter sketch of it even than those who on public authority set up memoranda of occasional happenings in chronological sequence, claim to have comprised in their work all events in Greece and abroad.

Polybius 5.33.1–5[25]

Polybius' statement hinges on the equivalence between his history and Ephorus' history: they both make the same boast (τὴν αὐτὴν φωνήν), that is, τὰ καθόλου γράφειν. Nevertheless, this fundamental correspondence has been queried, because, as Polybius frequently reminds us, his history involves explaining

πῶς καὶ τίνι γένει πολιτείας ἐπικρατηθέντα σχεδὸν ἅπαντα τὰ κατὰ τὴν οἰκουμένην οὐχ ὅλοις πεντήκοντα καὶ τρισὶν ἔτεσιν ὑπὸ μίαν ἀρχὴν ἔπεσε τὴν Ῥωμαίων, ὃ πρότερον οὐχ εὑρίσκεται γεγονός

by what means and under what system of polity the Romans in less than fifty-three years have succeeded in subjecting nearly the whole inhabited world to their sole government—a thing unique in history (Translation by E. S. Shuckburgh)

Polybius 1.1.5[26]

This master narrative only covers just over one hundred years, 264-146, even including the preliminary material covered in Polybius' first two books (the προκατασκευή), and the extension to include events down to the aftermath of the sack of Corinth in 146. That Polybius' own chronological coverage is so narrow has caused concern about how Polybius could equate his history with Ephorus' work, which covered, on modern 'calculations', approximately 750 years.[27]

Two recent discussions resolve this problem by arguing that Polybius is discussing multiple forms of 'Universal History' in this passage. For Sacks, this situation arises because Polybius "probably did not think the form through entirely": he is unwittingly confusing two separate criteria for 'Universal History', which Sacks terms "quantity" and "quality," where "quantity" focuses on the "sheer amount of material covered by a universal history," and was the criterion applicable to Ephorus' work, and "quality" emphasizes the existence

---

[25] Including FGH 70 T 7; revised translation of 5.33.5 following Walbank 1956, 1967, 1979.

[26] Cf. Polybius 3.1.4–10; Polybius 6.2.3; Polybius 39.8.7; Polybius 8.2.

[27] 'Calculations': e.g. Barber 1935:8–9, because Clement of Alexandria *Miscellanies* 1.139.3 = FGH 70 F 223 states that Ephorus allowed 735 years between the Return of the Heraclidae and Alexander's crossing to Asia.

of a "single unifying theme," and is applied to Polybius' history.[28] For Scafuro, by contrast, Polybius actively seeks the "redefinition of the universal orientation," and deliberately elides the difference between two different narrative orientations towards the past: one is "diachronic," an orientation which "covered events from an early period and was not confined to one event such as a war," and applies to Ephorus' history; the other is "synchronic," an orientation which "recounts events of the οἰκουμένη for one period and which is oriented toward showing the relationship between these events whether they are simply synchronic or of a more intimate nature," and applies to Polybius' work.[29]

Scafuro's interpretation is perhaps the more charitable, but the analyses are similar in their motivation: to preserve Polybius' testimony despite an apparent glaring contradiction. Despite their subsequent popularity,[30] they also share the same three overlapping weaknesses. First, we have no reason to believe that Ephorus' history was any less thematically unified than those of Herodotus, Thucydides, and Polybius himself, all of whom make their purpose explicit in their prologues. It is perhaps more difficult for us to identify Ephorus' theme, in particular on account of the loss of his prologues, but that would not have been a problem for Polybius or his readers, and should not be one for modern readers either.[31] Second, Polybius does not manifest any particular interest elsewhere in the duration of histories, or the respective chronological coverage of the works he discusses: even Timaeus, whom he faults on many other grounds in book twelve, is not censured on this point. It would thus be out of keeping for Polybius to be concerned with chronology, let alone motivated by a wish to elide a perceived chronological discrepancy between Polybius' and Ephorus' histories.[32]

---

[28] Sacks 1981:96–121, quotations from 104 and 105.

[29] Scafuro 1983:116–156, quotations from 131–132, 138, and 153; Scafuro's treatment is helpful in arguing that τὰ καθόλου was not a type or genre (114–115), and in her emphasis on the self-serving basis of Polybius' decision to appropriate the title (viz. "τὰ καθόλου or κοιναὶ ἱστορίαι, 'universal history'") for his "quite different history in order to facilitate its acceptance and success" (153); as this quotation suggests, however, her early position regarding τὰ καθόλου and genre is undermined by her subsequent treatment of τὰ καθόλου as effectively equivalent to 'Universal History', and lost in her later discussion.

[30] They are followed, among others, by Marincola 2007b:171 and Liddel 2010:15.

[31] For a discussion of the thematic structure of Ephorus' work, and of the importance of its ἀρχή to this structure, see below, pp. 178–184.

[32] We may also query whether Polybius would have understood the chronological bounds of his work in the way that modern scholars do, through their constant focus on his primary narrative. Polybius' chronology, including the Roman archaeologia in Book 6, actually stretched back at least to the foundation of the Republic (6.11), and more plausibly to the foundation of Rome itself. The reduced numerical difference that this approach suggests in the periods covered in Ephorus' and Polybius' histories (perhaps ca. 600 years versus ca. 750 years) is less significant than the structural and conceptual similarity which it involves: Ephorus' history stretching from

Third and most significantly, the point on which Polybius' statement turns is precisely that Ephorus made the attempt to do the same as he, τὰ καθόλου γράφειν, when others had not, despite their claims to the contrary. We have no other evidence that insists on such a unique connection between Polybius and Ephorus. Thus, to assume the existence of 'Universal History' as the independent constant uniting both Polybius and Ephorus, while at the same time denying the merits of the only statement on which that equivalence is based, and arguing that, in fact, *two* separate constants are involved, is to beg the question. If Sacks or Scafuro is right, and Polybius is engaging in rhetorically dubious practice here in equating two genres or historiographical approaches which were in reality distinct, it is entirely unclear why we or indeed any other Greek historiographer should be expected to accept Polybius' equation of their approaches!

If there were other evidence supporting the connection specifically between Ephorus and Polybius, this insistence might be justified. As it is, the restricted nature of these reinterpretations is more likely the result of the shadow of Jacoby continuing to influence analysis even as scholars seek to move beyond his paradigm. Given the strongly rhetorical context, the incomplete nature of these analyses, and the uncharacteristic concern for duration they involve, they are better set aside, and a fresh reading that takes greater account of the immediate and general historiographical context attempted. On account of the central role this passage has played in the debate, however, I first establish a frame for this re-interpretation by considering other 'cover-texts', most notably, those of Diodorus, that illuminate our understanding of Ephorus' position in the Greek historiographical tradition. Only then do I return to this passage.

4. Diodorus and 'Universal History'

Diodorus' perception of the earlier tradition is particularly important because he did claim to have written a history of the entire world, which scholars can unproblematically classify as a 'Universal History'.[33] As such, it might be expected that 'Universal History' would be an important factor in his self-representation and self-positioning relative to his predecessors. This is not quite the case.

---

the foundation of classical Greece by its current inhabitants, the descendants of the Heraclidae, to the present day is then more directly comparable to Polybius' history, which stretched from the foundation of Rome to the present day. This might not be the way we commonly choose to portray Polybius' work, but it is not necessarily illegitimate; indeed, Diodorus' description of Herodotus' history forms a direct parallel: see below, p. 170.

[33] See above, p. 161.

κειμένης γὰρ τοῖς ἀναγινώσκουσι τῆς ὠφελείας ἐν τῷ πλείστας καὶ ποικιλωτάτας περιστάσεις λαμβάνειν, οἱ πλεῖστοι μὲν ἑνὸς ἔθνους ἢ μιᾶς πόλεως αὐτοτελεῖς πολέμους ἀνέγραψαν, ὀλίγοι δ᾽ ἀπὸ τῶν ἀρχαίων χρόνων ἀρξάμενοι τὰς κοινὰς πράξεις ἐπεχείρησαν ἀναγράφειν μέχρι τῶν καθ᾽ αὑτοὺς καιρῶν, καὶ τούτων οἱ μὲν τοὺς οἰκείους χρόνους ἑκάστοις οὐ παρέζευξαν, οἱ δὲ τὰς τῶν βαρβάρων πράξεις ὑπερέβησαν, ἔτι δ᾽ οἱ μὲν τὰς παλαιὰς μυθολογίας διὰ τὴν δυσχέρειαν τῆς πραγματείας ἀπεδοκίμασαν, οἱ δὲ τὴν ὑπόστασιν τῆς ἐπιβολῆς οὐ συνετέλεσαν, μεσολαβηθέντες τὸν βίον ὑπὸ τῆς πεπρωμένης.

For although the profit which history affords its readers lies in its embracing a vast number and variety of circumstances, yet most writers have recorded no more than isolated wars waged by a single nation or a single state, and but few have undertaken, beginning with the earliest times and coming down to their own day, to record the events connected with all peoples; and of the latter, some have not attached to the several events their own proper dates, and others have passed over the deeds of barbarian peoples; and some, again, have rejected the ancient legends because of the difficulties involved in their treatment, while others have failed to complete the plan to which they had set their hand, their lives having been cut short by fate. (Translation by C. H. Oldfather)

Diodorus 1.3.2

Diodorus' evaluations of his predecessors can be read as explanations of how his predecessors failed to write 'Universal History', because the ideal of history presented by Diodorus and manifested in his work insofar as it survives equates to the modern notion of 'Universal History': by Diodorus' logic and utilitarian purpose, the best history was one that involved the most *exempla*, and so the broadest chronological and geographical range. Nevertheless, there is one crucial difference: Diodorus had no notion of such a project as a separate genre or type of historiography: it was the pinnacle of the entire historiographical enterprise. This ideal was also represented by Diodorus' history alone: from Diodorus' perspective, there was no other 'Universal History'. This was not a generic argument, but much more self-serving, emphasising how Diodorus' history was necessarily unsurpassed and unsurpassable as an example of histor-ical narrative as a whole: *all* other histories were ultimately failed attempts to achieve what Diodorus' history embodied.

An awareness of this broader context has to inform our understanding of Diodorus' discussions of Ephorus, such as in the prologue to book five:

Πάντων μὲν τῶν ἐν ταῖς ἀναγραφαῖς χρησίμων προνοητέον τοὺς ἱστορίαν συντατομένους, μάλιστα δὲ τῆς κατὰ μέρος οἰκονομίας. αὕτη γὰρ οὐ μόνον ἐν τοῖς ἰδιωτικοῖς βίοις πολλὰ συμβάλλεται πρὸς διαμονὴν καὶ αὔξησιν τῆς οὐσίας, ἀλλὰ καὶ κατὰ τὰς ἱστορίας οὐκ ὀλίγα ποιεῖ προτερήματα τοῖς συγγραφεῦσιν. (2) ἔνιοι δὲ καὶ κατὰ τὴν λέξιν καὶ κατὰ τὴν πολυπειρίαν τῶν ἀναγραφομένων πράξεων ἐπαινούμενοι δικαίως, ἐν τῷ κατὰ τὴν οἰκονομίαν χειρισμῷ διήμαρτον, ὥστε τοὺς μὲν πόνους καὶ τὴν ἐπιμέλειαν αὐτῶν ἀποδοχῆς τυγχάνειν παρὰ τοῖς ἀναγινώσκουσι, τὴν δὲ τάξιν τῶν ἀναγεγραμμένων δικαίας τυγχάνειν ἐπιτιμήσεως. (3) Τίμαιος μὲν οὖν μεγίστην πρόνοιαν πεποιημένος τῆς τῶν χρόνων ἀκριβείας καὶ τῆς πολυπειρίας πεφροντικώς, διὰ ἀκριβείας καὶ τῆς πολυπειρίας πεφροντικώς, διὰ τὰς ἀκαίρους καὶ μακρὰς ἐπιτιμήσεις εὐλόγως διαβάλλεται, καὶ διὰ τὴν ὑπερβολὴν τῆς ἐπιτιμήσεως Ἐπιτίμαιος ὑπό τινων ὠνομάσθη. (4) Ἔφορος δὲ τὰς κοινὰς πράξεις ἀναγράφων οὐ μόνον κατὰ τὴν λέξιν, ἀλλὰ καὶ κατὰ τὴν οἰκονομίαν ἐπιτέτευχε· τῶν γὰρ βίβλων ἑκάστην πεποίηκε περιέχειν κατὰ γένος τὰς πράξεις. διόπερ καὶ ἡμεῖς τοῦτο τὸ γένος τοῦ χειρισμοῦ προκρίναντες κατὰ τὸ δυνατὸν ἀντεχόμεθα ταύτης τῆς προαιρέσεως.

It should be the special care of historians, when they compose their works, to give attention to everything which may be of utility, and especially to the arrangement of the varied material they present. This eye to arrangement, for instance, is not only of great help to persons in the disposition of their private affairs if they would preserve and increase their property, but also, when men come to writing history, it offers them not a few advantages. (2) Some historians indeed, although they are worthy objects of praise in the matter of style and in the breadth of experience derived from the events which they record, have nevertheless fallen short in respect of the way in which they have handled the matter of arrangement, with the result that, whereas the effort and care which they expended receive the approbation of their readers, yet the order which they gave to the material they have recorded is the object of just censure. (3) Timaeus, for example, bestowed, it is true, the greatest attention upon the precision of his chronology and had due regard for the breadth of knowledge gained through experience, but he is criticized with good reason for his untimely and lengthy censures, and because of the excess to which he went in censuring he has been given by some men the name Epitimaeus or Censurer. (4) Ephorus, on the other hand, in the universal history which he composed (τὰς κοινὰς πράξεις ἀναγράφων) has achieved success, not alone in the style of his composition, but also as regards the arrangement of his work; for each one of his Books is so constructed as to embrace events which fall under a single topic. Consequently we also have given our preference to this method of handling our material, and, insofar as it is possible, are adhering to this general principle. (Translation by C. H. Oldfather)

Diodorus 5.1.1–4 (including Ephorus FGH 70 T 11)

Diodorus' focus is again here very broad. He is not offering his discussion as an analysis of the methodology of 'Universal History', but of historiography as a whole: all historiographers should take account of the utility and arrangement of their work, not a specific sub-group. In keeping with this approach, his selection of successful and less successful approaches to historiography is noteworthy: Ephorus, and Timaeus. This selection makes no sense if Diodorus is meaning solely to discuss 'Universal History': Timaeus' history, so far as we can reconstruct it, discussed Italy and Sicily; it was not 'Universal History'.[34] Ephorus' history seems similarly excluded from consideration as a 'Universal History' by Diodorus' statement in the previous passage censuring a range of predecessors: there, he specifically criticises those who had rejected the ancient legends (τὰς παλαιὰς μυθολογίας). One such historian, according to Diodorus using the very same words (τὰς . . . παλαιὰς μυθολογίας) in the prologue to his first book, was Ephorus himself:

διόπερ τῶν μεταγενεστέρων ἱστοριογράφων οἱ πρωτεύοντες τῆι δόξηι τῆς μὲν ἀρχαίας μυθολογίας ἀπέστησαν διὰ τὴν δυσχέρειαν, τὰς δὲ νεωτέρας πράξεις ἀναγράφειν ἐπεχείρησαν. (3) Ἔφορος μὲν γὰρ ὁ Κυμαῖος, Ἰσοκράτους ὢν μαθητής, ὑποστησάμενος γράφειν τὰς κοινὰς πράξεις, τὰς μὲν παλαιὰς μυθολογίας ὑπερέβη, τὰ δ᾽ ἀπὸ τῆς Ἡρακλειδῶν καθόδου πραχθέντα συνταξάμενος ταύτην ἀρχὴν ἐποιήσατο τῆς ἱστορίας.

For these reasons the writers of greatest reputation among the later historians have stood aloof from the narration of the ancient mythology because of its difficulty, and have undertaken to record only the more recent events. (3) Ephorus of Cymê, for instance, a pupil of Isocrates, when he undertook to write his universal history (ὑποστησάμενος γράφειν τὰς κοινὰς πράξεις), passed over the tales of the old mythology and commenced his history with a narration of the events which took place after the Return of the Heraclidae. (Translation by C. H. Oldfather)

Diodorus 4.1.2–3 (Ephorus FGH 70 T 8)

---

[34] Cf. Polybius 12.23.7; hence it is classified by Jacoby as *Sicelica*, not *Universal History*.

In this passage, Diodorus is using Ephorus' work as an example of his point that writers of great reputation had only discussed "the more recent events" (τὰς δὲ νεωτέρας πράξεις). For Diodorus nonetheless to be calling Ephorus' subject a 'Universal History' when he refers to Ephorus as ὑποστησάμενος γράφειν τὰς κοινὰς πράξεις would be highly paradoxical. The rhetorical thrust of this passage is precisely the reverse!

I prefer an alternative interpretation. To understand what the force of Diodorus' description of Ephorus' subject as τὰς κοινὰς πράξεις in these last two passages is, I instead compare it with Diodorus' elaboration of the content of τὰς κοινὰς πράξεις in his introduction, the first passage from Diodorus considered above.[35] There, Diodorus establishes a contrast between those writing τὰς κοινὰς πράξεις and narratives treating the isolated wars of a single nation or a single state (ἑνὸς ἔθνους ἢ μιᾶς πόλεως αὐτοτελεῖς πολέμους). This contrast immediately suggests that τὰς κοινὰς πράξεις is rather a broad notion, without a constraint requiring geographical or chronological universality. This suggestion is confirmed by the continuation, where Diodorus emphasizes that writers of τὰς κοινὰς πράξεις did not necessarily discuss the deeds of non-Greeks. The contrast here is not between universal and non-universal subjects but much looser, in keeping with the more open literal meaning of the phrase. Even a contrast between 'international history' and '*polis*-focused' or monographic history does not capture the force, not least because of the generic and specifically Jacobean implications involved in those terms. Instead, a more flexible translation is needed to match Diodorus' more flexible concept: to understand τὰς κοινὰς πράξεις as 'shared deeds' or 'common affairs' expresses this flexibility much better than 'Universal History', 'worldwide events', or 'world events'. Such translations read too much of Diodorus' own declared theme and aspiration, and of modern scholarly presuppositions, into this phrase.[36]

---

[35] Diodorus 1.3.2: see above, p. 166.

[36] Clarke 2008:96 "shared deeds"; Tuplin 2007:163 "common affairs"; Green 2006:9 "worldwide events," translating Diodorus 1.4.6; "world events": a translation of Diodorus 1.4.6 by Green praised by Marincola 2007b:171 as particularly "felicitous." See now also Pitcher 2009:115, where "common matters" is suggested for τὰς κοινὰς πράξεις. This translation seems fortunate, but the context suggests Pitcher is not entirely happy to pursue the ramifications of what he terms only "literally 'common matters'": thus he immediately juxtaposes the Loeb translation of τὰς κοινὰς πράξεις at Diodorus 1.3.2 as "events connected with all people," without further comment. Despite his cogent analysis of Polybius' rhetorical purpose, and common-sensical comments— "Some histories were more universal than others" (116)—Pitcher ultimately insists on narrow readings of crucial passages, such as Diodorus 1.3.2, and Diodorus 1.1.1, where he states that Diodorus "refers to 'universal' histories as *hai koinai historiai*" (226n13), and so continues to misunderstand the nature of the historiographical tradition. Thus, in this respect, his discussion is unfortunately still subject to the criticisms mentioned here.

I further support this more nuanced reading of τὰς κοινὰς πράξεις, and of Diodorus' approach to Ephorus, by comparing Diodorus' statements about Ephorus with his description of Herodotus' history:

> τῶν δὲ συγγραφέων Ἡρόδοτος ἀρξάμενος πρὸ τῶν Τρωικῶν χρόνων γέγραφε κοινὰς σχεδόν τι τὰς τῆς οἰκουμένης πράξεις ἐν βίβλοις ἐννέα, καταστρέφει δὲ τὴν σύνταξιν εἰς τὴν περὶ Μυκάλην μάχην τοῖς Ἕλλησι πρὸς τοὺς Πέρσας καὶ Σηστοῦ πολιορκίαν.

> And of the historians, Herodotus, beginning with the period prior to the Trojan war, has written in nine books a general history of practically all the events which occurred in the inhabited world, and brings his narrative to an end with the battle of the Greeks against the Persians at Mycalê and the siege of Sestus. (Translation by C. H. Oldfather)

> Diodorus 11.37.6

There is no suggestion here that Ephorus' history marked a radical departure from Herodotus' practice; quite the reverse. Where Ephorus' history had started in Diodorus' eyes with the return of the Heraclidae, Herodotus' work commenced still earlier: before the Trojan War. Given Herodotus' ultimate focus on the wars of 481–479, Diodorus' description of Herodotus' history may seem paradoxical, but it would be unwise to dismiss it as somehow invalid.[37] Diodorus is in good company: his approach is in keeping both with the prologue Herodotus wrote to his own work, and the description offered of Herodotus' history by Dionysius of Halicarnassus. Herodotus wrote his history

> ὡς μήτε τὰ γενόμενα ἐξ ἀνθρώπων τῷ χρόνῳ ἐξίτηλα γένηται, μήτε ἔργα μεγάλα τε καὶ θωμαστά, τὰ μὲν Ἕλλησι, τὰ δὲ βαρβάροισι ἀποδεχθέντα, ἀκλέα γένηται, τά τε ἄλλα καὶ δι' ἣν αἰτίην ἐπολέμησαν ἀλλήλοισι.

> so that things done by man not be forgotten in time, and that great and marvelous deeds, some displayed by the Hellenes, some by the barbarians, not lose their glory, including among others what was the cause of their waging war on each other. (Translation by A. D. Godley)

> Herodotus *praefatio*

---

[37] Vattuone 1998a:64. In Diodorus 1.3.2 (for text, see above, p. 166), Diodorus does not name any specific historian as among those who he felt had written τὰς κοινὰς πράξεις from (almost) the earliest times. The similarity in Diodorus' statements about Herodotus and Ephorus, however, surely suggests that he is as likely to have been thinking of Herodotus here as Ephorus, who we argue above likely is included given the echo of τὰς παλαιὰς μυθολογίας in Diodorus' later treatment of Ephorus.

According to Dionysius,

ἐκεῖνος μὲν γὰρ κοινὴν Ἑλληνικῶν τε καὶ βαρβαρικῶν πράξεων ἐξενήνοχεν ἱστορίαν, 'ὡς μήτε τὰ γενόμενα ἐξ ἀνθρώπων ἐξίτηλα γένηται, μήτε ἔργα' ... καὶ ἅπερ αὐτὸς εἴρηκε. τὸ γὰρ αὐτὸ προοίμιον καὶ ἀρχὴ καὶ τέλος ἐστὶ τῆς ἱστορίας.

He [Herodotus] has produced a national history of the conflict of Greeks and barbarians, 'in order that neither should the deeds of men fade into oblivion, nor should achievements,' to quote from his opening words. For this same proem forms both the beginning and the end of his History. (Translation by S. Usher)

Dionysius of Halicarnassus *Letter to Pompey* 3.3

It would perhaps be unwise to place too much weight on Dionysius' quotation of just the first half of Herodotus' self-description, excluding mention of the cause of the war. Nevertheless, the emphasis of these descriptions reminds us how different ancient perceptions of even famous works we think we know well may have been.[38] They also support Diodorus' emphasis on continuity between Ephorus and Herodotus: it is not self-evident that Diodorus' and Dionysius' descriptions of Herodotus and Ephorus show an active concern for genre, let alone that they mask an awareness of a significant shift in historiographical approach in the fourth century that could elsewhere have been conceived as equating to a different genre. Development and evolution, not disjunction and revolution, best summarise their approach to Ephorus and his position in the wider historiographical tradition.[39]

5. Polybius and 'Universal History'

In this context, I now return to Polybius, to consider what he meant when he referred to Ephorus as "the first and only writer who really undertook a general history" (τὸν πρῶτον καὶ μόνον ἐπιβεβλημένον τὰ καθόλου γράφειν).[40] Polybius' characterisation of the historians whom he felt had claimed yet had failed τὰ καθόλου γράφειν is noteworthy. Here, he does not choose historians whom he feels have omitted certain events or a certain area from their histories—or

---

[38] Compare the different possible formulations of Polybius' chronological bounds, above, p. 164, especially n32.

[39] On revolution in antiquity and contrasting ancient and modern approaches to change, see the essays in Goldhill and Osborne 2006, especially Osborne 2006.

[40] Polybius 5.33.1–5; translation revised following Walbank 1956, 1967, 1979: see pp. 162–163.

rather he does not characterise those historians as historians whom he feels have omitted certain events or a certain area from their histories. Instead, he characterises them as historians who discuss the war between the Romans and Carthaginians in three or four columns. The grounds of Polybius' criticism are clear: they do not fail because they do not discuss events earlier or later than the Punic War, or events in other locations; they fail because the Punic War deserves to be treated in greater detail.

Simply to mention the war is not enough. The brevity of these historians' descriptions indicates, to Polybius' eyes, that they do not correctly identify the significance of the events they are narrating. In short, it is a matter of an appropriate balance and perspective, not of chronological or geographical coverage—and so, by implication, is Polybius' associated praise of Ephorus. Polybius is acclaiming Ephorus not as the only historian who has truly covered a broad chronological span, or a broad geographical area, or even as the only historian (prior to himself) who has chosen an appropriate synthetic theme; instead, he is the only historian before Polybius himself who has even come close to producing a work which involves a balanced overarching perspective for each aspect of his history. For Polybius, this is not a question of 'Universal History'; indeed, Ephorus' genre is strictly irrelevant.

This reading is strikingly different from the approach that has been common in previous scholarship. It is, however, much more in keeping with Polybius' historiographical concerns elsewhere: a concern for overall balance and perspective, not extent of coverage, is Polybius' prime thrust. A particularly clear example is the extended analogy right at the start of book one, a prominent and programmatic location, between the inadequacies of an examination of the different separated parts of an animal, and the reading τῆς κατὰ μέρος ἱστορίας:

καθόλου μὲν γὰρ ἔμοιγε δοκοῦσιν οἱ πεπεισμένοι διὰ τῆς κατὰ μέρος ἱστορίας μετρίως συνόψεσθαι τὰ ὅλα παραπλήσιόν τι πάσχειν, ὡς ἂν εἴ τινες ἐμψύχου καὶ καλοῦ σώματος γεγονότος διερριμμένα τὰ μέρη θεώμενοι νομίζοιεν ἱκανῶς αὐτόπται γίνεσθαι τῆς ἐνεργείας αὐτοῦ τοῦ ζῴου καὶ καλλονῆς. (8) εἰ γάρ τις αὐτίκα μάλα συνθεὶς καὶ τέλειον αὖθις ἀπεργασάμενος τὸ ζῷον τῷ τ' εἴδει καὶ τῇ τῆς ψυχῆς εὐπρεπείᾳ κἄπειτα πάλιν ἐπιδεικνύοι τοῖς αὐτοῖς ἐκείνοις, ταχέως ἂν οἶμαι πάντας αὐτοὺς ὁμολογήσειν διότι καὶ λίαν πολύ τι τῆς ἀληθείας ἀπελείποντο πρόσθεν καὶ παραπλήσιοι τοῖς ὀνειρώττουσιν ἦσαν. (9) ἔννοιαν μὲν γὰρ λαβεῖν ἀπὸ μέρους τῶν ὅλων δυνατόν, ἐπιστήμην δὲ καὶ γνώμην ἀτρεκῆ σχεῖν ἀδύνατον. (10) διὸ παντελῶς βραχύ τι νομιστέον συμβάλλεσθαι τὴν κατὰ μέρος ἱστορίαν πρὸς τὴν τῶν ὅλων ἐμπειρίαν καὶ πίστιν. (11)

ἐκ μέντοι γε τῆς ἁπάντων πρὸς ἄλληλα συμπλοκῆς καὶ παραθέσεως, ἔτι δ' ὁμοιότητος καὶ διαφορᾶς, μόνως ἄν τις ἐφίκοιτο καὶ δυνηθείη κατοπτεύσας ἅμα καὶ τὸ χρήσιμον καὶ τὸ τερπνὸν ἐκ τῆς ἱστορίας ἀναλαβεῖν.

He indeed who believes that by studying isolated histories he can acquire a fairly just view of history as a whole, is, as it seems to me, much in the case of one, who, after having looked at the dissevered limbs of an animal once alive and beautiful, fancies he has been as good as an eyewitness of the creature itself in all its action and grace. (8) For could anyone put the creature together on the spot, restoring its form and the comeliness of life, and then show it to the same man, I think he would quickly avow that he was formerly very far away from the truth and more like one in a dream. (9) For we can get some idea of a whole from a part, but never knowledge or exact opinion. (10) Special histories therefore contribute very little to the knowledge of the whole and conviction of its truth. (11) It is only indeed by study of the interconnection of all the particulars, their resemblances and differences, that we are enabled at least to make a general survey, and thus derive both benefit and pleasure from history. (Translation by E. S. Shuckburgh)

Polybius 1.4.7–11

Here, Polybius does not envisage confusion arising because the viewer has overlooked a physical part of the animal. Instead, the difficulty arises because of the way the parts are arranged: they are διερριμμένα, dissevered, and so are seen in isolation from each other. Though the man may fancy he is able to conjure up a picture of the animal as it is when whole, in fact, he cannot, and realizes this when he does see the animal whole.

To pursue the analogy, Polybius is not here criticizing readers who have failed from κατὰ μέρος ἱστορία to learn about a particular important event, whether because of geographical or chronological oversight or simple forgetfulness. Instead, he is arguing that, no matter how well-informed the reader is, he falls short because the narrative structure involved in κατὰ μέρος ἱστορία does not offer the overarching synthesis between events that Polybius seeks, and thus prevents the correct connections from being made between the different events involved in the theme which the reader is investigating. Overall perspective, balance and structure with relevance to the theme in question—the body—are central here, not absolute extent of coverage, in keeping with the interpretation here of Ephorus' excellence at τὰ καθόλου γράφειν.

The same focus is visible in a similar later discussion of the inadequacy of κατὰ μέρος ἱστορία for those attempting to understand Polybius' own theme: how all parts of the known world came under one rule.[41] Here again, reading κατὰ μέρος ἱστορία is adequate to approach individual aspects of that process, such as how the Romans captured Syracuse and how they gained control of Spain, but it is inadequate for the overarching theme: the events are not interconnected, so that the reader remains unaware of the true significance and import of the events.

The emphasis in both of these examples is on synthesis, on making connections between the events narrated with concern for τὰ καθόλου in a way that κατὰ μέρος ἱστορία does not enable. The scope of each individual κατὰ μέρος ἱστορία is, however, superficially less clear. Two different interpretations are possible. Polybius could be suggesting that each κατὰ μέρος ἱστορία necessarily only covered a chronological or geographical part of the overall narrative, such that many κατὰ μέρος ἱστορίαι were required to cover all the material mentioned in one history written with regard for τὰ καθόλου. A second, stronger reading would involve Polybius allowing that κατὰ μέρος ἱστορία could potentially cover all the material, but without offering the synthetic aspect that writing with regard for τὰ καθόλου would provide: such a history would be perfectly adequate regarding the detail and analysis of the events themselves, but fail to offer the added level of analysis which Polybius claimed his history did.[42]

This distinction matters because of the implications for attempted generic approaches to Polybius' analysis: the second interpretation outlined above does not involve any strict geographical or chronological disjuncture between writing with regard for τὰ καθόλου and κατὰ μέρος ἱστορία. These two approaches could then be not mutually exclusive, but instead even complementary aspects of the same work, with both aspects, not just one, required for the perfect history. If so, Polybius might be expected to claim not just to have written τὰ καθόλου, as he does when discussing Ephorus in the passage with which we started, but to have written καὶ καθόλου καὶ κατὰ μέρος, both with an awareness of the broader picture and with reference to the particular event in question: unlike Ephorus, Polybius' own descriptions of battles were not lacking, and his history was perfect in every way.[43] This is, of course, precisely what Polybius does, not once, but three times, including at two prominent programmatic locations: the start of what he claims as the main narrative of his work in book three (the

---

[41] Polybius 8.2; cf. n26.

[42] To return to Polybius' analogy with the body: reading κατὰ μέρος ἱστορία equates, in the former case, to viewing a particular part of the body, and in the latter case to viewing all the parts of the body while they are disconnected.

[43] Polybius 12.25f1.

first passage noted below), and at what seems to have been the beginning of his epilogue in book thirty-nine (the third passage below):

ἐπεὶ δὲ τὰς ἐπιφανεστάτας τῶν πράξεων ἐπὶ κεφαλαίου διεληλύθαμεν, βουλόμενοι καὶ καθόλου καὶ κατὰ μέρος εἰς ἔννοιαν ἀγαγεῖν τῆς ὅλης ἱστορίας τοὺς ἐντυγχάνοντας, ὥρα μνημονεύοντας τῆς προθέσεως ἐπαναγαγεῖν ἐπὶ τὴν ἀρχὴν τῆς αὐτῶν ὑποθέσεως.

Now, having given a summary of the most important events, with the object of conveying to my readers a notion of this work as a whole and its contents in detail, it is time for me to call to mind my original plan and return to the starting-point of my history. (Translation by E. S. Shuckburgh)

Polybius 3.5.9

ἐπεὶ γὰρ οὐ τινά, τὰ δὲ παρὰ πᾶσι γεγονότα γράφειν προηρήμεθα, καὶ σχεδὸν ὡς εἰπεῖν μεγίστῃ τῶν προγεγονότων ἐπιβολῇ κεχρήμεθα τῆς ἱστορίας, καθάπερ καὶ πρότερόν που δεδηλώκαμεν, (7) δέον ἂν εἴη μεγίστην ἡμᾶς ποιεῖσθαι πρόνοιαν καὶ τοῦ χειρισμοῦ καὶ τῆς οἰκονομίας, ἵνα καὶ κατὰ μέρος καὶ καθόλου σαφὲς τὸ σύνταγμα γίνηται τῆς πραγματείας.

For since my design is to write the history not of certain particular matters but of what happened all over the world, and indeed, as I previously stated, I have undertaken, I may say, a vaster task than any of my predecessors, (7) it is my duty to pay particular attention to the matter of arrangement and treatment, so that both as a whole and in all its details my work may have the quality of clearness. (Translation by E. S. Shuckburgh)

Polybius 5.31.6–7

ἡμεῖς δὲ παραγεγονότες ἐπὶ τὸ τέρμα τῆς ὅλης πραγματείας βουλόμεθα, προσαναμνήσαντες τῆς ἀρχῆς καὶ τῆς προεκθέσεως ἧς ἐποιησάμεθα καταβαλόμενοι τὴν ἱστορίαν, συγκεφαλαιώσασθαι τὴν ὅλην ὑπόθεσιν, οἰκειώσαντες τὴν ἀρχὴν τῷ τέλει καὶ καθόλου καὶ κατὰ μέρος.

I, now I have reached the end of my whole work, wish, after recalling to my readers the initial scheme that I laid before them as the foundation of the work, to give a summary of the whole subject matter, establishing both in general and in particular the connection between the beginning and the end. (Translation by E. S. Shuckburgh)

Polybius 39.8.3

On the second analysis above, wherein writing καθόλου and κατὰ μέρος are complementary, these statements make perfect sense: Polybius is ostentatiously emphasizing his mastery of the historical discipline, both in narrating his overall theme, and with reference to each individual event mentioned. This approach is also entirely consistent with his use of καθόλου and κατὰ μέρος in the passages discussed above. By contrast, those who insist with Jacoby on a generic approach, that τὰ καθόλου elsewhere means 'Universal History', and that it is to be contrasted with accounts written κατὰ μέρος, which "clearly implies individual works on small topics, or monographs," have more difficulty. Even though Sacks, in discussing this passage, acknowledges that "*[k]atholou* must mean something like 'the general import' and *kata meros* 'particulars,' or 'details'," this does not cause him to question his previous conclusions regarding the meaning of τὰ καθόλου and κατὰ μέρος. Instead, it is "especially vexing" that Polybius could write so "offhandedly" in stating that he writes both καθόλου καὶ κατὰ μέρος.[44] On occasion, *non liquet* is an appropriate answer; authors can be self-contradictory. To suggest offhandedness when dealing with programmatic passages at significant locations in a work is, however, less than satisfying, especially when there is a clear, logical alternative: that Polybius is not concerned with genre, and even less with 'Universal History'.

The alternative solution I outline here may seem paradoxical. Any paradox arises, however, at least in part because of the weight of the scholarship that insists that τὰ καθόλου and κατὰ μέρος ἱστορία are mutually exclusive, and that reads these terms either implicitly or explicitly as generic, such that κατὰ μέρος ἱστορία equates to something close to Jacoby's 'Monographie', and τὰ καθόλου to 'Universal History'. The approach here is clearly to be preferred. If τὰ καθόλου and κατὰ μέρος ἱστορία are generic categories, scholars encounter and have to explain illogicalities in Polybius' discussions, such as why Polybius provides no separate generic category for *Hellenica* between 'Universal History'/ τὰ καθόλου and monography/ κατὰ μέρος ἱστορία, and why Polybius occasionally refers to histories of Greece or Persia in contexts where we might expect him to be discussing histories κατὰ μέρος.[45] There is, however, no need to read these phrases in such a technical way. The force of the adverbs suggests a concern for overarching perspective, and detailed discussion respectively, but these phrases

---

[44] Sacks 1981:103–104; Scafuro 1983:115, quotations from Sacks.
[45] Sacks 1981:103 with reference to Polybius 3.32 and 2.37.4.

do not imply that the philosophies and works represented by these categories were distinct or mutually exclusive.[46]

If we do not insist on such categorization, there is no difficulty, because Polybius' κατὰ μέρος ἱστορία is not a specific sub-genre of Greek History to be contrasted against *Hellenica*, 'Universal History', 'Monographie', or any other. Instead, it covers any history which Polybius felt failed to aim for and to achieve the correct overall perspective on the significance of the events which it narrated within its stated theme. Polybius can thus be self-consciously and deliberately referring to what modern scholars might term *Hellenica* and to histories of Greece and Persia as written κατὰ μέρος. By definition, such a history would disqualify itself from consideration as being written with regard for τὰ καθόλου, not because of any external characteristic, but because Polybius disagreed with its emphasis or tenor.

Polybius' history may have been geographically extensive, such that he felt that he could emphatically state that it covered events across the known world,[47] and he may have organised the various parts of his narrative round his overarching theme, but it does not follow that an awareness of modern generic categories must underlie his each and every discussion. Insisting on such an awareness only leads to confusion. Instead, not only was Polybius not concerned with notions equatable to modern concepts of 'Universal History', the interpretation here suggests that he was not interested in generic considerations at all.[48]

---

[46] Compare now Hartog 2010:37–38, which situates Polybius' discussion with reference to Aristotle's *Poetics*, but unfortunately continues to argue from the natural opposition of general and particular perspective that "'general' history opposes partial history (*kata meros*)" (38).

[47] τὰ δὲ παρὰ πᾶσι γεγονότα: Polybius 5.31.6; πάσας καθ' ἔκαστον ἔτος τὰς κατάλληλα πράξεις γενομένας κατὰ τὴν οἰκουμένην: Polybius 15.24a. Claims which, however, should be understood rhetorically, not literally, and compared to his repeated insistence on how the Romans conquered almost the entire known world (Polybius 1.1.5, etc.; see n26 for citations; for discussion of this claim, see below, p. 188).

[48] The argument here regarding non-prescriptive, non-generic readings of τὰς κοινὰς πράξεις, τὰ καθόλου, and κατὰ μέρος ἱστορία may be applied more widely. To treat, for example, *Hellenica* as a distinct genre of historiography, as has been the case in many modern analyses, or even to equate it with "Continuous Histories," as Tuplin 2007 does, for all his misgivings, is problematic not just because of the generic approach it authorises, but because it suggests that the modern generic category is based on ancient use. Such prescriptive readings are not, however, self-evident: τὰ Ἑλληνικά need mean no more than 'events concerning the Greeks'; τὰ Περσικά 'Persian affairs'. As such, they are descriptions of the content of a narrative, not its title, nor a description of its genre. Such phrases do not imply that the philosophies and works represented by these categories were distinct or mutually exclusive, any more than we have seen to be the case here for τὰς κοινὰς πράξεις, τὰ καθόλου, and κατὰ μέρος ἱστορία. Modern practice therefore facilitates perhaps unwitting retrojection of that categorization onto the 'cover-texts', causing confusion when it comes to interpreting those very 'cover-texts' that are simultaneously 'validating' the modern approach.

Examples could be multiplied of occasions where Polybius' phraseology is clearly at least as consistent with the above interpretation as with earlier genre-focussed argumentation.[49] Instead, I return to Polybius' claim about his relationship with Ephorus, that he was τὸν πρῶτον καὶ μόνον ἐπιβεβλημένον τὰ καθόλου γράφειν. It is clear that it is not a generic statement: that Ephorus was the first and only writer who had really attempted to undertake the specific type of history that Polybius himself did. Polybius' ideal of historiography is different: it requires writing both καθόλου and κατὰ μέρος. Polybius' claim is a much more ambitious, proud, and caustic statement: that Ephorus was the first and only writer who had really attempted to write a history with a correct synthetic awareness of the events mentioned. In one sentence, Polybius dismisses every previous Greek historiographer (including Ephorus) as his inferior. Whether scholars agree with Polybius or not about their relative statuses in the tradition is of little importance. What does matter is that such a tendentious and self-serving comment can under no circumstance be the basis for a generic analysis: even if Polybius and Ephorus were both, for independent reasons, considered 'Universal Historians', there would be no justifiable basis whatsoever to argue from this comment that Polybius saw any connection between them regarding 'Universal History', let alone that he was claiming Ephorus was his only predecessor in that regard.[50]

6. Ephorus without 'Universal History'

The discussion here of Diodorus' and Polybius' 'cover-texts' thus suggests a rather different picture from the one in current scholarship. It does not automatically follow that the modern emphasis on rupture is unhelpful. Nevertheless, I argue that, when we read Ephorus as part of a single tradition with Herodotus and Thucydides, we do gain insight, and so support the perspective of the ancient sources in de-emphasizing the importance of the shift from the fifth century to the fourth century in Greek historiography.

---

[49] Polybius 1.13.6, 9.44.2; 10.21.7; 29.12.1–8.

[50] It should be noted that Polybius does on one other occasion refer to τοὺς τὰ καθόλου γράφοντας, plural (Polybius 29.12.5), and also once during his discussion of Timaeus to τοῖς ὑπὲρ τῆς οἰκουμένης καὶ τῶν καθόλου πράξεων πεποιημένοις τὰς συντάξεις (Polybius 12.23.7). In the latter case, it probably refers only to Ephorus, whom Polybius has just said Timaeus vehemently attacked. In the former, as Sacks 1981:106 notes, the plural writers are probably just Polybius himself, who refers to himself in the plural in surrounding sentences. Thus, neither provides any sound basis for suggesting that Polybius is here contradicting his statement at Polybius 5.33.2, or for speculating which other ancient historians Polybius might have considered also wrote in the nuanced way he advocated under writing with regard for τὰ καθόλου. The clear answer is: none.

The analysis here starts with Parmeggiani's brilliant analysis of Diodorus' description of the ἀρχή of Ephorus' history as being the Return of the Heraclidae: Parmeggiani argued that the Return of the Heraclidae was the ἀρχή for Ephorus not only in the sense of being the start of the work, but also the start in a more philosophical sense, the point around which it was organised.[51] When Ephorus is read in isolation, this suggestion remains almost unverifiable. We can support it by noting that there are many surviving 'cover-texts' attesting to Ephorus' interest in the Spartan constitution, and in comparing it to those on Crete. Particularly significant, moreover, is Polybius' criticism of Ephorus for using the same words, names apart, when discussing the πολιτεῖαι of Sparta and Crete:[52] this suggests that Ephorus' comments were not just scattered, but that there was likely a structured comparison of their constitutions, perhaps similar to that which Polybius undertook for Rome in his sixth book. Nevertheless, precisely because we are now so aware of how surviving 'cover-texts' reflect the interests of the citing author as much as the author mentioned, this argument cannot be considered conclusive.[53]

The situation changes radically when we compare Diodorus' description of Ephorus' ἀρχή with Diodorus' similar description of Herodotus' history as ἀρξάμενος πρὸ τῶν Τρωικῶν χρόνων.[54] We do possess Herodotus' history, and we know that it did not just begin before the Trojan Wars, it also found its ἀρχή there in Parmeggiani's broader structural sense, through the investigation there of the themes of conflict, particularly between 'Greek' and 'Barbarian', and of the value of ἱστορίη. Both of these are themes we can trace through Herodotus' work right from the beginning of book one. In opening our perspective on Ephorus to resonances with Herodotus, we thus not only support Parmeggiani's interpretation of Ephorus' history, but also enrich our understanding of Herodotus' achievement, and of Diodorus' analytical skills.[55]

We can, moreover, powerfully confirm this argument when we turn to consider the end of Ephorus' history. Diodorus tells us that Ephorus' history ended with the Siege of Perinthus in 341/0, when Philip of Macedon failed to take

---

[51] Parmeggiani 1999:112: "il Ritorno degli Eraclidi non è solo *l'incipit* narrativo, ma anche il punto a partire dal quale il soggetto storico *viene organizzato*" (original emphasis); his suggested translation for Diodorus 4.1.2 = Ephorus FGH 70 T 8—τὰ δ' ἀπὸ τῆς῾ Ἡρακλειδῶν καθόδου πραχθέντα συνταξάμενος ταύτην ἀρχὴν ἐποιήσατο τῆς ἱστορίας: "organizzati i fatti a partire dal Ritorno degli Eraclidi, Eforo ne fece il principio delle *Storie*." For text, see p. 168 above.

[52] Polybius 6.46.10; cf. Strabo 8.5.4 = FGH 70 F 18b; Polybius 6.45.1 = FGH 70 F 148; Strabo 10.4.9 = FGH 70 F 33; Strabo 10.4.16 = FGH 70 F 149.

[53] See above, pp. 160–161.

[54] Diodorus 11.37.6.

[55] For positive reassessments of Diodorus' historiographical ability against earlier scholarship: Sacks 1990; Sacks 1994; Green 2006.

the city.[56] Such a conclusion has traditionally been considered problematic for a 'Universal History', and the lack of understanding of Ephorus' conclusion has encouraged speculation about the possibly unfinished nature of Ephorus' work, and what his intended end might have been.[57] A comparison with Herodotus' history is, however, again enlightening. As with Ephorus' conclusion, so too the ending of Herodotus' work has often been criticised, but recent scholars have been more kind: when the Athenians hang Artayctes, Herodotus invites us to reflect on later Athenian imperial behaviour, and on the Athenian story that is beginning even as the Persian story ends; when Cyrus advises the Persians to live on barren hills, not fertile plains, or else imperil their empire, questions of decay, decadence and their relationship are central.[58] Turning back to Ephorus, the significance of the Siege of Perinthus is not quite the same, but we should not expect that: Ephorus was not Herodotus. The Siege of Perinthus is, however, powerful in a related vein, as the prominent failure of the new hegemonical power even before it had reached its zenith: Macedon. We thus do not need to excuse Ephorus' decision to end here, explaining it as a sign of incompleteness. Instead, it was a historiographical masterstroke, just as Herodotus' conclusion had been.

We may, moreover, now go futher: the analysis of these two programmatic passages and the 'cover-texts' referring to Sparta supports and extends Parmeggiani's hypothesis: just as Herodotus' history was structured in one respect round the rise of the Persian empire, and proleptically looked forward to the rise of the Athenian, so too Ephorus' work was plausibly structured round the domination of the Spartans, and proleptically looked forward to the rise of the Macedonian. There is here no need to posit that Ephorus lived to see Alexander's domains riven by his generals' discord over the succession for this end to be understood as a comment on the likely durability of Macedonian hegemony: the succession of empires and the fragility of human success were notions embedded in Greek thought.[59]

Analyzing Ephorus' structure in this way is particularly valuable, because it both connects Ephorus into broader trends in Greek thought, and embeds him in contemporary political dialogue. Both these aspects are confirmed, moveover, when we consider the broader cultural context in which Ephorus'

---

[56] Diodorus 16.76.5 (= FGH 70 T 10).

[57] Drews 1963:254: "The penultimate stage in the siege of Perinthus is a most infelicitous conclusion to a universal history and can hardly have been arbitrarily selected as such by Demophilus; it is much more reasonable to assume that the awkward conclusion resulted from some exigency in Ephorus' own career."

[58] Herodotus 9.119–123. See Moles 1996; Dewald 1997; Pelling 1997; Flower and Marincola 2002; for a summary of earlier interpretations: Immerwahr 1966:146n119.

[59] See below, p. 189.

references to the myth of the Return of the Heraclidae are to be situated. Thus, Luraghi has persuasively demonstrated the importance of the Return in fourth-century Peloponnesian political discourse, that "the return had played a very prominent role in debates and conflicts throughout the century," including the emergence of Triphylia from the dependant allies of Elis and its later absorption into Arcadia, the establishment of a new Messenia, and the brief efflorescence of Pisatis.[60] If so, then Ephorus' choice of the Return of the Heraclidae as the point from which to structure his history was singularly appropriate, and suggests that he was as connected to the political atmosphere of his day as Thucydides and Herodotus had been to theirs. This valuable conclusion further calls into question previous statements depicting Ephorus as an 'armchair historian' beyond his predecessors, and supports Parmeggiani's re-analysis of the appropriate evidence emphasising both the limited range of Polybius' criticisms, and their rhetorical context.[61]

The Return of the Heraclidae was, however, not just a part of fourth-century Peloponnesian political discourse. We need to consider the 'pre-history' of the myth prior to the fourth century. Herodotus is again here helpful, because of the prominence the myth has in his narrative: Herodotus already presents the Spartan kings as descended from the Heraclidae.[62] Perhaps more important, however, are the arguments Herodotus offers before the Battle of Plataea, when the Tegeans and Athenians contested who should hold the place of honour on the second wing of the army along with the Spartans.[63] Herodotus' Tegeans argue their case through a retelling of the myth of the Return of the Heraclidae: in their earlier attempt to return, the King of the Tegeans, Echemus, defeated Hyllus, and so forced the Heraclidae to retreat for one hundred years. Herodotus' Athenians retort in the same terms: they helped the Heraclidae after their defeat, and in their eventual reconquest. Herodotus is, of course, not a direct reflection of contemporary political discourse. Nevertheless, both examples suggest that the Heraclidae, and their Return, were already an important reference when Herodotus was writing.[64] This discourse may perhaps have become

---

[60] See Luraghi's paper in this volume, p. 133f.

[61] See Parmeggiani, "On the Concept of Rhetorical Historiography," paper delivered at the Bologna Congress, December 13, 2007, to be published; Polybius envisaging Ephorus as an 'armchair-historian': e.g. Schepens 1977:96; Ephorus as 'armchair historian': e.g. Schepens 1987:329, and Hose 2006:677, depicting him as writing "without any attempt to find and explore new 'primary sources'," despite an awareness of the usefulness of inscriptions to Ephorus in his composition already in Barber 1935:127–128. The same criticism is also levelled at Timaeus from Polybius' criticisms, especially Polybius 7.28a3–4: Walbank 1972:31; Williams 2001:23; van der Stockt 2005:290. Both as 'typical armchair historians': Momigliano 1975:58.

[62] Herodotus 6.52.

[63] Herodotus 9.26–27.

[64] Compare also Euripides *Heraclidae*.

still more prominent in the fourth century, but it is at most a matter of degree, not a paradigm shift. Even if Ephorus is the first to structure his history round the Heraclidae, that does not make him a distinctively fourth century figure; rather, we again see the continuity between the fifth and the fourth centuries.

Ephorus was not *just* Herodotean, however. It is tempting to trace a narrative that connects Ephorus to Herodotus and effectively bypasses Thucydides and his model of historiography.[65] Indeed, there are undoubtedly features that these two share that are less prominent in Thucydides: thus, though we can never dismiss the difficulties caused by our evidence, even the few mentions of early foundations that survive and our few book references, involving Ephorus only reaching the Persian Wars in his tenth book, suggest that Ephorus was more interested in foundations than Thucydides, and that the distant past played a disproportionately larger role in his history than in that of Thucydides, just as it did for Herodotus.[66] Nevertheless, our comparanda have been Herodotean so far largely out of necessity: we do not have the end of Thucydides' work, nor do we possess Diodorus' vision of Thucydides' history to compare against his approaches to Herodotus and Thucydides, such that our other significant source of comparanda has been unavailable. Elsewhere, the similarity with Thucydides is more notable, and encourages us to think of all three historians as part of a broader milieu, with their coverage and emphases changing with their themes, but similar underlying concerns.

In keeping with this, Parmeggiani cogently emphasises that Ephorus' concern for the reliability of traditions of the distant past reflects Thucydidean influences (if not necessarily Thucydides' influence).[67] It is not, however, a matter of Thucydidean influence versus Herodotean: the reliability of his traditions, particularly the geographically and chronologically more distant, was equally a concern for Herodotus.[68] Each grapples in his own way with the difficulty of how to relate events known indirectly, whether through oral or documentary means.

A further example of underlying similarity, moreover, likely lies in their approach to incorporating history prior to their primary narrative: Herodotus discusses the history of each nation at the point in the narrative when the

---

[65] Vannicelli 1987:187.

[66] Early foundations mentioned by Ephorus included those of the Delphic Oracle: Strabo 9.3.11–12 = FGH 70 F 31b; Thebes: Strabo 9.2.2 = FGH 70 F 119; and Milesian colonies: Athenaeus 12.523e = FGH 70 F 183; the Persian Wars in Ephorus' tenth book: Stephanus of Byzantium s.v. Πάρος = FGH 70 F 63.

[67] Parmeggiani 1999:118–119.

[68] Herodotus 1.5.3–4; 1.171.1; 2.29.1; 2.123.1, 2.46.1; etc.; for discussion focussing on the significance of Herodotus' programmatic statements in his discussion of Egypt: Vannicelli 2001; for discussion of Herodotus' principles of source citation: Luraghi 2001b.

nation is first substantively presented as making contact with the Persians. Thucydides does just the same in his treatment of Sicily, presenting the geography and earlier history of Sicily when he wished to move it to centre-stage in his historical narrative at the start of book six.[69] So too, plausibly, did Ephorus: he likely wove his narrative round the actions of the Heraclidae, incorporating the earlier history of each nation around some significant early interaction with the Heraclidae.

Finally, this is also the context in which to approach the much-vexed question of Ephorus' κατὰ γένος structure. Vannicelli's argument for a looser, multivalent understanding of κατὰ γένος has much to recommend it against a narrower insistence on one of biographical, geographical or historical themes: it equates to organizing his history round central themes of varying types either inside or across books of his history.[70] His explanation of Ephorus' decision as connected with his writing 'Universal History', however, needs revision.[71] Insofar as it may be just a reference to the increased length, and so inherently increased complexity of Ephorus' history, it may have a certain justification, but it is insufficient in its own right; it does not explain why Ephorus should be credited with this shift rather than Theopompus, who wrote fifty-eight books of *Philippica* alone.[72] Similarly, our description of Herodotus' and Thucydides' narrative structure above suggests Ephorus cannot have been novel in writing κατὰ γένος: that is precisely what Herodotus and Thucydides had done in structuring the 'pre-history' of their narratives.

Diodorus' context is again helpful here: Diodorus' statement can instead be connected with Ephorus' innovation as being one of the first to structure his history as *books*. This decision might well have been spurred Ephorus to make the sort of repeated explicit programmatic statements explaining his organisational principles for those books which were not necessary or possible for Thucydides and Herodotus, as they did not write with such sub-divisions. The novelty would have been the regularity of those statements, and the way in which they frame those books. His decision to write κατὰ γένος was in itself

---

[69] Thucydides 6.2–5. Sicily had previously featured in the narrative, particularly through Laches' earlier expedition (3.86, 88, 90, 99, 103, 115; 4.1, 24–25, 48, 58–65), but it is structurally most important here.

[70] Vannicelli 1987:182: "Mi sembra infatti in pieno accordo con le conclusioni emerse [. . .] l'ipotesi che per Eforo, non meno che per Diodoro, narrare *kata genos* significhi (o almeno possa significare) conferire unità alla storia di un periodo ponendo in evidenza un tema centrale, senza che per questo lo storico riduca la sua visuale e faccia della sua opera una sorta di collezione di monografie: vicende parallele trovano ugualmente il loro posto nella narrazione, intrecciandosi con il tema centrale." A more wide-ranging summary of previous interpretations is offered by Drews 1963.

[71] Vannicelli 1987:183.

[72] Suda s.v. Θεόπομπος Χῖος ῥήτωρ (Θ 172 Adler) = FGH 115 T 1.

unnoteworthy, except in that he moulded this to a work divided into books, just as Diodorus also sought to do. Again, we here recognise that Ephorus was innovative, but there is no need for 'Universal History' as a paradigm to explain the innovation; instead, awareness of Ephorus' place in a continuous tradition is central to understanding Ephorus' own narrative choices.

7. Polybius and Ephorus

Analysis of Ephorus' structure thus supports the earlier analysis of Diodorus' and Polybius' 'cover-texts' in embedding all three historiographers into broad traditions where generic considerations play little role in self-presentation and discussion of predecessors. Instead, each historiographer is both more introspective and more ambitious than modern studies suggest: they are concerned with elucidating their own historiographical purpose, but feel a need to establish their primacy across historiography as a whole, not just 'Universal History'. Nevertheless, an important step remains. In denying the validity of 'Universal History' as a connection between Polybius and Ephorus, it remains to ask why Polybius made special mention of Ephorus in particular, rather than of any other prominent historiographer. There was, strictly, no need for him so to do.

Here, it is not so much the 'Universality' of Polybius' approach, as his parochiality that forms the key: namely, his strong sense of his Achaean identity. Polybius' Achaean heritage needs no introduction.[73] More important here is how these roots deeply influenced all aspects of Polybius' work. Polybius' favourable stance towards the policies of Aratus, Philopoemen and his father, Lycortas, is legendary. Equally noteworthy are his dislike of the Aetolians, who had been until recently the main competitor of the Achaeans for influence in mainland Greece, and his antipathy towards those Achaean politicians whom he felt had misdirected the League, notably Callicrates, Critolaus, and Diaeus. This view is perhaps clearest in Polybius' unashamedly patriotic representation of the earlier history of the Achaean League in his second book, and of events leading up to Sellasia: Aratus and his allies could do no wrong, but Aratus' personal and political opponents were consistently portrayed in a bad light.[74] It similarly

---

[73] The son of Lycortas, who was several times Strategos of the league; Polybius himself was appointed second-in-command, Hipparch, in 170 BCE; and he was prominent enough to be one of the thousand Achaeans sent for supervision in Rome after the Third Macedon War. In the aftermath of the sack of Corinth in 146, he was also involved in the resettlement of Achaea, perhaps a stronger incentive for continuing his history than he admits: Polybius 3.4.13; 39.4–5; cf. Plutarch *Philopoemen* 21.5–6.

[74] Polybius 2.37–71; see Lehmann 1967, and, more recently, Haegemans and Kosmetatou 2005; this section is occasionally referred to as the *Achaeca*, by analogy with *Hellenica* and *Persica* (e.g. Mendels 2005:14), but Polybius never refers to it as such.

affects Polybius' judgments of his fellow historiographers: Phylarchus is criticised for his description of the sufferings of Mantineia at the hands of Aratus and the Achaeans, not because Polybius denies that the events happened, but because Phylarchus overdramatises their suffering: if such exceptional treatment was meted out to the Mantineans, there was clearly an exceptional reason for their anger against them.[75]

This stance even encroaches on Polybius' main theme. One clear example is his judgment of the cause of the war with Antiochus: it was the Aetolians. There is no attempt here to analyse the reasons why Antiochus might have been susceptible to the Aetolian advances, whether because of pure expansionism, concern about Roman expansionism, a desire to retake control of land that he considered ancestrally his, or for any other reason. Instead, Polybius' sole concern is to note that the Aetolian claim to be liberating Greece was but a pretext.[76] Perhaps it was, but, as numerous studies have made clear, the Aetolians were not unusual in this regard—and there is no reason to be any more cynical about that claim than about that of Titus Flamininus in 196, when he declared the freedom of Greece at the Isthmian Games.[77] Polybius' hostility towards the Aetolians, which arose at least in large part from his Achaean roots, is such that it clouds his judgement, even when it comes to explicating a crucial stage of his theme: how the Romans and Antiochus came into conflict.

This is the context in which we should approach Polybius' connection with Ephorus' history, and specifically the role there of the Return of the Heraclidae. Our analysis above suggests that the actions of the Heraclidae formed a structuring motif for Ephorus' history.[78] The reason why such a view would have appealed to Polybius is clearest in Polybius' initial presentation of the Achaean League: with its remarkable power and political union, it had united the entire Peloponnese so effectively by the early second century that it could almost be considered a single city.[79] Polybius is here envisaging the Achaean League as the political manifestation of the entire Peloponnese, and so, in effect, the contemporary descendants of the Heraclidae. Thus, in acclaiming Ephorus, Polybius was

---

[75] Polybius 2.56–57, esp. 57.11, 15; see Haegemans and Kosmetatou 2005:131–138; Schepens 2005.

[76] Polybius 3.7.1–3; cf. Polybius' insistence on Aetolian responsibility for the Social War, and his description of their greedy and aggressive style of life, as though beasts of prey: Polybius 4.3–5, esp. 3.1 and 5.8. See Livy 35, especially 33.8 and 46.6, for Livy's narrative of the Aetolian wish to liberate Greece.

[77] Cf. Polybius' description of the reception of Flamininus' declaration: Polybius 18.46; for Antiochus' claims: Polybius 20.8.1 and Livy 35.32.11–12, 44.6, 48.8; 36.9.4, 11.2; see also Gruen 1984:2.635–636. Compare the rhetoric of liberation involved in the Peloponnesian War, as suggested by Thucydides 1.69.1, 3.32.2, et passim.

[78] See pp. 178–182.

[79] Polybius 2.37.8–11.

achieving two related goals. First, he was selecting as the canonical narrative of early Greek history the narrative in which the Peloponnese had the greatest structural prominence—just as he elsewhere indicated his preference for Aratus' narrative of the events up to 220 over those of such scholars as Phylarchus, and just as his own narrative often implicitly focalised the Achaean League's point of view (as he understood it) in its narrative. Second, he was commending a view that insisted on the unity of the Peloponnese, a politically important point both before and after the events leading up to the sack of Corinth in 146. Beforehand, it was important to insist on the unity against those member states, ironically including Sparta itself, that wished to break away from the League, disputes which occasionally involved Rome. After the sack, it was crucial, as the Romans debated whether to allow the League to continue to exist.[80]

None of these observations denies that Ephorus' history was recognised as a sound and prominent broad historical narrative before Polybius; it does, however, suggest that in his commendation of Ephorus beyond all other narratives, Polybius, like Diodorus later, was not entirely motivated by externally recognizable methodological criteria. As so often elsewhere, subjective considerations relevant to the historian himself, his theme, and the historical situation when he was writing are central: that the Peloponnesio-centric vision of Greek history which Ephorus advocated was more appealing than alternative visions, such as that of Herodotus, or of Theopompus in his *Philippica*. External characteristics of genre were far from his remit or concern, as might have been expected: central for our ancient sources are structure, approach to evidence, and historiographical perspective, not coverage, except insofar as coverage is bound up with source analysis.[81]

8. 'Universal History' without Ephorus

The consequences of this re-analysis on our understanding of Ephorus, and of early Greek historiography in general, are wide-ranging. Without the support of the internal Greek historiographical discourse, there is no reason to follow Jacoby in his narrow definition of 'Universal History' as a national, chronologically universal history, and still less to require Ephorus' work somehow to form a point of rupture in the tradition in a misguided attempt to preserve Polybius'

---

[80] Pausanias 7.16.9–10.

[81] Cf. Verbrugghe 1989 on the non-existence of a recognised sub-genre of *Annales* in Roman historiography, and Marincola 1999:301n373: "Sempronius Asellio's distinction between the two [*annales* and *historia*] . . . must be read in the exaggerative context of historiographical polemic, in which the writer tries to justify the superiority of his own work by criticizing that of his predecessors. Asellio's cricism is not about form or content, but about fullness of account and examination of causes and attendant circumstances."

testimony. The precise terminology used, however, is less important than the methodological approach. We may accept that Ephorus did write a wide-ranging history. Given its length it may well also have included more information about the distant and recent Greek past than Herodotus or Thucydides. We have, however, no reason to believe Ephorus' history extended those boundaries, was less thematically unified than his predecessors' works, or was thematically unified round its 'Universality' rather than particular historical themes, notably the rise and fall of the Heraclidae. Not only was Ephorus not the first 'Universal Historian', but to think in those terms is to misrepresent the nature of the contributions he and his contemporaries made to Greek historiography.

These conclusions are important because of the hermeneutic value that 'Universal History' has traditionally had in analysis of Ephorus, and fourth-century historiography. I have already illustrated how inadequate 'Universal History' is to explain the phenomenon of writing κατὰ γένος and to illuminate why Ephorus should have chosen to end his work with the Siege of Perinthus.[82] More important here is the way in which the rise of 'Universal History' in Greek historiography has been connected to a variety of factors including Alexander's conquests, a perceived growth of the Greek world, the 'decline of the *polis*', and an increased panhellenic awareness in the fourth century.[83] The argument here against rupture between Ephorus and his predecessors, and against character-ising that rupture in terms of 'Universal History' thus supports more recent scholarly approaches that downplay some of these trends. Thus, rather than the phenomenon of Hellenistic monarchy involving the 'decline of the *polis*', scholars now recognize that *poleis* continued to thrive much longer than earlier scholarly narratives allowed. Instead of envisaging an actual expansion of the Greek world in the fourth century, scholars are now much more aware than in the past of how the prominence of Thucydides and other Athenian sources in past scholarship has led to the normalisation of their perspective for the fifth century, and often has elevated them as a model against which the remainder of the classical tradition might be compared. Rather than insisting on the fourth century as a universally acknowledged new and different age, scholars now allow for a broader range of responses to their communal and several pasts.[84] So too, where Jacoby considered that all genres of historiography had been formed in

---

[82] κατὰ γένος: Vannicelli 1987:191, see above, p. 183; the siege of Perinthus: see above, pp. 179–180.

[83] Alexander's conquests inspiring a perception of universality: Mioni 1949:23; Châtelet 1962:285; as the Greek world grew, so necessarily did its history: Brown 1973:107; Mortley 1996:1; Marincola 2001:109; the 'decline of the *polis*' necessitating a new subject: Schepens 1977:97; inspired by Isocrates/panhellenism: Barber 1935:78; Alonso-Núñez 1990:190; Luce 1997:109.

[84] Nicolai 2006:695 for a recent espousal of this view; this is not to deny that for some Athenians, notably Isocrates, and at times Demosthenes, the imperial era from 477-404 BCE or into the early fourth century may have seemed quantitatively and qualitatively different from the middle to

the fifth century, that Thucydides was the ideal historiographer, and that after him there could only be decay, the argument here allows for a more dynamic relationship between the historiographers of the fifth century and those of the fourth century, and so for a re-evaluation of their efforts: it may well be queried whether any Greek historiographer was not a primary researcher, not a keen political analyst, and not discriminating in their use of sources, but it is certain that none of these criticisms can be applied to Ephorus, no more than the label 'Universal Historian'.[85]

This disconnect between Ephorus and 'Universal History' also urges a further reconsideration of later historiographers that can be classified in this way, such as Diodorus, and Nicolaus of Damascus. Not only has Ephorus suffered by his connection with 'Universal History', but these later historiographers have also suffered because of the confusion over the concept of 'Universal History', and insufficient allowance for the rhetorical force of 'cover-texts'. To argue from Polybius' rhetoric that his history was somehow synthetically more universal than his predecessors gives Herodotus, Thucydides, and Ephorus insufficient credit. To suggest that it was geographically universal is to give Polybius' rhetoric too much credence: Polybius may declaim the geographic universality of his narrative, but such statements are closely connected to his wish to dramatise his theme, to emphasise that the Romans conquered (almost) the entire known world. They also have to be understood in the same rhetorical light: the Romans did not conquer (almost) the entire known world, nor gain hegemony over it.[86]

This point has not been emphasized enough in previous scholarship; instead, having indicated the problematic nature of the link between 'Universal History' and historians prior to Diodorus, the standard narrative has been resumed, such that development through Ephorus has been implicitly, if not explicitly, posited.[87] This move is dissatisfying. Irrespective of what we may think of claims

---

late fourth century: Musti 1989:471. This perspective should not, however, be generalized, or transferred to affect our narrative of Greek Historiography.

[85]   Jacoby 1909, especially 98. Marincola 2007b:178: "Universal historians are often criticized for what they are not: not primary researchers, not keen political analysts, not discriminating in their use of sources."

[86]   On Polybius' claims of geographical universality, see n47. For an analysis of differences between Polybius' view of the Roman Empire and Roman perspectives: Richardson 1979. Polybius' deliberate restriction of his work's conceptual world to the Mediterrannean basin, which ignored such previously favoured 'others' of Greek historiography as the Scythians, and overlooked the Greek settlements around the Black Sea and in the interior of the Seleucid empire, may be stylistically helpful in maintaining this fiction, but it does not make it any more plausible.

[87]   Thus, Marincola 2007b opens by noting that a strict definition of 'Universal History' (citing Alonso-Núnez) would exclude some of the historians to be treated in the chapter, but immediately continues to offer a bipartite depiction similar to that of Scafuro, followed by biographies

of 'Universality', they are a phenomenon that deserves clear analysis, just as do the historiographers involved: Diodorus, Nicolaus, Strabo, Pompeius Trogus, Velleius Paterculus, and others. Hesiod's sequence of ages, and the succession of world-empires first attested in Greek thought in Herodotus are indicative of an urge to rationalize and to structure the rise of man,[88] but they do not explain the additional impulse making this structure the theme of a history. It is, moreover, implausible to assume that our authors were not as aware as modern scholars of how preposterous their claims to 'Universality' might appear when literally understood, and that they strictly could not achieve it—just as Polybius was, no doubt, aware that his claims to geographical universality in his history could only be understood in a very particular way. That at least Diodorus still wished to make the claim is still significant. Further discussion lies, however, beyond the scope of this essay.

Instead, we may return to Ephorus, and to the development of Greek historiography. There is, of course, a need to categorise the histories with which we are dealing. To emphasise extent and breadth of coverage as generic factors in the way that the scholarship on 'Universal History', 'Hellenica', and 'Local Histories' has encouraged, however, has its clear limitations: such classifications are often based on stronger readings of 'cover-texts', and of their representativeness than are now common. Coverage also necessarily varied with the themes a historiographer chose, and cannot automatically be meaningfully connected to broader historiographical questions.[89] If only because of the dominance of

---

of Ephorus, Theopompus, and Diodorus. He does not return to the implications of his initial comment, and any apparent doubt in the validity of the application has been lost by the conclusion, where the wide-ranging summary of 'Universal Historians' as a group at least implicitly covers all three authors treated in detail, Ephorus as much as Diodorus.

Similarly, Clarke 1999 initially states her allegiance to a strict definition of 'Universal History' (also citing Alonso-Núñez), and dismisses the relevance of either Herodotus or Polybius, both of whom are largely to be excluded from her discussion. Instead, the authors in question "belong to a single historical period, namely the mid-to-late first century." (250) She continues, however, to state that "Diodorus deliberately went beyond the range of his model, the great universal historian Ephorus." (255)

[88] Hesiod *Works and Days* 106–201. Herodotus: 1.95, 130; cf. Ctesias FGH 688 F 33a = Scholiast Aristeides *The Panathenaic Oration* 964.301Ddf, perhaps implying the same for Ctesias; Aristoxenus fr. 50 Wehrli = Athenaeus 12.546a; Polybius 1.2.

[89] This is not a novel claim, but the widespread awareness of the difficulties involved in this approach has yet to be translated into alternative conceptualisations of the Greek historiographical universe. Despite the clear argumentation against such divisions in Marincola 1999, especially the alternative taxonomy offered at 301–309, even Marincola 2007a still adopts this arrangement, juxtaposing chapters on such topics as "the Development of the War Monograph," "Continuous Histories (*Hellenica*)," and "Universal History from Ephorus to Diodorus," to the evident discomfort of the authors involved, including himself (see n87). Tuplin 2007 is typical in his acknowledgement of the difficulties he faced in his attempt to define the genre of "Continuous Histories (*Hellenica*)," in itself an equation many would find problematic (160): "This

this perspective in past research, there is now a need to move beyond it, to look across the apparent genres which our concern for chronological coverage has suggested to us, and to seek other perspectives on the tradition.[90]

Specifically regarding Ephorus, to emphasise disjunction, as the traditional focus on genre, and on the concept of 'Universal History' has done, ultimately occludes more than it reveals. We reduce our understanding of the historiographical context in which Ephorus wrote; we misrepresent the nature of the dialogue between the different historiographers; and we misunderstand Ephorus' achievement. Ephorus' history was not 'Universal History', quite the reverse: it was Ephoran history, a *personal* historiographical vision which reflected his time, his society, and his interests, and which was predicated, as all Greek historiography was, on a rich engagement with his predecessors. Only on this basis can we ever hope better to appreciate his achievement.

Bibliography

Alonso-Núñez, J. M. 1990. "The Emergence of Universal Historiography from the 4th to the 2nd Centuries BC." In *Purposes of History: Studies in Greek Historiography from the 4th to the 2nd Centuries BC.*, ed. H. Verdin et al., 173–192. Leuven.

———. 1999. "Die Entwicklung der Universalgeschichtsschreibung nach Polybios bis in die Epoche des Augustus." *Storia della storiografia* 35:5–14.

———. 2002. *The Idea of Universal History in Greece: From Herodotus to the Age of Augustus.* Amsterdam.

Barber, G. L. 1935. *The Historian Ephorus.* Cambridge.

Behrwald, R. 2005. *Hellenika von Oxyrhynchos.* Darmstadt.

Breglia Pulci Doria, L. 1996. "Eforo: l'ottica cumana di un storico «universale»." In *IVe siècle av J-C. Approches historiographiques*, ed. P. Carlier, 41–55. Paris.

———. 2001. "Storia universale e geografia in Eforo di Cuma." In *Storiografia locale e storiografia universale. Forme di acquisizione del sapere storico nella cultura antica (Atti del Convegno di Bologna, 16-18 dicembre 1999)*, ed. C. Bearzot et al., 139–164. Como.

Brown, T. S. 1973. *The Greek Historians.* Lexington, MA.

---

is, of course, a pretty loose criterion: it is easily met by authors such as Ephorus or Polybius who, as authors of so-called "universal history" (albeit in different modes), are normally regarded as clearly outside the genre with which we are concerned—and who should be so regarded, if the genre is to have any useful content at all."

[90] This is a general methodological point, but it is one that is particularly relevant to our understanding of fourth-century historiography: fourth-century historiographers have suffered even more than others from this focus on genre, because of their proximity to the fifth century and to Thucydides.

Brunt, P. A. 1980. "On Historical Fragments and Epitomes." *Classical Quarterly* 30:477–494.

Büdinger, M. 1895. *Die Universalhistorie im Alterthume.* Vienna.

Burde, P. 1974. *Untersuchungen zur Antiken Universalgeschichtsschreibung.* Munich.

Châtelet, F. 1962. *La naissance de l'histoire.* Paris.

Chávez Reino, A. L. 2005. "Los claroscuros del Éforo de Polibio." In Schepens and Bollansée 2005:19–54.

Clarke, K. 1999. "Universal Perspectives in Historiography." In Kraus 1999:249–279.

———. 2008. *Making Time for the Past: Local History and the Polis.* Oxford.

Cornell, T. 2010. "Universal History and the Early Roman Historians." In Liddel and Fear 2010:102–115.

Dewald, C. 1997. "Wanton Kings, Pickled Heroes, and Gnomic Founding Fathers: Strategies of Meaning at the End of Herodotus's *Histories.*" In *Classical Closure,* ed. D. H. Roberts et al., 62–82. Princeton.

Drews, R. 1962. "Diodorus and His Sources." *American Journal of Philology* 83:383–392.

———. 1963. "Ephorus and History Written KATA GENOS." *American Journal of Philology* 84:244–255.

Engels, J. 2008. "Universal History and Cultural Geography of the Oikoumene in Herodotus' Historiai and Strabo's Geographika." In *The Children of Herodotus: Greek and Roman Historiography and Related Genres,* ed. J. Pigón, 144–161. Newcastle.

———. 2009. "Demetrios von Kallatis 'Über Asien und Europa' (FGrHist 85 F 1-6): Universalhistorie und Kulturgeographie zwischen Ephoros und Strabon." In *Studien zur antiken Geschichtsschreibung,* ed. M. Rathmann, 187–202. Bonn.

Engels, J. 2010. "Strabo and the Development of Ancient Greek Universal Historiography." In Liddel and Fear 2010:71–86.

Flower, M. A. 1994. *Theopompus of Chios: History and Rhetoric in the Fourth Century B.C.* Oxford.

———. 1998. "Simonides, Ephorus, and Herodotus on the Battle of Thermopylae." *Classical Quarterly* 48:365–379.

Flower, M. A., and J. Marincola. 2002. *Herodotus. Histories, Book IX.* Cambridge.

Fornara, C. W. 1983. *The Nature of History in Ancient Greece and Rome.* Berkeley.

Fowler, R. L. 1996. "Herodotos and His Contemporaries." *Journal of Hellenic Studies* 116:62–87.

Goldhill, S., and R. Osborne, eds. 2006. *Rethinking Revolutions through Ancient Greece.* Cambridge.

Grant, M. 1970. *The Ancient Historians.* London.

———. 1995. *Greek and Roman Historians: Information and Misinformation.* London.

Green, P. 2006. *Diodorus Siculus, Books 11-12.37.1: Greek History 480-431 B.C., the Alternative Version.* Austin.

Gruen, E. 1984. *The Hellenistic World and the Coming of Rome.* Berkeley.

Haegemans, K., and E. Kosmetatou. 2005. "Aratus and the Achaean Background of Polybius." In Schepens and Bollansée 2005:123-139.

Hartog, F. 2010. "Polybius and the First Universal History." In Liddel and Fear 2010:30-41.

Hornblower, J. 1981. *Hieronymus of Cardia.* Oxford.

Hornblower, S., ed. 1994a. *Greek Historiography.* Oxford.

Hornblower, S. 1994b. "Introduction." In Hornblower 1994a:1-72.

Hose, M. 2006. "The Peloponnesian War: Sources Other than Thucydides." In Rengakos and Tsakmakis 2006:669-690.

Humphreys, S. 1997. "Fragments, Fetishes, and Philosophies: Towards a History of Greek Historiography after Thucydides." In Most 1997:207-224.

Immerwahr, H. R. 1966. *Form and Thought in Herodotus.* Cleveland.

Jacoby, F. 1909. "Über die Entwicklung der griechischen Historiographie und den Plan einer neuen Sammlung der griechischen Historikerfragmente." *Klio* 9:80-123.

Jacoby, F., ed. 1923-1958. *Die Fragmente der griechischen Historiker.* Berlin–Leiden.

———. 1926. "Ephoros." In Jacoby 1923-1958 IIC:22-35.

Kant, I. 1874. "Idee zu einer allgemeinen Geschichte in weltbürgerlicher Absicht." *Berlinische Monatsschrift* 385-411.

Kraus, C., ed. 1999. *The Limits of Historiography: Genre and Narrative in Ancient Historical Texts.* Leiden.

Lavagnini, B. 1933. *Saggio sulla storiografia greca.* Bari.

Lehmann, G. A. 1967. *Untersuchungen zur historischen Glaubwürdigkeit des Polybius.* Münster.

———. 1974. "Polybios und die ältere und zeitgenössische Geschichtsschreibung: Einige Bemerkungen." In *Entretiens sur l'antiquité classique,* ed. F. W. Walbank and E. Gabba, 145-205. Vandœuvres.

Lendle, O. 1992. *Einführung in die griechische Geschichtsschreibung: von Hekataios bis Zosimos.* Darmstadt.

Lenfant, D. 1999. "Peut-on se fier aux 'fragments' d'historiens? L'exemple des citations d'Hérodote." *Ktema* 24:103-121.

Levene, D. S. 2007. "Roman Historiography in the Late Republic." In Marincola 2007a:1.275-290.

Liddel, P. P. 2010. "Metabole Politeion as Universal Historiography." In Liddel and Fear 2010:15-29.

Liddel, P. P., and A. T. Fear, eds. 2010. *Historiae Mundi: Studies in Universal History.* London.

Luce, T. J. 1997. *The Greek Historians.* London.

Luraghi, N., ed. 2001a. *The Historian's Craft in the Age of Herodotus.* Oxford.

———. 2001b. "Local Knowledge in Herodotus' Histories." In Luraghi 2001a:138–160.

Marincola, J. 1997. *Authority and Tradition in Ancient Historiography.* Cambridge.

———. 1999. "Genre, Convention, and Innovation in Greco-Roman Historiography." In Kraus 1999:281–321.

———. 2001. *Greek Historians.* Oxford.

———, ed. 2007a. *A Companion to Greek and Roman Historiography.* Oxford.

———. 2007b. "Universal History from Ephorus to Diodorus." In Marincola 2007a:1.171–179. Oxford.

Marx, M., ed. 1815. *Ephori Cumaei fragmenta.* Karlsruhe.

Mazzarino, S. 1966. *Il pensiero storico classico.* Bari.

Meister, K. 1975. *Historische Kritik bei Polybios.* Wiesbaden.

———. 1990. *Die griechische Geschichtsschreibung: von den Anfängen bis zum Ende des Hellenismus.* Stuttgart.

Mendels, D. 2005. *Memory in Jewish, Pagan and Christian Societies of the Graeco-Roman World.* London.

Mioni, E. 1949. *Polibio.* Padua.

Moles, J. 1996. "Herodotus Warns the Athenians." In *Papers of the Leeds International Latin Seminar* 9:259–284.

Momigliano, A. 1972. "Tradition and the Classical Historian." *History and Theory* 11:279–293.

———. 1975. *Alien Wisdom: the Limits of Hellenization.* Cambridge.

———. 1978. "Greek Historiography." *History and Theory* 17:1–28.

———. 1982. "The Origins of Universal History." *Annali della Scuola normale superiore di Pisa, Classe di lettere e filosofia* 3.12.2:533–560.

Mortley, R. 1996. *The Idea of Universal History from Hellenistic Philosophy to Early Christian Historiography.* Lewiston.

Most, G., ed. 1997. *Collecting Fragments.* Göttingen.

Müller, K., ed. 1841. *Fragmenta historicorum graecorum* I. Paris.

Musti, D. 1989. *Storia Greca.* Rome.

Nicolai, R. 2006. "Thucydides Continued." In Rengakos and Tsakmakis 2006:693–711.

———. 2007. "The Place of History in the Ancient World." In Marincola 2007a: 1.13–26.

Osborne, R. 2006. "Introduction." In Goldhill and Osborne 2006:1–9.

Parmeggiani, G. 1999. "Mito e spatium historicum nelle Storie di Eforo di Cuma (Note a Eph. FGrHist 70 T 8)." *Rivista storica dell'Antichità* 29:107–125.

———. 2011. *Eforo di Cuma. Studi di storiografia greca.* Bologna.

Pédech, P. 1964. *La méthode historique de Polybe.* Paris.

Pelling, C. B. R. 1997. "East is East and West is West: Or are They? National Stereotypes in Herodotus." *Histos* 1.

Pitcher, L. 2009. *Writing Ancient History: An Introduction to Classical Historiography.* London.

Reekmans, T. et al., eds. 1977. *Historiographia antiqua. Commentationes Lovanienses in honorem W Peremans septuagenarii editae.* Leuven.

Rengakos, A., and A. Tsakmakis, eds. 2006. *Brill's Companion to Thucydides.* Leiden.

Richardson, J. S. 1979. "Polybius' View of the Roman Empire." *Papers of the British School at Rome* 47:1–11.

Rood, T. 2007. "The Development of the War Monograph." In Marincola 2007a:1.147–158.

Roussel, D. 1973. *Les historiens grecs.* Paris.

Sacks, K. 1981. *Polybius on the Writing of History.* Berkeley.

———. 1990. *Diodorus Siculus and the First Century.* Princeton.

———. 1994. "Diodorus and his Sources: Conformity and Creativity." In Hornblower 1994a:213–232.

Scafuro, A. C. 1983. *Universal History and the Genres of Greek Historiography.* Diss., Yale.

Schepens, G. 1977. "Historiographical Problems in Ephorus." In Reekmans, et al. 1977:95–118.

———. 1987. "The Phoenicians in Ephorus' Universal History." In *Phoenicia and the East Mediterranean in the First Millennium BC*, ed. E. Lipinski, 315–330. Leuven.

———. 1997. "Jacoby's FGrHist: Problems, Methods, Prospects." In Most 1997:144–172.

———. 2005. "Polybius on Phylarchus 'Tragic' Historiography." In Schepens and Bollansée 2005:141–164.

———. 2007. "History and Historia: Inquiry in the Greek Historians." In Marincola 2007a:1.39–55.

Schepens, G., and J. Bollansée, eds. 2005. *The Shadow of Polybius: Intertextuality as a Research Tool in Greek Historiography: Proceedings of the International Colloquium, Leuven, 21-22 September 2001.* Leuven.

Schwartz, E. 1907. "Ephorus (1)." *RE* VI 1:1–16.

———. 1957. *Griechische Geschichtschreiber.* Leipzig.

Sheridan, B. 2010. "Diodorus' Reading of Polybius' Universalism." In Liddel and Fear 2010:41–55.

Shrimpton, G. S., and K. M. Gillis. 1997. *History and Memory in Ancient Greece.* Montreal.

Starr, C. G. 1968. *The Awakening of the Greek Historical Spirit.* New York.

Stockt, L. van der. 2005. "'Πολυβιάσασθαι'? Plutarch on Timaeus and 'Tragic History'." In Schepens and Bollansée 2005:271–306.

Strasburger, H. 1966. *Die Wesensbestimmung der Geschichte durch die antike Geschichtsschreibung.* Wiesbaden.

———. 1977. "Umblick im Trümmerfeld der griechischen Geschichtsschreibung." In Reekmans et al. 1977:3–52.

Stylianou, P. J. 1998. *A Historical Commentary on Diodorus Siculus, Book 15.* Oxford.

Timpe, D. 2007. "Westgriechische Historiographie." In U. Walter, ed. 2007 *Antike Geschichtsschreibung: Studien zur Historiographie.* Darmstadt. 9–63.

Toynbee, A. J. 1934–1961. *A Study of History.* London.

Tuplin, C. 2007. "Continuous Histories (*Hellenica*)." In Marincola 2007a:1.159–170.

Usher, S. 1969. *The Historians of Greece and Rome.* London.

Vannicelli, P. 1987. "L'economia delle Storie di Eforo." *Rivista di filologia e di istruzione classica* 115:165–191.

———. 2001. "Herodotus' Egypt and the Foundations of Universal History." In Luraghi 2001a:211–240.

Vattuone, R. 1998a. "Koinai Praxeis. Le dimensioni universali della storiografia greca fra Erodoto e Teopompo." In *L'ecumenismo politico nella coscienza dell'Occidente: Bergamo, 18-21 settembre 1995*, ed. L. Aigner Foresti, 57–96. Rome.

———. 1998b. "Sul proemio delle Storie di Eforo di Cuma (Note a FGrHist 70 F 9)." *Rivista Storica dell'Antichità* 28:183–198.

Verbrugghe, G. P. 1989. "On the Meaning of Annales, on the Meaning of Annalist." *Philologus* 133:192–230.

Walbank F. W. 2005. "The Two-way shadow: Polybius among the Fragments." In Schepens and Bollansée 2005:1–18.

———. 1956, 1967, 1979. *A Historical Commentary on Polybius.* Oxford.

———. 1972. *Polybius.* Berkeley.

Wilamowitz-Moellendorff, U. von. 1908. *Greek Historical Writing.* Oxford.

Williams, J. H. C. 2001. *Beyond the Rubicon: Romans and Gauls in Republican Italy.* Oxford.

9

Greek Monographs on the Persian World
The Fourth Century BCE and its innovations

Dominique Lenfant

WHILE IT IS the best-known Greek monograph on the Persian world, Ctesias' *Persica* is often cited today as an illustration of the supposed decadence of the historical genre in the fourth century BCE. One symptom of this 'decay' is Ctesias' choice of subject matter: rather than a politico-military history focused on the contemporary Greek world, Ctesias' history concerns conflicts that took place within the Persian Empire—court intrigues, for example, and local revolts. The apparent decline has also been observed in Ctesias' historical method and is linked to his alleged motivation for writing history: the vain desire to supplant Herodotus, rather than the search for truth that is thought to lie behind the projects of Herodotus and Thucydides.[1] Ctesias has, moreover, been accused of ethnic prejudices, particularly in his malicious portrayal of the Persian court.[2] Similar charges have also been brought against Dinon, a later writer of a *Persica*, who tends to be seen in relation to Ctesias as Ctesias is to Herodotus, namely as a plagiarist who tweaks the text in order to conceal his plagiarism.[3]

Such views are for the most part overly simplistic, since they take into account neither the fragmentary nature of the evidence nor the biases of our sources. They compare Ctesias, moreover, only to the few historians whose works have survived intact, such as Herodotus, without paying any attention to other accounts of the same genre, about which we do indeed know something. As a result, they are unable to account for the distinctive features of the *Persica* as a whole. It is my purpose, therefore, to suggest another way of looking at these Greek monographs on the Persian world, a genre that may have assumed

---

[1] E.g. Jacoby 1922, Bleckmann 2007.
[2] E.g. Sancisi-Weerdenburg 1987.
[3] E.g. Drews 1973:117, Binder 2008:65.

a new scale in the fourth century BCE, but whose roots go back to the fifth.[4] I intend to point out some similarities and differences among the fourth-century *Persica*, before considering their relationship to earlier histories, both the fifth-century *Persica* and the histories of Herodotus and Thucydides.

1. Fourth-Century Persica: disparity and unity

Before defining the common features of the *Persica*, however, it is necessary to assess the state of our knowledge, which depends entirely on fragments.

What can we know about the *Persica*?

We know of three historians who wrote *Persica* in the fourth century: Ctesias of Cnidus, Dinon of Colophon, and Heracleides of Cyme.[5] The extent to which we are able to gain any insight into their individual works, however, differs considerably for each author. This disparity is a result, first of all, of the number of fragments available for each historian. We know a good deal more about Ctesias, whose *Persica* survives in 90 fragments, than we do about Dinon (35 fragments) or Heracleides (8 fragments), all the more so because Photius, Plutarch, and Nicolaus of Damascus preserve excerpts from Ctesias of exceptional length. A second explanation of this disparity is the range of citing sources: nearly 50 for Ctesias, some 15 for Dinon, and only three for Heracleides. So, while for Ctesias' work we may hope to have overlapping pieces of evidence from different sources, the same cannot be said of Dinon and Heracleides, both of whom are cited predominately by only two authors, Plutarch and Athenaeus.[6]

Given these circumstances, it may be the case that our vision of Dinon and Heracleides is influenced by the filter of these two citing authors—by their particular methods of selection and adaptation of their sources—so that the characteristics observed in the fragments may in fact only be those of the citers. For example, the fragments of each *Persica* share a marked interest in the material goods of the Persian court: Dinon writes about the Great King's golden footstool (FGH 690 F 26), his perfumed headdress (FGH 690 F 25), and his precious drinking cup (FGH 690 F 4); while Heracleides writes about the

---

[4] For a succinct presentation of *Persica*: Lenfant 2007a. For further developments: Lenfant 2009a. Edition, French translation, and commentary of Ctesias' *Persica*: Lenfant 2004; of Dinon's and Heracleides' fragments: Lenfant 2009a. Two English translations of Ctesias' *Persica* have been recently published: Llewellyn-Jones and Robson 2010; Stronk 2010 (Stronk is also preparing a detailed commentary). Summary and bibliography on Ctesias as a source on the Persian Empire: Lenfant 2011.

[5] On other authors who are said in the extant tradition to have written *Persica*, see Lenfant 2009b.

[6] Dinon: 10 fragments by Athenaeus, 7 by Plutarch; Heracleides: 4 fragments by Athenaeus, 2 by Plutarch.

golden royal throne, which was surrounded by small golden columns inlaid with precious stones (FGH 689 F 1). Such an attention to *realia* may in fact only reflect the interests of Athenaeus, to whom we owe all of these fragments, and this hypothesis becomes even more likely when we take a look at Athenaeus' treatment of Herodotus. For, if Herodotus were known to us only through the citations to his work in the *Deipnosophists*, we would assume not only that he was mainly interested in animals, food, natural products, table practices, and table ware of the barbarian world, but also that he was virtually silent about political history.[7] To understand the *Persica* of Dinon and Heracleides, then, we must rely on Athenaeus and Plutarch without any assurance that the themes to which they are drawn are in any way representative of the works as a whole.

There is much, therefore, that we cannot know with regard to Dinon and Heracleides in particular, and our ignorance extends beyond the topics treated by each work to the structure of the works themselves. While we have a good idea about how Ctesias arranged his *Persica*, thanks to Diodorus and Photius, who partially reproduced it, for Dinon we can attempt only an uncertain reconstruction[8] and things remain most obscure for Heracleides.[9] Another unknown is the proportion of narrative to description. For Ctesias, the abundance of narrative material in the fragments suggests that this was his chief interest. For Dinon and Heracleides, on the other hand, our impression depends on the citing source: Athenaeus tends to preserve descriptive elements, Plutarch prefers narrative, and as a result it is not easy to identify the predominating tendency in each original work.[10]

Some Clear Disparities

What we do not know about the *Persica*, however, does not prevent us from noting some undeniable disparities among them. The first distinction has to do with the date of composition of each work: Ctesias' *Persica*, which was finished about

---

[7] Lenfant 2007b:63–67.

[8] Dinon's work had a chronological scope ranging from the Assyria of Semiramis to the Persian Empire of the 340s, and a chronological structure can neither be excluded nor proved by the (inconclusive) indications of book division in the citing sources. Once again, citations of Herodotus in the *Deipnosophists* are a good warning against reconstructing a work by relying on Athenaeus alone, despite the precision with which he cites his sources (Lenfant 2007b:67–68).

[9] On Heracleides' *Paraskeuastika*, either a work distinct from, or a part of, his *Persica*, but evidently treating the Persian Empire in the same way, cf. Lenfant 2009a:257–261.

[10] This is why I have thought it better to speak of 'monographs' on the Persian world, rather than ethnographies or histories of Persia, terms that seem to suggest a descriptive or narrative tendency. An account of wars of conquest, local revolts, and crises of succession is well attested for Ctesias, thanks in particular to Photius. Although we are unable to rely on Photius for the work of Dinon or Heracleides, we can identify similar features in their work, especially for the period best covered by their fragments (the reign of Artaxerxes II).

390, is the oldest, and it was in fact completed and continued half a century later by Dinon and Heracleides.[11] It is impossible to say whether Heracleides' *Persica* was later or earlier than that of Dinon, nor can we rule out the possibility that each work was composed independently. That is to say, besides the fact that these three narratives were not conceived in the same historical context, they also do not fit into the same situation of intertextuality.

Another distinguishing feature is the length of each *Persica*: 23 books for Ctesias, probably more for Dinon,[12] but only five for Heracleides. Such a disproportion suggests another fundamental difference: whereas Dinon seems to have followed Ctesias' pattern, treating the same period and topics as Ctesias before moving on to the contemporary period, Heracleides endowed his *Persica* with more modest dimensions, and this may suggest that his project was unique.

In fact, Heracleides' work is generally thought to be distinctive in two regards: first, it contained more description than narration; and second, it was serious work and thus quite unlike Ctesias' fanciful account. One might certainly have reservations about labelling an author as either serious or fanciful,[13] about the influence of Athenaeus' method of selection, or about the qualities that modern scholars sometimes generously assign to works that are almost completely unknown.[14] But there are several arguments in favor of seeing Heracleides' work, if not as completely divergent from the other *Persica*, still as markedly different. It is striking, first of all, to note the quality of Heracleides' fragments, those that have been transmitted by Athenaeus at any rate, a quality that is due not only to Athenaeus' faithful reproduction of the original text in the *Deipnosophists*, but also to the significant information preserved by Heracleides himself.[15] In several fragments, for example, court customs are described with a great deal of precision, in particular the long passage about the King's dinner (FGH 689 F 2), which has no equivalent in Herodotus or in the other *Persica*. The phrases with which Athenaeus introduces this fragment, in fact, suggest that it comprises two verbatim quotations,[16] so that, even if it were not representative of the whole, *pars pro toto*, it is at least a piece from the whole, *pars ex toto*.

---

[11] Dinon continued the history of the Persian Empire at least until the 340s (Lenfant 2009a:51–53), whereas the *terminus post quem* for Heracleides cannot be defined very precisely: the 380–360s BCE (ibid. 257).

[12] Although the scarce sources suggest at least 15 books, it seems more likely that there were about 30. Cf. Lenfant 2009a:64–66.

[13] One may wonder how relevant it could be to consider, e.g., Herodotus as either a serious or fanciful historian.

[14] Thus, Olmstead 1948:380 considers that Ctesias' treatise *On the Tributes in Asia* was "a contribution to economic history whose loss is irreparable."

[15] On comparing Heracleides' information with local sources, see Lenfant 2009a, part 3. For a comparison with earlier Mesopotamian sources, see Lion 2013.

[16] At least this is to be deduced from Athenaeus' citations of Herodotus. Cf. Lenfant 2007b:51–52.

It should be once again emphasized that Heracleides' work was relatively brief: five books certainly do not allow for a narrative as developed as that of Ctesias,[17] and this supports the idea of a mostly descriptive account.[18]

Common features

Despite these clear disparities, the three fourth-century *Persica* share several common features. They all seem to present a kind of political ethnography: the "Persian" world has no ethnic connotation but refers rather to the Persian Empire. That is to say, the *Persica* treat people within the Empire who are not all Persian in a cultural or ethno-linguistic sense:[19] the political entity (the Empire) counts more than the ethno-cultural reality (the Persian people). Secondly, and most important, the topic best represented by our fragments is neither ethnography proper nor the customs of ordinary men, but the behavior and activity of the King and his court. In short, the *Persica* show a marked interest in the sphere of central power, and this is the focus of both the narrative and descriptive portions of the *Persica*. Alongside wars of conquest and local revolts, then, the *Persica* narrate court intrigues, conflicts, and stories of revenge, as well as crises of succession—a set of themes that modern scholars sometimes call *petite histoire* and that derives at least in part from Herodotus. The descriptive approach, in contrast, seems to be new, in particular the precise detail with which the daily life of the King and his court is depicted.

The description of the court circle is original in three respects. First, it pays especial attention to the general court staff: concubines playing music, royal guards,[20] eunuchs,[21] nobles taking part in the royal dinner, servants specifically charged with preparing meals[22] or dressing beds, and so forth.[23] Secondly, it reveals a novel interest in material goods (the general surroundings of the

---

[17] Or that of Dinon in probably even more books. See above n12.

[18] This is not to say that Heracleides' *Persica* included only description. No fragment, it is true, alludes to the Assyrian or Median Empire, so his account may have been limited to the Persian Empire in the strict sense of the word. In addition, no fragment mentions the Persian Wars or what preceded them. The two narrative allusions, moreover, do not even prove that his *Persica* comprised a continuous story, since they might have been used only to illustrate some aspects of court life. On the other hand, we should not disregard the fragmentary nature of our information, nor the fact that even brief works are capable of containing concise narratives, as in the case of Charon of Lampsacus (on this, see Lenfant 2009a:14–16).

[19] See Ctesias FGH 688 FF 11–12 on Dyrbaioi and Choramnaioi ; Dinon FGH 690 F 21, F 22, F 30 on Egypt, India, Ethiopia ; and Heracleides FGH 689 F 4 on "the country where frankincense is produced," whose king is in fact said to be independent.

[20] Heracleides FGH 689 FF 1–2.

[21] Ctesias, Dinon, and Heracleides, passim.

[22] Heracleides F 2.

[23] Heracleides F 5.

court, particular luxury objects, and items of food and their distribution), an interest, we should note, that is evident in many of the fragments of our three authors, not only in those transmitted by Athenaeus.

With respect to the physical setting, Ctesias describes the royal park (the so-called *paradeisos*) of Susa (688 F 34a-b), Heracleides the inner courts of the royal palace, which were covered with luxurious carpets on which no one but the King could walk, the aforesaid golden throne equipped with small, decorated columns on which the King sat when giving audience (689 F 1), and the room where the King had his meal, privately from his guests, whom he could see through a curtain without being seen himself (689 F 2). As for luxury items, Dinon mentions the golden egg from which the King drank (690 F 4) and the golden footstool on which he stepped when descending from his chariot (690 F 26). As for food, both Ctesias and Dinon provide details about the *rhyntakes*, a little bird that was consumed at the court;[24] Dinon mentions the ammoniac salt and Nile water that was sent from Egypt to the King (690 F 23a); and Heracleides discusses the bread and above all the meat that was cut at the King's dinner, of vast quantity (a thousand animals slaughtered daily) and great variety: horses, camels, oxen, asses, deer, sheep, birds, Arabian ostriches, geese, and cocks (689 F 2). In this way, the *Persica* provide a most vivid image of the court, its characters, scenery, and material components.

The third peculiarity of the *Persica* is their interest in explanation: not only are court practices described, but very often their meaning is expounded. For example, the kings of Persia store in their treasury water from the Nile and the Istros because, as Dinon points out,[25] they desire to "assert the greatness of their empire and their universal power."[26] But the most striking illustration of this explanatory tendency is provided by Heracleides in reference to the presentation of food at the King's dinner; the historian is not content merely to give a precise description of this meal but rather takes it upon himself to interpret its purpose and utility. The pieces of meat cut by the royal staff are distributed to the nobles who have been honored with an invitation to the royal table, who in turn redistribute at home what is left of their share. Food is also dispensed to the royal guards as payment, which Heracleides compares to the pay of mercenaries in the Greek world. He introduces his description of this process of distribution with the following judgment:

Τὸ δὲ δεῖπνον, φησί, τὸ βασιλέως καλούμενον ἀκούσαντι μὲν δόξει μεγαλοπρεπὲς εἶναι, ἐξεταζόμενον δὲ φανεῖται οἰκονομικῶς καὶ

---

[24] Ctesias F 27.70, F 29b (19.4) and F 29c*, Dinon F 15b.

[25] Dinon F 23b (= Plutarch *Alexander* 36.4).

[26] See also e.g. Dinon F 26, Ctesias F 40, Heracleides F 1.

ἀκριβῶς συντεταγμένον καὶ τοῖς ἄλλοις Πέρσαις τοῖς ἐν δυναστείᾳ οὖσι κατὰ τὸν αὐτὸν τρόπον.

The so-called King's dinner will appear sumptuous (μεγαλοπρεπές) to one who hears about it (ἀκούσαντι), but when one examines it carefully (ἐξεταζόμενον), it will be found to have been set up with economy and parsimony (οἰκονομικῶς καὶ ἀκριβῶς συντεταγμένον), and the same is true among other Persians who exercise power. (Translation by C. B. Gulick, modified)

Heracleides F 2 (Athenaeus 4.145d)

It is noteworthy not only that Heracleides praises the good management involved in the setting up of the King's dinner but also that he contrasts hearsay (ἀκούσαντι) with a precise examination (ἐξεταζόμενον), evidently both visual and intellectual. Two possible reactions are thus preempted here: first, a potential negative reaction to what could be interpreted as overindulgence at the King's table. When Heracleides uses the word *oikonomikos*, he expresses the idea of measure and rational control, in the same way that he will emphasize that each guest gets only a moderate portion (Καὶ μέτρια μὲν αὐτῶν παρατίθεται ἑκάστῳ τῶν συνδείπνων τοῦ βασιλέως, "Of these [meats] only moderate portions are served to each of the King's guests, and each of them may carry home whatever he leaves untouched at the meal"). The historian explicitly intends, then, to contradict an impression of ostentatious waste and useless outlay in order to avoid any misinterpretation and to contest the popular conception of the Great King's *tryphe*, of a continuous meal, at which people abandon themselves to an easy and weakening life of pleasure. But in precluding this cliché of Persian luxury, Heracleides also rejects a second tendency: to record *thaumasia* and describe sensational practices in order merely to provoke astonishment. The prototype of this attitude may well be the famous passage where Herodotus (2.35-36) describes the customs of Egyptian people as being exactly opposite to those of the rest of mankind (women go to the market, whereas men stay at home; women urinate standing, men sitting, and so on). Along these same lines, another passage from Herodotus' *Histories* provides an interesting point of comparison with Heracleides' *Persica*: Herodotus says that on their birthdays rich Persian men "serve an ox, a horse, a camel, an ass, roasted whole in ovens, while the poor men serve the lesser kinds of cattle" (1.133). In this way, he leaves the reader to his amazement without adding any further details or exegesis. Heracleides might also have contented himself with such a tactic. But, rather than simply mention the extraordinary quantity and variety of meat that was daily carved at court, he preferred to add an explanation.

One point remains doubtful, however: was this concern for such cliché-reversing explanations a distinctive feature of Heracleides alone? The fragmentary nature of the texts makes this a question quite impossible to answer, as is attested by a brief passage from the *Deipnosophists* that refers both to Ctesias and to Dinon and is thus considered a fragment of both historians: "The Persian king, as Ctesias and Dinon say in their *Persica*, used to dine in the company of 15,000 men, and four hundred talents were spent on the dinner."[27] This reference lacks any form of explanation, which makes the information contained here seem all the more sensational. And modern scholars would probably have read it in just this way had they not been aware of Heracleides' interpretation. The question, then, is whether the lack of an explanation here is due only to Athenaeus' editorial practice. For several reasons, this seems probable. First, the process of excerption often entails the suppression of context and explanatory details.[28] Secondly, Athenaeus gives here only a brief paraphrase,[29] not a long literal reproduction, as he does in the case of Heracleides' fragment on the King's dinner (F 2). Athenaeus is in fact comparing the costs of Alexander's meals with those of the King, so that any explanatory comments would be beside the point and might even interrupt the thread of his argument. Besides, just a few lines before, Athenaeus had cited the long passage from Heracleides,[30] and so he needs retain here only those numerical details that went unmentioned by Heracleides. It cannot be ruled out, then, that Dinon and Ctesias also explained the grounds and circumstances of these expenses. Ctesias' account certainly does not lack sensational aspects, but we must keep in mind that we have no literal citation of his work that could be compared in length and textual quality to Heracleides F 2. Nor have any personal comments been preserved, so that some of his explanatory material might well have fallen out.

In any case, the fourth-century *Persica* lead the reader far from mere caricatures of the Great King abstractly depicted as a despot devoted to sensual pleasures and ruling over a populace of slaves: they give a far more vivid, rich, and balanced picture. At the same time, with regard to material items, they are not content merely to list exotic marvels; even food, exported from the ends of the Empire or distributed at court, is seen as a political tool. By stressing the common features of the three fourth-century *Persica*, then, one arrives at an understanding far different from what would have resulted from a comparison between Ctesias and Herodotus alone.

---

[27] Ctesias F 39 = Dinon F 24 (Athenaeus 4.146c).
[28] The process of excerption can be an art of fabricating the wondrous, as is shown by Jacob and Schepens (Jacob 1983 and Schepens 1996:390–394).
[29] As the characteristic formula ὥς φησι shows. See Lenfant 2007b:48–51.
[30] 4.145a–146a.

2. The Relationship of Fourth-Century *Persica* to Fifth-Century Histories

Now that we have some idea of their common features, we are in a position to ask what distinguishes fourth-century *Persica* from histories written in the fifth century.

Thucydides

It is often said that fourth-century historiography on the whole follows in the footsteps of Thucydides. This is not the case with the *Persica*: they may follow Thucydides chronologically, but there is no genealogical relation nor any indication that the *Persica*-writers had any precise knowledge of Thucydides. In the case of Ctesias, in fact, a lack of engagement with Thucydides is explained by the fact that both historians published their histories at about the same time. But we should emphasize that the material common to Thucydides and the writers of *Persica* was rather limited: as has often been noticed, Thucydides says very little about the Persians,[31] and the mere difference of their subjects is enough to account for the scarcity of overlaps.[32] Last, there are few similarities with regard to method. In brief, the Thucydidean model plays no part in the fourth-century *Persica*, so that these writings are later than Thucydides' history only by virtue of the sequence of time: contrary to what has been said about the *Hellenica*, they are neither its heir, nor its opposite, nor a pale imitation.

Fifth-Century *Persica*

It is far more productive to question the links between *Persica* of the fourth century BCE and those of the fifth, of Dionysius of Miletus, Charon of Lampsacus, and Hellanicus of Lesbos.[33] Despite our limited knowledge of these works, we can say that all *Persica* shared the tendency to narrate the internal story of the Persian Empire and its kings, but there are several important distinctions.

The first is obvious: fifth-century *Persica* did not go beyond the fifth century, indeed not even beyond the first half of that century, and, as a consequence, the Persian Wars and the two kings who ruled the Empire at that time occupy a relatively large place in their narratives. In the fourth century, on the other hand,

---

[31] Andrewes 1961; Meiggs 1972:3; Wiesehöfer 2006.

[32] Among the few common subjects attested by the fragments are the revolt of Inaros (Thucydides, Ctesias) and the meeting between the exiled Themistocles and the Great King (Thucydides, Dinon F 13, Heracleides F 6 [= Plutarch *Themistocles* 27.1–2]). Whereas Ctesias probably had not read Thucydides, this is less certain for Dinon and Heracleides.

[33] Lenfant 2009a:9–24.

the Persian Wars no longer seemed so central: they constituted at the very most only a part of the long history of the relations between Greeks and Persians and a marginal one in the history of the Persian Empire itself. This is true even for Ctesias, whose account of these wars, although contradicting Herodotus in many details, was nevertheless quite brief.[34] As a result, the fragments of the fourth-century *Persica* give the impression that the history of the Empire was seen more on its own terms. A second disparity is that the fifth-century *Persica* tended to be rather short: two books for Charon, at least two (maybe no more) for Hellanicus, compared with the 23 books of Ctesias and probably more by Dinon (Heracleides being, as we have seen, unique in this respect). Such an amplification is linked, first of all, to the time at which these works were written: several decades had passed, in some cases even a century, and this resulted in the accretion of much new material. But there are literary grounds, as well—the intervening publication of Herodotus' account, for example, which is a third feature that separates fourth- from fifth-century *Persica*: while the latter are contemporary with Herodotus for the period that they cover and are, for this reason, probably independent from him, the fourth-century authors were well aware of Herodotus' account, and this is not without consequence.

Herodotus

Although Herodotus was not himself strictly a *Persica*-writer, he gave pride of place to the history and description of the Persian Empire—so much so, in fact, that in his day, his was likely the most detailed account available, far over-shadowing earlier and contemporary *Persica*. Ctesias certainly seems to know Hellanicus, whose claims he sometimes contests,[35] but it is mainly against Herodotus that he takes a stand, explicitly or not.

Polemic against Herodotus is a well-known feature of Ctesias' *Persica*, and its importance should certainly not be understated, whatever its motivation.[36] Yet we should keep several points in mind. First, Ctesias' *Persica* sets itself apart from Herodotus' account not only with regard to the details but also in the very nature of his project. Ctesias self-consciously places his work in the tradition of the earlier *Persica*: its guiding principle is the story of the Persian Empire, not the relations between Greeks and Persians, and the period he covers, therefore,

---

[34] Books 12 and 13 of Ctesias included no less than the reigns of Cambyses, the Magus, Darius, and Xerxes (T 8 and F 13.9).
[35] Ctesias F 16.62.
[36] On this well-known topic, see Jacoby 1922:2050-2059; Lenfant 1996; 2004:xxviiif.; Bichler 2004; Bleckmann 2007; Lenfant 2009a:27–30.

extends both before Herodotus' period of focus and after, continuing on into the early fourth century. This makes the Persian Wars even more marginal than they had been in the earlier *Persica* and endowed them with rather a different significance.[37]

Secondly, whereas divergences between Ctesias and Herodotus have often been noted, especially by Photius, convergences have generally been neglected, and there were probably many. Let us turn, for instance, to the description of the Choaspes river. Herodotus (1.188) says that the Choaspes is "the only river from which the King will drink," that "its water is boiled, and very many four-wheeled wagons drawn by mules carry it in silver vessels, following the King wherever he goes at any time." Athenaeus, after paraphrasing Herodotus' passage, adds further information that he has drawn from Ctesias: "Ctesias of Cnidus also explains how this royal water is boiled and how it is put into the vessels and transported for the King, adding that it is very light and pleasant."[38] Far from contradicting Herodotus, then, Ctesias here confirms and supplements his account. While the shadow of Herodotus undeniably influences Ctesias' *Persica*, or rather a limited part thereof, it can hardly be detected in the fragments of successive *Persica*. Indeed, some scholars have erred in identifying in Dinon an interest in contradicting Herodotus[39] rather than a rivalry with Ctesias,[40] which seems more likely.

That being said, we should note that Herodotus' shadow generally had more of an impact on *Persica* than did Thucydides' on the *Hellenica*, for the simple reason that, unlike the *Hellenica*, which undertook to continue Thucydides' project, Ctesias and Dinon obviously aimed at replacing Herodotus' account with a modified, expanded, and updated version. This expansion is evident in two respects. First, because Persia was so different from the Greek world, *Persica* provide a description, indeed an explanation, of the Empire's components and customs, with a predilection for practices and people of the royal court, all of which is lacking in *Hellenica*. Secondly, circumstances had changed since the period with which Herodotus ends his history: the Persian Wars were now long in the past, and Persian rule had again imposed itself on Greek cities of Asia Minor. How could a Greek's view of Persia remain unchanged?

---

[37] Note that the Persian Wars only covered some 4% of Ctesias' *Persica*, compared to 40% for Herodotus' *Histories* (see Lenfant 2009a:315–316).

[38] Athenaeus 2.45a–b = Ctesias FGH 688 F 37.

[39] See Lenfant 2009a:238–242 on Dinon F 28.

[40] That clearly emerges from the divergences between Dinon and Ctesias about the events surrounding Cyrus the Younger's rebellion (Dinon F 15–17).

3. Conclusions

The extended historical monograph devoted to a foreign people, namely the Persians, appears to be one of the new trends of Greek historiography in the fourth century BCE. By focusing on the Persian world, these works distinguish themselves not only from political historiography of the fifth century but also from the contemporary *Hellenica*, another sort of specialized history but one that was focused on the Greek world. At the same time, the *Persica* differ from the nascent universal histories, which encompass a larger geographical area, although both genres, *Persica* and universal history, have in common the fact that they go back to a far remote past and make a claim to supplant previous accounts. Thus, far from being merely a failed attempt to surpass fifth-century historiography, *Persica* of the fourth century paved a new way in a varied historiographical field.

This is not to say that these *Persica* should be seen outside of time and space as mere reactions to literary tradition, uninfluenced by their own time. It is important to keep in mind the geo-political, biographical, and chronological conditions in which the genre developed in the fourth century: these works were composed by Greeks from Asia who lived in contact with Persians at a time when the Persian Wars no longer accounted for the concrete reality of relations between Greeks and Persians, still less for the history of the Empire itself. These works, as we have seen, focus mainly on the sphere of central power in recounting its history and describing and explaining its administration.

The fact that *Persica* ceased to be composed after the Persian Empire was incorporated into Alexander's Empire can be explained by the fact that Greeks were henceforth faced with a world that was larger and far more complex, where it was more difficult to distinguish the fate of Persians from the rest of humanity.[41] But we should also think about what might have motivated the Greeks to write *Persica* in the first place: a very specific political relationship, a Persian domination that, depending on the *polis* and on the moment in time, could be past, potential, or present, a foreign civilization often viewed as a cultural counterpoint. In fact, as a political ethnography, *Persica* were by necessity a history of the present.

---

[41] What Tuplin has said about the death of *Hellenica* (Tuplin 2007:168–169) applies all the more to *Persica*.

Bibliography

Andrewes, A. 1961. "Thucydides and the Persians." *Historia* 10:1–18.

Bichler, R. 2004. "Ktesias "korrigiert" Herodot. Zur literarischen Einschätzung der Persika." In *Ad fontes!: Festschrift für Gerhard Dobesch zum fünfundsechzigsten Geburtstag am 15. September 2004*, ed. H. Heftner, and K. Tomaschitz, 105–116. Vienna.

Binder, C. 2008. *Plutarchs Vita des Artaxerxes. Ein historischer Kommentar.* Berlin.

Bleckmann, B. 2007. "Ktesias von Knidos und die Perserkriege: Historische Varianten zu Herodot." In *Herodot und die Epoche der Perserkriege. Realitäten und Fiktionen. Kolloquium zum 80. Geburtstag von Dietmar Kienast*, ed. B. Bleckmann, 137-150. Cologne.

Drews, R. 1973. *The Greek Accounts of Eastern History.* Cambridge, MA.

Jacob, C. 1983. "De l'art de compiler à la fabrication du merveilleux. Sur la paradoxographie grecque." *Lalies* 2:121-140.

Jacoby, F. 1922. "Ktesias (1)." *RE* XI 2:2032–2073.

Lenfant, D. 1996. "Ctésias et Hérodote, ou les réécritures de l'histoire dans la Perse achéménide." *Revue des Études Grecques* 109:348–380.

———. 2004. *Ctésias. La Perse. L'Inde. Autres fragments.* Paris.

———. 2007a. "Greek Historians of Persia." In Marincola 2007:200–209.

———. 2007b. "Les "fragments" d'Hérodote dans les Deipnosophistes." In *Athénée et les fragments d'historiens*, ed. D. Lenfant, 43–72. Paris.

———. 2009a. *Les Histoires perses de Dinon et d'Héraclide. Fragments édités, traduits et commentés.* Paris.

———. 2009b. "Des Persica indépendants de l'empire perse? Enquête sur les usages d'un titre." In *Ingenia Asiatica. Fortuna e tradizione di storici d'Asia Minore*, ed. F. Gazzano et al., 15–33. Rome.

———. 2011. "Ctésias de Cnide." In *Les Perses vus par les Grecs*, ed. D. Lenfant, 96–107. Paris.

Lion, B. 2013. "Les banquets perses d'après le livre IV d'Athénée : points de vue grecs, points de vue orientaux. " In *À la table des rois . Luxe et pouvoir dans l'oeuvre d'Athénée*, ed. C. Grandjean et al. Rennes and Tours, 107–125.

Llewellyn-Jones, L., and J. Robson, eds. 2010. *Ctesias' History of Persia. Tales of the Orient.* London.

Marincola, J., ed. 2007. *A Companion to Greek and Roman Historiography* I. Oxford.

Meiggs, R. 1972. *The Athenian Empire.* Oxford.

Olmstead, A. T. 1948. *History of the Persian Empire.* Chicago.

Sancisi-Weerdenburg, H. 1987. "Decadence in the Empire or Decadence in the Sources? From Source to Synthesis." In *Achaemenid History* I, ed. H. Sancisi-Weerdenburg and A. Kuhrt, 33–45. Leiden.

Schepens, G. 1996. "Ancient Paradoxography: Origin, Evolution, Production and Reception, Part I." In *La Letteratura di consumo nel mondo greco-latino*, ed. O. Pecere and A. Stramaglia, 375–409. Cassino.

Stronk, J. P. 2010. *Ctesias' Persian history, Part 1: Introduction, Text, and Translation.* Düsseldorf.

Tuplin, C. 2007. "Continuous Histories (*Hellenica*)." In Marincola 2007:159–170.

Wiesehöfer, J. 2006. "'. . . Keeping the Two Sides Equal': Thucydides, the Persians and the Peloponnesian War." In *Brill's Companion to Thucydides*, ed. A. Rengakos and A. Tsakmakis, 657–667. Leiden.

10

The Sick Man of Asia?

CHRISTOPHER TUPLIN

If you will take, I don't say unlimited time or many generations, but only these last fifty years immediately preceding our generation, you will be able to understand the cruelty of Fortune. For can you suppose, if some god had warned the Persians or their king, or the Macedonians or their king, that in fifty years the very name of the Persians, who once were masters of the world, would have been lost, and that the Macedonians, whose name was before scarcely known, would become masters of it all, that they would have believed it? Nevertheless it is true that Fortune, whose influence on our life is incalculable, who displays her power by surprises, is even now I think, showing all mankind, by her elevation of the Macedonians into the high prosperity once enjoyed by the Persians, that she has merely lent them these advantages until she may otherwise determine concerning them. (Translation by E. Schuckburgh)

Demetrius of Phalerum FGH 228 F 39 (Polybius 29.21)

T HE QUESTION that this paper seeks to address is simple: did fourth-century Greek historiography about Persia give the lie to Demetrius by displaying any sense that the Achaemenid Empire might not be a permanent part of the geo-political landscape? The question is only truly significant if we are speaking of historiographical texts produced before the Empire's non-permanence was revealed by the Macedonian conquest. But that line of demarcation is not always easy to establish and, in any case, the topic evokes the slightly wider question of the types of explanation given (at whatever date, though relatively early) for the potential or actual vulnerability of the Empire. The range of texts under consideration must therefore be extended a little. Moreover, at least to provide some sense of context, there needs to be an extension that is not only chronological: texts that are not strictly or at all historiographical come into view too. Let me start, therefore, by defining a little more precisely the authors with whom I am concerned.

First, there are the authors of historical works specifically devoted to Persia, i.e. Ctesias, Dinon, and Heraclides. Ctesias' work was produced towards the beginning of century and is certainly that of someone who had not seen the fall of the empire. We cannot affirm this for sure with regards to the other two—nor can we deny it. That uncertainty already means that we cannot be doctrinaire about the 334 BCE limit, since it would paradoxical to exclude one, or even two, of the *Persica*-writers from our investigation.[1] It is perhaps worth stressing that, while something can be said of Ctesias' explicit posture as a historian (cf. Tuplin 2004a), no programmatic statements survive from Heraclides or Dinon, and the scope of their works is rather obscure. (Did Heraclides provide much in the way of narrative history? Did he actually write two different works? How long a historical period did Dinon cover?) Next are the historical works that included material about Persia because the states that were the principal focus of their interest came into contact and conflict with the Achaemenid Empire: this category embraces works on pre-Alexandrine Greek history by Xenophon, Theopompus, Cratippus, the Oxyrhynchus historian, Callisthenes, Anaximenes, and Ephorus—at least some of which were products in part of the conquest era.[2] We should also put Thucydides' Book 8 here, since it is reasonable to regard it as an early fourth-century product. Thirdly, we have the Alexander historians: *ex hypothesi* an intellectual product of the conquest era or its aftermath, they cannot simply be ignored as a possible source for explanations of Persian weakness, albeit *ex post facto* ones. Going back to the pre-conquest era, we then have, fourthly, a more miscellaneous bunch of texts: two works of Xenophon, viz. *Anabasis* and *Cyropaedia*, each *sui generis* but each in some sense historiographical;[3] commentary on Persia in philosophical publications (notably Plato's *Laws*, but also—straying again into the early Hellenistic era—Aristoxenus or Clearchus); the works of pamphleteers and deliberative orators; and even poetic evocations of a Persian past from the pens of Timotheus and Choerilus.

---

[1]   The fifth-century authors of the so-called *Persica*, Charon, Dionysius, and Hellanicus, fall outside this investigation—although I do not know that we can prove that Hellanicus might not belong at the start of the long fourth century (cf. below at n4). But it makes little odds, because we know nothing that would illuminate their attitude to Persia's exposure to collapse.

[2]   Duris (who covered 370–281) and Diyllus (who covered 357/6–297) exemplify a much later generation of historians, who had occasion to write of events in the later history of the empire but who would be of no relevance here, even if we knew anything about what they said.

[3]   I do not include Sophaenetus, whose existential status is decidedly dubious.

(Both might be wholly or partly late fifth-century authors, but both also reflect a resurgence of interest in Persia following her reappearance as a direct player in Aegean Greek politics—an event which is arguably the real start of the fourth century for our purposes.[4]) Finally, we should not forget that many of the writings in these four categories survive in only fragmentary form. If we are asking ourselves about what 'fourth-century historiography' had to say, we are bound to take account of non-fragmentary texts (not necessarily themselves historiographical) written well after the fourth century that preserve material about Achaemenid history that is not attributed to any specific source but presumably derives ultimately from classical authors, and perhaps predominantly from fourth-century ones.

What we aim to discover from these documents is (a) whether there was a discourse uttered before 334–323 about the prospects for the collapse of the Achaemenid Empire and (b) whether any such discourse was produced, elaborated, or exploited by writers of history. The topic overlaps with the theme of Persian decadence—a notion that Dominique Lenfant (2001) has identified as a distinctively fourth-century epiphenomenon of the clash between Artaxerxes and Cyrus in 404–401 and the view that Artaxerxes was the unworthy winner—and the question of how Achaemenid historians should actually explain the fall of the empire.[5] A survey of that question by Josef Wiesehöfer (1996) reminds us that—both as historians of reality and students of fourth century Greek representation of reality—we should distinguish between decadence and abiding systemic weakness.

Many readers will be familiar enough both with the rhetoric of academic discourse and the substance of the material in question to have begun to suspect that the array of texts listed above is more impressive for extent than the degree of illumination it will cast upon our topic. The suspicion is justified. My paper (which focuses on Greek receptions, rather than modern historical explanations, and spends quite a lot of time with non-historiographical texts) is a report upon this sad fact.

---

[4]   Plutarch *Agesilaus* 14 has people quote Timotheus ("Ares is Lord; Greece has no fear of gold") in the context of Agesilaus' defeat of Persians, who are figured as διαρρέοντες ὑπὸ πλούτου καὶ τρυφῆς. But that does not get us far. We have no reason to suppose the intellectual context of his *Persians* extended beyond Salamis to some larger proposition about the empire. What succeeds the narrative at the end of the poem is actually what seems to be a coded attack on Sparta for encouraging Persia back into Greek politics.

[5]   It is odd against such a background that the *Anabasis* is so totally lacking in hostility to Artaxerxes. Among other papers on decadence are Briant 1989 (which suggested *inter alia* that perceptions of Persian decadence were not simply a fourth-century phenomenon) and Sancisi-Weerdenburg 1987.

1. Collapse or Weakness in Historiographical Texts

Our ideal would be to discover a surviving historiographical text that explicitly and unambiguously addressed the possibility of imperial collapse in advance of 334 BCE, and did so in the voice of the historian, not that of some actor in the historical drama. (The latter qualification rules out *Hellenica* 6.1.10, where Jason claims the King can easily be mastered because his subjects are slaves and his weakness is shown by the state to which he was reduced by the 10,000 and Agesilaus.) As far as I can see there is no such ideal text. There is, of course, *Anabasis* 1.5.9, where Xenophon comments that the empire's lengthy roads and scattered military forces are a source of weakness, if someone makes war quickly, because of the time required to assemble a royal army. This is a serious observation, and a sign that Xenophon was minded to generalise from his observation of the younger Cyrus: the hypothetical war may even be to dismantle the empire, not merely usurp its throne. But the events of 401 demonstrated the difficulty of turning theory into practice. Indeed, the comment tends to point up Cyrus' failure and its appearance is primarily to be seen in the light of the unsupportive overall attitude of *Anabasis* towards contemporary panhellenist ideas rather than as a contribution to a theory of imperial collapse.[6]

Denied an ideal source, we must look instead for historiographical texts presenting material that might have been part of an analysis of the empire's potential vulnerability. To be more precise, we are looking for historians who dealt with an episode or an institution or other topic that could raise issues about the empire's likely survival and who did so in a fashion that, whether by virtue of explicit evaluation or less tangible features such as disproportionate emphasis or literary manipulation, highlighted those issues. In searching for such material we can be guided either by our own imagination or by our awareness from non-historiographical texts of the sorts of topics that were sometimes adduced in the pre-conquest fourth century as signs of the empire's weakness. Either way we are mostly deep into the realm of conjecture because we are characteristically dealing with fragmentary authors or an indirect epitomized or contextless tradition. I say that because, in the case of non-fragmentary authors, we can usually see immediately that what we are looking for is not really there.

Thucydides' Book 8 presents a narrative about Tissaphernes that, visible in its totality, offers no reason to believe that the author saw in the Empire anything but a powerful and dangerous adversary.[7] The situation is not significantly

---

[6] Cf. Tuplin 2004b, 181–182; Rood 2004.

[7] Hyland 2007: 15–16 writes that "for Thucydides Achaemenid Persia was a dangerous neighbor, trusted too much by the gullible population of Athens, a natural enemy to any Greek *polis* with ambitions for empire. It was not . . . a strange 'Other' . . . but a great power that used its might

different with Xenophon's *Hellenica* and *Anabasis*. With a complete text before us there is no way that we can claim that occasional 'negative' features in *Hellenica*—e.g. Tissaphernes' oath-breaking (3.4.5–6.11) or Pharnabazus' mistreatment of Spithridates (3.4.10, 4.1.7[8])—are symptoms of a greater moral malaise that threatens the viability of the Empire. For it is plain that Xenophon is not concerned with any thesis about Persian weakness. Even the account of the 368/7 peace-conference, ending with Antiochus' famous sound-bites—there are 10,000 cooks and servants but no men capable of fighting Greeks; the golden plane-tree is too small to shade a cricket—is much more about the inadequacy of Thebes than of Persia.[9] As for *Anabasis*, leaving aside Tissaphernes (who gets a distinctively poor press throughout the historical tradition), there is little real animus against Persia or the Persians and (as I have already suggested) the scattered hints at panhellenist themes constitute more of a warning against lack of realism than a considered argument that Persia is weak. This is particularly striking, of course, in view of the willingness of some to adduce the escape of the 10,000 as proof of Persian military inadequacy. In fact, to find Xenophon talking about the weakness of Persia one has to go to *Cyropaedia*. This is a historiographical text of sorts, but, in recognition of its peculiar generic status, I defer discussion until a later point in the argument. But I note now that near the end of his life Xenophon speculated that kings, tyrants, and satraps might be willing to invest money in the Athenian economy (*Poroi* 3.11). This does not sound like someone who thought the Persian system was going to collapse any time soon, even though (when it did) there were still people called 'satraps'.

So, sticking to 'normal' historiography, the rest of this search for engagement by pre-Alexander historians with the intrinsically weak or actually decadent (but in either event potentially destroyable) Achaemenid empire has to be conducted amidst fragments and epitomes. And the truth is that it is next to impossible to find anything that really seems to count. Demonstrating a negative of this sort is potentially a rather tiresome exercise. But I do need to illustrate some of the possibilities that do not work, so the reader can see my criteria and assess my judgment. Turning this into an elegantly fluent discourse is not easy, and what follows is going to be little more than a list of various sorts of failure.

---

in ways quite familiar to fifth-century Athenians . . . Above all, for Thucydides and his contemporaries, the Achaemenid empire was not a power in decline." He adds that there is no sign of Persian decadence and no suggestion that Persia relied upon gold because of military weakness. This seems a fair summary to me.

8 Revealed in *Agesilaus* 3.3 to be a plan to have his daughter as a concubine.

9 Xenophon *Hellenica* 7.1.38. Compare Plutarch *De Alexandri Magni fortuna aut virtute* 342b: Alexander asked about armies, the position of the King in battle, and roads, not about hanging gardens, the golden vine, or the King's *cosmos*.

(1) I am prepared to guess that Dinon told the story of the visit of the wrestler Pulydamas to the court of Darius II and of his victory in a fight with three of the Immortals.[10] Someone certainly did, for it is in Pausanias (6.5.7). The story is emblematic of the superiority of Greek over Persian, but hardly a sign that Dinon (or whoever) elaborated a broader critique of Persian military qualities. Nor can I feel confident that there is any special point in the fact that, when telling the story, Pausanias labels Darius as "the bastard son of Artaxerxes, who had become king by killing the legitimate son Sogdius." Darius' success in emerging as the last one standing in the Year of Four Kings was certainly predicated *inter alia* on military resources, so one could, I suppose, say that Pulydamas' demonstration has a special piquancy. But, as Dinon well knew, Darius was the king under whom a process was set in train that resulted in the Persian recovery of western Anatolia and the re-subjection of Asiatic Greeks to Achaemenid rule. So the victory of a freakish Greek wrestler might well in the long run seem embarrassing rather than substantively significant.

(2) Having started in the 350s to write a continuation of Thucydides (a work with no demonstrable specific Persian angle), Theopompus switched to the history of Philip of Macedon. But we have no reason to think he did so specifically because he saw Philip's Macedonia as the power that could defeat Persia (and had seen this before the 330s)—indeed the absence of any report that he said anything like this is close to being a clinching *argumentum e silentio* against any such thesis. There are quite a lot of Persian historical fragments from *Philippica*, but we cannot be quite sure that there was a solid chunk of Persian history in Books 11-19 and there is no persuasive way of extracting a message of imperial vulnerability even from e.g. the mercenary-general Nicostratus (who took his son to court and made daily offerings to the King's *daimôn*: FGH 115 F 124) or the famous description of Artaxerxes' march to Egypt (FGH 115 F 263). The observation that there is a long established tariff for contribution to the King's Dinner like that for tribute (FGH 115 F 113) is arguably a celebration of organizational strength, not a critique of decadent self-indulgence. (See below on Heraclides' treatment of the same topic.) Artaxerxes' comment (FGH 115 F 179) about the greedy extravagance of the Paphlagonian King Thys when a prisoner at the Persian court—to the effect that he ate as though he were about to die—might even pass as a pleasingly sardonic observation that reflects well upon the Great King.[11]

---

[10] Dinon FGH 690 F 2 relates to Heracles being defeated when fighting two opponents, which evokes the story of Pulydamas confronting three opponents.

[11] That is especially true if, as seems to be the case, the story was told out of chronological context.

(3) The historian Anaximenes wrote a work with the evocative title *Metallagai Basileôn* (FGH 72 FF 18–19).[12] Two fragments survive: one names Pasargadae as the location of Cyrus' defeat of Astyages; the other reports the competitive extravagance of Straton of Sidon and Nicocles of Salamis and notes that both suffered a violent death. Pasargadae is obviously a matter of Persian history, and Straton and Nicocles were prominent Achaemenid subjects in areas that saw significant disturbance at various times in the fourth century. Other sources claim Straton died (in the 350s and at the hands of his wife) after an alliance with the Egyptians, though nothing survives to link the death of Nicocles (before 354/3) with rebellious behavior.[13] One might spin from these data the image of a work that put the *metallagê* of Darius III into some wider historical context of the fate of kings and empires and perhaps dwelt on such familiar potential 'weakness-of-Persia' themes as extravagant *truphê* and provincial disturbance. But to do so would plainly be the merest conjecture – and assumes a post-conquest date.

(4) The Oxyrhynchus Historian famously commented on the unreliability of the King's financial support to those fighting his wars (22.2–3): this would later attract comment from Isocrates (*Panegyricus* 142), but the awkward truth was that it did not in fact inhibit the King's achievement of his goals. Indeed, the point of the historian's report is that Conon was able to get the money he needed—and indeed secured more later by visiting the King, as we learn from Diodorus.[14] One could say that financial brinkmanship was a bit silly but since the King's actual wealth is never denied, it would be hard for a historian to detect a potentially fatal weakness here. Where was the evidence that this sort of delay or the inclination to manipulate with money rather than deploy huge armies or the length of time it took to deploy large armies, all of which appear in the general historical tradition, were in the long run destructive of imperial power? This was not what caused major reverses such as the failure to conquer Greece or the late fifth century Egyptian revolt, and such reverses had anyway not caused the empire to unravel. The empire's size did have implications (and not just those Xenophon noted in *Anabasis*): historians duly reflect this, as when Pharnabazus explains to Iphicrates that the King's ultimate control from afar slows things down (Diodorus 15.41), but in their subsequent invasion of Egypt Pharnabazus' on-the-spot decisions were a more important cause of failure than the length of time it had taken to mount the attack in the first place.

---

[12] The term is used in *Marmor Parium* 109 (FGH 239 B 8) of the end of Alexander's rule ("from the *metallagê* of Alexander and Ptolemy's seizure of Egypt…").

[13] Jerome *adversus Jovinianum* 1.45. The date was 351 according to most recent calculations in Elayi 2006.

[14] Diodorus 14.81.4–6. Note also Tiribazus going to the King to get 2000 talents in Diodorus 15.4.2.

(5) The tension between Iphicrates and Pharnabazus exemplifies a phenomenon that recurs elsewhere in the historical record, that of conflict, often categorized as 'jealousy,' among members of the elite: one thinks of Themistocles at the Persian court, the uneasy relationship between Tissaphernes and Pharnabazus, the defection of Datames, or the clash between Tiribazus and Orontes during the war with Evagoras. The final two items, like the problems between Iphicrates and Pharnabazus, certainly had locally disadvantageous consequences, but it is not clear that historians actually highlighted systemic weakness here. Significantly, perhaps, it is a theme apparently absent from non-historiographical critique of the empire.[15]

(6) Another interesting absence is satrapal rebellion. Isocrates happily lists regions over which the King (allegedly) had no control in ca. 380 or 346 or 339, but these are ethnically defined areas, and the only individual satraps ever said to be actually or potentially disaffected are the Carians Hecatomnus and Idrieus (*Panegyricus* 162, *Philippus* 104).[16] *Philippus* 104 does add that other satraps will throw off the King's power if the Greeks promise them freedom (one thinks of Agesilaus tempting Pharnabazus with talk of autonomy in 394[17]), but he does not seek to prove this by alluding to the historical dissidence among Iranian satraps and any more general idea that the empire's systemic weakness is demonstrated by such dissidence is never broached. So far as the historiographical tradition goes we can point to the fifth-century revolts of Megabyzus, Pissuthnes, and Terituchmes in Ctesias,[18] fourth-century troubles represented by Nepos' *Datames*, scattered material in Trogus and the stratagem-writers, and a narrative in Diodorus.[19] Nepos' categorization of Tissaphernes as a rebel who had apparently provoked the Spartan invasion of Asia Minor as a dissident act (*Conon* 2.2) is not a sign that someone had a doctrinaire view that satraps can be assumed to be rebellious. Rather, it is a *post eventum* Persian *parti pris* 'clarification' of history. What these have in common is that in the long run the King comes out on top. The Diodoran Satraps' Revolt is particularly interesting: on the one hand, half the empire's revenues were cut off, which sounds really serious; on the other hand, the rebels were spectacularly unable to maintain any cohesive unity. Modern accounts of the era doubt there ever was a unitary

---

[15] It is different from the claim that commanders treated subordinates and subjects badly.

[16] In 15.11 Demosthenes argues that, since the King is apparently doing badly in Egypt, Artemisia will fear that he might want to use Rhodes against a move on her part and so will not mind Athens having it, and will not take it herself (which would put it in the King's hands). This convoluted reasoning takes for granted that a failure in Egypt might prompt satrapal dissidence—though (again) in a Carian satrap.

[17] Xenophon *Hellenica* 4.1.35.

[18] FGH 688 F 14.40–42, 15.53, 15.55–56.

[19] Trogus *Prologue* 10; Polyaenus 7.14.2–4, 21.3, 6, 7, 26.1, 29.2; Diodorus 15.90–92.

plan in the first place.[20] But, even if this were the case, we cannot be certain that historiographical claims to the contrary were meant to demonstrate imperial vulnerability: for the more rebel unity is falsely postulated, the more plain is its failure. As for uncoordinated dissidence, if Isocrates neglected it, I doubt the historians invested it with any more than anecdotal significance.

(7) This is the place to notice another oddity. Isocrates is not interested in Achaemenid succession crises; nor is at least part of the historiographical tradition. Ctesias retailed the Year of Four Kings, and Plutarch reports the deadly plots of the future Artaxerxes III (perhaps from Dinon), but both are absent from Diodorus.[21] This may be because the non-*Persica* tradition was in general unconcerned with events located in the court, unless they linked directly to stories from western imperial politico-military history. Two comments follow. First, this neglect means that the non-*Persica* tradition offered no thesis about Achaemenid weakness that centered on the luxury of the court or the unhealthy role played there by women or eunuchs:[22] Bagoas is an exceptional case and women barely feature. (Diodorus' image of Mandane whipping up a mass popular protest against Themistocles and forcing the King to put him on trial is an odd exception in more than one sense of the word.[23]) Secondly, when such neglect extends to convulsions around the throne it underlines the extent to which any Persian history outside the *Persica* is an epiphenomenon of Greek history. Any appetite for systematic presentation of Persian weakness would surely have seized greedily upon the instability of royal succession. The silence of Isocrates' surviving discourses may be due to their dates, but historians had no such excuse. In these circumstances one has to be wary of assuming that anyone was thinking about the empire as such enough to be consciously formulating ideas about its future.

(8) We should bear this in mind when approaching items of *histoire événementielle* that are adduced in Isocrates as signs of Persian weakness, i.e. the escape of the 10,000, Agesilaus' successes in 395/4, Evagoras' revolt (and associated disturbances in the Levant), continuing Egyptian independence, and the Cypriot-Phoenician rebellions of the early 340s. All figure in the historiographical tradition preserved in Diodorus, Plutarch, and Nepos, and in some cases the mere telling of the relevant stories certainly offers an unwelcome spectacle from a Persian point of view. For example, it is hard to see how Evagoras could have got away with such favorable terms of surrender if Orontes had not accused

---

[20]   Weiskopf 1989, Debord 1999:302–366.
[21]   Ctesias FGH 688 F 15.47–51; Plutarch *Artaxerxes* 26–30.
[22]   Actually I am not sure we can really prove that *Persica*-writers did so either.
[23]   11.57. In Plutarch *Themistocles* 29, hostility to Themistocles is simply ascribed to οἱ ἐπὶ θύραις.

Tiribazus of treason;[24] and the six aborted or failed attempts to regain Egypt before 343 are an embarrassing history, even if we cannot prove that all figured fully in Ephorus or elsewhere.[25] Our problem is that we cannot tell whether the presentation or explicit evaluation of such material exploited the opportunity for critique, and we certainly cannot say whether this happened in any pre-conquest text: for example, the Diodoran observation that Artaxerxes II's failures in Egypt were due to lack of personal military ambition and reliance on generals deficient in courage or experience is presented as a foil to Artaxerxes III's very different qualities. The Ephoran original is dangerously likely to be a post-conquest text but, in any event, since the context is Artaxerxes III's success in repossessing Egypt, the critique would be at best rather ambiguous. But there are two things we can say on other episodes. First, the account of the 10,000 in Diodorus discloses nothing interesting, and Xenophon's treatment is more about Greek success in very precise circumstances than Persian weakness in general terms.[26] Second, whereas Xenophon gives only a vague account of Agesilaus' brief incursions into inland Asia Minor, produces evasive rhetoric about the results of the Battle of Sardis, and avoids any claim that either the Persian King's life-style or Agesilaus' political and military activities have actually done anything to weaken the empire,[27] the tradition in Diodorus (15.31), Nepos (*Agesilaus* 2.1) and Plutarch (*Pelopidas* 30) sees Agesilaus as planning the conquest of cis-Taurine Anatolia, aiming to attack the King in person, and fighting for possession of Susa and Ecbatana. This hype may go back to fourth-

[24] Diodorus 15.8–9. Crucially, it was bad morale among the Persian troops caused by the accusation of Tiribazus that rendered Orontes' pursuit of the siege of Salamis difficult.

[25] They certainly do not all appear in Diodorus. Stevenson 1997 notes on more than one occasion that Dinon did not provide a proper description of all the Egyptian attacks. (She thinks, for example, that 385–383 and 373 were somehow run together and dealt with before the Cadusian War and end of Evagoras' rebellion—hence the foreshortening in Diodorus, consuming Dinon *via* Ephorus, around the withdrawal of Chabrias and arrival of Iphicrates.) She stops short (142) of attributing this to Dinon's absorption of royal propaganda, preferring to think that it is simply that Dinon's history was too court-oriented to be interested.

[26] Plutarch *Artaxerxes* 20 says that the escape of 10,000 proved τὰ Περσῶν καὶ βασιλέως πράγματα χρυσὸν ὄντα πολὺν καὶ τρυφὴν καὶ γυναῖκας but otherwise τῦφον καὶ ἀλαζονείαν which is neat, but probably Plutarch, rather than a fourth-century source. Polybius' analysis of the enabling cause of the Macedonian attack as Philip's perception from the 10,000 and Agesilaus that the Persians were cowardly and indolent by comparison with the military εὐεξία of the Macedonians (3.6.12) is not necessarily directly drawn from a fourth-century historian's analysis (and certainly not a pre-conquest historian).

[27] *Agesilaus* 1.33–35. *Agesilaus* 8–9 draws what is essentially a moral contrast between Agesilaus and the Persian King and, while it is said at the end of 9 that Agesilaus' aim was have as many cities and people as possible friendly to himself, his motive turns out to be outdoing others in benefiting his own state, getting his own back on his 'rivals' (ἀντίπαλοι), and becoming greatly celebrated in life and death. There is no actual claim that the Persian King's behaviour has actually made him weak or that Agesilaus' behavior has made him strong.

century, and perhaps to pre-conquest texts, but, since the whole point was that events in Greece involving Persian financial intervention wrecked Agesilaus' ambitions, it does not seem to serve the thesis of Persian weakness very well.

(9) The most fully preserved fragmentary historian of Persia is, of course, Ctesias. Nuance and evaluation are elusive, but we are free to believe that the presentation of powerful eunuchs or scary royal women conveyed a message of difference, not inadequacy, and there is no plain sign that Ctesias postulated a decline in Persian strength or character since the early days of the empire (the same is true for the non-*Persica* tradition) or that Persian luxury masked or caused systemic weakness. (Ctesias does not even appear in Athenaeus' major cluster of citations on *truphê.*) His record as military historian discloses no systemic criticism of Achaemenid armies: a comment on the lack of siege machinery was a purely factual one in an Assyrian context; and Artaxerxes' apprehension about viewing Cyrus' body while Greek mercenaries were still on the loose is no basis for large conclusions.[28] But there is one feature of Ctesias' work (unique in what is preserved of *Persica* and other fourth century historiography) that makes it possible that he thought about the end of the Achaemenid Empire. This, of course, is the fact that it embraced the fall of two other near eastern empires. Were the lessons to be learned here? Can we imagine Ctesias pondering them?

In the case of Assyria the central features of the story are: (a) Arbaces' contempt for the extremely enclosed, luxurious, and effeminized life of Sardanapalus' court, (b) a Median and Persian desire for freedom, (c) the prolonged series of military actions (including repeated defeat for the rebels) required to bring about Sardanapalus' defeat, and (d) the dependence of eventual success upon a conviction of divine support, an episode of complacency on the part of the loyalist army, and the exceptional weather conditions that finally fulfil a prophecy and break the siege of Nineveh.[29] This is quite a striking story. The Assyrian Kings had abandoned the military aggression of Semiramis and given themselves over to secluded self-indulgence generations earlier;[30] yet its troops still prove able to mount a strong defence—one that only fails because some higher force wants the empire to fall. Why is that so? Well, Ctesias is clear that Sardanapalus' effeminization distinguished his life-style from that of his predecessors: we may say that it is this change (or decline) that engenders sufficient human contempt to provoke an insurrection and divine distaste to ensure its success. We might also say that effeminization is emblematic: it symbolizes a degree of *truphê* that is capable of undermining the capacity for self-defence.

---

[28] FGH 688 F 1 (Diodorus 2.27.1), F 20 (Plutarch *Artaxerxes* 12). See Tuplin 2011.
[29] FGH 688 F1b 23–27, 1oβ,1pα,1pε, 1q.
[30] FGH 688 F1b 21.

But if so, we must also insist that this is a model in which a less offensive degree of *truphê* can coexist with imperial power over huge periods of time.

The subsequent fall of the Median empire is a different affair.[31] Cyrus' revolt is prompted by his mother's prophetic dream, as interpreted by an anonymous Babylonian and further encouraged by the good-omened appearance of the Persian Oebaras. There are also hints that the Persians were suffering under a Median yoke,[32] but one has to say that in the surviving material these hints are not greatly developed and Astyages is not depicted in particularly lurid colours. There is certainly no discourse about *truphê*. What the process does have in common with the Assyrian story, however, is that the overthrow of empire requires immense military effort. Once again, the rebels are repeatedly defeated, and their eventual victory is put down to the desperation of a last stand (symbolized in the famous story about the Persian women's obscene gesture to their menfolk) and the fact that (in some sense) fate was on their side.

Empires fall, then, only when their time has come—something that may, but need not, be the consequence of a change for the worse in their character—and only with great difficulty and amidst extensive violence. Fate may be unpredictable, but there is no reason why kings who enjoy their wealth and the luxury it affords in an appropriate fashion, and who do not play the role of military aggressor, should not rule for many generations. Looking at things in these terms Ctesias would have little cause to imagine that the Achaemenid realm had anything but a great future.

We cannot know whether he even confronted the question; but there are two observations that can be made.

First, there was no strong reason for Ctesias' intertextual engagement with Herodotus to have prompted consideration of the issue, because Herodotus does not at all plainly propose a view on the matter. If we look at his treatment of the fall of earlier empires, we see that the end of the Median Empire attracts quite extensive narrative (1.107-130) and the underlying factors include Astyages' cruelty (πικρότης) toward the Medes, Harpagus' personal motive for fomenting the overthrow of Astyages, and the Persians' desire to be free and to exchange hard labor for enjoyable leisure. In the case of the Assyrian Empire (1.103-106), what strikes one in the narrative is the story of the Medes attacking Assyria, winning a battle but then being interrupted by a Scythian incursion. Only when the Scythians are disposed of is war with Assyria resumed and Nineveh captured. But this does not technically represent the demise of the Assyrian empire, because that has apparently already taken place. The Medes have

---

[31] FGH 688 F 8d 1–46.
[32] FGH 688 F 8d 14–15.

already become an independent kingdom (courtesy of Deioces) and acquired an *arkhê*, and other peoples have also asserted their freedom from Assyria: Nineveh is simply the seat of an isolated (albeit still prosperous) kingdom. So the fall of the Assyrian empire is not in fact described by Herodotus at all, and is only explained inasmuch as its subjects are represented as achieving freedom. That does, of course, recall Persian self-liberation from the Medes (so there is a common thread) and, in view of the fact that *Histories* ends with the Greeks of Asia securing freedom from the Persian yoke and with an example of what one might call Xerxes' (or at least his wife's) πικρότης to the Persians in the shape of the Masistius story, one could wonder whether Herodotus is speculating about the Achaemenid Empire's vulnerability to a historically validated pattern. But there is no explicit sign of this in the text; there was no actual sign of such vulnerability by the time the text of Herodotus' work reached the definitive form we now have before us; many readers think that the imperial future with which Herodotus was concerned, albeit *sub rosa*, was more that of Athens than of Persia; and the tantalizing final chapter which recalls Cyrus' advice that the Persians should not emigrate en masse from their homeland if they do not wish to become subjects rather than rulers, while certainly inviting us to contemplate 479 in the light of the empire's origins, is arguably as much a reminder that the fundamental change Cyrus feared has not happened as (for example) a hint that the mere fact of having conquered an empire and therefore gained access to wealth and the potential for leisure has undermined the imperial project's viability. Reading Herodotus could, of course, have prompted Ctesias to explicit thought about Persian imperial collapse, just because any consideration of relevant parts of the historical past (presented by any source) might prompt such thought. But there is no reason to assert any special or specially peremptory influence.[33] Secondly, no hint survives that Ctesias commented openly on the issue at the end of *Persica* any more than Herodotus had at the end of *Histories*. The end of *Persica* was, of course, rather distinctive in the sense that the stopping point is not provided by any particular watershed event, but simply by the historian's departure from the Persian court. The claim to autoptic and autecoic authority is central to Ctesias' posture (or pose) as a historian, and it is this methodological feature that determines the scope of the work. It is true that the context of Ctesias' departure means the introduction into the narrative of the latest part of a Greek political and military story that had begun in ca. 414 but (despite its implicit presence in the origins of Cyrus' revolt) had been essentially absent from *Persica*. But I cannot see any reason to assign this more than

---

[33] It is perhaps worth saying explicitly that the idea of succession-of-empires (whether it be attributed to Herodotus or the Achaemenids) does not appear to bear *particular* significance in this context. See Wiesehöfer 2003, 2005.

contingent significance. The effect will have been that the steady continuum of Persian history was carrying on and it was simply an accident that Ctesias would no longer be in a position to report on it. By the time he published his work everyone may have known that this Greek story had ended in Artaxerxes' favour with the King's Peace, but it does not really matter. Moreover, if Ctesias' story ended abruptly, the final element of the book was a description of the road from Ephesus to Bactria and India, and a list of the Kings of Asia from Ninus and Semiramis to Artaxerxes. This will have done nothing to undermine the assumption that the empire, vast in extent and heir to over 50 generations of history, was here to stay. The model for imperial collapse required a rebel from among the empire's subject-nations. Where was that to be found? Cyrus' rebellion was a story of usurpation, not empire-destruction and not one demonstrably intended to prove that the 'wrong' claimant had won, thus setting the empire on a downward path. It is not clear if Ctesias even mentioned the late fifth century revolt of Egypt and, although Evagoras would later give Isocrates a stick with which to beat the empire, his appearance at the end of *Persica* will hardly have struck Ctesias' readers as the first appearance of a new Arbaces or Elder Cyrus.

2. Xenophon and Plato

I wish to turn now to two other fourth-century texts, in which the end of a non-Persian empire also appears in the context of a discourse about Persia, though their importance largely lies elsewhere. One is Xenophon's *Cyropaedia*, the other Plato's *Laws*, and so we are moving away from normal historiography. I have already deployed some tropes of non-historical criticism of Persia in the preceding discussion, but we need to confront certain non-historiographical texts more directly, since the characteristics and limitations of their discourse are intrinsically interesting and may cast light on what is likely to have been found in the lost historiographical discourse. It is worth stressing at the outset that there were, of course, people in the real world (not the historian's study) who did not see a weak Persia. Demosthenes' *Oration* 14 shows that people could believe the King might attack Greece—whether as a result of Athenian aggression or for some other reason, and whether after an eventual reconquest of Egypt or with preparation of an Egyptian campaign as the cover.[34] This fear of attack casts Persia as dangerous, and Demosthenes argues that the incurability

---

[34] Aristotle *Rhetoric* 2.20.1393b (Darius and Xerxes attacked Greece after securing Egypt) illustrates a possible line of argument in the context. Compare the idea in Isocrates *Panathenaicus* 159 that Argos and Thebes helped the Egyptian expedition in order that he could win great power and plot against Greece.

of Greek internal dissension means one cannot envisage fighting the King except in a critical end-game, involving direct attack on Greece. Only for such a context can one produce any arguments to suggest that the King's undeniable wealth and military power, including that derived from Greek mercenaries, might be less than they seem. And the evidence that Greeks would win a last-stand contest is precisely that they did so in 480; the claim is not based on any proposition about the character of current Persians or their military capacity. I would also stress that Isocrates' position fundamentally differs from this only in its willingness to speculate that Greek political dissension might be cured. The alleged occasional or systemic weaknesses of Persia are primarily deployed as supports for the thought-experiment of Greek unity: Isocrates is saying that you can dare to think the unthinkable because Persia is not a wholly solid and impervious politico-military entity. We are dealing with an *a fortiori* argument, not with the listing of objective signs of imminent collapse. Some of the King's successes may be due to Greek folly or his own exploitative φρόνησις rather than brute strength, but his local difficulties with dissident subjects are not irreversible (left to himself he may take firmer control of Asia again: *Panegyricus* 163) and, without Greek unity, the King is far too powerful to be confronted.

What, then, do Xenophon's *Cyropaedia* and Plato's *Laws* bring to the topic? In a nutshell, a clear, if differently articulated, thesis of decline. I have alluded to the idea of decadence earlier, but this is our first direct encounter—and may be our last as well.

The final chapter of *Cyropaedia* paints a picture of contemporary Persia in which the decent habits of the past have been abandoned or subverted to produce a world of spiritual and physical decay. The first four sections of the analysis each contain explicit or implicit remarks about military consequences,[35] and the final section (8.8.20–26) addresses the matter directly with a claim that the ranks of cavalry are being filled with cooks, waiters, and body-servants. So we are certainly being told that Persia's capacity to defend itself or attack others is compromised by a change in character for the worse that includes but is not confined to a surrender to *truphê*.

When did this occur? There are three chronological levels in *Cyropaedia*.[36] One is the time of Cyrus (that is, of the main narrative). One is the present to which the final chapter refers—in the reign of Artaxerxes and even as late as the later 360s. The third is elusive—it is the time to which many passages in the main narrative refer that say that a practice or institution still applies among the Persians even now (ἔτι καὶ νῦν), and it sits somewhere between Cyrus and

---

[35] I.e. 8.8.2–7, 8–12, 13–14, 15–19.

[36] Tuplin 1997:103–105.

the reign of Artaxerxes. The final chapter sets out to prove that, after Cyrus, πάντα ἐπὶ τὸ χεῖρον ἐτρέπετο ['everything turned to the worse'], but this did not wholly happen immediately: the mercenary generals in 401 could hardly have been deceived by a belief that the oath of the Persian King or his representative could be trusted, if the morality had plainly dropped out of Persian behavior generations earlier. But Xenophon's primary interest is not to define the rate or stages of this decline. His concern is different: he has constructed a quasi-historical narrative which provides a paradigm of excellence in *arkhê*. He now needs to protect the validity of this historical paradigm by (a) making clear that contemporary, mid-fourth-century Persians have changed, are not paradigmatic of good qualities, and cannot be adduced to disprove what is said about Cyrus (hence the final chapter) and (b) claiming that what Cyrus achieved, though not perfectly maintainable, was sufficiently grounded and historically real to apply in some respects for a considerable time after his death (hence the ἔτι καὶ νῦν statements). The two stages of change (dissension following immediately upon his demise; the subversion of good habits into their opposite characteristic of contemporary Persia) exist for rhetorical reasons, not historical ones, and it is no surprise that they cannot be tied down. Still one change—excessive and ill-controlled drinking together with the abandonment of regular hunting—is explicitly attributed to Artaxerxes (and evokes Cyrus' reported critique of his brother in Plutarch *Artaxerxes* 6), and there is no reason to imagine Xenophon considered current Persian degradation to be of any great historical depth.

This real, but limited concern with post-Cyrean history also means that it is not Xenophon's business to worry about the future fate of the current empire. Despite real stress on military consequences in the final chapter, no conclusion is drawn that the empire is vulnerable to destruction, and there is no inclination even hypothetically to say "if a serious force came against them they would be in bad trouble." One might even say that the almost parodically satirical tone adopted to denounce contemporary Persia reflects Persia's actual continuing status as a powerful force: in order to insist on the distinction between his historical paradigm and a contemporary national enemy Xenophon outdoes denunciations of the latter by politicians and pamphleteers. But in any case the focus of *Cyropaedia* is backwards to the days of the Elder Cyrus, not forwards to the prospect of a different geopolitical environment. There is a sort of parallel with Aeschylus' *Persians*: that too provides an historical *exemplum* (one not about modes of rule so much as maintenance of bounds) and the future after Xerxes' lament-filled return home is no more the issue than it would be if the 'historical' material were drawn from mythology rather than the contemporary world. Individual spectators may have been conscious of a dissonance between the 'destruction of Asia' bewailed in the play and the fact that in 472

BCE Achaemenid Asia was pretty much intact. But the play was no invitation to think about the end of the Achaemenid Empire.

Xenophon, then, provides an example of the 'decadent Persian' model of thought. The same is true of a passage in Plato's *Laws* about the deleterious effects of Persian education of royal children (3.694a–697b). Cyrus and Darius, not brought up as sons of kings, were good and egalitarian rulers. The education of Cyrus' sons, however, led them to τρυφή and ἀνεπιπληξία ['impunity' or 'licentiousness']. Cambyses killed his brother, was driven mad by drink and ἀπαιδευσία ['lack of education'], and fell victim to a coup. Xerxes experienced similar παθήματα ['misfortunes'], and since all that time ago pretty much no King has been Great, except in title. After an interlude Plato continues ἀνευρίσκομεν δὲ ἐπὶ ἔτι χείρους αὐτοὺς γεγονότας ('they reached an even worse position', not 'their corruption increased year by year', as Saunders 1970 has it) because they were too strict in depriving people of liberty and bringing on *to despotikon*; this removed τὸ φίλον . . . καὶ τὸ κοινὸν ['friendship and communal spirit']. Policy is driven by the interest of the ruler and even a slight prospective advantage means they make cities ἀνάστατοι ['ruined'] and ruin and destroy friendly nations (ἔθνη φίλια ἀνάστατα πυρὶ καταφθείραντες). There is pitiless reciprocal hatred. The result is that they discover that, when they approach the *demoi* in need of soldiers, although they have countless myriads of subjects they are useless for warfare because there is no community-spirit encouraging them to fight. Hence, as though there were a population shortage, they have to hire soldiers, and they think they will be kept safe by mercenaries and foreigners. Their actions proclaim a belief that compared with gold and society, τὰ λεγόμενα τίμια καὶ καλὰ κατὰ πόλιν ['those things that are regarded as honorable and good in society'] are just nonsense. The Persian set-up οὐκ ὀρθῶς διοικεῖται διὰ τὴν σφόδρα δουλείαν τε καὶ δεσποτείαν ['is not well-regulated because of excessive servitude and despotism'].

A number of observations may be made:[37]

1. Plato has found an ingenious way to reconcile the fact that early kings conquered an empire with a claim that the Persian system was intrinsically weak—a weakness consistently present since Xerxes and already present under

---

[37] Plato expressed a different view about Persian royal education in the *Alcibiades*, a work of the early 350s, so written before *Laws*. That calls the seriousness of the historical analysis into some question (though perhaps it is *Alcibiades* where he is being consciously playful and paradoxical). But we can still legitimately analyse the argument laid out here. The *Alcibiades* passage assumes Sparta and Persia to be the major adversaries with which Alcibiades would have to deal; so far as Sparta goes that was out-of-date in the early 350s and Plato is consciously assuming a fifth century setting, as indeed the explicit reference to Artaxerxes (I) shows. (Since Artaxerxes was already king before Alcibiades was born, the specific comparison is not terribly *à propos* either.) So nothing emerges usefully about views of fourth century Persia.

Cambyses. Plato does say that the Persians became worse, but the seeds go back very early: Cyrus and Darius are the accidents in this story. There is no mention of the Persian Wars in the remarks about Xerxes (they are reserved for a subsequent discussion of Athenian history) and what Plato means by his references to demolished and burned cities is unclear; if things got worse it is simply that the accident of history provided no further kings who had not been educated as royal princes and perhaps because the consequential effects mount up. But the mechanism, the rate, and future trajectory are not of much interest to him. (The statement "as of now Persian affairs are badly run because of despotism" even theoretically allows the possibility of change for the better.)

2. The basic principle is that lack of virtue and experience of restraint makes children inimical to κοινωνία ['communal partnership'] and ἰσότης ['equality'] and so forth. And it is the wider absence of these community virtues that matters. Τρυφή is mentioned but seems to be no more than an epiphenomenon. This focus matches the context in *Laws*: Plato's concern is with political structures and the immediate context is a contrast between monarchy (Persia) and democracy (Athens), on the one hand, and a Spartan-Cretan model of polity, on the other. But it is not unique to *Laws*: Isocrates *Panegyricus* 150-151 is also more concerned with lack of equality than with *truphê*, and even in the Xenophontic analysis *truphê* is not the unique source of trouble.

3. It is notable that a specifically military conclusion is drawn. In a parallel passage about Athens the consequence of extreme liberty is figured in general terms as misery such as that suffered by the Titans (3.701c): since in the good old days before extreme liberty Athenians had been able to fight off two Persian invasions (3.698b–699d), one may assume that the Titans' character as the victims of crushing defeat is of pertinence and that, at least implicitly, military ineffectiveness is the consequence of the faults of democracy just as it is of the faults of monarchy. Since, in Plato's view, extreme democracy results in everyone thinking he knows best and so in a breakdown in respect for authority and the laws, one can certainly see that military effectiveness would suffer—especially as (again in Plato's view) what made the Athenians able to defeat Xerxes was the beneficial fear that is learned by being subject to an ancient code of laws. But a question remains: is it a predetermined desire to figure the consequence of poor political structure as military weakness that dictates the allusions to this point in the two case studies? Or is it a predetermined idea that contemporary Persia is paradoxically greedy for Greek mercenaries that dictates the crafting of a parallel element in the Athenian case? One's first inclination may be for the latter, on the ground that the point is implicit, and perhaps a touch artificial, in the Athenian case. But the wider context pits Persia and Athens against a Spartan model (which naturally evokes military excellence) and the

historical discourse in the immediately preceding section of *Laws* speaks of the Dorian League (3.682e–686a) and its function as a military protection for the Peloponnese and Greece against, for example, the threat of an Assyrian attack in revenge for the Greek sack of Troy. (Modern Sparta is the only bit of that old league that retains its character and expectations.) So I think the question may remain open. In any event, of course, Plato is incorporating in his argument an externally given proposition: that Persia proved her weakness by employing foreign mercenaries was an idea already in the air.

4. What might follow from this is unclear. Both Persian and Athenian discourses end with a steady state—in the case of the Titan-like Athenians, presumably one stretching into eternity!—and it is not Plato's business to speculate about the end of the Persian empire. The situation is thus like that in Xenophon, even if the processes that produce it are rather differently figured.

There is another difference. Unlike Plato,[38] but like Ctesias, Xenophon has a narrative embracing the fall of another empire—though only one, since there is no Median empire here and Cyrus incorporates the Median kingdom into his own realm via matrimony and the demise of the previous king. We thus move directly from an Assyrian to a Persian empire, thanks to Cyrus' invasion of Assyria, defeat of the Assyrians' allies, acquisition of Anatolia, and eventual capture of Babylon. All this starts because of Assyrian aggression and ends as it does because of Cyrus' faultless excellence as a leader of men. If there is a transferrable principle, it is that empires fall when a tyrant's greed for power provokes an exceptionally gifted opponent. That is a different model from the one in Ctesias, which depends upon rebellion by existing subjects inside an empire, not successful resistance to aggression by the empire against potential new subjects outside. It is also a model that Xenophon could not rationally have thought applicable to the current Achaemenid state: for it is hard to see how a state whose military arm is as totally corrupted as Xenophon suggests would be likely to engage in the sort of proactive aggression against new outside victims that the model requires. Should we, then, infer that Xenophon was consciously, if implicitly, arguing that the empire had no reason to worry about its future? Probably not. The model of Assyrian imperial failure is entirely a by-product of Xenophon's need for a version of history in which Cyrus won an empire with no taint of aggression on his own part and against a background in which Persia and Media provide parallel inputs into his educational and therefore political make-up (hence a

---

[38] A passage in the discussion of the Dorian League says that the reason that it broke down was that kings in that era fell prey to aggressive and illegal greed because their life of *truphê* had made them arrogant (3.691a). I do not know if Plato thought the *truphê* of early Dorians (a rather wonderfully paradoxical idea) comparable with that of Artaxerxes, and I am wary of supposing that he would have thought of applying the model to the Persians.

fight for freedom against Median imperial rule had to be eliminated). The applicability or otherwise of the model to contemporary Persia is simply not part of Xenophon's project. It turns out, then, that, although both Xenophon and Plato are engaging in political analysis rather than historical anecdote and might in theory be more likely to think about the consequences of systemic weakness (especially when it involves an element of decline and therefore raises questions about change), they are in the event just as hidebound as everyone else. Perhaps what this really illustrates is how difficult it was for anyone to contemplate the possibility of a world without the Achaemenid Empire.

3. Decadence, Military Weakness, Despotism, and Luxury

I shall end with some further remarks on four themes raised by Plato and Xenophon. First, decadence. The acknowledgment of change for the worse appears in Xenophon and Plato for specific reasons that are not primarily to do with actual judgments about Persian history. In Xenophon it is needed to protect his historical paradigm from the distaste for Persia that he assumes will characterise many of his readers. In Plato it arises because his big project is construction of an ideal *polis* and his definition of some of the parameters operates within the model of serial constitutional change already established in Greek political thought.[39] For both of them Persia is a tool with which to think about non-Persian things. When this was not the case the issue of systemic change and decay was less important. I have already noted the general absence of obvious reasons to identify it as an element in historiographical texts—or at least the absence of evidence for its presence. More positively one might mention the surprisingly positive view of Artaxerxes I, whom various texts label as mild, peaceful and successful,[40] and whose evaluation in such terms may be unconsciously reflected in Plato's contextually senseless statement that since Xerxes 'almost' no Persian kings have been great except in name. This is an aspect of the historical tradition's way of dealing with the Persian defeat in 480/479: instead

---

[39] The possibility of influence from, or intertexting with, Xenophon might be considered too. But the whole issue of Plato's supposed reaction to, even attack on, *Cyropaedia* is rather tricky: after all, Plato's attack on Persian royal education is not an attack on the actual education of Xenophon's Cyrus.

[40] Ammianus Marcellinus 30.8: Artaxerxes I's invention of gentle modification of punishments (cutting off hats or bits of hats, rather than heads or ears), won his subjects' support and he was enabled to perform wonderful deeds chronicled by Greek writers. Plutarch *Artaxerxes* 1.4: Artaxerxes I was gentle and μεγαλόψυχος. Diodorus 11.71: Artaxerxes I governed the empire ἐπιεικῶς; 15.93: he ruled well, and was εἰρηνικός and ἐπιτυχής. Nepos *Reges* 1.5 credits him with *virtus belli*. I am inclined to think that Athenaeus 12.548e really applies to Artaxerxes I, not to Artaxerxes III Ochus.

of any suggestion that the empire went into decline at that point (an idea that is not to be read into Herodotus and is vanishingly elusive in fourth century texts),[41] we have a positive evaluation of the abandonment of large-scale schemes for the conquest of new lands. Again, although Artaxerxes III is a less attractive character, there is a story that the *magi* foretold for his reign a great deal of death but also a great deal of prosperity (Aelian *Varia Historia* 2.17). The prosperity is figured as agricultural, but I think we have here the reflection of an assessment of his reign as pragmatically quite successful.[42] The trajectory of a king's reign may have ups and downs (the aged Artaxerxes II cuts a rather pathetic figure) but with each new reign the story, so to say, starts again: the Alexander historians do not construe Darius III as intrinsically weaker than his predecessors (though some express more hostility towards him than others, and Arrian is particularly critical). A different version of this sort of continuity is the way in which in Isocratean discourse the King is generally anonymous and a strangely unchanging entity—so that, for example, one can speak of defeating the King in 480/79 and then making a shameful treaty with that same King in 387/6. More generally, indeed, it seems to me that decadence is not a very powerful feature of the Isocratean discourse about Persia. His tendency to adduce contemporary 'proofs' of Persian weakness is primarily a function of his wish to prompt contemporary action, rather than a belief that contemporary Persia is peculiarly enfeebled. A passage such as *Panegyricus* 150–151, explaining the impact of Persian upbringing and education upon military failure, seems comparatively timeless, while *Philippus* 124 postulates that the Persians were already ruined by *truphê* by Darius' time.[43] Furthermore, though in some circumstances Cyrus can be deployed as an admirable *exemplum*, *Philippus* 66 and 139 picture the empire created by a foundling as from the start necessarily feeble compared with the realm of Philip of Macedon. On the whole, the idea that Greeks have suffered decline since the good old days is a much greater concern for Isocrates and other fourth-century observers than any comparable idea about Persians. And with

---

41 On Herodotus I agree with Lenfant 2001:423; cf. also Bichler 2010. *Menexenus* (239df.) stresses that Athens brought an end to the conquest era, but is not interested in articulating any idea that this set Persia on a road to decline. In the course of arguing against Philip exposing himself to personal danger, Isocrates (*Epistle* 2.7) is even prepared to remark that Xerxes, despite a calamitous defeat, kept his throne, handed it over to his children, and administered Asia so it was no less fearful to Greeks than before. The Persian Wars are adduced by fourth-century orators not as a proof of Persian weakness (for that other arguments are required) but as a means of raising contemporary Greek consciousness, of proving that in the right circumstances Greeks can beat Persians, or of claiming that one's own state's contribution to that great event was better than that of some other state.

42 Cf. Mildenberg 1999 for a modern appreciation of the King's qualities.

43 According to Critias, the Thessalians invited a Persian invasion of Greece because they admired Persian τρυφή and πολυτέλεια (88 B 31 D.K. = Athenaeus 14.662f–663a).

good reason: in the clash of Greek and Persian, at least, the King had won in 386, and the diplomatic and political history of the next four decades repeatedly reminded everyone of this fact. This is as likely to have affected historians as pamphleteers. [44]

Second, military weakness. Xenophon and Plato encapsulate this in the proposition that Persians cannot recruit useful troops of their own and must depend upon Greek mercenaries. Isocrates makes similar observations. All three are talking about a phenomenon that, as a matter of fact, did not go back through the whole history of the Empire. Xenophon and Plato evidently knew this. Isocrates surely did too—after all Greek mercenaries as a class were for him a sign of a change for the worse in Greek society—but he does not exploit it as a sign of diachronic Persian decline. Instead it is simply a fact about the present that makes it particularly reprehensible that the Greeks fight one another instead of attacking Persia, as Persians had attacked Greece 135 years earlier. Readers of historiographical sources will find plenty of references to fourth-century Persian employment of Greek mercenaries—and may suspect that they are sometimes (e.g. in the Diodoran narrative of the reconquest of Egypt) accorded a greater prominence than the actual facts justified. But there is no way of validating that suspicion, and contemporary historians generally think it reasonable that the Persians should have made heavy use of them— indeed, even that the willingness to use foreign military technology is a sign of self-confidence and strength. Fourth-century historians are really displaying Greek chauvinism (there is more pride in the Greek contribution than criticism of the Persian use), and even in the accounts of the empire's actual fall, presentation of Darius' mercenaries is sufficiently nuanced to suggest that no one has radically misrepresented the facts. No one suggests either that he would have done better without them or that he needed (and knew he needed) many, many more or that he did not know how to use them—even if there could be awkward

---

[44] Callisthenes' choice of 386 as the start for his Hellenica must reflect its perceived status as an epochal moment. Book 1 also spoke of the Atheno-Spartan treaty of 369 and may have offered remarks about the Peace of Callias (FGH 124 F 8): perhaps, having picked the King's Peace as a starting point, Callisthenes looked backwards and forwards to other significant diplomatic moments. That would be consistent with the panhellenist angle with which some have credited Callisthenes, but it hardly demands it. The bulk of the work concentrated on 378–357 and cannot be demonstrated to have had a substantial Persian element. The account of Mausolus' synoecism of Halicarnassus (FGH 124 F 25) need not be from Hellenica and, if the 373 Persian invasion of Egypt figured in Book 4, all we have is a digression on Etesian winds and Nile-flooding (FGH 124 F 12) and, perhaps, one on the relationship between Athens and the Saite kings (FGH 124 F 51). Mausolus' emergence as a regional power and the 373 invasion are topics that could have allowed the historian to question the health of the Achaemenid Empire. But it seems a bit of a long shot that Callisthenes did so.

(even fatal) moments of culture clash between Persians and their Greek employ-ees.[45] Stress on the misfortune of Memnon's death is again, at worst, Greek chau-vinism. Meanwhile there are certainly non-Greek troops capable of fighting well, if eventually unsuccessfully, in defence of the empire. The chances at Issus were fatally compromised by bad choice of battle-site and, in one strand of the tradition at least, the outcome of Gaugamela is made to turn on a false belief that Darius had been killed. In the *Politics* (7.2.1324b11) Aristotle still counted Persians among the barbarian races who valued the ability to fight: I do not imagine that his view was eccentric.

Thirdly, freedom and despotism. The corrupting effects of despotism are integral to Plato's analysis of the poor state of Persia and prominent in Isocrates *Panegyricus* 150–151. Compare Jason of Pherae's comment that the Persians prac-tice slavery not ἀλκή (Xenophon *Hellenica* 6.1.12). Desire for freedom is also an element in the historical models for imperial collapse in Ctesias and Xenophon, but it is presented as a sentiment that contributes to the process rather than one that sets it going. Isocrates speaks of sowing the word *eleutheria* (the word that destroyed the power of Athens and Sparta) in Asia—at least among the ruling elite: the generality of barbarians are to be exposed to Greek supervision (ἐπιμέλεια)—but this is only relevant when the world has already been changed by an outbreak of Greek unity. Empires do not collapse just because people would prefer not to be ruled by others and, as Alexander showed, it is not necessary to offer much unambiguous freedom to displace an imperial dynasty. After all, when we are dealing with the succession of empires, not their complete demoli-tion, freedom is a dangerous weapon. (What really destroyed the Achaemenid empire was not Darius' replacement by Alexander but the power vacuum caused by Alexander's death, and the only freedom that mattered then was that of one ambitious satrap in relation to another.)

One place where despotism and freedom play no part in the analysis is the final chapter of *Cyropaedia*. Xenophon wanted readers to draw appropriate lessons about leadership from his historical account of the creation and char-acter of a benevolent autocracy in charge of an imperial super-state, and he needed to put distance between this benevolent autocracy and the 'real' Persian empire as known, or imagined, by those readers. So why did he not write a final chapter contrasting Cyrus' state with the non-benevolent and tyrannical autoc-racy of contemporary Persia? Because he thought it would be hard to describe the latter without reinforcing the complaint that the work was an invitation to admire an alien political form. One of the lessons of *Cyropaedia* is that achieve-ment of significant power involves a delicate balance between republican and

---

[45]   Charidemus (Diodorus 17.30, Curtius 3.2.17–19); Iphicrates and Pharnabazus (Diodorus 15.43).

monarchic modes of rule. Even in the terms of the *Cyropaedia* narrative, there are rather uncomfortable features to the rule of Cyrus in Book 8. Drawing a contrast with a stereotype image of contemporary Persian kingship (while concentrating solely on methods and strategies of rule) might not make readers acknowledge the actual necessity for manipulative autocracy in any effective exercise of power over others. To say that Cyrus' nice version has degenerated into the contemporary nasty version may provoke the response that Cyrus' version is actually nasty too. The whole thing would be additionally difficult if, as I suspect, Xenophon did not believe the current Persian system (as a system of *arkhê*) to have become fundamentally corrupted. The general principle of king, court, and satrapal elite, and of the control exerted by the first over the others through manipulative patronage still held and remained fit for purpose. What was wrong—or could safely be said to be wrong for the purpose of calming the reader's prejudices—lay in the moral health of the rulers, not in the system within which they were trying to rule. Since Cyrus had been an effective general and Xenophon had a particular interest in military matters, it is the military consequences of moral corruption that are highlighted—including the repeated observation that enemies can wander around imperial territory unimpeded. That is an incontestable failure in a basic function of government, but it does not prove that the type of government involved is wrong.

Finally, luxury. The story here is not uniform. Xenophon makes recent *truphê* comparatively important among the causes of military inadequacy. Plato and Isocrates register it merely as one aspect, already present far in the past. The philosopher Clearchus is represented as highlighting it as a component of imperial failure. In one passage he says that Darius "gave prizes to those who catered to his pleasures, but brought his kingdom to defeat through all these indulgences, and did not perceive that he was defeating himself until others had seized his sceptre and were proclaimed rulers." In another we read that the untimely and senseless (παράκαιρος καὶ μάταιος) luxury of the Median lance-bearers had led to the fall of the Medes (and turned the Medes into something like ἀγύρται ['mendicant priests']) and that the Persians adopted the practice of having (gold or silver) apples on their spear butts to remind the Medes of their former power and its loss. Does that imply that the Persians also succumbed to untimely *truphê*—and an untimely *truphê* that had always been there?[46] The claim has sometimes been advanced that a contrary view was developed of *truphê* as a beneficial aspect of Persian power. This is based particularly on a passage of Heraclides Ponticus:

---

[46] Clearchus fr. 49–50 Wehrli. For a recent brief account of Clearchus' *peri Biôn*, see Tsitsiridis 2008.

Tyrants and kings, masters of all the good things in life, of which they have experience, put their pleasures in first place, because pleasure renders human nature more noble. In any case, all those who devote themselves to pleasure and choose a life of luxury are noble and generous: this is true of the Persians and the Medes since, more than any other people in the world, they devote themselves to pleasure and luxury and yet at the same time are the most noble and most courageous of the barbarians. In fact, to enjoy pleasure and luxury is the mark of free men: doing so frees and elevates the spirit, whereas to live a life of work is the mark of slaves and men of low birth. (Translation by C. B. Gulick)

Heraclides Ponticus fr. 55 Wehrli (Athenaeus 12.512a–d)

This is a remarkable text—so remarkable that it should be treated with considerable caution. What we know otherwise of Heraclides does not encourage the idea that he would have praised *truphê* in his own voice and, as Dominique Lenfant has recently argued, there must be a strong suspicion that Athenaeus has quoted out of context an argument that it was Heraclides' purpose to refute.[47] There must be a similar worry about a passage of Aristoxenus' *Life of Archytas* in which an envoy of Dionysius of Syracuse is represented as suggesting that hedonism empowered the imperial conquests of the Medes and Persians[48]—and there is perhaps a general danger that Athenaeus' own agenda imposes a moral color on his treatment of this general area that was less pronounced or absent in the sources he is excerpting. Still the fact (if it is one) that Heraclides or Aristoxenus saw fit to invite their readers' scepticism may count as evidence that the views in question were sometimes articulated, perhaps as a provocatively extreme version of the more general point that the Persian King was extremely rich and therefore, in principle, extremely, and enviably, powerful.[49] The frequency with which Persian *truphê* is, in fact, royal *truphê* is, as Lenfant has observed, a sign of its association with power.

Another text to note in this connection is Plutarch *Artaxerxes* 24. During the withdrawal from a disastrous expedition against the Cadusians, Artaxerxes made a sterling show of qualities of leadership amidst scenes of extreme deprivation and death. This showed (Plutarch says) that cowardice and weakness are

---

[47] Lenfant 2007.
[48] Aristoxenus fr. 50 Wehrli = Athenaeus 12.545a–546c. This may well have been penned in the post-conquest era, though it attributes the observation to a pre-conquest observer. The problem is that Aristoxenus' intention may be to expose the incorrectness of Polyarchus' general defence of hedonism.
[49] cf. Tuplin 1996:162.

not always the result of *truphê* and extravagance, as most think, but of a nature that is evil, base, and controlled by evil opinions. The effect of this apparent, if indirect, praise of the King is qualified, of course, by Artaxerxes' execution of certain leading men after the safe return home—in which context Plutarch attributes to him the cowardice that drives tyrants to kill. Perhaps tyranny can create cowardice irrespective of character. But it is still not cowardice produced by *truphê*, and there really is a hint here that the luxury of the Persian environment is not in itself a systemic cause of weakness.[50] Was this derived from Dinon or is it entirely due to Plutarch's moral assessment of the facts? We cannot tell, but the former option is not to be ruled out. In any event, we may compare, on the one hand, Ctesias' treatment of the Assyrian empire and, on the other hand, two fragments of the other Heraclides, the historian from Cyme. These are the famous long piece about the King's Dinner (FGH 689 F 2) and a shorter one about the independent king of incense-bearing Arabia (FGH 689 F 4). The latter displays excessive *truphê* and idleness, and spends 15 talents per day on himself, his women, and his friends. One could conjecture a telling contrast between him and the Achaemenid monarch, whose great daily expenditure on his Dinner is not μεγαλοπρεπής ['magnificent'] but οἰκονομικῶς καὶ ἀκριβῶς συντεταγμένον ['arranged economically and carefully']. Heraclides seems to be arguing against denunciation of Persian luxury and consciously articulating the view that the system of which it is part is well-designed and robust: moreover, those supported by the King's table include the King's *doruphoroi* and *peltastai*; like Greek mercenaries getting silver, they receive food from the king εἰς ὑπόλογον. The precise significance of that unusual phrase is elusive, but it is not inconceivable that Heraclides was *inter alia* questioning claims about Persian military weakness— and indeed specifically criticizing views that linked such weakness with the consequences of *truphê*. We do not know when Heraclides wrote this, but the fragment is in the present tense and may predate the fall of the empire. Here, at least, is a Persian historian who cannot be said to have seen what was coming.

That the Achaemenid dispensation could eventually succumb to invasion by a grotesquely outnumbered adversary certainly suggests that something was amiss. It was not a system that most subject peoples were going to do much to defend on their own cognisance, so the invader had some freedom of movement except when a satrapal or royal army was on the scene, and when Xenophon

---

[50] The historical tradition behind Strabo 15.3.22 contrasts generally moderate (σωφρονικά) customs with a tendency for wealth to induce *truphê*. (The sign of this is that the Kings bring wheat from Assus, Chalydonian wine from Syria, and water from the Eulaeus. The articulation of this with the previous paragraph from Polyclitus about Persians keeping metal for equipment or as gifts or deposits rather than turning it into coinage is not entirely clear.) There may be a model implicit here of decline from an earlier age of greater innocence but no particular consequences are articulated.

said Persia's enemies were able to move armies around within imperial territory, he was touching on what turned out to be a relevant point. On the other hand his theory about quick attack finds no close reflection in the events of 334-331 and was, perhaps, more appropriate to usurper than external conqueror. Still, in the end, nothing definitive could be achieved by either usurper or conqueror except at the moments of major confrontation between the two sides and it is on the devilish details of strategy, tactics, and the battle-field success and failure of men as individuals and groups that much depended. If no one predicted an appropriate scenario we can hardly be surprised. Fourth-century criticism of Persian morality, and celebration of Persian use of Greek mercenaries are expressions of frustration at Persian power, not confidence in its weakness. If pressed, many would have said the empire's fall required a miracle; so if Demetrius, even in retrospect, chose to put the whole thing under the aegis of unpredictable Fortune, we can hardly blame him.[51]

Bibliography

Bichler, R. 2010. "Der Hof der Achämeniden im Augen Herodots." In *Der Achämenidenhof*, ed. B. Jacobs and R. Rollinger, 155-188. Wiesbaden.

Briant, P. 1989. "Histoire et idéologie: les Grecs et la 'décadence perse'." In *Mélanges P. Lévêque II*, ed. M.-M. Mactoux and E. Geny, 33–47 . Paris. Translated as "History and Ideology: The Greeks and 'Persian Decadence'." In *Greeks and Barbarians*, ed. T. Harrison, 193–210. Edinburgh.

Debord, P. 1999. *L'Asie mineure au IVe siècle*. Bordeaux.

Elayi, J. 2006. "An Updated Chronology of the Reigns of Phoenician Kings During the Persian Period." *Transeuphratène* 32:11–44.

Hyland, J. 2007. "Thucydides' Portrait of Tissaphernes Re-Examined." In Tuplin 2007:1–26.

Lane Fox, R., ed. 2004. *The Long March*. New Haven.

Lenfant, D. 2001. "La "décadence" du Grand Roi et les ambitions de Cyrus le Jeune." *Revue des études grecques* 114:407–438.

———. 2007. "On Persian Tryphê in Athenaeus." In Tuplin 2007:51–66.

Mildenberg, L. 1999. "Artaxerxes III Ochus (358-338 BC). A Note on the Maligned King." *Zeitschrift des Deutschen Palästina-Vereins* 115:201–227.

Rood, T. 2004. "Panhellenism and Self-Presentation: Xenophon's Speeches." In Lane Fox 2004:304–329.

---

[51] This paper was written during tenure of a Leverhulme Major Research Fellowship. I gladly take the opportunity to express my gratitude to the Leverhulme Trust for its support.

Sancisi-Weerdenburg, H. 1987. "Decadence in the Empire or Decadence in the Sources? From Source to Synthesis: Ctesias." In *Achaemenid History* I, 33–46. Leiden.

Saunders, T. J. 1970. *Plato: The Laws.* Harmondsworth.

Stevenson, R. B. 1997. *Persica.* Edinburgh.

Tsitsiridis, S. 2008. "Die Schrift *Peri Biôn* des Klearchos von Soloi." *Philologus* 152:65–76.

Tuplin, C. J. 1996. *Achaemenid Studies.* Stuttgart.

———. 1997. "Xenophon's *Cyropaedia*: Education and Fiction." In *Education in Greek Fiction*, ed. A. H. Sommerstein and C. Atherton, 65–162. Bari.

———. 2004a. "Doctoring the Persians: Ctesias of Cnidus, Physician and Historian." *Klio* 86:305–347.

———. 2004b. "The Persian Empire." In Lane Fox 2004:154–183.

———, ed. 2007. *Persian Responses. Political and Cultural Interaction with(in) the Achaemenid Empire.* Swansea.

———. 2011. "Ctesias as Military Historian." In *Ktesias' Welt*, ed. J. Wiesehöfer et al., 449–488. Wiesbaden.

Wiesehöfer, J. 1996. "Dekadenz, Krise oder überrachendes Ende? Überlegungen zum Zusammenbruch der Perserherrschaft." In *Das Ende von Grossreichen*, ed. H. Altichter and H. Neuhaus, 39–78. Erlangen.

———. 2003. "The Medes and the Idea of the Succession of Empires in Antiquity." In *Continuity of Empire (?). Assyria, Media, Persia*, ed. G. B. Lanfranchi et al., 391–396. Padua.

———. 2005. "Herodotus and Darius the Mede." In *Von Sumer bis Homer: Festschrift Manfred Schretter*, ed. R. Rollinger, 647–653. Münster.

Weiskopf, M. 1989. *The So-Called 'Great Satraps' Revolt'. 366-360 BC.* Wiesbaden.

11

Local History, *Polis* History, and the Politics of Place

Rosalind Thomas

THE GREEK *POLIS* was, as we all know, the central and abiding socio-political institution of the Greek world, continuing in the Hellenistic period and even into Roman times, but with vastly reduced political power. Yet it was inherently changeable in ways which make the identification of what constituted 'the *polis*' extraordinarily elusive; even identifying whether such and such a place was really a '*polis*' is sometimes difficult, as the deliberations of the Copenhagen Polis Centre have shown. *Stasis* was common throughout the Greek world in the fifth and fourth centuries. Aristotle's manner of identifying the *polis* with its citizens even led him to ask whether a given *polis* would remain the same *polis* if its constitution was radically changed (*Politics* 3.3.1276b). The fourth century, our theme here, saw radical changes in the relative political roles and positions of the major city-states.[1] Those city-states all had to readjust to a changed image and sense of importance in the Greek world; fourth-century theories about the ideal *polis* imply considerable anxiety about the *polis* and a disjuncture with the changing realities of the Greek world.

One way of following the development of these numerous *poleis* would be to trace the evolution of what is conventionally known as 'local history' and what it is about a *polis*' past that the local historians think worthy of narration.[2] The genre of 'local history' was mostly written by citizens within the city-state they examined; when we are in a position to judge, they tend to be written by apparently prominent and politically active citizens, sometimes men with office, priesthoods and a prominent public role who might combine diplomatic activity with historical lectures (e.g. in Athens, Androtion, Philochorus, Phanodemos;

---

[1]   For discussion of the question of '*polis* decline', see for instance Pečirka 1976, Davies 1995, and Eder 1995.

[2]   As Schepens 2001 makes clear.

Semos of Delos (below); Syriscos of Cherronesos), though we should also not forget the travelling historians.[3] Cults, cultic peculiarities, important shrines, and local legends were a common element of local histories; so was much else. It is likely from everything else we know about the Greeks that their 'local histories' might have striven to differ from those of their neighbors, and their local emphasis likewise. Above all, though, we can dwell on the fact—and surely it is a fact—that writing down a history of a particular *polis* was a major step in cementing or crystallizing a particular vision of that *polis*, its past and therefore its present character, its 'identity'. Whatever memories and local knowledge had existed before in people's minds, traditions and memories vaguely passed down, and everyday habits, the sheer fact of having a written *polis* history will have done something to create a new entity.

We should, in short, consider these local histories in terms of political, social, or cultural changes in the Greek world and in individual city-states, and not simply in terms of the internal development of the genre of historiography (whether in methodological or literary terms). 'Local history' is conventionally and under Jacoby's authoritative aegis seen in terms of what history-writing had achieved before. Jacoby insisted that local history came after Herodotus and that it was in some vague way a response to the 'grand history' of the Greek struggle against Persia, the cities either correcting Herodotus, or trying to insert themselves into the historical record; or else because Hecataeus, Herodotus, and Hellanikos "roused the historical sense and interest" of these writers in their own home towns.[4] Yet if we rely on Plutarch's attempt to undermine Herodotus' account of the Persian Wars in the *De Malignitate*, he does not seem to have found so much material in the local historians that was either very extensive or that really undermined Herodotus' account in any serious way (cf. Lysanias of Mallos' history of Eretria, 861c, Naxian *horographoi*, 869b[5]): one wonders whether that was really all he could find. Besides, the debate has inevitably been couched in terms of the question of the priority of Herodotus and the particularly shadowy early writers of the fifth century about which we know very little. While that is not uninteresting, it detracts attention from the great mass of later local

[3]   See most recently Chaniotis 2009 on particular travelling envoys/historians; Chaniotis 1988:290-326 and esp. 365-382 for itinerant historians honoured in decrees, and 'wandering historians'; Schepens 2006 for a wider perspective, and Clarke 2008:346–354, 360–367.

[4]   Jacoby 1949:68–70 with 289nn110–111; Jacoby 1909; cf. Jacoby 1954:1f. ('Introduction' to Hellanikos). Critique in Fornara 1983:16–22 (stressing the scientific spirit of late 5th century), although cf. Fowler 1996:62–69, arguing that local history as a genre did predate Herodotus. Contrast the stimulating and very different approach of Ambaglio 1998 and 2001.

[5]   More extensive defence of the Thebans against Herodotus' account of Thermopylae, chapters 31–33, 864c–867b: perhaps derived from Aristophanes of Boiotia, who is cited at 864c–d on Herodotus, and 867a for the identity of the Theban commander, which corrects Herodotus.

historians and the possibility that their writings had other routes, other causes of momentum than the presence of Herodotus. Most local historians spent their energies in other directions than (solely) the Persian Wars, and one suspects that the Greek city-states were too important to their citizens for them to have to wait to insert their historiography into wider developments of the genre. It is very striking that the vast mass of *polis* histories or local histories belong to the fourth century (possibly the late fourth century) and third centuries BCE. The appearance of the Athenian *Atthides* from ca. 350 BCE onward, with Kleidemos the first Athenian Atthidographer, then, is not surprisingly late, but absolutely conventional. The study of these histories as a mass phenomenon raises very interesting questions about the relation of history-writing to contemporary perceptions of the Greek *poleis'* place in the world.

Some numbers give an idea of the scale of the phenomenon. There is an initial question of how you count the writers of local history. As everyone knows who has used Jacoby's *Fragmente*, his organization of the historians into categories and volumes reflecting their main interests and the overall development of historiography (in his view) can lead to some distortion, the artificial separation of sub-genres, and the separation of individual writers across volumes.[6] Hellanikos of Lesbos thus appears under several FGH numbers (4, 323a, 601a, 687a), but most historians are listed in the volume and with an appropriate number that reflects their main historical output (as Jacoby saw it). Thus Charon of Lampsakos, who wrote a *Horoi of Lampsakos*, is number 262 in part III A, which is devoted to writers who wrote on several cities, while the interesting list of historians who wrote on the Black Sea, an extension of the Greek world, or any of its Greek cities, is relegated to the end of volume III C, which deals (effectively) with marginal or non-Greek areas, and the FGH numbers in the 800's. Any arrangement will have its problems, of course: the important point to make here is that volume III B, numbers 297–607, just over 300 writers, does not include writers of local or *polis* history who wrote some other form of history and have a first home and number in another Jacoby volume. Nor does it include Aristotle's *Politeiai*, nor the large scattering of histories of cities or areas which are not considered central and which are listed in Part III C (including Macedonia and Cyprus, as well as India). In the Register I have made to clarify this, the works listed in Part III B alone (even if their author is not necessarily given a III B number), in other words the number of works treating local history in some way, is nearly 500 (in fact this includes most of the works listed in III A, writers who wrote on several cities). The precise number is 496, though inevitably this will include a few dubious authors; it includes the Aristotelian *politeiai*

---

[6]   See esp. Marincola 1999, Schepens 1997; Humphreys 1997.

as listed in Jacoby, but not the works in III C, which admittedly raise almost insuperable category problems.[7] Ephorus is a good example: he wrote a history of Kyme, but is listed as FGH 70, and the scarce attestations to his Kymean history are only cited in that volume.

The numbers alone imply that this was a phenomenon of some significance. They are all histories of place, securely tied to a particular area, often a *polis*, sometimes a wider area like Boiotia or Euboia. I prefer the term '*polis* history' to local history, because in English at least local history has connotations more appropriate to tiny obscure places, villages, parishes, and is a byword for the parochial, but the interesting fact is that areas like Boiotia tend to produce 'Boiotian' histories rather than those for individual *poleis*. Why such vigorous interests in producing *polis* or local histories? Miletus has 9 histories attested (10 if we count Aristotle), Samos 13, Argos 12. Athens has 7 with the title *Atthis* and at least 73 writers in total who devoted themselves to a work on some aspect of Athens. One cannot think that these are produced simply out of pure objective interest in the past for its own sake. They must have a local audience—and indeed Chaniotis' study has focused sharply on the way *poleis* were highly appreciative of their own local historians, and of other travelling historians who came from outside and gave talks on the history of a city.[8] They attest to a deep love of place.

But this brings us to another problem with 'local history', which in the scholarship can take on very different guises according to the way it is approached (not unlike the *polis* itself).[9] It is the ugly duckling of Greek historiography: it is identified with *Horoi* and 'horography' by Jacoby, Fornara, and others, and therefore seen as a genre of dull lists in chronicle form, a year by year treatment.[10] In fact, works with the title *Horoi* are remarkably rare, and the fragments of both *Horoi* and other local histories that we still have attest lively, often rather 'Herodotean' stories and anecdotes. One of the most vivid and tantalizing is perhaps the story of the dancing horses of Cardia, found in Charon of Lampsakos (FGH 262 F 1): Cardia is on the opposite side of the Hellespont to Lampsakos, and the story involved war between Cardia and Bisaltae, which is to the west of the River Strymon. The story tells of a Bisaltian barber in Cardia, who gets to

---

[7] Since it is reasonable to include Cyprus or the Pontus, but not so obviously Bithynia. This number also omits *Sammelzitaten* and *Schwindelautoren*. I have included writers who, as listed in Jacoby, may be either one or two people; also all writers listed even if they are virtually unattested.

[8] See Chaniotis 1988, and 2009.

[9] Cf. Murray's remark about the *polis* in French, German, and English and American scholarship: Murray and Price 1990:2-3.

[10] Jacoby 1954:1-2 ('Introduction' to Hellanikos): "town chronicles"; though Jacoby 1949:68 admits almost casually that not all local history had chronicle form. Cf. Möller 2001:244, who admits it is difficult to prove that *Horoi* were structured as annals.

know the local Cardian music and passes it back to Bisaltae: the trick is adopted by the Bisaltian attackers of playing the favorite tunes of the Cardian horses as they attacked. Cardian horses could dance, and this therefore produced terrible havoc in the Cardian ranks. Quite how this featured in Charon's *Horoi of Lampsakos* is unclear, but feature it obviously did, and we need to accommodate this in any vision we might have of 'horography'. Thus whether or not *Horoi* did indeed attempt chronicle-like treatments, they may have been only a sub-genre of local history, and the attested fragments indicate at the very least that this did still allow varied, amusing stories, folktales, and other material quite unsusceptible to strict chronicle form.[11]

If we approach *polis* history via Parthenius, Plutarch, Conon, and (for example) the interesting preliminary study by Gabba, local history is a subspecies of history posing under the guise of romantic tales verging on the novelistic, full of exotica and with elements that might be described as dear to 'Hellenistic tastes'—that is, simply not real history at all.[12] Or it is approached under the category of antiquarian: cults, local details, and so on, which are thus damned with faint praise by the professional historian.[13] But this begs the question of the importance of such details for the *poleis* in question and their citizens and audiences, and we might plausibly reverse the picture: perhaps, for instance, the lively tales of *polis* history helped feed the romantic genres of the Hellenistic period.

Dionysius of Halicarnassus remarked on the stylistic monotony (*monoeideis*) and the chronological framework of local histories in *Roman Antiquities* 1.8.3. But on closer inspection it turns out that he was referring specifically to the 'chronicles' (ταῖς χρονικαῖς) produced by authors of the Atthis as *monoeideis* and tedious to the hearers.[14] Elsewhere, in his essay on Thucydides, Dionysius says that writers on *ethne* and *poleis* included ancient stories, myths and stories of *peripeteiai* that now seem foolish. But, he continues, their style was "clear, ordinary (*koinen*), pure, concise, appropriate to the narrative," and they had a charm (*charis*) which was why they still survived:

λέξιν τε ὡς ἐπὶ τὸ πολὺ τὴν αὐτὴν ἅπαντες ἐπιτηδεύσαντες ... τὴν σαφῆ καὶ κοινὴν καὶ καθαρὰν καὶ σύντομον καὶ τοῖς πράγμασι προσφυῆ καὶ μηδεμίαν σκευωρίαν ἐπιφαίνουσαν τεχνικήν: ἐπιτρέχει μέντοι τις ὥρα τοῖς ἔργοις αὐτῶν καὶ χάρις.

---

11 I deal with this more fully elsewhere (forthcoming).
12 See e.g. Gabba 1981.
13 See Momigliano 1966 and 1990.
14 *Roman Antiquities* cited by Schepens 2001:9 as evidence for tedium, but his note does point out that this is said of *Atthides*. All translations of Dionysius of Halicarnassus here are mine.

. . .mostly employing the same diction . . . clear, normal, pure and concise, appropriate to the narrative and without any rhetorical embellishment. A certain grace and beauty suffuse their works.

Dionysius of Halicarnassus *On Thucydides* 5

This was a remark on the historians he thought early, especially the supposedly 'pre-Thucydidean historians', and scholars may argue about the relative dating or his accuracy; since, however, he had more text in front of him than we do, and he was talking about those who wrote on *ethne* and *poleis*, we should probably take this seriously as a testimony to some aspect of the genre's content and style, whatever their date. It fits with the strictures of Polybius about most types of history except his own (below). And slightly later (*On Thucydides* 7) Dionysius says of those who wrote "tribal or local histories" (ἐθνικὰς καὶ τοπικὰς ἐκφέροντες ἱστορίας) that when they came across fictional stories (τῶν μυθικῶν . . . πλασμάτων) carefully told and handed down, they could not bear to leave them out: they were regarded too fondly to be omitted (cf. also *On Thucydides* 23).

As for Polybius, his polemic in Book 9, a pseudo-apology for the austerity of his own history, suggests that most other historians made use of many branches of *historie*: the genealogical side, he says, appeals to the φιλήκοον, 'one who loves a story', the accounts of colonies and foundations and *syngeneia* attract the πολυπράγμονα καὶ περιττὸν, 'active and curious', while the acts of *ethne*, cities and monarchs interest τὸν πολιτικὸν, the 'student of politics' (Polybius 9.1.3–5).[15]

This is in fact reflected in the fragments that are preserved. The indirect descriptions of *polis* or local history testify to a chronicle form for Athenian history, but they are mostly silent for other *poleis*:[16] and while that is not a certain indication of absence, there is evidence that much else came into *polis* history than lists of officials, if, indeed, such lists featured at all. I find it hard to believe that all city-states could produce a year-by-year account in any case, even if they had the officials for each year; and while the Parian Chronicle 'gives' a fairly detailed list, it is mostly Athenian in tenor, with much on the victors of dramatic festivals at Athens, as well as on wider, non-Parian, events: Parian

---

[15] My translations. *Polypragmosyne* is important in Polybius. Note that Diodorus 1.37.4 uses *polypragmosyne* of Herodotus in approval and it is translated/interpreted there as 'a curious enquirer'. Odysseus can of course be thought of as the archetypal Greek *polypragmon*.

[16] Dionysius of Halicarnassus *Roman Antiquities* 1.8.3 (above); cf. Clarke 2008:208f., 325–335, who seems largely to accept Jacoby's insistence on a framework of officials outside Athens—relying heavily on the Parian Marble—while also stressing the existence of different chronological frameworks.

history is actually conspicuous by its absence in the Parian Chronicle (it can be found at FGH 239: 264/3 BCE).[17]

But *polis* history is above all about people and place with an intense interest in locality: this is best pursued by looking more closely at the histories of particular areas. I turn now to some particularly revealing case studies to examine more closely the variety and local significance of 'local history': we will examine Delos as a fascinating case where local history-writing seems to reflect local independence and pride; and the Ionian cities of Asia Minor, Ephesus, Miletus, and (briefly) Chios where we seem to find a mass of lively and mutually contradictory tales of origins which raise important questions about the role of *polis* histories.

1. Delos

Delos, sacred island of Apollo, was an important cult centre and *polis* during the archaic and classical period but it had a checkered political history.[18] Its more prosperous neighbour Naxos adorned its sanctuary, without necessarily controlling it. Polycrates, tyrant of Samos, intervened in the late sixth century, but afterwards Delos fell increasingly under the sway of Athens. It was purified by Peisistratos, and then again in 426 by the Athenians, who three years later felt it necessary to remove the entire population of Delians from the island on the grounds of some offence and pollution (Thucydides 5.1). They were ordered by Delphi to return the Delians to Delos in 421, and we are told the Athenians did this (Thucydides 5.32.1). But one wonders how many Delians did actually return, since Thucydides in Book 8 tells us almost accidentally that while they were relocated to Atramyttium in the Northern Troad, on an invitation from the Persians, a Persian played a trick on the men. He invited the leading men to dinner and had them all killed (Thucydides 8.108.2). One wonders about continuity of traditions and knowledge in these circumstances—circumstances of relocation, dislocation, and then disappearance of the leaders. After this, so far as we can make out, the Athenians controlled the sanctuary again during 394–314, and some nasty incidents occurred (they perhaps did not control the *polis* in a formal sense, but in a three-mile island dominated by the shrine it is doubtful how independent the Delians could really be). A short period of independence

---

[17] See now Clarke 2008 for full discussion and analysis of chronological structuring in local history: 193–244, esp. 208f. on magisterial and priestly time, and the Parian Marble (which she sees as more Parian than I do). For a different view, see Boffo 1988:39.

[18] Recent work on Delian political and economic history: Constantakopoulou 2007 for Delos in the Cycladic network; Tuplin 2005 and Rhodes and Osborne no. 28, for political and imperial history of 5th–4th centuries; Reger 1994 for 3rd century. Cf. also Hornblower 2003:517f. on the question of purification; Bruneau 1970 for Delian cults.

in 404–394 is signalled by an enigmatic inscription partly in Laconian and partly in Attic/Ionic (Rhodes and Osborne no. 3).[19] Then in 314, Antigonus created the League of Islanders, and Delos was at least nominally independent during 314–166 BCE. Benefactors and kings lavished buildings and offerings upon the island, and there was recurring Antigonid, Ptolemaic, and Rhodian activity.

This tiny island was treated by Herodotus and Thucydides with reverence when its activities impinged on the wider Greek world: compare the famous contradictory remarks of both about what was supposedly the 'first' and only earthquake on Delos, a portent of disaster—Herodotus putting it at the beginning of the Persian wars, Thucydides at the start of the Peloponnesian War (Herodotus 6.98.1, shaken after Datis' visit; Thucydides 2.8). But Delos actually had several local historians, both Athenian and Delian, who concentrated upon Delos in her own right.

The best known was Semos of Delos (FGH 396) who wrote eight books on Delos and who was widely consulted by later authors, including (fortunately for us) Athenaeus. He was dated to ca. 230/200 BCE by Jacoby, with the help of local inscriptions. As Bertelli points out in the Brill New Jacoby, confirming previous identifications, he is most likely to be the Semos (II) mentioned in Delian inscriptions as *epistates* in 229, owing a debt in 207, and dead by 201/200 BCE. A *terminus post quem* of 250 BCE is given by F 9, and thus his floruit lies securely in the second half of the third century.[20] Phanodikos was also a Delian (FGH 397) and relatively late. Deinarchos of Delos (FGH 399), of whom little is known, was dated by Jacoby to the late fourth century. Before Semos, in addition, there was a *Politeia* of Aristotle, around the mid-fourth century. A group of Athenian writers was also listed by Jacoby, but Philochorus is the only one securely attested as writing specifically on Delos: his work would have been late fourth century or early third century (his dates are ca. 340–263 BCE).[21] He also wrote works on divination, sacrifices, and much else. An Antikleides of Athens also wrote a *Deliaka* (FGH 140 F 2, date unknown). Two or three shadowy epic poets wrote on Delos, one early enough to be cited in Aristotle's *Poetics* (FGH 398, from Andros). Another Andrian poet was honored and praised by the Delians in an inscription for writings "about the temple and the *polis* of the Delians and the myths of the land (τοὺς μύθου[ς] τοὺς ἐ[π]ιχωρίους)." This can be dated by letter forms to the first half of the third century.[22]

---

[19] See Tuplin 2005:37f. for the complexities and problems of the 4th century.

[20] See Bertelli BNJ s.v. Semos, biographical essay and commentary on F 9; this disposes of a recent attempt (by Boshnakov) to date Semos to the late second century.

[21] There is little clear evidence that Phanodemos (FGH 325) wrote a *Deliaka*, though F 2 mentions Erisychthon, who elsewhere (Hesychius) is said to have brought the first wooden statue of Apollo to Delos (Pausanias 1.31.2 mentions his *theoria* to Delos as if well known).

[22] FGH 400; Chaniotis 1988 E 53 = IG XI iv 544.

It is tempting, then, to see Athenian political and religious interest in Delos as mirrored in the beginnings of Athenian 'historical' works about the island: when Athens had a large stake in Delos, Athenians wrote about it, perhaps appropriating it on some level. With the island's independence from 314, it started to honor poets who wrote about it, and to produce its own local historians. The appearance of *polis* history for Delos seems to symbolize and reflect the growth of Delos as an entirely self-generating and upstanding *polis*. This is most clear from the overall pattern of authors, and from Semos of Delos.

Even from the fragments and testimonia, Semos of Delos is a fascinating and serious writer. He had much to say about Delian place names, nearby islands, special Delian words, sacrifices, and different kinds of bronze tripods (F 16, the kind of erudite detail loved by the Deipnosophists). He described the local cult of Brizo, the interpreter of dreams on Delos, who was honored by Delian women with offerings in miniature boats (F 4), details of particular local festivals (F 14, F 5), and of course the great offerings including the beautiful golden drinking bowl (*hedypotis*) dedicated by a local Delian woman, Echenike (F 9; also F 18). He offered a special Delian claim on the origin of the musical instrument called the *phoinix* (F 1). There are hints of local stories connected with wider Aegean history, such as a tale about fish being found in the lustral water when some Athenians visited, an extraordinary sign which clearly predicted their maritime supremacy (F 12).[23] Semos also had much to say about different kinds of music and song (F 11; cf. F 23 and F 24 supposed to be from *On Paians*). There are two stories that indicate the story-telling aspect of Semos' work. Plutarch tells a story not expressly attributed to Semos, concerning some exiled Delians who were told by Delphi to find the place of Apollo's birth, and to make a sacrifice there. As good Delians, they thought they knew the answer, but hanging around in Chaironeia one day, they found to their surprise that Tegyra also claimed to be the place of Apollo's birth—and all ended happily.[24]

Another story, this time explicitly attributed to Semos, may well have been attached to an offering (F 10). A certain Parmeniskos of Metapontum had visited Trophonius and re-emerged from the experience entirely unable to laugh. The Delphic oracle told him that "the mother will give it to you at home." He wandered around without success, till finally at Delos he saw the shrine of the Letoon. But he had expected the statue of this famous shrine to be *axiologos* and so little was this true that he laughed out loud at the ancient crudity of the statue. Thus

---

[23] It is an interesting question whether Semos might have had more on Theseus and Minos with implied connections to either the Athenian or Minoan thalassocracy and control of Delos: suggestively cited by Tuplin 2005:17n15, in connection with the Theseus legend and Athenian assertion of influence over Delos.

[24] See Semos FGH 396 F 20 and Plutarch *De Defectu Oraculorum* 412b–d.

cured, he honored the goddess. A silver bowl dedicated by Parmiskos is listed in one of the inventories. This is very probably a story attached to an offering and preserved by it, rather like Herodotus' accounts of Croesus and his dealings with Delphi (Herodotus 1.50–56.1).[25]

Impressed by Semos' learning and erudition, Jacoby guessed that he must have been educated in Alexandria. He took the Suda's remark that he wrote also on Pergamon to indicate that he must have been a third-century writer. But it is not clear that this must make him a *late* third-century writer.[26] In his recent study, Lanzillotta was more impressed by Semos' affinity with, or rather, what he called 'the influence of', the Atthidographers.[27] There is a danger, however, that this becomes a circular argument. Semos' detailed knowledge of local cult and customs looks like Alexandrian erudition and Hellenistic antiquarianism from afar when it is unfamiliar. But for a prominent citizen actually living in this strange boot-shaped island amidst larger predatory Greek rulers, such details could surely have had a different significance. Such stories and details were easily ascertainable if someone wished to do so. Probably many Delians knew some or much of this, or thought they could if they ever needed to know. We do not know, unfortunately, how far Semos (or the others) dealt with the tangled political history of Delos *polis*, let alone the wider currents of international activity swirling around it, Ptolemaic or Rhodian actions in the Aegean. But from what we have seen, it seems plausible to think of him as writing up or recording the dedications, places, cults, customs, and traditions of his homeland from a familiar standpoint of a fellow citizen, rather than some strange erudite oddity bringing his foreign tastes back home.[28]

The oddity lies not so much in the cult or dedication details but the idea that they should be recorded in a long literary work: why write them down at all? The type of subject matter itself is not entirely new. After all, Herodotus gave his audience details of offerings at sanctuaries, especially Delphi; stories connected with the dedicator or dedications; interesting and curious information about cult practice; geographical curiosities of a region; *nomoi*, though

---

[25] Jacoby 1955, *ad loc.*, identified a silver crater dedicated by a Parmiskos in an inventory of 278 BCE; Bertelli BNJ, *ad loc.*, commentary on F 10 for other possible offerings. Athenaeus 14.614a (= Semos F 10) has 'Parmeniskos'.

[26] Jacoby 1955:203. Pergamon is first attested in the very late fifth century. Cf. Bertelli, BNJ s.v. Semos, agreeing on the importance of the Pergamum connection, suggests he lived there for a while.

[27] Lanzillotta 1996a:283. But his reasons for this argument are not clear. Cf. Bertelli, BNJ, commentary on F 2, also seeing influence of Atthidography (but see below).

[28] Note Bertelli's commentary in BNJ. Ambaglio 2001, on the content and tenor of local history, finds a general emphasis very similar to that suggested here for Semos.

most often for non-Greek peoples.[29] What makes someone write a sustained work on this kind of subject matter for his city in eight books?—and, for all we know, its political history too, though admittedly Delos' fame lay primarily in her religious importance. It is the sheer scale and the local focus rather than the subject matter itself that is exceptional. Third-century Delos was independent, but there was recurring Antigonid and Ptolemaic rivalry in the Cyclades, not to mention Rhodian activity. It is only during its period of independence that local historians of Delos write histories of the island.[30] To see this in purely literary terms, as a response to Athenian antiquarian interest in Delos or the Atthidographers, as Bertelli does,[31] seems to underestimate the extraordinary political importance of Delos to Athens, and also the continuing cultural and political cachet of Delos and its cults.

It is tempting, then, to suspect a combination of local pride, sheer love of *polis*, and a determination to record traditions, dedications, and cults before they might disappear, to set in writing the critical elements which were part of Delos' religious identity at a time of continuing powerlessness in the wider world. Perhaps an act of memorialization and nostalgia combined. Perhaps a product of self-absorption in the period of 'independence' as an act both of defiance to outside powers and of self-advertisement to persuade them to treat the Delians with respect. The two might be intimately connected. The very act of writing a work on Delos was a statement of self-assertion.

2. Ionia and the Greek Cities of Asia Minor.

In Ionia we find a quite different situation. This is another area with a very rich number of local *polis* histories—nine attested for Miletus (ten if we include Aristotle), five for Colophon, six for Ephesus, four for Chios, 13 for Samos. There were also communal histories of Ionia, *Ionika*, and this goes back of course to Panyassis' poem *Ionika* (FGH 440). One or two cities produce nothing at all (Myous, Phokaia, perhaps even Priene), but the general impression is of great

---

[29] E.g. Herodotus 1.50–52, 92 on Croesus' offerings at Delphi and elsewhere; 2.54–57 on cult practice and tales at Dodona.

[30] We do not know if Semos made a lot of the new third-century festivals and big dedications. But Delos' fame lay in its sanctuary, and it is conceivable that local historians dwelt less on purely political activities.

[31] In his excellent BNJ entry for Semos, under F 2: "The Delian local historiography (Semos, Phanodikos BNJ 397, Nikokares BNJ 398) arose during the independence of the island probably as a response to the antiquarian interest in Delos shown by Attic orators and Atthidographers (Philochorus . . . Antikleides . . .)".

activity in telling or recording local history, particularly *polis* history.[32] Apart from the 'early' historians listed in Dionysius of Halicarnassus as 'predecessors' of Thucydides, and early poets, the great mass of activity lies in the fourth and third centuries. The fourth century was a period of great upheaval and uncertainty in Asia Minor for Greek cities, with the freedom of the Greeks of Asia a political slogan, Persian rule, satrapal revolts, Athenian ambitions to regain maritime supremacy, and the uncertain internal stability that was an accompaniment of these various wider ambitions.[33]

It is difficult to know how much of this messy recent history was treated by *polis* historians of Ionia, but what is clear in the extant testimony is an intense preoccupation with origins and foundation myths, and it is these we concentrate upon here. They are particularly interesting because the remaining fragments have much to do with intermarriage and mixtures of peoples, and we might guess that their situation on the edge of the Persian empire and larger non-Greek areas of Anatolia gave particular urgency and piquancy to their stories of Greek origin. It reminds us forcefully that such a preoccupation with remote stories of origin was not a feature of Herodotus' time and *Histories* which then went out of fashion. More than this, however, it gives us a glimpse of non-Athenian *poleis'* views of their own origins, stories that are sometimes very surprising. The fragments, and indeed the whole topic of these cities' 'origins' are immensely complicated, and we can only examine a fraction of the material here (we will also have to consider versions not strictly attested in local historians but very probably related to their versions). I wish to take each city separately (Ephesus and Miletus especially), since this is most illuminating, and to make no attempt to combine the different and often incompatible accounts that exist even for a single city.

Let us take Ephesus first: there are several versions of *ktisis* from various authors that suggest political anxiety and rivalry in claiming origins between Athenian (or Athens-based) writers and the Ionians themselves.

Kreophylos of Ephesus (FGH 417), about 400 BCE (according to Jacoby)[34] is the source for a delightful story in Athenaeus about the original founders of

---

[32] Priene is puzzling: in the protracted and well-documented territorial disputes between Samos, Miletus, and Priene, several historians are mentioned by name but none are from Priene. See I.Priene 37 and OGIS 13, letter of Lysimachus to Samians. OGIS 13 does mention the Prienians as citing histories and documents (lines 12-13). Yet it is odd that no Prienian is actually named among the several historians cited and named in I.Priene 37; perhaps, as Prof. Hornblower has suggested to me, Myron of Priene might have written about his home town. Or did they instead specialise in keeping and publicizing the documents?

[33] See Debord 1999 for excellent recent analysis; also Seager and Tuplin 1980 on 'the freedom of the Greeks of Asia Minor'.

[34] Dowden, in BNJ, Kreophylos, puts Kreophylos in the 3rd century as response to Duris of Samos and to the relatively new third-century significance of Ephesus. But this relies overly on the

Ephesus suffering, unable to find a suitable place, and living on an island for 20 years. They receive an oracle about following in the direction shown by a fish and being led by a wild boar. While some fishermen are cooking lunch, a fish leaps out, the thicket catches fire, and a wild boar runs out of the thicket. Accordingly, they settle there, and the main landmarks of Ephesus are lovingly explained: how they established a temple to Artemis in the agora, the spring, the hill, the temple of Athena (FGH 417 F 1 = Athenaeus 8.361c–e). The story is precisely located in the landscape; the temple of Artemis is new and therefore of course entirely Greek; the temple to Pythian Apollo presumably recalled Apollo's help with the foundation. It is a foundation myth that can generate further foundation myths—for temples, for other buildings—and which implies pure Greek origins. Unfortunately, Athenaeus does not recall where in Greece the founders originated. The group emphasis, with no founder named, may be significant if it is not simply due to Athenaeus' own omissions.

But we may note the idea that a single, separated group founded Ephesus, and that they had difficulties at first. In other traditions about the Ionian colonization we get the impression of a single large expedition for the whole of Ionia. In Pherecydes of Athens from the early fifth century, paraphrased by Strabo, Carians and Leleges lived in the land first of all, then "Androcles, legitimate son of Codrus king of Athens, was the leader of the Ionian colonization ... and he became the founder of Ephesus" (FGH 3 F 155, from Strabo 14.1.3). For Hellanikos, in the late fifth century, Neleus the son of Codrus founded the 12 cities (FGH 4 FF 48, 125). This sounds like the version favorable to Athens and her fifth-century claims to the Ionian cities of Asia as colonies of hers.

Strabo, on the other hand, paraphrasing the fifth-century Athenian writer Pherecydes, had said that the Ionian *paralia* or seaboard was first inhabited by Carians and (in Samos) Leleges (14.1.3). A little later, weaving together the testimony of the early Ionian poets, Strabo claimed a close relationship between Ephesus and Smyrna: Ephesus was called Smyrna in ancient times, and Ephesians and Smyrnians lived together, then the Smyrnians left Ephesus (Strabo 14.1.4). Again we find a tradition about movement, difficulty, violence and different stages in the settlement of the cities. "Smyrna was originally an Amazon who took possession of Ephesus," according to Strabo (ibid.), our first encounter in this paper with the idea of the founding Amazon.[35] Ephesus and Miletus were the first areas to be settled (14.1.4).

---

claim that Ephesus was not important earlier (cf. however Thucydides 3.104.3, Herodotus 1.92, 142 etc.) and assumes that only very large cities got local histories.

[35] Smyrna itself had a complex set of foundation myths: Strabo 14.1.4 cites Mimnermus about the original settlers coming from Pylos the city of Neleus, settling in Colophon, then taking lovely Smyrna from the Aeolians (and Strabo also says they had been driven out of Smyrna and taken

Malakos, on the other hand, a local historian of Siphnos, had a story about Ephesus being populated by 1000 slaves from Samos who on the advice of an oracle left Samos for Ephesus: "Ephesians were descended from these" (Malakos FGH 552 F 1: *Siphnian Horoi*).[36] Surely this is part of the continual rivalry between Samos and Ephesus.

I present these not in order to claim that one or another are more accurate or closer to the original events, for stories of origin were always far too important to remain wholly loyal to original happenings.[37] Rather, they show that a striking variety of tales, mutually incompatible, existed in the *polis* histories about the foundation of Ephesus, and they continued to have currency well after Herodotus. Scholars sometimes think of Herodotus' foundation stories as belonging primarily or exclusively to the earlier periods, the stress on remote origins and original founders as an archaic or early classical phenomenon in the conceptualization of the past, and something that historians grew out of with the onset of greater sophistication. Yet of course it is now very clear from the work of Curty, Christopher Jones, and others that origins and founder genealogies continued to have political and diplomatic significance well into the Hellenistic period and beyond.[38] Indeed one may even wonder if they become more important in certain respects as other factors behind status and diplomatic energy declined. They seem to have taken up a great deal of energy in the *polis* histories of the Ionian seaboard.

The various stories about the *ktisis* of Ephesus imply strongly that the citizens of Ephesus maintained—and continued to develop—their own tales of foundation, tales that were tied precisely to the prominent buildings and natural landmarks of the place. Each area probably had a story. The grand legend of Ionian colonists all setting out from Athens had given Athens a suitable prominence in Ionian history and assumed a neat linear line from Athens, but these are contradicted by the traditions propagated by the Ionian cities themselves (and quite how Herodotus fits in with his claim that the Ionians were expelled from Achaea by the Achaeans [1.145] is unclear). We have just seen four different versions of the founding of Ephesus, one with Androcles as leader of the whole expedition (Pherecydes), one with Neleus as founder of all 12 cities (Hellanikos),

---

refuge in Colophon). Herodotus implies another version again, 1.143.3: the Smyrnaians were the only city which asked to join the Panionion; cf. Strabo ibid., Smyrna was later added to the 12 Ionian cities, induced by Ephesus.

[36] See Jacoby 1955, *ad loc.* for further speculations about this writer and Strouk, BNJ, Malakos.

[37] See e.g. Nilsson 1951; Calame 1996; contrast Huxley 1966, which attempts to make sense of certain local historians in the context of a history of early Ionia. Hall 2002:67–73 stresses the lack of an early unitary tradition of an 'Ionian migration'.

[38] Curty 1995, Jones 1999. See also Strubbe 1984–1986 for Asia Minor in particular.

one claiming foundation by Samian slaves (Malakos), and the story narrated by Kreophylos from Ephesus itself, of the founders as a group.

The Asian Greek or Ionian historians also gave much attention to the Carians and Lydians in the process. Thus, to pursue only the relations with non-Greeks, Pausanias repeated some interesting traditions which confronted the possibility (or problem) of Greeks coexisting with non-Greeks, perhaps a hint at further local traditions now lost: according to Pausanias, Androklos, a grandson of Codrus [of Athens] expelled the Leleges and Lydians from the upper city of Ephesus, but left the natives living around the ancient temple of Artemis (Pausanias 7.2.4–5). These natives turn out to be Amazons, one example of several from Asia Minor where Amazons play a prominent and positive role. The Amazons remaining at Ephesus have been seen very plausibly by Josine Blok as a legendary way of accommodating Greek and indigenous populations, and their rival claims to the land, by projecting them into the remote past.[39] In a complex and tangled web of tales, Pausanias also claimed that Androklos, in his war against Carians, expelled all the Samians from Samos, because they sided with Carians against Greeks; and the Samians suffered a ten-year exile (Pausanias 7.2.5–6; 4.2–3).[40]

Pausanias is a relatively late source: we do not know which local historians he used here, and he may well have used later transformations of the traditions, as well as early poets (this is a question which needs more attention). But in the late seventh century Mimnermus of Colophon retold the tale of the *ktisis* of Smyrna as a direct journey straight from Pylos in the southwest Peloponnese to Colophon, and then on to Smyrna; in other words, with no sojourn in Athens (F 9 W = Strabo 14.1.4). This at least makes clear that the fifth-century version of the Athens-based colonization of Ionia was not the sole or canonical version even then. It is, of course, another version of the founding of Smyrna that we may contrast with the Ephesian story in Strabo mentioned above. And Pausanias disagreed with Pindar's (evidently at least fifth-century) claim, that the sanctuary of Artemis at Ephesus was founded by Amazons (Pausanias 7.2.6–9).

Ion of Chios was paraphrased at length by Pausanias, and his account of Chios centred upon the founder Oinopion: this founder, whose name conveniently hints at Chios' claims to viticulture, seems to be no relation to Codrus and indeed is expressly said to come from Crete, as do his sons (Ion FGH 392 F 1

---

[39] Blok 1996, esp. 94f. for further discussion of the Amazonian presence in Ephesus.

[40] Pausanias is quite possibly using early Ionian poets: certainly he cites Asios of Samos, epic poet, on early Samos and the legendary founders, 7.4.1, just before this section (then also states that the Samians accepted the Ionians as settlers "more out of necessity than of *eunoia*" 7.4.2).

= Pausanias 7.4.8).[41] Ion of Chios also told of waves of Carians and Abantes from Euboia coming to Chios; Amphiklos came from Euboia, and his great-grandson Hector, also king, slaughtered or expelled the Carians and Abantes. Under Hector they united with the Ionians at the Panionion. As Pausanias puts it, Ion does not explain how the Chians were allowed to join the Ionians and sacrifice at the Panionion. Thus, the complications of many sets of Greeks in the years of the establishment of Chios appear early in the traditions.[42] Strabo, however, had a completely different version, or rather two versions: citing Menecrates of Elaea, he claimed that the whole Ionian coast was inhabited initially by Pelasgians, but that the Chians say that the Pelasgians from Thessaly were their founders, then Ionians came to Asia, and the Pelasgians disappeared (13.3.3): in Book 14, he talks of Leleges driven out by the Chians, here following Pherecydes of Athens (early fifth century); apparently still following Pherecydes, he declares that Chios was founded by Egertios, "with a mixed crowd" (14.1.3). The version of Ion of Chios cannot have been much later, yet it is totally incompatible; the tomb of Oinopion long visible at Chios (Pausanias 7.5.13; cf. Theopompus FGH 115 F 276) and the inscribed list of "those who came with Oinopion" and Oinopion's wives, suggests that this was the abiding local tradition.[43] Where does this leave us? With a host of invented traditions of community, and yet traditions which also imply struggle and conflict, expulsions, and no clear Ionian fraternity from the start. Barbarian Leleges and Pelasgians, Greeks, Euboians, Cretans: there seem to be layers and layers of symbolic relationships between Chios and various other parts of the Greek and non-Greek world interwoven in these traditions, and no single version.

Miletus' foundation traditions have a similarly potent mixture, and are almost impossibly complicated. Herodotus knew of the tradition that Miletus was founded by Neleus, son of the Athenian King Codrus. This is implied by his remark at 1.146.2–3 about those setting out from the Athenian prytaneion being the true Ionians, but that they killed the men whose Carian wives or daughters they then married: "and this happened at Miletus." He also later remarks about "Philistos ... following Neleus son of Codrus to found Miletus" (9.97). But he also said, of course, that Neleus and his party married the wives and daughters of the men they killed (1.146.2–3), which seems to be pointing deliberately at the mixture of peoples involved in the eventual creation of these Ionian cities. The collective Milesian traditions in Pausanias have a strong Cretan element

---

[41] Schepens 2001:17–19 for a lucid discussion of this *ktisis* story as characteristic of *polis* histories' gradual transition from mythical times to more recent history.

[42] Huxley 1966:162n67 suggests that there is significance in the fact that Ion of Chios tried to claim Athamas, founder of Teos, as a son of Oinopion (Ion FGH 392 F 1 [=Pausanias 7.4.8] again).

[43] Condoléon [Kontoleon] 1949:5 = Chaniotis T 9; with Hornblower and Morgan 2007:14n48 and Hornblower 2004:155.

(FGH 496 F 2, from Pausanias: "the Milesians themselves say," surely indicating local Milesian historians): Miletus was originally called Anactoria after Anax, an autochthonous ruler, and his son Asterios. Then Miletos (a man) arrived from Crete and took the city, and Cretans and Carians lived together (it is interesting that an elaboration in Nicander of Colophon gave an exposure story for the baby Miletos who was nourished by wolves).[44] We may note here the merging of the ethnic origin of the ruler with that of the inhabitants, and the significant vagueness about the mixture as waves of inhabitants of (apparently) quite different ethnicities take over one after the other. Then, Pausanias continues, the Ionians took over, killing the entire male population and marrying their wives (Pausanias 7.2.3).

The Milesian local historian Aristokritos had more on the ruler called Miletus, his Cretan origins, how he got the name, and the fact that he was a grandson of Minos (if we can believe the scholia). His date is uncertain, but at least he reveals the Cretan element considerably earlier than Pausanias' account.[45] In any case, Strabo, who earlier cited Pherecydes, talked of the Cretan origins of the pre-Ionian inhabitants of Miletus, and he cited Ephorus, thus taking back the tradition of Cretan origins at least to the early fourth century: "Ephorus says" that the Cretans first founded and fortified Miletus, formerly inhabited by Leleges, coming from Crete with Sarpedon, and naming the new city Miletus after their city Miletus in Crete; "later Neleus and his followers fortified the present city" (Strabo 14.1.6; FGH 70 F 127). Aristokritos also related the story of the children of Miletus (the man), Kaunos and Bublis, and their forbidden love, which led to Kaunos founding the city of Kaunos, genealogy symbolizing and maintaining a link with Miletus that was evidently important in later centuries.[46] While the Milesian historian had Kaunos as a son of the man/founder Miletos, so presumably a second generation settlement, Herodotus declared that Kaunians were in his opinion autochthonous, although they thought they came from Crete (1.172).

What emerges as especially interesting is the way these traditions and/ or historians talked of waves of settlement: Leleges, Carians, Cretans, and, finally, Ionians. Herodotus was clearly familiar with traditions that Carians

---

[44] See Sourvinou-Inwood 2005:269 with comments.

[45] Aristokritos FGH 493 F 3. Jacoby says he is early third century, but we know only that he was pre-Parthenius (first century BCE). The Cretan element in these versions seems to be ignored by Huxley and Nilsson—perhaps understandably—but see now Sourvinou-Inwood 2005:268f. for a thorough treatment. (Lightfoot 1999:433f., on Aristokritos F1, has long note on different versions of Ionian *ktisis* but does not discuss symbolic origins.)

[46] For the sake of completeness note that Miletus had an early historian (fifth century) Kadmus of Miletus; Klytos, a pupil of Aristotle; and several others who might be late fourth century or third century, certainly pre-200 BCE.

had a Cretan connection, living in the islands as subjects to Minos, while the Kaunians and Lycians said they came from Crete (1.171–173). But the Cretan and non-Greek mixture continues too in later local historians of east Greece and it is interwoven in the stories of the current inhabitants, and is thus not simply an antiquarian detail from the remote past and of no present significance. We should add to these tales of conquest and expulsion the other stories of fighting between Ionian cities in the very early period—Ephesians taking over Samos, for instance—and the shadowy Melian War which permanently divided up the territory of the town of Melia between various Ionian cities, and which was discussed by the eight historians mentioned on the Priene Inscription (I.Priene no. 37).[47] We have here the shadows cast by a long and complex set of traditions narrating the forging of the 12 proud Ionian cities of Asia Minor and the Panionion and their extremely checkered history.[48]

It is easy to say that these traditions are part of each city's identity. But what kind of identity? Or, more precisely, what kind of identity in different periods (and to different writers)? These local historians seem to offer a picture of varied origins for the Ionian cities, and a checkered settlement history: it is one that is surprisingly similar to Herodotus' wry comment that the 12 Ionian cities did in fact originate from very many places, Abantes from Euboia, Minyans, Kadmeians, etc., and not just from Achaea: ἄλλα τε ἔθνεα πολλὰ ἀναμεμίχαται (1.146.1). Even those thought most noble, he added, starting from the Athenian prytaneion, took Carian wives (1.146.2–3). Herodotus' comment seems at first to be a jibe at Ionian pretensions to Ionian purity and status, but in that case it is then surprising that the local historians of such cities produced similar images. It cannot really be the case that they were still uncritically peddling a Herodotean account simply because it was there already—that assumes a totally passive attitude to previous writings and the central question of each city's origins. The most economical interpretation is that the citizens of the Ionian cities simply held similar views themselves and continued to do so for several generations later: they had traditions which embraced the complexity and the local historians crystallized this in literary form. Herodotus' implied critique may rather have been aimed at Athenian claims to have a monopoly of the 'Ionian migration' than at the Ionians' own claims.[49]

---

[47] The inscription is divided up between cities in FGH (longest quotation at FGH 491–492, Miletus): see Curty 1989 for excellent discussion and now Magnetto 2008, for new edition of the whole inscription. For Lysimachus' earlier judgment, see OGIS 13, and Bagnall and Derow 2004: 26–27.

[48] The story of the canonical 12 Ionian cities replicating the 12 Achaean communities (Herodotus 1.145) is presumably a back-formation on the part of the Ionian cities. I discuss the rich Milesian traditions and local histories in more detail elsewhere.

[49] Cf. Thomas 2004 for Herodotus' complex attitude to the Ionians; cf. also Thomas 2000.

Indeed one can suggest that the Ionian cities perpetuated the traditions that they themselves originated from layers of different peoples for several reasons: in part they were not (or were no longer) attracted by the idea of single Athenian origin after the fifth century, when the loss of the Athenian empire made that version both less attractive and less necessary. A second suggestion is that their very make-up and geographical situation meant that they were living cheek by jowl with Carians, Lydians, Lycians (cf. Herodotus 1.147.1, mentioning Lycian kings descended from Glaukos son of Hippolochos). They had to explain through legend how the political dominance of the Greek speakers had emerged, for example by Ionians coming and killing or expelling Leleges, Carians, and others. The importance of Amazons as founders or original inhabitants of some cities (see Blok, above) brings out clearly and symbolically their recognition of the indigenous female contributions. Thirdly, they also reflect the communal need to explain through narrative how they all came to be Ionians, the 12 special cities, and how they came together in the Panionion. The interlocking myths and legends of rivalries, and of oikist groups moving from one area to another seem to create an image of conflict, the overcoming of difficulties, mutual accusations of siding too much with the non-Greeks, perhaps even heroic struggle. This would be politically useful or powerful as a charter myth for Greeks holding tight to the edge of a non-Greek-speaking continent. The combination of early poetic treatments of *ktisis* and rich local histories in prose imply elevated, even heroic, treatments of these origins. The links with different parts of the Greek world other than Athens could then go on to facilitate alliances and contacts with many other places. But the heroic forging of 'Ionia' out of these conflicts between Greeks and between Greeks and Carians or Leleges or Cretans, would no doubt be a powerful charter myth for the Panionion. One can well see how it was that Ionian Greeks of Asia produced early histories of 'Ionia' and of their cities. It would have been all the more necessary during the fourth century of Persian rule of the mainland of Asia.

Finally, let us turn to the striking Cretan element. Why would so much be made of Miletus as a Cretan man, and Miletus the town as originally populated by Cretans fleeing from King Minos? Even if there had been some distant Cretan connection in the Dark Age, the question still remains why anyone felt it worth remembering (or inventing?) in the fourth or third centuries. There were various ties with Crete and cities of Asia Minor in the fourth and third centuries. Mausolus of Caria gave privileges to the people of Knossos, for example and there are other links, not to mention the frequent *asylia* declarations in the third century. The French scholar Debord suggests the links were fostered in the fourth century to facilitate acquiring mercenaries and sailors from Crete.[50]

---

[50] Debord 1999:383, citing Hornblower 1982:135. Hornblower 2011 discusses different explanations for the Mausolid attempts to foster connections with Crete. Cf. Curty 1995:no.56.

It must have been useful and desirable for some reason to continue to celebrate Cretan origins. The Cretan origins are so persistent and common that it is tempting to think that these links were indeed also deep-seated and probably maintained through cult and cultic traditions from far earlier. One wonders, too, if the links to a powerful Cretan thalassocracy had particular value during the Athenian thalassocracy, and even more after the decline of Athens' power. Cretan links gave a highly reputable and very ancient connection to that other great thalassocracy, and elegantly trumped the Athenian claims.

3. Some Conclusions

The vast numbers and geographical spread of *polis*- and local-histories in the fourth century and later demands a political-cultural explanation that rises above the internal literary developments of the genre of historiography. Yet individual case studies seem to show a diversity in content and emphases which must also reflect the rivalries between neighboring city-states, played out in their differing sources of pride and identity. Delos' powerful cultic role in the Greek world was celebrated by its historians particularly in its period of independence, and this late independence gave room for what we must call an overflowing of local patriotism. The tangled web of stories of origin and foundation of the *poleis* of the Ionians seems by contrast to tell a tale (or rather many tales) of struggle and interaction between Greeks of many different origins and the Anatolian peoples already there; and it is significant that such tales continue to be told for generations.

To call this antiquarianism seems to beg the question—this is not really an answer, but rather a categorization that implies an explanation. This type of historiography does not offer or partake of the grand march of international Greek history, but in the fourth and third century there could be many sensible reasons to reject that: compare the *aporia* of Xenophon at the end of his *Hellenika*, faced with the collapse of the world order he knew. Successive hegemonies could perhaps engender historiographical indifference to the tradition of the grand Greek narrative. Individual *poleis* and their customs and history seem to have become an acceptable topic for written literature, indeed a much sought after topic in the fourth century and later. Ancient history and present day cults could all be useful in diplomacy, inter-*polis* relations, and relations with the kings. There is also a large element of simple escapism and local patriotism, even nostalgia. The loving enumeration of Delian cults and the traditions of place seems to testify to simple love of homeland as well as to the international or diplomatic uses of such tradition. There were, after all, other possible routes in historiography not taken here: for example elaborate family histories,

histories of grand houses and their families, a genre familiar in English history, and other sub-genres which were also divisive. These local histories of the Greek world are, it seems, mostly about community and unity: they are community building. In the Ionian cities, the conflicts and struggles are in the remote past, part of the story of how they came to be as they were now. This could be vitally important in an era of violence, *stasis*, external interference from greater powers, successor wars—and the need to impress a powerful overlord. When the present and future were so uncertain, origins and one's own *polis* could be more comforting, an area of familiar certainty. Origins would be even more useful and reassuring when the future posed real threats. But the '*polis*' being presented here is a different kind of *polis* from the more political animal of the mid and late fifth century. The origin tales gave literary and concrete form to the idea of an imagined community that fed both interest in the remote past and a need to foster the sense of *polis* in the present.

Bibliography

Ambaglio, D. 1998. "Per il reperimento di materiali di storia locale greca: Diodoro, Strabone e Pausania." In Συγγραφή. *Materiali e appunti per lo studio della storia e della letteratura antica*, ed. D. Ambaglio, 93–109. Como.

———. 2001. "Ἐπιχώριος: un termine tecnico storiografico?" In Bearzot et al. 2001:7–21.

Ampolo, C., ed. 2006. *Aspetti dell'opera di Felix Jacoby*. Pisa.

Bagnall, R., and P. Derow, eds. 2004. *The Hellenistic Period: Historical Sources in Translation*. Oxford. New edition.

Bearzot, C. et al., eds. 2001. *Storiografia locale e storiografia universale. Forme di acquisizione del sapere storico nella cultura antica, Bologna 16–18 Dec. 1999*. Como.

Blok, J. 1996. "A Tale of Many Cities. Amazons in the Mythical Past of Greek Cities in Asia Minor." In *Proof and Persuasion: Essays on Authority, Objectivity and Evidence*, ed. S. Marchand and E. Lunbeck, 81–99. Shelby Cullom Davies Centre. Brepols.

Boffo, L. 1988. "Epigrafi di città greche: un' espressione di storiografia locale." In *Studi di storia e storiografia antiche*, ed. E. Gabba, 9–48. Como.

Bruneau, P. 1970. *Recherches sur les cultes de Délos à l'époque hellénistique et à l'époque impériale*. Paris.

Calame, C. 1996. *Mythe et histoire dans l'Antiquité grecque: La création symbolique d'une colonie*. Lausanne. Also pub. 2003. *Myth and History in Ancient Greece. The Symbolic Creation of a Colony*, trans. D. W. Berman. Princeton.

Chaniotis, A. 1988. *Historie und Historiker in den griechischen Inschriften*. Stuttgart.

———. 2009. "Travelling Memories in the Hellenistic World." In *Wandering Poets in Ancient Greek Culture. Travel, Locality and Pan-Hellenism*, ed. R. Hunter and I. Rutherford, 249-269. Cambridge.

Clarke, K. 2005. "Parochial Tales in a Global Empire: Creating and Recreating the World of the Itinerant Historian." In *La cultura storica nei primi due secoli dell'impero romano*, ed. L. Troiani and G. Zecchini, 111-128. Rome.

———. 2008. *Making Time for the Past. Local History and the Polis*. Oxford.

Constantakopoulou, C. 2007. *The Dance of the Islands. Insularity, Networks, the Athenian Empire, and the Aegean World*. Oxford.

Condoléon [Kontoleon], N. M. 1949. "Inscriptions de Chios." *Revue de philologie, de littérature et d'histoire anciennes* 75:5-16.

Curty, O. 1995. *Les parentés légendaires entre cités grecques*. Geneva.

———. 1989. "L'historiographie hellénistique et l'inscription no. 37 des Inschriften von Priene." In *Historia Testis. Mélanges d'épigraphie, d'histoire ancienne et de philologie offerts à Tadeusz Zawadzki*, ed. M. Piérart and O. Curty, 21–35. Fribourg.

Davies, J. K. 1995. "The Fourth-Century Crisis: What Crisis?" In Eder 1995:29–39 (including discussion).

Debord, P. 1999. *L'Asie Mineure au IV e siècle (412-323 a.C.)*. Bordeaux.

Eder, W., ed. 1995. *Die athenische Demokratie im 4. Jahrhundert v. Chr.* Stuttgart.

Fornara, C. 1983. *The Nature of History in Ancient Greece and Rome*. Berkeley.

Fowler, R. L. 1996. "Herodotus and his Contemporaries." *Journal of Hellenic Studies* 116:62–87.

———. 2001. "Early Historiê and literacy." In *The Historian's Craft in the Age of Herodotus*, ed. N. Luraghi, 95–115. Oxford.

Gabba, E. 1981. "True History and False History in Classical Antiquity." *Journal of Roman Studies* 71:50–62.

Hall, J. 2002. *Hellenicity. Between Ethnicity and Culture*. Chicago.

Hornblower, S. 1982. *Mausolus*. Oxford.

———. 1994. "Introduction." In *Greek Historiography*, 1–72. Oxford.

———. 1995. "The Fourth-Century and Hellenistic Reception of Thucydides." *Journal of Hellenic Studies* 115:47–68.

———. 2003. *A Commentary on Thucydides* I, Books I–III. Oxford.

———. 2004. *Thucydides and Pindar. Historical Narrative and the World of Epinikian Poetry*. Oxford.

———. 2011. "How Unusual were Mausolus and the Hekatomnids?" In *Labraunda and Karia: Proceedings of the International Symposium Commemorating 60 Years of Swedish Archaeological Work at Labraunda*, ed. L. Karlsson and S. Carlsson, 355–362. Uppsala.

Hornblower, S., and C. Morgan, eds. 2007. *Pindar's Poetry, Patrons and Festivals.* Oxford.

Humphreys, S. 1997. "Fragments, Fetishes and Philosophies. Towards a History of Greek Historiography after Thucydides." In Most 1997:207–224.

Huxley, G. 1966. *The Early Ionians.* London.

Jacoby, F. 1909. "Über die Entwicklung der griechischen Historiographie und den Plan einer neuen Sammlung der griechischen Historikerfragmente." *Klio* 9:80–123. Reprinted 1956, in F. Jacoby, *Abhandlungen zur griechischen Geschichtsschreibung,* 16-64. Leiden. Also reprinted in Ampolo 2006:301–344.

———. 1949. *Atthis. The Local Chronicles of Ancient Athens.* Oxford.

———. 1950. *Die Fragmente der griechischen Historiker. Dritter Teil: Geschichte von Städten und Völkern (Horographie und Ethnographie). B. Autoren über einzelne Städte (Länder). Nr. 297-607.* Leiden.

———. 1954. *Die Fragmente der griechischen Historiker. Dritter Teil: Geschichte von Städten und Völkern (Horographie und Ethnographie). b Supplement. A Commentary on the Ancient Historians of Athens (Nos. 323a-334). I. Text.* Leiden.

———. 1955. *Die Fragmente der griechischen Historiker. Dritter Teil: Geschichte von Städten und Völkern (Horographie und Ethnographie). b. Kommentar zu Nr. 297-607. Text.* Leiden.

Jones, C. P. 1999. *Kinship Diplomacy in the Ancient World.* Harvard.

Lanzillotta, E. 1996a. "Note di storiografia delia." In Lanzillotta and Schilardi 1996:275–284.

———. 1996b. "Semo di Delo." In Lanzillotta and Schilardi 1996:285–326.

Lanzillotta, E., and D. Schilardi, eds. 1996. *Le Cicladi ed il mondo egeo.* Rome.

Lenfant, D., ed. 2007. *Athénée et les fragments d'historiens. Actes du colloque de Strasburg (16-18 Juin 2005).* Paris.

Lightfoot, J. L. 1999. *Parthenius of Nicaea: The Poetical Fragments and the Erotika Pathemata.* Oxford.

Magnetto, A., ed. 2008. *L'arbitrato di Rodi fra Samo e Priene. Edizione critica, commento e indici.* Pisa.

Marincola, J. 1999. "Genre, Convention and Innovation in Greco-Roman Historiography." In *The Limits of Historiography. Genre and Narrative in Ancient Historical Texts,* ed. C. S. Kraus, 281–324. Leiden.

Möller, A. 2001. "The Beginning of Chronography: Hellanicus' *Hiereiai.*" In *The Historian's Craft in the Age of Herodotus,* ed. N. Luraghi, 241–262. Oxford.

Momigliano, A. 1966. "Ancient History and the Antiquarian." In *Studies in Historiography,* 1–39. London.

———. 1990. "The Rise of Antiquarian Research." In *The Classical Foundations of Modern Historiography,* 54–79. Berkeley.

Most, G., ed. 1997. *Collecting Fragments.* Göttingen.

Murray, O., and S. Price, eds. 1990. *The Greek City from Homer to Alexander.* Oxford.

Nilsson, M. P. 1951. *Cults, Myths, Oracles and Politics in Ancient Greece.* Lund.

Orsi, D. P. 1994. "La storiografia locale." In *Lo spazio letterario della Grecia antica III 1.*, ed. G. Cambiano et al., 149–179. Rome.

Pečirka, J. 1976. "The Crisis of the Athenian Polis in the Fourth Century B.C." *Eirene* 13:5–29.

Porciani, L. 2001. "La storia locale in Grecia secondo Dionigi d'Alicarnasso." In Bearzot et al. 2001:287–297.

———. 2006. "Il problema della storia locale." In Ampolo 2006:173–184.

Prinz, F. 1979. *Gründungsmythen und Sagenchronologie.* Munich.

Reger, G. 1994. "The Political History of the Kyklades 260-200 B.C." *Historia* 43:32–69.

Schepens, G. 1997. "Jacoby's FGrHist: Problems, Methods, Prospects." In Most 1997:144–172.

———. 2001. "Ancient Greek City Histories. Self-Definition through History Writing." In *The Greek City from Antiquity to the Present. Ideological Construction, Literary Representation*, ed. K. Demoen, 3–25. Leuven.

———. 2006. "Travelling Greek historians." In *Le Vie della Storia. Migrazioni di popoli, viaggi di individui, circolazione di idee nel Mediterraneo antico. Atti del II Incontro Internazionale di Storia Antica (Genova 6-8 ott. 2004)*, ed. M. Gabriella et al., 81–102. Rome.

Seager, R. and C. Tuplin. 1980. "The Freedom of the Greeks of Asia Minor. On the Origins of a Concept and the Creation of a Slogan." *Journal of Hellenic Studies* 100:141–154.

Sourvinou-Inwood, C. 2005. *Hylas, The Nymphs, Dionysos and Others. Myths, Ritual, Ethnicity.* Stockholm.

Strubbe, J. H. M. 1984-1986. "Gründer kleinasiatischer Städte: Fiktion und Realität." *Ancient Society* 14-17:253–304.

Thomas, R. 2000. *Herodotus in Context. Ethnography, Science and the Art of Persuasion.* Oxford.

———. 2004. 'Herodotus, Ionia and the Athenian Empire." In *The World of Herodotus*, ed. V. Karageorghis and I. Taifacos, 27–42. Nicosia.

———. Forthcoming. "The Greek Polis and the Tradition of Polis History: Local History, Chronicles and the Patterning of the Past." In *Patterns of the Past. Epitedeumata in the Greek Tradition*, ed. A. Moreno and R. Thomas. Oxford.

Tuplin, C. 2005 [2006]. "Delian Imperialism." In *ΑΡΧΑΙΟΓΝΩΣΙΑ* 13:11–68.

12

The Tools of Memory
Crafting Historical Legacy in Fourth-Century Greece

SARAH FERRARIO

1. Introduction

CAN INDIVIDUALS CONTROL the ways in which they are remembered? Achilles saw κλέος ἄφθιτον, 'undying fame', as a possible outcome of his own decisions;[1] Alexander undertook a complex campaign of self-promotion that was imitated by the Hellenistic monarchs[2] and was surpassed in scope and scale perhaps only by the efforts of the Roman emperor Augustus.[3] But while the Homeric world generally equated memorialization with oral recollection, often in song,[4] Alexander brought with him on his Eastern expedition not only poets (e.g. Curtius 8.5.7–8, Arrian 4.9.9), but also a designated historian, Callisthenes (FGH 124). By the later fourth century,[5] memory had gained historical context,[6] and historiography had become one of its many tools.

Alexander's public program, which involved image-making across a wide variety of media and contexts, was both ambitious and potent, but it was not without precedent. By his time, there were many ways for an eminent individual to script (to borrow from Thucydides 1.22.4) both a presentation for the contemporary public and a story for the ages. Some of these 'tools of memory,'

---

[1] *Iliad* 9.412–416; cf. below.
[2] See Stewart 1993:229–340.
[3] E.g. Zanker 1988.
[4] *Iliad* 6.357–358; cf. below.
[5] All dates in this chapter are BCE. All translations are my own unless otherwise noted.
[6] Starr 1968 traces the evolution of this concept, in the form of an "intellectual history of early Greece" (5), from the time of the Homeric poems through the fifth century; see also Derderian 2001, esp. 161–188.

such as the commissioning of poetry, have their origins in the more distant past. Others, however, seem to have blossomed during the classical period. In the course of the fifth and earlier fourth centuries, individual historical responsibility and accomplishment gradually received greater acknowledgment both in the public sphere and in historical writing, and certain well-placed men in turn took advantage of the wider range of expressive resources available to them. By the time of Xenophon, outstanding individuals interested in shaping their own legacies could, for example, erect or accept statues or other monuments during their lifetimes, deliberately perform services that merited honorific inscriptions, and perhaps even, under certain circumstances, exercise some control over their reception in historiography.

This essay treats the eminent individual's attempt during the earlier fourth century to craft what I will call here a 'historical memory' of himself: the recollection, in tangible media and beyond his lifetime, of his contributions to the political and military life of his state.[7] I first characterize some of the general opportunities for historical commemoration available to eminent individuals, particularly at Athens, during this time (section 2). Next, I use several case studies drawn from Athens, Sparta, and Thebes to show that the construction of historical memory was by no means an isolated or localized concern (section 3). Finally (section 4), I suggest that certain individual historiographic *characters* demonstrate an understanding of historical memory that not only validates and valorizes the literary genre that created them, but also constructs a sympathetic and engaged audience. On these terms, then, historiography itself may be read as a partial guide to the establishment of historical memory for those who would aspire to its text.

2. The 'Tools of Memory' in Fourth-Century Greece

The developed concept of 'historical memory' as observed in the fourth century BCE finds its earliest literary roots in the heroic paradigm.[8] Achilles sees fighting at Troy as a necessary condition for gaining κλέος ('fame'), and suggests that he can determine how he is remembered according to whether or not he remains at war (*Iliad* 9.412–416); Helen speculates that she and Paris will be ἀνθρώποισι... ἀοίδιμοι ἐσσομένοισι, "made famous in song for the generations to come" (*Iliad* 6.358). In Achilles' reflections, therefore, recollection is bound up with *deeds*; in Helen's, it is attached to *words*. But while *logos* may transform

---

[7]   On the essence of this concept as 'historical' in classical Greece, see Momigliano 1972, esp. 283–284, 290.

[8]   M. Flower, critical correspondence of 4-30-06; Starr 1968, esp. 12–23, 91–96.

ergon into memory, this process alone does not constitute the crafting of history, which by the fourth century can be articulated as requiring specific, as opposed to paradigmatic, content (Aristotle *Poetics* 9.1451a–b).[9] The specificity that Aristotle recognizes derives not only from the report of factual information, but also from historical context, the grounding of actions in a particular time, place, and set of circumstances. The fact that Aristotle famously takes Alcibiades as his exemplar is an appropriate reminder that an essential part of that context for the Greek individual of the classical era is his membership in his state. Indeed, the relationship between individual and *polis* can both enhance and limit opportunities for the creation of historically contextualized memory. During the fifth century, one place where this can be observed is in Pindar.[10]

Pindaric poetry stands at the intersection not only of deed and word, but also of individual and civic life.[11] In the Pindaric world, κλέος and memory derive from the productive relationship of poet and honorand. The athletic victor performs deeds in the 'real' world that in turn furnish subject-matter for the poet, who both notes their specific qualities and explores their universal ones by analogizing them in myth. That which is ephemeral, the single act achieved in time, is transformed into a twofold eternal, consisting firstly of the song, ever reproducible in performance and (probably also) in written text; and secondly (and more importantly) of the κλέος that the song can bring to the victor by inscribing his achievement in memory.[12] But unlike the Homeric hero, the Pindaric athletic victor is also a member of a state, and the careful reconciliation of his individual glory with the honor of his native *polis*, as Kurke has shown, is one of the central concerns of the poetry. The athlete must be productively incorporated not only into the universalizing realm of myth, but also into the broader history of his people.[13]

Poetry was also employed as a tool of *historical* memory at Athens in the recollection of the Tyrannicides, whose deeds inspired not only what was probably the first public sculpture of non-divinities (the Harmodius and Aristogeiton

---

[9] On the evolving relationship between memory and historical context during the fifth century, see Derderian 2001, esp. 102–111, 161–188, 192–194. Both this discussion and Starr's (see n10, below) have been very influential upon my thinking about the issues discussed here.

[10] On Pindar as a potential bridge between heroism and history, see Starr 1968:124–130.

[11] Kurke 1991, esp. 163–224; Starr 1968:124–130. I am grateful to P. Hari Prasad for discussion of Pindaric issues in conversation and in class presentation that made the points expressed here increasingly clear and significant to me.

[12] See Segal 1989 and Prasad 2007:4–5, both of whose articulations influenced my discussion of the 'Pindaric world' here.

[13] Kurke 1991, esp. 163–94.

group by Antenor),[14] but also a well-known group of *skolia*.[15] History-making actions during the early and mid-fifth century were further recollected in the 'songs' of the Persian War epigrams,[16] and, in a few cases, in metrical funerary inscriptions.[17] The later fifth century, however, witnessed a significant expansion of the 'vocabulary' of memory, yielding the earliest surviving public commemorations of individuals in document reliefs and inscribed honorific decrees.[18] Earlier on, most of these are for non-Athenians,[19] but by the fourth century, some important changes are evident. Not only does the quantity of extant inscriptions rise throughout Greece during this period,[20] but at Athens in particular, there is a marked increase in document reliefs and honorific decrees for individuals, which are now much more frequently offered for Athenian citizens, not only for *proxenoi* or other foreign benefactors.[21]

Such public inscriptions are themselves history-making gestures: the inscription, as an act of writing, reifies the memory of the benefactor's meritorious action, records the transaction of more ephemeral honors (such as entertainment in the *prytaneion*), and, through its physical presence in the landscape of the city, also symbolically recollects the impact that the honorand has made.[22] That these documents were considered to be an integral part of the history of the *polis* as well as memorials of individuals is suggested by the retrospective

---

[14] On the Antenor group, see Taylor 1981:33–37; on the unique position of these statues in Athenian artistic and political history, see also Keesling 2003:174–176, esp. n25, and Ajootian 1998:1, esp. n4. The most important ancient testimonia cited by these and other analyses are Aristotle *Rhetoric* 1.9.1368a and Demosthenes 20.70, but a fuller survey of the literary and epigraphical evidence for both statue groups may be found in Brunnsåker 1971.

[15] Texts: Page 1962:474–475 nos. 893–896.

[16] See n55, below, and Derderian 2001:109–110.

[17] During the mid-fifth century, these more elaborate, historically contextualized epitaphs, exceedingly rare in the archaeological record in any case, seem generally to have been confined to foreign benefactors. The two best-known examples from this time are probably the epitaphs of Pythagoras of Selymbria (IG I³ 1154, ca. 460–450) and Pythion of Megara (IG I³ 1353, ca. 446/5). From the later fifth century, when metrical epitaphs for Athenian citizens are slightly more common in the epigraphical record, see e.g. the epitaphs of Glauciades and -ULOS [*sic*], discussed in Ferrario 2006a:91–95.

[18] See Ferrario 2006a:87–88.

[19] As noted in Ferrario 2006a:87n29, approximately 16 proxenies of Athens are attested before 450, and 78 (of which 68 are referenced in extant inscriptions) from the years 450–400 (Walbank 1978:ix–xiv). On the first appearance of honors for Athenian citizens in the archaeological record (as opposed to the literary testimonia), see e.g. Henry 1983:13, 22–23; on *proxenoi* in the Attic document reliefs, see Lawton 1995, esp. 32.

[20] Hedrick 1999:391–392.

[21] Ferrario 2006a:96–97.

[22] Thomas 1989:49–53.

monuments and documents that seem to have been construed—and even constructed—during the fourth century.[23]

By the later classical period, then, an ambitious individual who wished to design his own historical legacy might, for example, ensure impact upon the material record by deliberately performing public service that tended to result in public recollection. Proxeny in particular had long since been construed as a public honor, and many such relationships were recorded in inscriptions.[24] Civic benefaction might also merit commemorative returns, and perhaps more frequently in the later fourth century than before, the benefaction itself might be an inscribed or labeled monument.[25] Even just proposing a significant decree might result in one's name being 'immortalized' in stone.

The erection of statuary was also a potential avenue for the creation of historical memory during the fourth century, particularly because the vocabulary of commemoration that was considered 'appropriate' seems to have been expanding. Names now appear more frequently, for example, on honorific statue-bases.[26] Living men are observed inspiring or accepting statues at public expense, and while privately-funded dedications of various types had long been acceptable adornments in sanctuaries,[27] special commemorations of individual historical deeds in those contexts (such as Lysander's 'Nauarch's Monument' at Delphi: see below) seem to find parallels in the growing attribution of military victories to prominent commanders, rather than to their cities or their citizens.[28]

Such opportunities, however, were simply not available to all. Anecdotal evidence suggests that inexperienced speakers were frequently shouted down in the Athenian Assembly;[29] proxenies were the province of the wealthy and

---

[23] E.g. Thomas 1989:83–94; Robertson 1976. For a brief history of scholarship on this issue and a methodological discussion, see Davies 1996.

[24] E.g. Henry 1983:116–162; Walbank 1978. Perlman 1958 briefly treats the use of proxeny outside of Athens (including in Boeotia, *op. cit.* 189–190); for more on Boeotian proxenies (holding that they seem to have borne much resemblance to Athenian practices, which may have provided their political models), see Gerolymatos 1985. Proxenies and other honors could be hereditary, too, offering a real-life parallel to the endurance of the inscription that recorded the privileges: see Henry 1983:137–140; Perlman 1958:187–188.

[25] See Umholtz 2002, who holds that the surviving dedicatory inscriptions of the fourth century, while more numerous than those of previous periods, represent continuity with the past rather than an abrupt change.

[26] Keesling 2003:167.

[27] Keesling 2003:170–185.

[28] See esp. Demosthenes 23.198; Burnett and Edmonson 1961:89. West 1969:14 and nn35–36, with references, notes that by the fourth century, "generals, not the army as a whole, are given credit for setting [trophies] up after a victory." Keesling 2003:175 holds that athletic victors were part of the narrow class of individuals whose self-representation in sanctuaries had been acceptable prior to the changes evident at this time.

[29] Blackwell 2003, accessed 11-29-07.

well positioned; and those without adequate education and military training were highly unlikely to be elected generals.[30] While athletic victories remained a significant motivation for the erection of statues in certain sanctuaries,[31] such achievements of strength or sponsorship (*pace* Thucydides' Alcibiades in the debate about the Sicilian expedition)[32] seem not to have been construed as the exclusive means for the construction of lasting historical impact. Warfare and political leadership have left more significant traces both in historiography and in the material record, suggesting that these legacy-building behaviors were probably largely the province of social, economic, and political elites. As in earlier periods of Greek history, such favorably situated individuals seem to have expressed certain common interests in similar ways that transcended the boundaries of their respective *poleis*.[33] Case studies from Athens, Thebes, and Sparta highlight some of these connections.

3. The Legacy-Builders: Case Studies

The Athenians

Demosthenes says that the portrait statue of Conon in the Agora was the first of a man (as opposed to a god) to be erected by the state since the Tyrannicides.[34] To what extent might Conon himself have helped to motivate such an extraordinary gesture?

That Conon was a conscious manipulator of public perception is suggested by the tradition that he advocated 'autonomy' for the Greek territories from which he and Pharnabazus expelled the Spartans during the middle years of the 390s.[35] Conon may have been acting in part out of expediency, but his ongoing rivalry with Thrasybulus was also a likely motivation for his careful attention to his image, as Strauss has observed, suggesting that "it is hard to avoid the

---

[30] On "qualifications for citizenship" (author's heading) and for the various governmental and military positions in classical Athens, e.g. Samons 2004:45–49, with both ancient and modern references; see also Raaflaub 1996:154–159. The ephebate, once it became a recognized institution, may or may not have been open to the poorest individuals: see Samons 2004:47n26 and Raaflaub 1996:157.

[31] See Keesling in n28, above.

[32] Alcibiades is notably defensive in any case: see his speech at Thucydides 6.16.1–3, and cf. Nicias' attack at 6.12.2.

[33] On inter-state relationships, both personal and political, between Greek elites during the later classical era, see Mitchell 1997.

[34] Demosthenes 20.69–70, cited and summarized by Keesling 2003:176; see also Burnett and Edmonson 1961:89.

[35] Perlman 1968:261nn32–33, 262–263nn45–46 (with references).

suspicion that Athens was not big enough for two liberators."[36] The honors that took place upon Conon's return from the victory at Cnidus are striking. Strauss collects the awards that Conon received (citing an inscription, the Agora statue, an Acropolis statue, and freedom from taxes), iterates the benefits that Conon bestowed in kind (new fortifications for the city, a temple to Cnidian Aphrodite, and a "festival liturgy for the entire citizenry"), and further notes that "the cities of Ionia, ever alert, exchanged statues of Lysander for images of the hero of Cnidus."[37] Most significant here is the *cycle* of these honorific transactions. Conon, in a conscious, symbolic gesture, effectively proclaims to the Ionians the freedom that Athens failed to win for them a century before, during the great revolt against the Persians. In return, the Ionian Greeks grant Conon himself a series of honors expressed in tangible form.[38] Next, at Athens, Conon engages in public benefactions that are familiar—in kind if not perhaps in scope—from the fifth century. Like Nicias and even Alcibiades before him, he indulges, for example, in grand religious gestures:[39] the Piraeus temple of Cnidian Aphrodite is probably a tangible attempt to construct an historical legacy along with a building.[40] Most striking of all, however, would have been his large-scale support, both financial and logistical, for the rebuilding of Athens' Long Walls.[41] The walls themselves would not only memorialize Conon's patronage, but also in effect portray him as a re-founder of the Athenian Empire,[42] a Themistocles or Pericles reborn in an age that could offer him increased opportunities for memorialization as repayment for his achievements, his leadership, and his philanthropy.

Chabrias, the victorious commander in the battle of Naxos, also received high honors from the Athenian *dêmos*, most notably a statue in the Agora and a golden crown.[43] The Agora statue, as Burnett and Edmonson observe, was probably the next major public dedication after Conon's: its elaborate, inscribed base survives, and records a series of honors conferred upon Chabrias by a variety of foreign and civic entities.[44] A disputed story even suggests that Chabrias insisted

---

[36] Strauss 1984:38.

[37] Strauss 1984:39–40, with references.

[38] The ironic fact that Conon was essentially under contract to the Persians seems to have posed little or no difficulty: see Perlman 1968:262 and n9, citing Xenophon *Hellenica* 4.8.9 and Diodorus 14.85.2.

[39] E.g. Nicias' famous festal benefactions at Delos (Plutarch *Nicias* 3.4–6), and Alcibiades' celebration of the procession for the Eleusinian Mysteries upon his return to Athens from exile (Xenophon *Hellenica* 1.4.20; Plutarch *Alcibiades* 34.4).

[40] On this general concept, see e.g. Umholtz 2002:278–282, esp. 281n78.

[41] See Seager 1967:103.

[42] This in spite of the fact that the reconstruction was begun prior to Conon's intervention: see Seager 1967:103.

[43] Burnett and Edmonson 1961:89, with references.

[44] Burnett and Edmonson 1961:89 and passim.

on a particular *pose* for this statue to commemorate the specific battle tactics he had employed against Agesilaus at Thebes.[45] Regardless of what the actual physical stance of the figure might have been, as Anderson points out, Aristotle's examples in the *Rhetoric* show that the statue itself could be construed as a testimonial to a specific view of the man's deeds.[46] Like Conon, then, Chabrias earned the approbation of his fellow citizens and transformed their approval into a more permanent form of self-commemoration, in this case through his own monument to an historical deed: the enshrining of his golden crown on the Acropolis.[47]

The Thebans

Lukewarm or hostile historiographic traditions,[48] probably combined with the distractions of near-constant warfare in a semi-rural and semi-federalized region[49] and a somewhat less intensive 'epigraphical habit'[50] than that of Athens, have left only limited near-contemporary evidence for the self-presentation and reception of the leaders of fourth-century Thebes. However, there are some signs that certain Thebans probably also attempted to exercise control over their historical legacies.

The most significant evidence in this regard is a famous inscription from Thebes itself, probably dating to shortly after the Battle of Leuctra:[51]

Ξενοκράτης,
Θεόπομπος,
Μνασίλαος.
ἁνίκα τὸ Σπάρτας ἐκράτει δόρυ, τηνάκις εἷλεν
  Ξεινοκράτης κλάρωι Ζηνὶ τρόπαια φέρειν,
οὐ τὸν ἀπ' Εὐρώτα δείσας στόλον οὐδὲ Λάκαιναν
  ἀσπίδα. "Θηβαῖοι κρείσσονες ἐν πολέμωι."
καρύσσει Λεύκτροις νικαφόρα δουρὶ τρόπαια,
  οὐδ' Ἐπαμεινώνδα δεύτεροι ἐδράμομεν.

[45] Burnett and Edmonson 1961:89, citing Diodorus 15.33.4 and Nepos *Chabrias* 1.3.
[46] Anderson 1963:412–413.
[47] Burnett and Edmonson 1961:89 and n43, citing Demosthenes 24.180.
[48] Shrimpton 1971.
[49] E.g. Buckler and Beck 2008:12–15 (with cross-references), 133–139.
[50] Hedrick 1999 uses this phrase for his title, explaining that it has been borrowed from MacMullen 1982.
[51] Shrimpton 1971:313 discusses the Leuctra inscription, along with the Delphi Pelopidas statue base, for slightly different reasons, noting: "Fortunately, we do possess some inscriptional proof of the prestige being won by the Theban heroes in central Greece while they were being ignored in Athens ... We must conclude, then, that very shortly after the actual events there existed glowing stories of Pelopidas and Epaminondas (whether literary or oral) waiting to enter Athenian literary traditions from central Greece."

Xenocrates,

Theopompus,

Mnasilaus.

When the Spartan spear was dominant, then

    Xenocrates took by lot the task of offering a

trophy to Zeus, not fearing the host from the

    Eurotas or the Spartan shield. "Thebans are

superior in war," proclaims the trophy won

    through victory (*or* bringing victory) by the spear

at Leuctra; nor did we run second to Epaminondas.

Rhodes and Osborne 2007:151 no. 30 (text and translation)

The first two dedicators of the monument (though not the third) are known figures: Xenocrates was a boeotarch; Theopompus was involved in the liberation of the Theban Cadmeia from the Spartans.[52] The inscription is of especial interest not only for its poetical features, but also for its attempt to *correct* historical memory.[53]

Commemoration of individuals in elegiac couplets, as here, is known at least as early as the archaic period, when this poetical form was commonly used for epitaphs.[54] This private practice seems to have continued through the fifth century and into the fourth (with a mid-fifth century break at Athens). But elegiacs were also occasionally employed for important public monuments to history-making individuals and groups: in the Athenian Agora, for example, both the statue-base for the Tyrannicides and the monument for the Persian Wars carried epigrams in elegiacs.[55] A common feature of such inscriptions, especially when they reference or describe historical events, is the use of appropriately heroic language to glorify their content and their agents.[56] This inscription participates in that tradition, but most notable are the *Pindaric* resonances: the word root νικαφορ-, though not Homeric, occurs a dozen times in Pindar, and the phrase δεύτεροι ἐδράμομεν similarly recalls athletic competition.[57]

---

[52] Tod 1948:93–94n130, with ancient references.

[53] Tod 1948:93 suggests that the last line "might be interpreted as a veiled protest against the undue glorification of [Epaminondas]," although Rhodes and Osborne 2007:151 disagree.

[54] E.g. the entries in Pfohl 1967.

[55] Cf. n16, above. Tyrannicide base epigram: Meritt 1936:355–358 (edition); Page 1981:188 et al. Persian War epigrams: bibliography collected at IG I³ 503/504 (edition); Clairmont 1983:106–111; Meiggs and Lewis 1969:54–57 no. 26; cf. also Jacoby 1945:161nn19–20 and passim for extensive references to earlier discussions.

[56] See Derderian 2001, esp. the detailed treatment of Homeric and other poetical resonances in the Persian War epigrams at 102–103; Day 1989; cf. also Day 1994.

[57] The Pindaric quality of this poetry is mentioned (but not explored in detail) by Rhodes and Osborne 2007:150.

The elevation of the individual military commander may have been some-what problematic during the earlier fifth century. The Athenian orators, for example, recollect (although likely with exaggerated fondness) only limited public commemoration for the famous generals of the past, but changes in the norms of commemoration in the later fifth and earlier fourth century meant that Conon and Chabrias might accept—or even invite— honorific statues, along with other types of acclaim.[58] The Theban Leuctra inscription should probably also be understood in this context. Xenocrates, Theopompus, and Mnasilaos are here not merely attempting to guarantee their own historical legacy by reifying it in an inscription. They are also crafting a corollary to the legacy of another, more famous individual, Epaminondas, and perhaps even attempting to aggrandize themselves through comparison with him. The memorable last line of the epigram both performs a literal rewriting and demands a metaphorical reconsideration of what Shrimpton suggests was already becoming Theban legend,[59] and the reader is thereby implicitly invited to use the historical account contained in the epigram to adjust his understanding of the historical event.

Did Epaminondas in turn concern himself with his own historical legacy? He was perhaps best known for his daring military exploits, and in this both his immediate reputation and his lasting fame would have benefited not only from the growing tendencies of his age to honor individual generals, but also from the potential associations to be made with the Iliadic heroes. But one of the lasting monuments to his achievements in war was couched in highly traditional terms: his refoundation of Messene. Diodorus reads the city's creation as being at least in part a strategic decision, due to the location of the site and Thebes' ongoing conflicts with Sparta. But he also suggests, just beforehand, that Epaminondas was a man φύσει μεγαλεπίβολος ὢν καὶ δόξης ὀρεγόμενος αἰωνίου . . . τόπον δ ᾽ εὔθετον ἔχουσαν κατὰ τῆς Σπάρτης, "by his [very] character a planner of great things and grasping for eternal glory" (Diodorus 15.66.1). If there was any of this in Epaminondas' motivations, casting himself in the role of colonial founder was a superb choice to ensure that he left his mark upon the historical record.

In most traditional Greek colonial narratives, once the founder, or κτίστης, and his colonists have separated from their mother-city, that founder serves as both a political and a religious leader. In addition to setting up the new city, he also selects or creates its laws and other institutions. Most significantly, after his death, the κτίστης is often heroized.[60] Diodorus' account of Epaminondas' activities at Messene is very much in keeping with this pattern—and is doubtless

---

[58] See n28, above, and Aeschines 3.177–191.

[59] See n51, above.

[60] E.g. Herodotus on the colonization narratives of Cyrene (Herodotus 4.150–159), and Thucydides on the colonization narrative of Sicily (Thucydides 6.2.1–5.3). This brief summary of the role of

influenced by it. But the fact that this tradition of the heroic founder was still alive in the fourth century is suggested by *Constitution of the Athenians* 58.1, the earliest known reference to Harmodius and Aristogeiton receiving sacrifices as nominal κτίσται of the Athenian democracy.[61] Epaminondas may have deliberately presented himself as κτίστης of Messene not only because it was a symbolic gesture for the moment, but also because it would ensure him lasting remembrance as the liberator of the district's people from Spartan domination.

Was potential heroization something one could actually aim at in the fourth century? Currie contends that "historical persons' emulations of heroes (preeminently Herakles) constitutes a bid *in those persons' lifetime* and *on their initiative* to be regarded as the equals of established heroes."[62] In his examination of the athlete Euthymus of Locri, who received heroic honors during his lifetime, Currie suggests that the process of heroization might best be understood as a communicative exchange between the honorand and his audience, that is, his community. The aspirant hero behaves in a manner that invites others to associate him with an established figure, and then welcomes the assumption that he should be understood—and revered—in the same way as the object of his imitation. Both sides are therefore active participants in the transaction.[63] Euthymus lived during the fifth century BCE, allowing Currie to argue that the conferral of heroic (and perhaps even divine) honors on living men must be recognized as having begun earlier than is conventionally recognized.

Another potential model for Epaminondas' behavior, however, may have been the Spartan general Brasidas,[64] remembered in particular by Thucydides both for his military talents and for his individual daring.[65] Brasidas also received heroic honors as a colonial founder at Amphipolis,[66] but this occurred only after his death in 422. The phenomenon was therefore in one sense consistent with established colonial practices, in that it is the deceased founder who typically receives heroic attentions. But Amphipolis already possessed a founder in Hagnon, who had led out the colony in the year 437/6.[67] Regardless of the extent

---

the κτίστης is based upon the points iterated by Osborne 1996:8–17, 115–129, 202–207, 232–242; and Murray 1993:102–123.

[61] Cited by Taylor 1981:20–21; cf. also Kearns 1989:55, 150.

[62] Currie 2002:37, emphasis original.

[63] Currie 2002:26, 36–38, 43; cf. also Currie's discussion of Connor's analysis of a somewhat similar pattern from the archaic period: Currie 2002:39, citing Connor 1987.

[64] McCauley 1993:244n596 notes the suggestion in Cartledge 1987:85 that Brasidas' experiences anticipate *Lysander's*.

[65] E.g. Thucydides 4.11.4, 81.1–2, 112.1–2, 5.10.6, et al.; see also Harley 1942:68–83. I am grateful to S. Saporito for discussion of Brasidas in conversation and in class presentation that called my attention to and helped to shape my interpretations of some of the material that I treat here.

[66] Thucydides 5.11.1.

[67] Thucydides 4.102.3.

of Hagnon's cult,[68] the reassignment of the privilege of memorialization is especially striking in that it happened within a single generation. It may have been
presaged in any case by the reaction of the inhabitants of Scione to their liberation by Brasidas, where the supreme civic approbation suggested by the award
of a golden crown[69] is coupled with hints of heroization: Thucydides compares
the treatment of Brasidas to that conventionally accorded an athlete.[70] It is well
worth considering whether Brasidas might have served as a potential model for
some of Epaminondas' later choices.

The Spartans

Currie also connects the phenomenon of Euthymus of Locri with the experiences of Lysander of Sparta,[71] who is said to have received honors as a god at
Samos during his own lifetime,[72] and who is still the best-attested (if conten-
tious) example of such acknowledgement prior to the Hellenistic kings. To what
extent might Lysander might have attempted to foster such reception through
his own behavior?

The commemoration of individual achievements in sanctuaries was by no
means unknown at this point in Greek history. Individual dedications of arms
and armor, both personal items and (especially) those taken from enemies,
were a long-standing tradition;[73] extravagant and personalized 'gifts' to the
gods also contributed to the reputations of their givers.[74] But the erection of
individual monuments to historical successes in (especially) warfare seems to

---

[68] See Currie 2002:37–38, esp. n134; cf. also McCauley 1993:243. I do not necessarily agree that
the Thucydidean passage implies a wholesale transfer of honors from Hagnon to Brasidas; the
emphasis appears to be upon the rituals established for the new κτίστης, rather than upon those
existing for the old one.

[69] Henry 1983:22–23 demonstrates that inscriptions recording the award of golden crowns are
exceptionally rare in the fifth and earlier fourth centuries. On literary testimonia and other
evidence for such crowns, see e.g. Gygax 2006, esp. 490–496.

[70] ἰδίᾳ δὲ ἐταινίουν τε καὶ προσήρχοντο ὥσπερ ἀθλητῇ, "individually they placed bands upon his
head and presented him accolades as if for an athletic champion" (Thucydides 4.121.1).

[71] Currie 2002, esp. 37n133, 43. I am grateful to M. Flower for the recommendation some time ago
that I expand this study to include Lysander (especially his 'Nauarch's Monument' at Delphi) and
other non-Athenians.

[72] Plutarch *Lysander* 18.3–4, cited by Flower 1988:128 and n21, who notes that Plutarch explicitly
references Duris of Samos on this subject; if the reference is acceptable at face value, then the
literary evidence for this cult may be not only locally grounded but also much closer in time to
the actual events (Flower 1988:132).

[73] Jackson 1991, esp. 230.

[74] At Delphi, the most famous named examples from the archaic period are probably Croesus (see
Herodotus 1.50.1–55.1) and the Alcmaeonids, who restored the Temple of Apollo after a fire in
548/7 BCE (the Alcmaeonid marble façade on that temple is dated to 514–505: see Bommelaer
and Laroche 1991:20).

have been somewhat restrained in the fifth century and often posthumous.[75] As Crane highlights, however, only some 75 years after the erasure of Pausanias' epigram from the Serpent Column's tripod, Lysander, during his lifetime and of his own accord, erected a spectacular, highly symbolic monument at Delphi.[76] The epigram from the base of Lysander's statue may be preserved in a recut inscription from the later fourth century (ca. 350–300 BCE), in the now-expected elegiac couplets:

εἰκόνα ἑὰν ἀνέθηκεν [ἐπ'] ἔργωι τῶιδε ὅτε νικῶν
    ναυσὶ θοαῖς πέρσεν Κε[κ]ροπιδᾶν δύναμιν
Λύσανδρος, Λακεδαίμονα ἀπόρθητον στεφανώσα[ς]
    Ἑλλάδος ἀκρόπολ[ιν, κ]αλλίχορομ πατρίδα.
ἐχσάμο ἀμφιρύτ[ου] τεῦξε ἐλεγεῖον· Ἴων.

Lysander set up his image here on this monument when as conqueror
    with swift ships he destroyed the Cecropidan force,
having crowned Lacedaemon undefeated,
    the acropolis of Greece, homeland of beautiful dancing-grounds.
Ion, from sea-girt Samos, created this poem.

Meiggs and Lewis 1969:288 no. 95 (= FD III.1.50)

Like the Leuctra inscription from Thebes, this epigram emphasizes the historical contributions of its subject and employs poetical language. Despite the prominent mention of his state, the emphasis upon Lysander himself is striking for its reversal of commemorative expectations: under ordinary circumstances, it is the city that crowns the individual, but here it is Lysander who crowns Sparta. The monument itself apparently showed the god Poseidon crowning Lysander (Pausanias 10.9.7), and so if the epigram indeed belongs to the monument, the overall message would have portrayed Lysander as a kind of conduit to the divine on his city's behalf. It might also have invoked the extensive reach of Lysander's power and authority. On Attic document reliefs, for example, individuals who

---

[75] The Spartan general Pausanias, victor of Plataea, was forbidden to memorialize himself by name on the collective Greek monument to the Persian Wars at Delphi (Thucydides 1.132.2–3), and both the Miltiades statue group there (Pausanias 10.10.1–2; Bommelaer and Laroche 1991:110–111, with additional references) and the Callimachus monument on the Athenian Acropolis (Raubitschek 1940:53–56) seem to have been posthumous.

[76] Plutarch *Lysander* 18.1; Pausanias 10.9.7–10. For a summary of the monument, see Bommelaer and Laroche 1991:108–109; on the problems of its reconstruction, see Vatin 1991:103–138; for the inscriptions on the statue bases, see Meiggs and Lewis 1969:287–290 no. 95 and Tod 1946:228–231 nos. 94–95; for an analysis of the potential impact of Lysander's monument in its historical and physical context, see Crane 1996:177–179, 205–206 (making the comparison with Pausanias).

had benefited the *dêmos* might be shown being crowned by Athena, patroness of the *polis* and returner in kind of benefits received.[77] Casting Poseidon in a similar position here implies that Lysander is the benefactor of the sea itself.[78]

Crane further observes that "the Lysander monument fully exploits the devices by which the famous could give permanent physical shape to their triumphs, and thus perpetuate their moment of glory," noting that the epigram for Lysander's statue is itself a signed work of art by the poet Ion of Samos.[79] As described above, poetry had been construed as a means of memorialization in the Greek world at least as early as the Homeric oral tradition, but its use for the glorification of the living had expanded over time, moving from the acknowledgement of athletes (as, for example, in Pindar) to encompass the praise of agents of political and military history.[80] Now, an individual seeking historical memory might well deliberately employ verse to record his deeds. Plutarch even suggests that Lysander was possessed of an actual poetical following (Plutarch *Lysander* 18.4–6). Admittedly, the retinue of artists could be a contamination from the Alexander tradition (e.g. Curtius 8.5.7–8; Arrian 4.9.9). But it is worth noting that the Delphi monument Lysander erected again evokes the kind of memorialization earlier reserved for athletic victors,[81] and that the kind of heroized attention Lysander seems to have deliberately sought was previously modeled by athletes like Euthymus, participating in a paradigm that was traceable by the Greeks themselves all the way back to Heracles.[82]

The Lysander monument at Delphi may have itself helped to inspire the Lysander cult and the *Lysandreia* on Samos;[83] at a minimum, it suggests Lysander's intention to present himself in a suitably heroic vein, and to open himself to the embrace of his 'audiences.'[84] For a variety of political reasons, it

---

[77] Lawton 1995:31–32.

[78] Hornblower 2002:183; Shur 1931:31.

[79] Crane 1996:177.

[80] On the evolution of the civic function of *mousikê* from the archaic into the classical era at Athens, see Kowalzig 2004; cf. Murray and Wilson 2004:3.

[81] Crane 1996:177.

[82] Flower 1988:132.

[83] See the discussion by Flower 1988:132–133, with references. Rose's understanding of C. Habicht's argument provides additional insight (see Rose 1957:340): "[Habicht] holds, rightly as I believe, that the institution of worship of any human being has nothing to do with his character, but is invariably, in the case of the Greek cities, a response to some one specific act resulting in great benefit to the community in question, such as deliverance from a dangerous enemy, restoration of its constitution after a period of tyranny or foreign domination, or the like."

[84] McCauley 1993:245–248, 257–260 sees the escalation of heroic honors, especially in the course of the fifth century, as pointing towards Lysander's reception ("It was already apparent in the time of Lysander that if athletes and other generals could become heroes, then the only thing left for an outstanding individual to do was to become a god," 260), but also notes the other side of the

appears that the Samians were the ones who were most receptive to the message he was sending,[85] but it is unlikely that even Lysander could have predicted the apparent magnitude of their response. He may have hoped to be honored as a hero after his lifetime and perhaps even during it, but little to no real precedent seems to have existed for him to aim directly at the status of divinity on political and military grounds.[86]

It is remarkable, however, how quickly the concept seems to have been taken up. The Plutarchan anecdote that the Thasians offered to pay Agesilaus divine cult, and that he ostentatiously refused the honor, has been defended as historical and near-contemporary by Flower, who holds that Plutarch's source for the story was Theopompus. For Flower, Agesilaus' rejection of divine status may have postponed the development of true ruler cult until the time of the *Diadochoi*.[87] This arrest, however, seems to have been not only temporary and artificial, as Flower suggests, but also compartmentalized, in that other ways of honoring and elevating the individual seem to have continued in their development uninterrupted down to and beyond the time of Philip II. One of these ways was historiography.

4. Legacy Building and Historiography

Herodotus' preface suggests that historiography itself is a medium for the creation of memory,[88] and it is perhaps no surprise, therefore, that one of his own characters, Leonidas, appears to demonstrate awareness of that stance. Before the final struggle at Thermopylae, Herodotus examines Leonidas' possible motivations for dismissing most of the other Greek contingents, noting in particular that μένοντι δὲ αὐτοῦ κλέος μέγα ἐλείπετο, καὶ ἡ Σπάρτης εὐδαιμονίη οὐκ ἐξηλείφετο, "great fame would be left him if he stayed, and the good fortune of Sparta would not be erased" (Herodotus 7.220.1–4, quotation at 7.220.2). Herodotus is clearly modeling his Leonidas here upon Achilles, given not only the reference to κλέος but also the idea of remaining at war to gain it, despite the promise of an early death. But this Spartan Achilles has wider-ranging concerns: beyond himself, he is also invested in the future of his city. Here, the character Leonidas seems not only to have taken the glory of the state to himself

---

transaction, citing (245–246) ancient perceptions that Lysander was a conscious manipulator of religious symbolism.

[85] Flower 1988:133.

[86] McCauley 1993:247–248.

[87] Flower 1988:133–134.

[88] Luraghi 2006, esp. 87.

in the manner of a Pindaric victor,[89] but even to have read the opening of the text in which he appears, given the connections between Leonidas' thoughts here and the author's words in the preface:[90] ὡς μήτε τὰ γενόμενα ἐξ ἀνθρώπων τῷ χρόνῳ ἐξίτηλα γένηται, μήτε ἔργα μεγάλα τε καὶ θωμαστά . . . ἀκλεᾶ γένηται, "so that what has happened among men may not fade with time, and that acts both great and amazing, some accomplished by Greeks and others by barbarians, may not lack fame" (Herodotus *praef.*).[91]

Herodotus here ascribes thoughts to Leonidas that seem to prove the essential function of the historian's own mission. Leonidas may be sketched as a quasi-epic hero, but his concern for the εὐδαιμονίη of his state grounds him in historical reality, and Herodotus, through his diction, makes the character himself appear to understand that fact. For Leonidas, as for Herodotus, historiography is now the medium of memorialization, a path towards κλέος, and a means for crafting historical memory. It is too much to claim that the historical Leonidas was acting for the proverbial cameras, but it seems safe to say that the character Leonidas is certainly performing for the text—and that incidences like this might serve to remind readers and audiences of the memorializing potential of historiography.

Similar metatextual awareness seems to be displayed by some characters in Xenophon. An examination of Agesilaus and of Xenophon himself suggests that Xenophon the writer, much as he may admire the Spartan king, still demonstrates a pronounced difference between the character Agesilaus and the *character* Xenophon in their attitudes towards the construction of their respective historical legacies.

Flower, as already noted, contrasts Lysander's acceptance of divine cult with Agesilaus' refusal of it.[92] My examination here treats a slightly different feature of this important distinction and highlights some other places where Xenophon's particular version of Agesilaus is also shown deliberately rejecting methods of historical memorialization available during the earlier fourth century. This does not mean, however, that Xenophon's Agesilaus character has no ego, no desire for honor or fame, no long-term plans. He is possessed of all these things: one might note, in the Asian expedition sequence of the *Hellenica* alone, his negative reaction to the popularity of Lysander, his aspirations to

---

[89] See n11, above.

[90] For other analyses of this echo, e.g. Baragwanath 2008:68–70 and nn41–42; Pelling 2006:93–94 and n51. On Herodotus' deliberate establishment of interactions between the "authorial voice" of the historian and the content of the text, see Dewald 1987, esp. 153.

[91] On literacy as a means for the construction of memory, see Shrimpton 1997:48–72, 88–91, 186–190; Thomas 1989, esp. 118–154; cf. also Derderian 2001, esp. 63–113.

[92] Flower 1988:128 and passim.

detach part of the Persian Empire, his disappointment at being recalled from Asia and thereby deprived of opportunities for achievement, and even his personal pride in the outcome of a cavalry battle in Thessaly.[93] But in both the *Hellenica* and the *Agesilaus*, he repeatedly either spurns or ignores opportunities to shape his historical legacy under the terms explored here.

Xenophon's encomiastic *Agesilaus* shows the king refusing to allow the raising of statues to himself, presumably during his lifetime. (Plutarch has him explicitly prohibiting this after his death as well, something that may, like Lysander's poets, also represent some contamination from the Alexander tradition.)[94] This 'rejection of fame' motif also occurs in the tale told by Xenophon (and repeated by Plutarch), that Agesilaus would not race horses at Olympia and in fact encouraged his sister Cynisca to do so instead, to show that this activity did not display *aretê* (Xenophon *Agesilaus* 9.6; Plutarch *Agesilaus* 20.1). In this anecdote, Agesilaus deprives himself of one of the major paths towards commemoration in a panhellenic sanctuary: given the famous (and rather innovative) monument that his early rival erected to an historical deed, it is difficult not to read into the literary Agesilaus' rejection of even one of the more traditional 'tools of memory' a deliberate contrast to Lysander.

Perhaps the most dramatic gesture in Xenophon's accounts, mentioned in both the *Hellenica* and the *Agesilaus*, is Agesilaus' withdrawal from Asia when he is summoned back to Greece by the Spartans. In both works, although the accounts differ in style and emphasis, the king's decision is portrayed as a deliberate choice of country over self, and duty over prospective honor.[95] As Xenophon narrates it, Agesilaus' choice to return from Asia is inherently unselfish, which is doubtless part of the reason why he implies that it is virtuous. The decision to return to 'help Sparta' does therefore garner a certain kind of honor for Agesilaus, but one that bears little resemblance in either degree or kind to what he may really have been contemplating.

The lack of self-commemorative effort on the part of the Agesilaus character also emerges in vivid scenes such as the military preparations at Ephesus, complete with competitive games, intensive work upon military crafts, and religious processions. The sum total of the variety of activities feels not dissimilar to the shield of Achilles or the funeral games for Patroclus in the *Iliad*;[96] and like Achilles' shield, which Hephaestus promises that men will gaze upon

---

[93] Xenophon *Hellenica* 3.4.7–10 (Lysander), 4.1.1–2, 41 (Persian Empire), 4.2.3 (recall), 4.3.9 (cavalry battle, with Agesilaus setting up a trophy afterwards).

[94] Xenophon *Agesilaus* 11.7; Plutarch *Agesilaus* 2.2, both sources are cited by Flower 1988:127, who also mentions this story. On the (spurious) tradition of Alexander's artistic 'edict' upon his own image, see the references collected by Stewart 1993:360–362; see also Stewart 2003:32.

[95] Respectively, Xenophon *Hellenica* 4.2.2–3; Xenophon *Agesilaus* 1.36.

[96] Xenophon *Hellenica* 3.4.16–18; cf. *Iliad* 18.483–608 (shield), 23.257–897 (funeral games).

with amazement (*Iliad* 18.466–467), Agesilaus makes Ephesus ἀξίαν . . . θέας ("deserving of sight," Xenophon *Hellenica* 3.4.17; cf. verbatim, Xenophon *Agesilaus* 1.26). Why, then, does the character Agesilaus seem unconcerned with the historical memorialization of the great deeds that Xenophon says he wishes to inspire? There are a number of possible responses to this question—including that Xenophon's ethical interests may have guided his presentation of this material.[97] But the Homeric connection noted here invites reflection upon a passage from Pericles' Funeral Oration in Thucydides that may help to illuminate what Xenophon is doing:

> καὶ οὐδὲν προσδεόμενοι οὔτε Ὁμήρου ἐπαινέτου οὔτε ὅστις ἔπεσι μὲν τὸ αὐτίκα τέρψει, τῶν δ' ἔργων τὴν ὑπόνοιαν ἡ ἀλήθεια βλάψει, ἀλλὰ πᾶσαν μὲν θάλασσαν καὶ γῆν ἐσβατὸν τῇ ἡμετέρᾳ τόλμῃ καταναγκάσαντες γενέσθαι, πανταχοῦ δὲ μνημεῖα κακῶν τε κἀγαθῶν ἀΐδια ξυγκατοικίσαντες.

> We have no requirement to be the object of Homer's tribute, nor that of any other who will provide fleeting pleasure through his words, but to whose version of events the truth will do injury. We have forced the whole sea and earth to be open to our boldness, and have sowed everywhere eternal monuments to both our vengeance and our benefactions.

Thucydides 2.41.4

The Funeral Oration, of course, emphasizes throughout, as here, the tension between *logos* and *ergon*.[98] But in its surface rejection of Homeric poetry and its emphasis on the creation of memory through action, this passage also offers a way of thinking about Xenophon's characterization of Agesilaus. The deeds of the deceased and the achievements of the *polis* are here converted into memory through words, not once, but *twice*—once by the ostensible speaker, Pericles, and once by Thucydides, the historian. Encomium is therefore acknowledged both implicitly and explicitly within the text as one of the new 'tools of memory.'

And it is thus that Xenophon may claim to be himself the crafter of Agesilaus' historical legacy, playing if not a Homer to Agesilaus' Achilles, then perhaps at least a kind of Pindar for a king whom he records as deliberately refusing to embrace the role of heroic victor. It has long been noted that Xenophon's

---

[97] An important formulation of Xenophon's interest in leadership paradigms is Breitenbach 1967; see also Dillery 1995.

[98] My reading of this passage is indebted to the interpretation of the *epitaphios logos* as an agonistic and historically contextualized genre by Derderian 2001, esp. 163–178, 182–185 (the latter specifically on the *logos-ergon* dichotomy); cf. also, as Derderian does, Loraux 1981.

encomium is connected in style and thought with Isocrates' *Evagoras*,[99] and Race has shown that the *Evagoras* in fact employs styles and methods of praise that owe much to Pindar.[100] Whether or not this outcome was one of the goals of the 'real-life' king, the character in the *Hellenica* and in the *Agesilaus* has his historical memory deliberately and, I would argue, explicitly, 'rescued' by Xenophon.

This leads naturally to the question of Xenophon's depiction of himself as a character in the *Anabasis*. For all of the historian's highlighting of Agesilaus' restraint, the *character* Xenophon still behaves in ways that show him planning specifically for his own historical legacy. The fact that Xenophon the character is not more closely modeled upon the modesty paradigm of Agesilaus may suggest that Xenophon the historian is using the figure of himself to communicate with a receptive public about the construction of historiographic memory, and to demonstrate how to understand his text.[101]

An important passage in this regard is the controversy over whether the remains of the Ten Thousand should found a colony. The idea begins in Xenophon's own mind and expands outward through rumor until it becomes the subject of a military assembly, climaxing in a defensive speech by Xenophon himself. At issue are both the possibility of the soldiers settling in a new land far from their homes and the rewards that might accrue to Xenophon as a result. The quasi-heroic position of κτίστης is on offer, but so are immediate power and access to wealth.

The colony-idea is first raised in Xenophon's mind late in Book 5 of the *Anabasis*:

ἐν δὲ τούτῳ τῷ χρόνῳ Ξενοφῶντι, ὁρῶντι μὲν ὁπλίτας πολλοὺς τῶν Ἑλλήνων, ὁρῶντι δὲ πελταστὰς πολλοὺς καὶ τοξότας καὶ σφενδονήτας καὶ ἱππέας δὲ καὶ μάλα ἤδη διὰ τὴν τριβὴν ἱκανούς, ὄντας δ' ἐν τῷ Πόντῳ, ἔνθα οὐκ ἂν ἀπ' ὀλίγων χρημάτων τοσαύτη δύναμις παρεσκευάσθη, καλὸν αὐτῷ ἐδόκει εἶναι χώραν καὶ δύναμιν τῇ Ἑλλάδι προσκτήσασθαι πόλιν κατοικίσαντας. καὶ γενέσθαι ἂν αὐτῷ ἐδόκει μεγάλη, καταλογιζομένῳ τό τε αὐτῶν πλῆθος καὶ τοὺς περιοικοῦντας τὸν Πόντον. καὶ ἐπὶ τούτοις ἐθύετο πρίν τινι εἰπεῖν τῶν στρατιωτῶν Σιλανὸν παρακαλέσας τὸν Κύρου μάντιν γενόμενον τὸν Ἀμπρακιώτην.

---

[99] For a summary of the ancient sources, see Marchant 1925: intro. xvii–xx; for more information, see Flower 1994:149–150.

[100] See Pownall 2004:32–35 on the relationship between Xenophon's *Agesilaus* and Isocrates' *Evagoras*, referring on this topic (32n125) to Race 1987.

[101] While this suggestion might be used to bolster the interpretation of the *Anabasis* as an apologetic work (recently on this issue, e.g. Rood 2004:322–326; and cf., in the same collection, Cawkwell 2004), I am not here attempting to engage with this particular problem.

To Xenophon at that moment, as he looked upon the large numbers of Greek infantry, light-armed troops, archers, slingers, and cavalry—especially because they were at the ready due to their experience—present in Pontus, where such a vast military force would have been otherwise readied only at significant expense, it seemed that it would be a good idea for them to acquire land and influence for Greece by settling a city. And it seemed to him that it would be a large one, as he calculated their own numbers along with those who lived in the surrounding region of Pontus. And so, before saying anything to any one of the soldiers, he sacrificed towards these goals, after sending for Silanus the Ambraciot, formerly the prophet of Cyrus.

Xenophon *Anabasis* 5.6.15–16

Clustered within this passage is the vocabulary of colonial foundation (χώραν, gaining significance by association; προσκτήσασθαι; κατοικίσαντας), and even a potential oblique connection to the traditional preparatory rituals, in the reference to sacrifice (ἐθύετο). The precise context and purpose of this particular sacrifice, however, are deliberately misrepresented by Timasion and perhaps even misconstrued by Xenophon's own men.[102] The problem suggests that the reader, too, may not be out of bounds in expecting for a moment that this sacrifice is intended as a prologue to the usual foundation rites, particularly given the word order of the sentence, which mentions the ritual before indicating its audience.

Following this scene, the colony idea is deconstructed almost immediately by Silanus the *mantis*. The rumor he spreads amongst the men is presented in terms that echo—but alter—Xenophon's initial thoughts (Xenophon *Anabasis* 5.6.17). Silanus repeats the general concept, but changes Xenophon's motivations from apparently altruistic and 'panhellenic' ones to selfish ones. While the character Xenophon was shown contemplating the future and assessing the resources of the potential colony, Silanus instead implies more immediate concerns about personal acclaim. The central issue for the men becomes not the foundation of a potentially great city, but simply the question of whether to remain where they are now: Xenophon's motivations are minimized in the face of the soldiers' concern for their own fate (Xenophon *Anabasis* 5.6.19). Timasion and Thorax reduce the issue once again in their report to the local merchants (Xenophon *Anabasis* 5.6.19-20), focusing upon whether or not the army may put pressure upon them by taking up permanent residence. The idea of the colony

---

[102] Xenophon *Anabasis* 5.6.22 and 27, respectively.

has now drifted far away: when it is recollected by the Achaeans Philesias and Lycon, it is depicted as a private rumor started by Xenophon himself, accompanied by secret machinations (Xenophon *Anabasis* 5.6.27). Xenophon capitulates and abandons his plans (Xenophon *Anabasis* 5.6.28–31).

When the colony idea is first introduced in the report of Xenophon's thoughts, it is presented in terms that tend towards the general, the ennobling, and the eternal. However, as it is debated and gradually dismissed, the emphasis moves to immediate benefits and liabilities, and finally to shallow motivations and open distrust. The implication here seems to be that Xenophon the character is able to conceive of himself as a κτίστης, but his men are irrevocably focused on baser, more transient concerns. Xenophon the writer is therefore here able to ennoble Xenophon the character in two ways: firstly, through the contemplation of the image of the colonial founder, regardless of whether that image is actually activated; and secondly, through the character's 'selfless' inclination to yield to the wishes of his men (see especially Xenophon *Anabasis* 5.6.28). And it is, ironically, in this final rejection of the potential honor that the character Xenophon can imitate Agesilaus—having already demonstrated that he knows full well what he is giving up.

5. Conclusion

In fourth-century Greece, a highly developed vocabulary of commemoration permits appropriately positioned individuals both to script (in literature and in the epigraphical record) and to stage (in public works of art) their own historical significance. By making careful choices about their own activities and behaviors, by demonstrating receptivity to acknowledgements offered by others, and even by deliberately memorializing themselves, such individuals demonstrate their conscious ability to harness public discourse to their advantage, both during their lives and after their deaths.

The shifting political divisions and near-constant conflicts between the major *poleis* of the Greek mainland during the earlier fourth century created a situation that was ripe for exploitation by any state that could gain a decisive upper hand, but they also provided highly advantageous conditions for those who aspired to the creation of historical memory. And the receptivity of the Greeks to image-making by eminent leaders in turn groomed hospitable audiences for the notable 'performances' that would follow during the Hellenistic age.[103] The picture that emerges from the evidence here, therefore, not only

---

[103] E.g. the surveys by von Hesberg 1999 and Kuttner 1999.

suggests a very sophisticated and self-conscious exploitation of both public and literary resources, but also shows that Alexander and his successors had many possible examples to whom they might have turned for programmatic inspiration.[104]

Bibliography

Ajootian, A. 1998. "A Day at the Races: The Tyrannicides in the Fifth-Century Agora." In Hartswick and Sturgeon 1998:1–13.

Anderson, J. K. 1963. "The Statue of Chabrias." *American Journal of Archaeology* 67:411–413.

Baragwanath, E. 2008. *Motivation and Narrative in Herodotus.* Oxford.

Bergmann, B., and C. Kondoleon, eds. 1999. *The Art of Ancient Spectacle.* Studies in the History of Art 56. Center for Advanced Study in the Visual Arts Symposium Papers 34. New Haven.

Blackwell, C. W. 2003. "An Introduction to the Athenian Democracy." In Lanni 2003. Republished as "Athenian Democracy: A Brief Overview," in *Dēmos: Classical Athenian Democracy,* http://www.stoa.org/projects/demos/ article_democracy_overview?page=1&greekEncoding=UnicodeC. Project of The Stoa: A Consortium for Electronic Publication in the Humanities.

Bommelaer, J-F., and D. de Didier Laroche. 1991. *Guide de Delphes: Le Site.* Paris.

Breitenbach, H. R. 1967. "Xenophon von Athen." *RE* IX A2:1567–1910.

Brunnsåker, S. 1971. *The Tyrant-Slayers of Kritios and Nesiotes: A Critical Study of the Sources and Restorations.* Stockholm.

Buckler, J., and H. Beck. 2008. *Central Greece and the Politics of Power in the Fourth Century BC.* Cambridge.

Burnett, A. P., and C. N. Edmonson. 1961. "The Chabrias Monument in the Athenian Agora." *Hesperia* 30:74–91.

Carlier, P., ed. 1996. *Le IVe siècle av. J.-C.: Approches historiographiques.* Paris.

Cartledge, P. 1987. *Agesilaos and the Crisis of Sparta.* Baltimore.

Cawkwell, G. 2004. "When, How, and Why Did Xenophon Write the *Anabasis*?" In Fox 2004:47–67.

Clairmont, C. W. 1983. *Patrios nomos: Public Burial in Athens during the Fifth and Fourth Centuries BC.* 2 vols. Oxford.

Clarke, M. J. et al., eds. 2006. *Epic Interactions: Perspectives on Homer, Virgil, and the Epic Tradition Presented to Jasper Griffin by Former Pupils.* Oxford.

---

[104] Some of this material, particularly in section 2, first appeared in my dissertation (Ferrario 2006b), and I remain very grateful to the organizers, Nino Luraghi and Riccardo Vattuone, and to the other Bologna conference participants for the opportunity to explore these ideas in new ways. I would also like to thank Giovanni Parmeggiani for his editorial work and support.

Connor, W. R. 1987. "Tribes, Festivals, and Processions: Civic Ceremonial and Political Manipulation in Archaic Greece." *Journal of Hellenic Studies* 107:40–50.

Crane, G. 1996. *The Blinded Eye: Thucydides and the New Written Word.* Lanham, MD.

Currie, B. 2002. "Euthymos of Locri: A Case Study in Heroization in the Classical Period." *Journal of Hellenic Studies* 122:24–44.

Davies, J. K. 1996. "Documents and 'Documents' in Fourth-Century Historiography." In Carlier 1996:29–39.

Day, J. W. 1994. "Interactive Offerings: Early Greek Dedicatory Epigrams and Ritual." *Harvard Studies in Classical Philology* 96:37–74.

———. 1989. "Rituals in Stone: Early Greek Grave Epigrams and Monuments." *Journal of Hellenic Studies* 109:16–28.

Derderian, K. 2001. *Leaving Words to Remember: Greek Mourning and the Advent of Literacy.* Leiden.

Dewald, C. 1987. "Narrative Surface and Authorial Voice in Herodotus' Histories." *Arethusa* 20:147–170.

Dewald, C., and J. Marincola, eds. 2006. *The Cambridge Companion to Herodotus.* Cambridge.

Dillery, J. 1995. *Xenophon and the History of His Times.* London.

Easterling, P. E., and B. M. W. Knox, eds. 1989. *The Cambridge History of Classical Literature.* Vol. I, *Greek Literature.* Part 1, *Early Greek Poetry.* Cambridge.

Ferrario, S. 2006a. "Replaying Antigone: Changing Patterns of Public and Private Commemoration at Athens c. 440–350." In Patterson 2006:79–117.

———. 2006b *Towards the 'Great Man': Individuals and Groups as Agents of Historical Change in Classical Greece.* PhD diss., Princeton.

Flower, M. 1988. "Agesilaus of Sparta and the Origins of the Ruler Cult." *Classical Quarterly* 38:123–134.

Flower, M. 1994. *Theopompus of Chios: History and Rhetoric in the Fourth Century BC.* Oxford.

Fox, R. L., ed. 2004. *The Long March: Xenophon and the Ten Thousand.* New Haven.

Gerolymatos, A. 1985. "Fourth Century Boeotian Use of the *Proxenia* in International Relations." In Roesch and Argoud 1985:307–309.

Gygax, M. D. 2006. "Plutarch on Alcibiades' Return to Athens." *Mnemosyne* 59:481–500.

Harley, T. R. 1942. "A Greater Than Leonidas." *Greece and Rome* 11:68–83.

Hanson, V. D., ed. 1991. *Hoplites: The Classical Greek Battle Experience.* London.

Hartswick, K. J., and M. C. Sturgeon, eds. 1998. *ΣΤΕΦΑΝΟΣ: Studies in Honor of Brunilde Sismondo Ridgway.* Philadelphia.

Hedrick, C. 1999. "Democracy and the Athenian Epigraphical Habit." *Hesperia* 68:387–439.

Henry, A. S. 1983. *Honours and Privileges in Athenian Decrees: The Principal Formulae of Athenian Honorary Decrees*. Subsidia epigraphica 10. Hildescheim.

von Hesberg, H. 1999. "The King on Stage." In Bergmann and Kondoleon 1999:65–75.

Hornblower, S. 2002. *The Greek World, 479–323 BC*. London.

Jackson, A. H. 1991. "Hoplites and the Gods: The Dedication of Captured Arms and Armour." In Hanson 1991:228–249.

Jacoby, F. 1945. "Some Athenian Epigrams from the Persian Wars." *Hesperia* 14:157–211.

Kearns, E. 1989. *The Heroes of Attica*. Bulletin of the Institute of Classical Studies Suppl. 57. London.

Keesling, C. M. 2003. *The Votive Statues of the Athenian Acropolis*. Cambridge.

Kowalzig, B. 2004. "Changing Choral Worlds: Song-Dance and Society in Athens and Beyond." In Murray and Wilson 2004:39–65.

Kurke, L. 1991. *The Traffic in Praise: Pindar and the Poetics of Social Economy*. Ithaca.

Kuttner, A. 1999. "Hellenistic Images of Spectacle from Alexander to Augustus." In Bergmann and Kondoleon 1999:97–123.

Lanni, A., ed. 2003. *Athenian Law in its Democratic Context*. Center for Hellenic Studies Online Discussion Series. http://chs.harvard.edu/cgi-bin/WebObjects/workbench.woa/wa/pageR?tn=ArticleWrapper&bdc=12&mn=1184.

Lawton, C. L. 1995. *Attic Document Reliefs: Art and Politics in Ancient Athens*. Oxford.

Loraux, N. 1981. *L'invention d'Athènes: histoire de l'oraison funèbre dans la 'cité classique'*. Paris. Also pub. as *The Invention of Athens: The Funeral Oration in the Classical City*, trans. A. Sheridan. Cambridge, MA, 1986.

Luraghi, N. 2006. "Meta-*historiê*: Method and Genre in the Histories." In Dewald and Marincola 2006:76–91.

MacMullen, R. 1982. "The Epigraphic Habit in the Roman Empire." *American Journal of Philology* 103:233–246.

Marchant, E. C., ed. 1925. *Xenophon: Scripta Minora*. London.

McCauley, B. A. 1993. *Hero Cults and Politics in Fifth Century Greece*. PhD diss., University of Iowa.

Meiggs, R., and D. Lewis, eds. 1969. *A Selection of Greek Historical Inscriptions to the End of the Fifth Century BC*. Oxford.

Meritt, B. D. 1936. "Greek Inscriptions." *Hesperia* 5.3 (*The American Excavations in the Athenian Agora: Tenth Report*):355–430.

Mitchell, L. G. 1997. *Greeks Bearing Gifts: The Public Use of Private Relationships in the Greek World, 435–323 BC*. Cambridge.

Momigliano, A. 1972. "Tradition and the Classical Historian." *History and Theory* 11:279–293.

Murray, O. 1993. *Early Greece*. 2nd ed. Cambridge, MA.

Murray, P., and P. Wilson, eds. 2004. *Music and The Muses: The Culture of* 'Mousike' *in the Classical Athenian City*. Oxford.

Ober, J., and C. Hedrick, eds. 1996. *Dêmokratia: A Conversation on Democracies, Ancient and Modern*. Princeton.

Osborne, R. 1996. *Greece in the Making, 1200–479 BC*. London.

Page, D. L., ed. 1962. *Poetae melici Graeci*. Oxford.

———, ed. 1981. *Further Greek Epigrams*. Cambridge.

Patterson, C., ed. 2006. *Antigone's Answer: Essays on Death and Burial, Family and State in Classical Athens*. Special Issue, *Helios* 33.

Pelling, C. 2006. "Homer and Herodotus." In M. J. Clarke et al. 2006:75–104.

Perlman, S. 1968. "Athenian Democracy and the Revival of Imperialistic Expansion at the Beginning of the Fourth Century BC." *Classical Philology* 63:257–267.

———. 1958. "A Note on the Political Implications of *Proxenia* in the Fourth Century BC." *Classical Quarterly* 8:185–191.

Pfohl, G., ed. 1967. *Greek Poems on Stones*. Vol. 1, *Epitaphs from the Seventh to the Fifth Centuries BC*. Leiden.

Pownall, F. 2004. *Lessons from the Past: The Moral Use of History in Fourth-Century Prose*. Ann Arbor.

Prasad, P. H. 2007. "A Comparative Analysis of Pindar's Victory Odes and Vedic Poetry, with a Commentary on Olympian 1." Unpublished paper. Washington, DC.

Raaflaub, K. A. 1996. "Equalities and Inequalities in Athenian Democracy." In Ober and Hedrick 1996:139–174.

Race, W. H. 1987. "Pindaric Encomium and Isokrates' Evagoras." *Transactions of the American Philological Association* 117:131–155.

Raubitschek, A. E. 1940. "Two Monuments Erected after the Victory of Marathon." *American Journal of Archaeology* 44:53–59.

Rhodes, P. J., and R. Osborne, eds. 2007. *Greek Historical Inscriptions, 404–323 BC*. Oxford.

Robertson, N. 1976. "False Documents at Athens: Fifth Century History and Fourth Century Publicists." *Historical Reflections* 3:3–25.

Roesch, P., and G. Argoud, eds. 1985. *La Béotie antique: Lyon, Saint-Etienne, 16–20 mai 1983*. Paris.

Roisman, J., ed. 2003. *Brill's Companion to Alexander the Great*. Leiden.

Rood, T. 2004. "Panhellenism and Self-Presentation: Xenophon's Speeches." In Fox 2004:305–329.

Rose, H. J. 1957. Review of *Gottmenschentum und griechische Städte*, by C. Habicht, 1956. *Journal of Hellenic Studies* 77.2:340–341.

Samons, L. J., II. 2004. *What's Wrong with Democracy? From Athenian Practice to American Worship*. Berkeley.

Seager, R. 1967. "Thrasybulus, Conon and Athenian Imperialism, 396-386 BC." *Journal of Hellenic Studies* 87:95–115.

Segal, C. 1989. "Pindar." In Easterling and Knox 1989:185–194.

Shrimpton, G. S. 1997. *History and Memory in Ancient Greece*. Montreal.

———. 1971. "The Theban Supremacy in Fourth-Century Literature." *Phoenix* 25:310–318.

Shur, E. G. 1931. *Sculptured Portraits of Greek Statesmen*. Baltimore.

Starr, C. 1968. *The Awakening of the Greek Historical Spirit*. New York.

Stewart, A. 2003. "Alexander in Greek and Roman Art." In Roisman 2003:31–66.

———. 1993. *Faces of Power: Alexander's Image and Hellenistic Politics*. Berkeley.

Strauss, B. S. 1984. "Thrasybulus and Conon: A Rivalry in Athens in the 390s B.C." *American Journal of Philology* 105:37–48.

Taylor, M. W. 1981. *The Tyrant Slayers: The Heroic Image in Fifth Century BC Athenian Art and Politics*. New York.

Thomas, R. 1989. *Oral Tradition and Written Record in Classical Athens*. Cambridge.

Tod, M. N. 1948. *A Selection of Greek Historical Inscriptions*. Vol. II, *From 403 to 323 BC*. Oxford.

———. 1946. *A Selection of Greek Historical Inscriptions*. Vol I, *To the End of the Fifth Century BC*. 2nd ed. Oxford.

Umholtz, G. 2002. "Architraval Arrogance? Dedicatory Inscriptions in Greek Architecture of the Classical Period." *Hesperia* 71:261–293.

Vatin, C. 1991. *Monuments votifs de Delphes*. Archaeologia Perusina 10. Rome.

Walbank, M. B. 1978. *Athenian Proxenies of the Fifth Century BC*. Toronto.

West, William C., III. 1969. "The Trophies of the Persian Wars." *Classical Philology* 64:7–19.

Zanker, P. 1988. *The Power of Images in the Age of Augustus*. Trans. A. Shapiro. Ann Arbor.

13

Aristotle and History

Lucio Bertelli

THE TITLE OF MY PAPER may wrongly suggest that I am going to discuss Aristotle's famous—I should perhaps say infamous—comparison in the *Poetics* between tragedy and history (*Poetics* 9). In fact, this passage from the *Poetics*, one of the rare occasions where Aristotle uses the word *historia* to refer to historiography, is perhaps so famous precisely because of the tendency of modern historians to read it as confirmation of the fact that history was underestimated by Aristotle in comparison with poetry (tragedy as well as epic, if we take *Poetics* 23 into account) and that the term referred only to the exposition of particular actions or stories of particular individuals ("what Alcibiades did or suffered") without any overarching significance (*to kath'hekaston*) (*Poetics* 9.1451b10–11). It is evident that I cannot escape this subject, but I will save it for the last course of this Aristotelian *satura lanx*.

A short 'doxographic' introduction is necessary to focus my inquiry: the problem of the relationship between Aristotle and history in fact depends more on scholars' opinions than on Aristotle's own statements about *historia* or his *modus operandi* as a historian – for after the discovery of the *Constitution of the Athenians*, it became necessary to judge Aristotle not only as a philosopher but also as an historian. And, as is well known, Aristotle's ability as an historian has often been criticized, from Wilamowitz, who thought that "Aristoteles keine geschichtlicher Forscher ist," to Jacoby, who questioned the value of Aristotle's historical work and doubted that he had intended to write a real history.[1] And this, despite the fact that Wilamowitz—and Jacoby implicitly—admitted that the discovery of the *Constitution of the Athenians* had made it far easier to reconstruct Athens' constitutional history. This critical judgment at any rate has persevered and gained force in part because of the perception that Aristotle's historical research about the constitutional development of Athenian democracy is

[1] Wilamowitz 1966:i373; Jacoby 1949:210.

actually an a priori reconstruction based on categories developed in his *Politics*.[2]
Those scholars who consider that Aristotle was an historiographer and that his
inquiries do indeed possess some historical value are in fact quite rare: I will
mention only those who seem to me most important.

In his still fundamental work, *Aristote et l'Histoire. Essai sur la "Politique"* (note
the subtitle) Raymond Weil approaches the problem by considering quantity—
the huge spread and variety of Aristotle's historical researches—more than
quality. How is it possible, he asks, to conclude that Aristotle was not an historian or that he made no contributions to the field of history when the catalogue
of his works includes 158 constitutions, *Nomima Barbarika*, a study of Solon's
axones, accounts of local land claims (*Dikaiomata*), catalogues of Olympic and
Pythian winners, *didaskaliai* of the tragic and comic competition winners, and
historical works on tragedy, on poets, and so on?[3] According to Weil, Aristotle's
'condemnation' of history in *Poetics* 9 and 23, must be read in the context of his
anti-Platonic polemic and not as a final judgment on history itself. However,
as Weil argues, Aristotle here makes a distinction between 'ordinary', popular
historical works (*synetheis*) and works of great philosophical commitment, such
as those of Herodotus and Thucydides: Weil based his conclusion, we should
note, on a doubtful reading of the text (*Poetics* 23.1459a21f.): *synetheis* 'popular,
customary' instead of commonly accepted *syntheseis* 'structures'.[4]

On several occasions, Kurt von Fritz has also had recourse to reappraise
Aristotle's innovations as an historian. He concludes that, in light of the boundless breadth of his inquiries, Aristotle was the first, indeed the only one in antiquity, to make use of a team of researchers, and he extended his inquiry beyond
the traditional bounds of historiography to comprise subjects that had not yet
been studied in any systematic way (e.g. biology, philosophical doxography,
medicine, and physical sciences), as well as those more closely related to historiography, such as biography. With respect to history in the proper sense, says
von Fritz, the unavoidable comparison between history and poetry in the *Poetics*
was only a matter of nuances: poetry was 'more' philosophical than history,
which is itself concerned with the universal, if 'less' so than poetry.[5]

In the most exhaustive work on the subject, Renate Zoepffel rejects von
Fritz's conciliatory solution to *Poetics* 9, suggesting in fact that the *kath' hekaston*
'particularity' of *historia* is not at all compatible with the *kath'holou* 'generality'
of poetry and therefore that Aristotle's concept of *historia* cannot be compared

---

[2]   See e.g. Day and Chambers 1962.
[3]   Weil 1960.
[4]   Weil 1960:163–178; for the text, see Gudeman 1934:388f. and Gallavotti 1974:88.
[5]   Fritz 1958a; 1958b.

with ours, nor even with that of Thucydides.[6] Zoepffel's approach has the merit of setting the famous passage of *Poetics* 9 in the general framework of Aristotelian research and epistemology in order to explain his idiosyncratic view of *historia*. But after following Zoepffel's lengthy theorization of Aristotelian research, her discussion of Aristotle's conception of history—in her view, Aristotle did not consider history to be cyclical—and her detailed examination of *Poetics* 9 and 23, we are still unable to answer the question, "Was Aristotle an historian?" We want to know, in other words, whether Aristotle was an historian in accordance with von Fritz's four requirements of historical work: identification and criticism of traditions and sources, chronological arrangement of facts, explanation of causes, and demonstration of the forces operating within history.[7] Let us see whether we are able to answer this question by relying on the Aristotelian corpus itself.

When Aristotle discusses *historia* in the *Poetics* (9.1451b6f. and 23.1459a21f.), he is no doubt thinking about historical works; at 9.1451b2, in fact, he mentions Herodotus as an example of an *historikos*; his work, he says, would be historical even if it were put into verse. The semantic horizon of the word, *historia* in Aristotle, however, extends beyond a simple account of *genomena ex anthropon* 'the things having happened among men', beyond even the *erga megala* 'great deeds' of Herodotus and Thucydides; indeed, *historia* covers all *phainomena*— including *legomena* 'the things said'—of every *techne*, or science. Closely tied to the Ionic concept of *historie*, *historia* in Aristotle in fact plays a fundamental role in his theory of scientific research, which in turn is connected to his theory of the origin and evolution of human knowledge.

At the beginning of the *Metaphysics* (1.980a28–981b25), Aristotle explains the process of knowledge acquisition through different levels of comprehension: first there is *aisthesis* 'perception or sensation', which is common to all animals; next comes *mneme*, the memory of sensation, which is peculiar to some animals (man included); belonging to man alone is *empeiria*, the third stage, which is produced by the fixing of this memory of perception through a process of synthesis; and it is through knowledge of the particular (*gnosis ton kath'hekaston*) that it is possible to obtain *techne* and *episteme*: "art arises when from many notions gained by experience one universal judgment (*mia katholou hypolepsis*) about a class of objects is produced." (1.981a6–8; translation by W. D. Ross)

Although it is a lower level of knowledge, Aristotle continues, *empeiria* is nevertheless significant in the field of praxis (*prattein*), where the knowledge of the particular is enough to get good results. A theoretician without experience

---

[6]   Zoepffel 1975.
[7]   Fritz 1936:315.

will fail on the practical level; the achievement of scientific knowledge (*eidenai*) is the result of a combination of knowledge of particular facts (*hoti*) and knowledge of causes (*dioti*), and it is accessed only by a person who possesses *techne* or *episteme*. *Empeiria*, then, plays a role—a fundamental role, inasmuch as only *empeiria* leads to universal judgment (*katholou hypolepsis*) and allows for causal inference—in the field of the particular (*kath'hekaston*).

We find this same gnosiological sequence at the end of *Posterior Analytics*, this time applied to the scientific method (2.19): in the final analysis, the "first principles" (*protai archai*) of demonstration (*apodeixis*) come from *aisthesis* and lead to *mneme* and *empeiria*—that is, the fixing of the memory of perception in order to gain unified knowledge, which itself leads to the principle (*arche*) of *techne* in the field of becoming and of *episteme* in the field of being. This inductive process is even more clearly stated in the *Prior Analytics*:

> But most of the principles pertaining to each science are peculiar to it. Consequently, it is the business of experience (*empeiria*) to give the principles which belong to each subject. I mean for example that astronomical experience supplies the principles of astronomical science: for once the phenomena were adequately apprehended, the demonstrations of astronomy were discovered. Similarly with any other art or science. Consequently, if the attributes of the thing (*ta hyparchonta peri hekaston*) are apprehended, our business will then be to exhibit readily the demonstrations. For if none of the true attributes of things had been omitted in the historical survey (*kata ten historian*), we should be able to discover the proof and demonstrate everything which admitted of proof, and to make that clear, whose nature does not admit of proof. (Translation by A. J. Jenkinson, modified)

> Aristotle *Prior Analytics* 1.30.46a19–29

At the end of this chapter, where he discusses the choice of general principles (*eklegein tas protaseis*) that are necessary for demonstration (*apodeixis*) or for explicative arguments (*phaneron poiein*), Aristotle refers to a work on this specific subject, namely his treatise on dialectic better known as the *Topics*: here, perfectly consistent with the methodological and gnosiological assumptions of the *Analytics*, the philosopher explains the meaning of *eklegein tas protaseis* from the point of view of their contents:

> As for propositions, they should be selected in a number of ways corresponding to the number of distinctions drawn in regard to the proposition: thus one may first take in hand the opinions held by all or by most

men or by the philosophers, i.e. by all, or most, or the most notable of them [. . .] Moreover, all statements that seem to be true in all or in most cases, should be taken as a principle or accepted position [. . .] We should select also from the written handbooks (*gegrammenoi logoi*) of argument, and should draw up sketch-lists (*diagraphai poieisthai*) of them upon each several kind of subject, putting them down under separate headings, e.g. 'On Good', or 'On Life'—and that 'On Good' should deal with every form of good, beginning with the category of essence [. . .] Of propositions and problems there are—to comprehend the matter in outline—three divisions: for some are ethical propositions, some are on natural philosophy, while some are logical. (Translation by W. A. Pickard-Cambridge)

Aristotle *Topics* 1.14.105a34–b21

But dialectic is not only a *logica inventionis*, an art of finding the data or the principles of argumentation; it is also a *techne* of analysis (*exetastike*) and proof (*peirastike*) of the selected data, as Eric Weil correctly emphasized in a famous article.[8] The dialectical process, then, can be applied to all fields of knowledge, in different ways depending on the nature of object at hand. Therefore it can be applied also to the field of objects *allos endechomena* 'contingent objects', and it is not by chance that in the passage from the *Topics* cited above Aristotle mentions ethical propositions (*protaseis ethikai*) beside propositions of natural philosophy and of logic (*protaseis physikai* and *logikai*). And *protaseis ethikai* bring us to a field of research overlapping with that of *historia qua* history, i.e. the field of *praxeis*. This is demonstrated by the precise reference to the dialectic method that we have seen employed in the *Topics*—to discover (*heurein*) and examine the propositions (*exetazein tas protaseis*)—in the treatises of Aristotle concerned with *praxis*.

In the methodological prelude on the treatment of "best life and perfect life" in the *Eudemian Ethics* (1.3.1214b28–1215a8), Aristotle stresses the necessity of "investigating the opinions" (*episkopein tas doxas*) on the subject, but he "scrutinizes" (*exetazein*, a term that points to the relationship of this process to the dialectic method) only the opinions of wise men, not those of "boys, sick, and mad people." In the *Rhetoric* (2.22.1396a5f.), in a passage that treats "discussions or reasonings about politics or every subject"—with a clear reference to the *Topics* about the necessity of having at hand "a choice of probable and more suitable premises" for each subject—Aristotle says that "it is necessary to possess the elements of the argument (*hyparchonta*), all or part of them." It is true that

---

[8]   Weil 1951.

in the following examples, divided as they are according to the circumstances of discourse (deliberative, encomiastic, or invective), the philosopher does not separate historical *hyparchonta* (Athens and Sparta) from mythical ones (gods, Achilles); but when we must deliberate about whether or not to go to war, the 'premises' from which our conclusions come are based strictly on knowledge that is factual (the availability of military forces, economic resources, alliances, and hostilities) and 'historical' (past wars and their consequences). When dealing with discourses of praise and condemnation, moreover, Aristotle recalls not only the mythical precedent of the Heraclids but also the historical battles of Salamis and Marathon and, in the case of invective (*psogos*), the enslavement of former allies during the Persian Wars (such as the Aeginetans and Potidaians), all of which requires a knowledge of history.

The use of examples from the past (*paradeigmata*) is a technique explained, as Roberto Nicolai has shown in his excellent book, by Aristotle's principle that "future cases are usually similar to past ones" (*Rhetoric* 2.20.1394a5).[9] If we replace Aristotle's cautious *hos epi poly* 'for the most part, usually' here with the more absolute *kata to anthropinon*, 'according to human nature', we in fact obtain Thucydides' justification of historiography (1.22.4). In a frequently quoted chapter of the *Rhetoric*, moreover, where Aristotle lists the most popular subjects of political discourse—*poroi* 'ways and means', peace and war, *phylake* 'defence' of the territory, import and export, and legislation—he demands not only that the political speaker have personal experience in the field but also that he be *historikos*, 'a searcher' of other men's solutions and facts of the past. This latter kind of knowledge is particularly necessary in legislation (*nomothesia*):

> But while he must, for security's sake, be able to take all this into account, he must before all things understand the subject of legislation; for it is on a country's laws that its whole welfare depends. He must, therefore, know how many different forms of constitution there are; under what conditions each of these will prosper and by what internal developments or external attacks each of them tends to be destroyed. When I speak of destruction through internal developments I refer to the fact that all constitutions, except the best one of all, are destroyed both by not being pushed far enough and by being pushed too far. Thus, democracy loses its vigour, and finally passes into oligarchy, not only when it is not pushed far enough, but also when it is pushed a great deal too far [here Aristotle has recourse to one of his favorite analogies, a nose that is either too aquiline or too snub]. It is

---

[9]   Nicolai 1992:42–46.

useful, in framing laws, not only to study the past history of one's own country (*ek ton paralelythoton theoria*, i.e. historical knowledge), in order to understand which constitution is desirable for it now, but also to have a knowledge (*eidenai*) of the constitutions of other nations, and so to learn for what kinds of nation the various kinds of constitution are suited. From this we can see that books of travel (*ges periodoi*) are useful aids to legislation, since from these we may learn the laws and customs of different races. The political speaker will also find the researches of historians useful.[10] But all this is the business of political science and not of rhetoric. (Translation by W. Rhys Roberts, modified)

Aristotle *Rhetoric* 1.4.1360a18-38

Aristotle's conclusion here is perfectly correct, inasmuch as what he lists as necessary for *nomothesia* well summarizes the contents of the *Politics* and corresponds for the most part to his proposed plan for that treatise appended to the end of *Nicomachean Ethics* (10.9). I will avoid the insoluble—or almost insoluble—problem of the chronology of Aristotle's treatises, aside from pointing out that the collected constitutions (*synegmenai politeiai*, describing 158 *politeiai*), which clearly underlie the concluding passage of the *Nicomachean Ethics* about the causes of destruction and salvation of cities and their *politeiai*, did not exist when Aristotle wrote the first book of the *Rhetoric* (usually considered to be one of his earliest works). The same can be said of his treatises on the laws of non-Greek peoples. It is, of course, possible to say that in the chapter of the *Rhetoric* cited above, Aristotle is speaking about a (political) speaker's socio-political culture, not explaining his own research project. Nevertheless, if the works on which he based the argumentation of the *Politics*, not to mention the *Politics* itself, had already been written, we would expect Aristotle to have alluded to them in the *Rhetoric*, by way of a source citation, for example.

In fact, in the *Rhetoric* Aristotle mentions only works of others: the descriptions of the earth (*ges periodoi*) of the ancient Ionic tradition (he cites Scylax of Caryanda in the *Politics*) and anonymous historical works (*praxeis*). And his reference to politics as the *techne* of legislation makes sense also according to a broader point of view concerning the very structure of the *Politics* as a treatise. As Raymond Weil astutely observed in his article on Aristotle's *Politics*, a palinode to his conclusions in *Aristote et l'histoire*, if it is true that Aristotle's political philosophy depends on his historical knowledge—and the conclusion of the *Nicomachean Ethics* seems to me to be the final proof of this—the reciprocal

---

[10] Rhys Roberts's translation in this point is not correct. It must be: "and an aid to political proposals (*politikai symboulai*) comes from the researches on the authors of historical works (*historiai ton peri tas praxeis graphonton*)."

is true as well, i.e. that "the historiographer Aristotle remembers himself to be something other than an historian."[11] If we want to understand Aristotle as historian, then, we must make a synthesis of the two positions.

Up to this point in my argument, the assertions, methodological principles, and practical applications displayed by Aristotle as a collector of *phainomena* (including past events), that is as an *historikos* in the larger sense of the word, can be used more as evidence for his views on the "utility of history"—intended as a "mine of informations to exploit" as said by Nicolai[12]—than to answer the question that we originally posed, namely, "Was Aristotle able to construct an historical argument or an historical *récit* in accordance with von Fritz's criteria?" It would, of course, be possible to answer this question by analyzing the only work of Aristotle's (problems of authorship apart) that is ostensibly historical, namely the *Constitution of the Athenians*. But, it is precisely the author of the *Constitution of the Athenians* who has been accused of not being a proper historian. To defend Aristotle as an historian, then, it will be necessary to look elsewhere.

Unfortunately, we cannot rely on the evidence from the fragments of the other 157 constitutions—in fact, only 148 constitutions, Athens included, are attested—because they tend to be antiquarian remarks made by scholars interested in curious particulars and not in the historical quality of the information they cite. No help comes from Herakleides Lembus' *Excerpta*. If Ptolemy VI had to learn how the Athenian constitution worked, he would have had better success consulting Aristotle's still extant originals than his secretary's summaries: certainly it was not enough for him to be informed that in Athens there were *astynomoi* overseeing the measures of balconies on the streets, that the Eleven took care of prisons, that there were nine archons, among which there was one—the *Basileus*—who dealt with matters of religion and war, or that the six *thesmothetai* swore not to take bribes, or else they would "set up a golden statue." Not to mention other amenities of the summary. And, in my opinion, the summary of the Spartan constitution is no better. . . .[13] I would prefer to examine as examples of historical reasoning the 'unintentional' evidence contained in Aristotelian works whose aim is not to provide an account of historical events.

I will begin with Aristotle's 'cameo' of cultural history in the first book of the *Metaphysics*, a passage that immediately follows his theory of the epistemological

---

[11]   Weil 1965:161.

[12]   Nicolai 1992:47.

[13]   Herakleides' summary of Aristotle's *Constitution of the Lacedaimonians* is very much along the same lines; this is not, however, to say that there were no other benefits to Herakleides' work. See Bertelli 2004.

process (*aisthesis-mneme-empeiria-techne* or *episteme*) and that aims to confirm this sequence with historical facts:

> At first he who invented any art whatever that went beyond the common perceptions (*aistheseis*) of man was naturally (*eikos!*) admired by men, not only because there was something useful (*chresimon*) in the inventions, but because he was thought wise and superior to the rest. But as more arts were invented, and some were directed to the necessities of life (*anankaia*), others to recreation (*diagoge*), the inventors of the latter were naturally always regarded as wiser than the inventors of the former, because their branches of knowledge (*epistemas*) did not aim at utility. Hence when all such inventions were already established, the sciences which do not aim at giving pleasure or at the necessities of life were discovered, and first in the places where men first began to have leisure (*schole*). This is why the mathematical arts[14] were founded in Egypt; for there the priestly caste was allowed to be at leisure. (Translation by W. D. Ross)

Aristotle Metaphysics 1.981b14–26

In this encapsulation of cultural history, Aristotle scrupulously follows the rules of scientific inquiry that he set out in the *Analytics*, namely the relationship between *hoti* (here, the discovery of mathematics in Egypt) and *dioti* (the theory of the evolution of knowledge), but the reconstruction, despite its brevity, also satisfies von Fritz's conditions of historical writing: (1) Collection and criticism of sources. The source for the discovery of mathematics in Egypt is Herodotus 2.109, supplemented—as seems clear from scholia—with a passage from Isocrates (*Busiris* 21). We cannot exclude the possibility that there were other influences, as well, a passage from Democritus's *Mikros Diakosmos* (68 B 5 D.K.), for example, regarding inventions for recreation (*pros diagogen*) and for pleasure (*pros hedonen*). But we can note that Plato's mythical version of the Egyptians' contributions (*Phaedrus* 274) goes completely unnoticed. (2) Chronological ordering. The sequence of knowledge is chronologically arranged, emphasized by the adverbial progression *proton-eita*; in fact, the reference to the Egyptians is itself a chronological marker, already evident in Herodotus. (3) Causal connections. This is quite clear in the teleology for movers of inventions: first there is use/necessity (*chreia/ananke*), then recreation (*diagoge*) and leisure (*schole*), which is the prerequisite of *techne/episteme*. This last causal connection clearly demonstrates (4) the "evolutionary forces" in action.

---

[14] Aristotle uses *technai* and not *epistemai*; probably the reason of this choice is hidden in the source or sources he is using here.

The Egyptians evidently also play a part in the second piece of evidence that supports my contention about Aristotle's validity as an historian, namely a short historical and cultural *excursus* from the *Metaphysics* about the divinity of heavenly bodies and the origin of this belief:

> Our forefathers in the most remote ages (*para ton archaion kai pamp-alaion*) have handed down (*paradedotai*) to their posterity a tradition, in the form of a myth (*en mythou schemati kataleleimmena*), that these bodies are gods, and that the divine encloses the whole of nature. The rest of the tradition has been added later in mythical form with a view to the persuasion of the multitude and to its legal and utilitarian expediency (*pros ten peitho ton pollon kai pros ten eis tous nomous kai to sympheron chresin*); they say these gods are in the form of men or like some of the other animals, and they say other things consequent on and similar to these which we have mentioned. But if one were to separate the first point from these additions and take it alone—that they thought the first substances to be gods—one must regard this as an inspired utterance, and reflect that, while probably (*kata to eikos*) each art and each science has often been developed as far as possible and has again perished, these opinions, with others, have been preserved until the present like relics (*leipsana*) of the ancient treasure. Only thus far, then, is the opinion of our ancestors (*patrios doxa*) and of our earliest predecessors (*proteron*) clear to us. (Translation by W. D. Ross)

Aristotle Metaphysics 12.8.1074a38–b16

En mythou schemati kataleleimmena 'a tradition in the form of a myth', *leipsana* 'relics, remains': we feel Thucydides, perhaps, behind these words. In fact, if we apply Aristotle's argument to the material conditions of Greece at its origin, taking also into account his revaluation of *mythologountes* 'mythologizers' or *leipsana* as evidence for the past, we would approximate some passages from Thucydides' *Archaiologia*.

In this short discussion of the origin of the *doxa* 'belief' about the divinity of stars, Aristotle not only reveals his global view of history—the repetition in time of human experiences, which is a Thucydidean principle—but also criticizes the *paradedomena* 'the views handed down' of much of the ancient tradition, resorting without problems to rather dangerous prompters as Critias, to whom, I believe, Aristotle points with the phrase, *pros ten peitho . . . sympheron chresin* 'with a view to the persuasion. . .and utilitarian expediency'.

There is another text that explicitly demonstrates Aristotle's ability to place the historical *kath'hekaston* into a causal chain—and what a causal chain!—where it serves as evidence for the necessary and natural evolution of events. This 'unintentional testimony' comes from a treatise completely extraneous to the history of human events, the *Meteorologica*. In a passage from Book 1, Aristotle explains why lands and seas change over time, why at one time there may be sea where once there was land, and vice versa, and why rivers sometimes appear and sometimes dry up (1.14). All of these things, he says, depend on the alternate cycle of hot and cold and their inherent qualities, dry and humid. All of these things happen according to a cyclical order, but this order concerns not the whole *kosmos*, but only those parts of earth that change cyclically in a sort of seasonable cycle, similar to the biological one of growth and senility. This cycle manifests itself differently in different parts of earth because physical bodies—that is, terrestrial elements—change differently from place to place, in accordance with the course of the sun (*periphora*), which sometimes moves away and sometimes moves close to earth. Animal bodies, on the contrary, change simultaneously in all their elements. Therefore there are not only seasons of the year but also 'seasons' of the earth, with an alternation between hot and cold and their consequences.

Up to this point, Aristotle's physical theory is totally consistent with his astronomical conceptions and offers a sufficient explanation of the phenomenon. Next, Aristotle introduces a comparison between human and geological time in order to show why men cannot directly perceive geological changes. It is possible, he insists, to perceive this change by taking into account the evidence offered by human history, provided we examine it on the basis of *dioti*, the necessary sequence of phenomena.

But the whole vital process of the earth takes place so gradually and in periods of time which are so immense compared with the length of our life, that these changes are not observed, and before their course can be recorded from beginning to end whole nations perish and are destroyed. Of such destructions the most utter and sudden are due to wars; but pestilence or famine cause them too. Famines, again, are either sudden and severe or else gradual. In the latter case the disappearance of a nation is not noticed because some leave the country while others remain; and this goes on until the land is unable to maintain any inhabitants at all. So a long period of time is likely to elapse from the first departure to the last, and no one remembers and the lapse of time destroys all record even before the last inhabitants have disappeared. In the same way a nation must be supposed to lose account of the time when it first settled in a land that was changing from a marshy and watery state and becoming dry. Here, too, the change is gradual and lasts a long time and men do not remember who came first, or when, or what the land was like when they came. This has been the case with Egypt. Here it is obvious that the land is continually getting drier and that the whole country is a deposit of the river Nile. But because the neighbouring peoples settled in the land gradually as the marshes dried, the lapse of time has hidden the beginning of the process. However, all the mouths of the Nile, with the single exception of that at Canopus, are obviously artificial and not natural. And Egypt was nothing more than what is called Thebes, as Homer, too, shows, modern though he is in relation to such changes. For Thebes is the place that he mentions; which implies that Memphis did not yet exist, or at any rate was not as important as it is now. That this should be so is natural, since the lower land came to be inhabited later than that which lay higher. For the parts that lie nearer to the place where the river is depositing the silt are necessarily marshy for a longer time since the water always lies most in the newly formed land. But in time this land changes its character, and in its turn enjoys a period of prosperity. For these places dry up and come to be in good condition while the places that were formerly well-tempered some day grow excessively dry and deteriorate. This happened to the land of Argos and Mycenae in Greece. In the time of the Trojan wars the Argive land was marshy and could only support a small population, whereas the land of Mycenae was in good condition (and for this reason Mycenae was the superior). But now the opposite is the case, for the reason we have mentioned: the land of Mycenae has become completely dry and barren, while the Argive land that was formerly barren owing to the water has now become fruitful. Now the same process that has taken place in this small district must be supposed to be going on over whole countries and on a large scale. (Translation by E. W. Webster)

Aristotle *Meteorologica* 1.14.351b8–352a17

R. Zoepffel also discusses this extraordinary passage of the *Meteorologica*, but she uses it to question whether or not Aristotle had a cyclic view of the world and history, and does not consider it as evidence, which it surely is, of Aristotle's noteworthy ability to construct an historical account.[15] He starts from the premise that there is a disproportion of time between geological and human events, an observation based on the factual data of the shorter duration of people's life and the mechanism of nations' decay (*phthorai*)—due in part to chance (*polemoi* 'wars', *nosoi* 'sicknesses'), in part to necessity (*aphoriai* 'famines',

[15] Zoepffel 1975:45–51.

caused by the geological cycle of hot and cold)—and proceeds to the analysis of *symbebekota*—Egypt, Argos and Mycenae. Through the criticism (*exetasis*) of signs (*tekmeria*)—the mouths of Nile, the name of Egypt in Homer, the comparison between ancient and contemporary conditions of the two Greek cities—he confirms (*peira*) the premise. We recall, perhaps, that Thucydides also alludes to Argos and Mycenae in his *Archaiologia*.

As further evidence that Aristotle fulfils the criterion of the "collection and criticism of sources," note his 'proof' at the end of the same chapter (*Meteorologica* 1.14.352b24–31) that serves to validate his theory of local geological changes (*metabolai*), namely the story of the canal dug from Bubastis to the coast of the Red Sea (the Erythrean Sea). Herodotus also records this event (2.158), but his version does not seem to lie behind that of Aristotle, for Aristotle ascribes the canal not to Nekos, as had Herodotus, but to Sesostris. Furthermore, Aristotle claims that the project was abandoned by Sesostris (and again by Darius) out of fear that salty waters would seep into the Nile and spoil the river, since the sea was higher than the land. Herodotus, on the other hand, had supposed that Nekos ceased digging because an oracle predicted that the canal would end up benefiting the Barbarians and the work would be completed by Darius. We cannot tell what source Aristotle was using here, but it was certainly not his favourite one, Herodotus.

If we want to take the *Politics* into consideration, a work that befits the formula "sans histoire, pas de matière pour la politique," a paraphrase of what Eric Weil once said about the *Topics* and dialectical syllogism,[16] we find that historical events (*genomena*) are cited not only to show indications (*martyria*) or signs (*semeia*) of constitutional changes but also as evidence for the evolution of political and sociological institutions according to a logic not based on chance but subject to strict causal connections (see, for example, 1.8 on nourishment (*trophe*) and nations; 3.13 on ostracism; 3.14 on forms of monarchy; and 7.11 on forms of cities). Think, too, of the sequence, monarchy-archaic polity, at *Politics* 4.13, which is caused by the evolution of military forces (cavalry to hoplites) and by the widening of political participation to include hoplites.

Having explored Aristotle's use of the concept of *historia*, let us conclude by returning to the starting point of our inquiry, to the famous chapters of the *Poetics* and to Aristotle's allegedly 'scandalous' underestimation of history. As should be evident from our survey of the role of *historia* as a preliminary inquiry into the *kath'hekasta* in Aristotle's research method, valid—as Aristotle makes clear—for every *techne* and *episteme*, we can conclude that in *Poetics* 9 there is no limit put on the function of *historia* and that the philosopher in no way claims that the historical *kath'hekasta* cannot be used to construct arguments that are

---

16   Weil 1951:292.

philosophoterai (causal according to verisimilitude and necessity). In fact, in the examples we have examined he does precisely this. It is certainly true that the example chosen to illustrate the historical 'particular' in *Poetics* 9 is a little trifling—what Alcibiades did and what he suffered—but we must consider that Aristotle is here dealing with the actions (*praxeis*) and speeches (*logoi*) of tragic characters and so the historical object must be analogous. The 'scandal', if it is a real scandal, is the way in which Aristotle describes *historiai*:

> Epic compositions (*syntheseis*) will differ in structure from histor-
> ical compositions (*historiais*), which of necessity present not a single
> action, but a single period, and all that happened within that period
> to one person or to many, little (*hos etuchen*) connected together as
> the events may be. For as the sea-fight at Salamis and the battle with
> the Carthaginians in Sicily took place at the same time, but did not
> tend to any one result, so in the sequence of events, one thing some-
> times follows another, and yet no single result is thereby produced.
> (Translation by S. H. Butcher)

Aristotle Poetics 23.1459a21-29

Several interpretations are possible: perhaps Aristotle has not yet written the *Constitution of the Athenians*; perhaps, alternatively, we should eliminate from the *Constitution of the Athenians* the passage in which causal connections explain the chronological sequence of eleven changes (*metabolai*) in the Athenian constitution (*Constitution of the Athenians* 41). But there is a third option, too: the philosopher may be thinking here of another kind of history, a pure chronicle, similar to the precursors to the *The Parian Chronicle* (*Marmor Parium*).

In my opinion, it is not necessary to change *syntheseis* (structures, compo-sitions) into *synetheis* (sc. *historias*: ordinary, popular histories) or to embark on syntactical tightrope walks—as does Weil—to justify this lesson in the text. Aristotle is here comparing the supreme Homer to the epical poetasters who make mythical chronicles and not unitary epical compositions whose narrative has a beginning, a middle and an end; in the same way, he elliptically compares the unitary epical action to the historical chronicle. In so doing, he in fact suggests that there is another kind of history, quite different from the simple chronicle. I am certainly aware that I am using an *argumentum ex silentio*, which may perhaps convince, but which lacks scientific rigor. But, if we do not accept this explanation, we must assume either that Aristotle is using historical facts here in a way that is inconsistent with his usual method, or that, in the *Poetics*, he has reduced history to 'random' chronicle.

I am inclined without hesitation to give a positive answer to the question with which I began: "Was Aristotle able to write history?" Aristotle's history is a peculiar history based on a theory of scientific research and knowledge that we do not usually find in historians, but we cannot deny that Aristotle's circumstantial processes are very similar to those of Thucydides. In conclusion, it is hard to deny that a person who affirms that we must rely more on observation than on theory, when the facts have not yet been satisfactorily verified, and that we must rely on theory only when it matches facts already ascertained (see *De Generatione Animalium* 760b30–33) has the *forma mentis* of an historian, of an *Erforscher*. Aristotle certainly did not lack any of the principles necessary for discovering the causes of events.

Bibliography

Bertelli, L. 2004. "La Sparta di Aristotele: un ambiguo paradigma o la crisi di un modello?" In *Sparta fra tradizione e storia*, ed. R. Vattuone, 9–71. Bologna.

Day, J., and M. Chambers, eds. 1962. *Aristotle's History of Athenian Democracy.* Berkeley.

Gallavotti, C. 1974. *Aristotele. Dell'arte poetica.* Verona.

Gudeman, A. 1934. *Aristoteles. Perì Poiêtikês.* Berlin.

Jacoby, F. 1949. *Atthis. The Local Chronicles of Ancient Athens.* Oxford.

Fritz, K. von. 1936. "Herodotus and the Growth of Greek Historiography." *Transactions of the American Philological Association* 67:315–340.

———. 1958a. "Die Bedeitung des Aristoteles für die Geschichtsschreibung." In *Histoire et Historiens dans l'antiquité*, ed. K. Latte, 85–128. Entretiens Hardt IV. Vandoeuvres-Genève.

———. 1958b. *Aristotle's Contribution to the Practice and Theory of Historiography.* Berkeley.

Nicolai, R. 1992. *La storiografia nell'educazione antica.* Pisa.

Weil, E. 1951. "La place de la logique dans la pensée aristotélicienne." In *Revue de métaphysique et de morale* 56:283–315.

Weil, R. 1960. *Aristote et l'histoire. Essai sur la 'Politique'.* Paris

———. 1965. "Philosophie et histoire. La visione de l'histoire chez Aristote." In *La 'Politique' d'Aristote*, ed. R. Stark et al., 159–189. Entretiens Hardt XI. Vandoeuvres-Genève.

Wilamowitz-Moellendorff, U. von. 1966. *Aristoteles und Athen* I-II. 2nd ed. Berlin. Orig. pub. Berlin 1893.

Zoepffel, R. 1975. *Historia und Geschichte bei Aristoteles.* Abhandlungen der Heidelberger Akademie der Wissenschaften, Philosophisch-historische Klasse 2. Heidelberg.

Index Locorum

Subject Index

CPSIA information can be obtained
at www.ICGtesting.com
Printed in the USA
FSHW011454181019
63161FS